Horror Noir

Horror Noir

Where Cinema's Dark Sisters Meet

PAUL MEEHAN

McFarland & Company, Inc., Publishers

Jefferson, North Carolina, and London

LIBRARY OF CONGRESS CATALOGUING-IN-PUBLICATION DATA

Meehan, Paul, 1948–
Horror noir : where cinema's dark sisters meet / Paul Meehan.
p.   cm.
Includes bibliographical references and index.

ISBN 978-0-7864-4597-4
softcover : 50# alkaline paper ∞

1. Film noir — History and criticism.
2. Horror films — History and criticism.
I. Title.
PN1995.9.F54M44   2011   791.43'655 — dc22   2010036610

British Library cataloguing data are available

Front cover: Publicity photo for Rouben Mamoulian's *Dr. Jekyll
and Mr. Hyde* (1931) with Fredric March

Manufactured in the United States of America

*McFarland & Company, Inc., Publishers
Box 611, Jefferson, North Carolina 28640
www.mcfarlandpub.com*

Table of Contents

Acknowledgments

First and foremost, I would like to thank my wife, Theresa, for her invaluable assistance in the preparation of this manuscript, and my daughter, Kelly, for her inspiration. I also wish to extend my profound thanks to Eddie Muller, San Francisco's Czar of Noir (www.eddiemuller.com), author John Kenneth Muir (www.reflectionsonfilmandtelevision.com) and blogger John W. Morehead (www.theofantastique.com) for their interest in, and encouragement of, my work.

Preface

This book was conceived as a natural follow-up to my previous book *Tech-Noir: The Fusion of Science Fiction and Film Noir*. While film noir is considered to be a realistic genre, it can also be shown to contain an element of the fantastic. The American science fiction, horror and film noir genres all ultimately came out of the milieu of the German expressionist films of the silent and early sound period.

When it first emerged as a genre during the 1940s, film noir derived its distinctive visual style from the horror film. Like horror, film noir exists inside a shadow realm of fear, darkness, fate and death. Both forms exhibit a propensity toward nightmarish dream imagery and surrealism.

While it's more difficult to discern commonalities between the realms of science fiction and film noir, the connection with the horror genre is much more obvious. The modern horror and mystery literary genres both had their origin in 18th and 19th-century gothic fiction, where the workings of human perversity were played out amid the trappings of the supernatural. The works of authors Edgar Allan Poe, Robert Louis Stevenson and Arthur Conan Doyle defined the emerging mystery genre in these early years, and the grotesqueries of gothic fiction were later reflected in the works of proto-noir American writers like Dashiell Hammett and James M. Cain.

Unlike science fiction, the classic film noir canon contains works that are clearly influenced by the horror genre. The gothic influence has long been recognized in noirs such as *Sunset Boulevard* and *The Night of the Hunter*, for instance. Critics have long discerned a strain of noir in 19th-century historical melodramas like *The Lodger, Hangover Square* and *The Spiral Staircase*, films that are frequently consigned to the horror genre as well.

The series of horror films produced by Val Lewton, including *Cat People* and *The Seventh Victim* which were made during the formative period of film noir, have long been acknowledged as having had a profound effect on the development of the noir genre. Eric Somer's 2004 article "The Noir-Horror of *Cat People*" analyzed this influence in great detail. Chris Fujiwara's 1998 book *Jacques Tourneur: The Cinema of Nightfall* also addressed the sway that Lewton's most talented director exerted over the evolution of film noir.

Other writers on noir have pointed out the confluence between the two genres. In his 1988 book *The Devil Thumbs a Ride*, critic Barry Gifford lists the Lewton films, along with horror movies like *Cult of the Cobra, House of Horrors, Invaders from Mars, Invasion of the Body Snatchers* and *Island of Lost Souls* alongside recognized works of the noir canon. Similarly, Arthur Lyons in his 2000 book on B-noirs, *Death on the Cheap* cited the influence of Universal horror films like *Dracula's Daughter* on the genesis of noir. These books and essays were critical in guiding my analysis of the linkage between the two dark genres.

Introduction

They call her film noir. Black film. Personified as a woman, lady noir is a clever, darkly beautiful *femme fatale* who executes the grimmest and most mysterious decrees of fate. Death and lust attend her, murder and obsession are her companions. Deadly yet desirable, like a beautifully colored but poisonous serpent, she lies coiled, waiting, daring all to come near so she can inflict her excruciating venom upon her victims.

But wait — noir has a twisted sister, a twin of even blacker reputation. Morbid and irrational, she is even more depraved and given to violence than her sibling. She also travels in dark realms of fate and death, madness and murder, but journeys even deeper into the blackness. She consorts with monsters out of hell and demons of the void. She is horror itself.

These are horror and noir, the two dark sisters, the evil twins of the cinema.

There is an interzone, a twilight realm that exists somewhere between mystery and imagination, murder and fate, flesh and fantasy. This nightmare world is inhabited by criminals, murderers, and monsters of many kinds, human and inhuman: phantom ladies, brute men, wolfen, cannibals, vampires, magicians and serial killers. It is a world of shadows and depravity, madness and obsession, cloaked perpetually in the gloom of night.

The macabre has been an element of the mystery story since the inception of the genre. Edgar Allan Poe's short story "The Murders in the Rue Morgue," first published in 1841, is considered the first example of detective fiction. Poe's eccentric sleuth M. Auguste Dupin cracks a multiple murder case in which the perpetrator turns out to be a homicidal ape. Arthur Conan Doyle's most memorable Sherlock Holmes adventure is surely his 1901 novel *The Hound of the Baskervilles*, in which Holmes squares off against a phantom hound and a ghostly family curse. The Victorian writer Wilkie Collins incorporated the trappings of the supernatural into his seminal detective novels *The Woman in White* (1860) and *The Moonstone* (1868). All of these writers (and Poe in particular) are also known for their horror fiction.

Morbidity has always been a prime feature of detective/mystery fiction, where ghastly murders and dire plans constitute the soul of the plot. The noir fiction of Dashiell Hammett, James M. Cain, Cornell Woolrich and Raymond Chandler, although realistic in nature, is populated with characters who are monstrous grotesques. The gross Fat Man and the oily, effeminate Joel Cairo in Hammett's novel *The Maltese Falcon* (played by Sydney Greenstreet and Peter Lorre in John Huston's 1941 film version), are cases in point.

The obsessive quest of these human monsters for the titular avian talisman has a touch of gothic horror. Similarly, Raymond Chandler's Philip Marlowe novel *Farewell, My Lovely* exhibits a cast of similarly grotesque characters, including the Frankenstein-like Moose Malloy, the mysterioso phony psychic Jules Amthor and his sinister American Indian henchman. The psychotic killer in Woolrich's novel *Black Alibi* disguises his crimes as the grisly work of an escaped leopard.

The most horrific character in classic noir fiction, however, is certainly Phyllis Nirdingler in James M. Cain's 1936 novella *Double Indemnity*. A much more terrifying creature than her cinematic counterpart (renamed Phyllis Dietrichson and portrayed by Barbara Stanwyck in Billy Wilder's screen version), Cain's Nirdingler is depicted as the angel of death personified as a woman. She is a psychotic serial killer and child murderer, a former nurse who uses her medical skills to dispense the boon of death to individuals suffering the travails of life. In one passage, her daughter surreptitiously observes Phyllis's psychodrama while dressed in Lady Death drag, "with some kind of foolish red silk thing on her, that looked like a shroud or something, with her face all smeared up with white powder and red lipstick, with a dagger in her hand, making faces at herself in front of a mirror."[1] Phyllis dons the outfit once more at the tale's conclusion, where she plays her death scene prior to throwing herself off the fantail of a ship to be devoured by a waiting shark. "She's made her face chalk white, with black circles under her eyes and red on her lips and cheeks," the novella's protagonist observes. "She's got that red thing on. It's awful-looking ... her hands look like stumps underneath it when she moves them around. She looks like what came aboard the ship to shoot dice for souls in the *Rime of the Ancient Mariner*."[2] These images of this *femme fatale* are as macabre as anything in a standard horror movie, and they are even more disturbing because the monster is human.

Supernatural vs. Psychological Horror

The horror film comes in basically two flavors: supernatural and psychological. In supernatural horror, the threat to societal order comes from something preternatural or anomalous: a haunted house, a curse, or a monster like a vampire or werewolf. These threats are external to any human agency and are inflicted upon the characters by the designs of fate. Typical of this is the supernatural lycanthropy visited upon the hapless protagonist of *The Wolf Man* (1941), an individual "who is pure in heart and says his prayers by night," as the film's bit of Hollywood verse proclaims. In his human form he has no wish to kill, but he is transformed into an inhuman murderer through no fault of his own, having defended a woman from a ravenous werewolf and being bitten by the beast and given the curse. Torn by the whims of fate, the Wolf Man is like many a film noir protagonist, doomed by a cruel destiny.

The supernatural horror film had its genesis in the German expressionist films of the 1920s and early '30s. Beginning with Robert Weine's grim tale of insanity and hypnotism *The Cabinet of Dr. Caligari* (1919), German cinema began to mass-produce a parade of mordant terrors, the so-called "shudder films" that featured vampires in *Nosferatu* (1922), deals with the devil in *The Student of Prague* (1926) and *Faust* (1926), and assorted terrors in *The Chronicle of the Grey House* (1925), *Warning Shadows* (1923), *The Hands of Orlac* (1925), *The Golem* (1920) and *Waxworks* (1924). The German expressionist style utilized low-key lighting to produce deep shadows and employed unusual camera angles and other means of cinematic distortion to create a nightmarish netherworld of supernatural fear. The expressionist style also provided an iconic template for Fritz Lang's crime melodramas *M* (1931) and *The Testament of Dr. Mabuse* (1933) in the early sound period, and this style would later be adapted for American films noir beginning in the early 1940s.

Supernatural horror was the dominant cinematic mode of the genre during the period of the commercial heyday of the Universal Studios horror movie product, which extended from *Dracula* (1931) to *House of Dracula* (1945). These films also borrowed the expressionist style of the German film-makers, some of whom had fled Germany and were working in Hollywood. As the source material, chiefly the novels *Dracula* and *Frankenstein*, had an old world, 19th-century setting, the films were set in a mythical Transylvania or other Eastern European locale, in an unreal fantasy world far divorced from the everyday. In a sense, this served to make the creatures of the night that populated these films into harmless chimeras comfortably ensconced in the faraway past.

This formula began to change in the 1940s, as the Universal monsters came to America in movies like *The Mummy's Tomb* (1942) and *Son of Dracula* (1943). And a new crop of intelligent and financially successful fright films produced by Val Lewton for RKO, set in '40s-era urban America, redefined the supernatural horror movie. Lewton's films, in particular *Cat People* (1942), *The Leopard Man* (1943) and *The Seventh Victim* (1943), exploited some of the same urban angst that inspired the early films noir of the period. Revamping the supernatural horror film for the contemporary world brought it into the realm of mystery and crime melodrama in unusual fare from other studios like *The Undying Monster* (1942), *Return of the Vampire* (1944) and *Night Monster* (1942).

By the early 1940s the supernatural horror film had become passé, and began to be superceded by a new brand of psychological horror film. This was a trend that began with *Dracula's Daughter* (1936) and continued with *The Wolf Man* (1941) and *Cat People* (1942). The movie monsters began to be psychoanalyzed, and pseudo-scientific explanations for their homicidal conditions (like "lycanthropy" in *The Wolf Man* and *The Undying Monster*) were put forth. Within the landscape of the supernatural horror film, this represented a skepticism about the methods and assumptions of psychoanalysis, because the audience has been apprised of the reality of the film's supernatural situation. In these films, the penalty for disbelief was total annihilation. In *Cat People*, a psychiatrist's theories about the mental fantasies of his patient are put to the test as she shapeshifts into a panther and mauls him to death. As America entered World War II in the early 1940s, however, audiences began rejecting the tired formulas of the supernatural horror film in favor of a more contemporary, realistic approach.

But this shift away from the preternatural and toward the psychological provided a fresh direction for the horror film, and one that brought it closer to the orbit of film noir. The screen began to be populated less by supernatural creatures and more by human monsters. Evil was not external, deriving from a non-human source, but internal, reflecting the darkness in men's souls. Like film noir, horror movies became studies in the psychopathology of evil. The psychological horror film emerged at the same time as film noir, and the two forms developed along parallel courses contemporaneously.

Popular radio programs of the period also constituted a venue in which horror and the crime melodrama commingled. Shows like *Inner Sanctum* and *Lights Out!* alternated between murder mystery plots and tales of the supernatural. The Shadow, a crime-fighter with occult powers, would open each show with the rhetorical (and very noir) question, "Who knows what evil lurks in the hearts of men?" Similarly, the eponymous character on *The Whistler* program lent his mysterious presence to a series of morbid crime stories. *The Shadow*, *The Whistler* and *Inner Sanctum* all incarnated on celluloid in the 1940s, where they provided a potent mixture of horror and film noir.

Another cross-genre development was the "gothic" and "costume" noirs of the early '40s. These were works that transposed elements of the film noir genre formula into a 19th-century setting. Many of them adopted the haunted conventions of the gothic novel: the innocent heroine in peril, the mysterious *homme fatal*, the ghostly mansion hiding a terrible secret. For the most part, the horrors depicted in these films were of the psyche, explorations of the many dimensions of human darkness. Some examples include Victor Fleming's *Dr. Jekyll and Mr. Hyde* (1941), Edgar G. Ulmer's *Bluebeard* (1944), Joseph L. Mankiewicz's *Dragonwyck* (1946), Robert Siodmak's *The Spiral Staircase* (1946), John Brahm's *The Lodger* (1944) and *Hangover Square* (1945) and Robert Florey's *The Beast with Five Fingers* (1946).

The supernatural horror film met its demise in the mid-'40s, concurrent with the end of World War II and all its attendant ghastliness, as supernatural horrors paled before the awful realities of Auschwitz and Hiroshima. By the 1950s, supernatural horror motifs had been largely replaced by those of science fiction. Astro-zombies, atomic insects and flying saucer occupants populated this new world of scientific terrors. Typical of this new landscape of horror were films like Georges Franju's *Eyes Without a Face* (1960), which mixed gothic motifs with sci-fi chills. Despite a revival of the Universal monster movie by England's Hammer Studios, beginning with *The Curse of Frankenstein* (1957), the psychological horror film continued to gather momentum during the '50s. By the end of the decade this new form had taken hold in popular and acclaimed thrillers such as Henri-Georges Clouzot's *Diabolique* (1955), Michael Powell's *Peeping Tom* (1960) and Alfred Hitchcock's mega-hit *Psycho* (1960). Since then, psychological horror has remained a robust form of the genre, and has eclipsed the popularity of the supernatural horror film to a great extent.

The realism of psychological horror brings it closer to the spirit of film noir. Both forms revolve around the homicidal pathology of psychotic individuals. Like many noirs, some of these films (i.e., *Psycho*, Peter Bogdanovich's *Targets*) were inspired by true crime stories. Madness, obsession, misogyny, murder and sociopathology are common elements of both genres. The evil manifested in these films is purely internal and disturbingly human. The psychopathic borderland between horror and noir would be explored in such memorable works as William Wyler's *The Collector* (1965), David Cronenberg's *Dead Ringers* (1988) and Jonathan Demme's *The Silence of the Lambs* (1991).

This is not to say that the supernatural is totally inimical to noir, for although noir is grounded in realism, it also shades into the realms of surrealism and nightmare. Roman Polanski's *Rosemary's Baby* (1968) brilliantly updated the gothic noir formula into a modern urban context. More recently, Alan Parker's *Angel Heart* (1987) combined diabolism and voodoo with '50's-era film noir motifs, while Clive Barker's *Lord of Illusions* (1995) pitted a tough New York P.I. against an evil cult leader with sorcerous powers.

Styles and Themes

The most obvious resemblance between film noir and the horror film is in the realm of cinematic style. Both horror and noir exist inside a haunted universe of night and fear first conjured by Germany's expressionist film-makers in the 1920s. The dark shadows of Weimar cinema were replicated in America as many of the luminaries of the German film industry migrated to America during the 1930s, first in the popular Universal horror movies of the period, and later, during the 1940s, in film noir. As European film-makers fled the horrors of Nazi-occupied Europe, they brought the shadows and terrors of the war with them.

Noir visual stylistics included the use of low-key ratio lighting and the absence of "fill light" to create stark contrasts and shadow areas of deep black. Actors are frequently photographed in darkness while their forms are silhouetted in light. Unusual camera placements, offbeat lighting setups and the use of wide-angle lenses in facial close-ups serve to distort the actors' faces into masks of fear and menace. The use of wide-angle lenses allowed for shooting in low-light conditions, provided enhanced depth-of-field, and distorted and abstracted space within the frame. This expressionist cinematic style is equally applicable to either horror or noir. The portability of this style between the two genres is illustrated in the elegant visual look of *Cat People* (1942), a shadow world of tension and dread created by director Jacques Tourneur, cinematographer Nicholas Musuraca and art director Albert S. D'Agostino, which was replicated by the same trio for the classic noir *Out of the Past* (1947). Film writer Dale Ewing sums it up nicely by stating, "From horror films, such as *I Walked with a Zombie* and *Cat People*, film noir gained a mise-en-scène of repulsion and dread."[3]

In addition to stylistic resemblances, the two forms share several "antitraditional" narrative techniques, including the use of flashbacks and voice-over narration. In his book *Bright Darkness*, Jeremy Dyson notes that in Jacques Tourneur's *I Walked with a Zombie* (1943), voice-over narration is used to describe events that will transpire in the future: "This is exactly the kind of technique that would become familiar through film noir a good two years before *Double Indemnity* (1944) and *Laura* (1944) were made."[4]

Noir and horror share a number of common themes as well. A profound morbidity is common to both, where the threat of imminent death hangs in the air like a black cinematic miasma. The characters are frequently caught in an escalating cycle of violence from which they cannot escape. Corpses are lovingly depicted onscreen in horror and noir, both of which exploit the existential terrors of death. Horror is more morbid than noir, often dwelling on the grim mechanics of mortality while exploiting the terrors of death up close and personal. Both have been described as "body genres" that affect the senses directly and activate the "fight or flight" adrenaline response in the viewer as a physiological reaction caused by stress induced by cinematic suspension of disbelief.

It should be noted that the film noir concept of the *femme fatale*, the "fatal" woman who corrupts and destroys the male protagonist, derives in part from conceptions of the female vampire in horror literature. Famous 19th-century horror tales such as Sheridan Le Fanu's *Carmilla* and Bram Stoker's *Dracula* featured feminine bloodsuckers, while Rudyard Kipling's poem "The Vampire" casts the female monster in a non-supernatural light as "a rag, a bone and a hank of hair" that brings men to ruination. By the 1920s the term had been shortened to "vamp," which had come to mean a *femme fatale*, and celebrated in the persona of silent film star Theda Bara and in songs like, "Hard-Hearted Hannah, the Vamp of Savannah." Thus, the monstrous femmes of *Dracula's Daughter* and *Cat People* are the direct antecedents of the deadly psychopathic ladies that inhabit film noir. Following the gothic model, many horror films feature a *homme fatal*, a mysterious man who attracts the heroine but who conceals a strange and often deadly secret in gothic noirs like *Rebecca*, *Dragonwyck*, and *Bluebeard*.

Noir is an intensely urban genre, and there is a strain of big-city angst in many of the most effective horror films. While the Universal horrors initially took place in mythical Germanic or Eastern European locales, by the 1940s, with war clouds looming, these settings had become quaint and dated. Horror thrillers began to be set in urban America of the '40s, in the same filmic environment that would spawn film noir. The lurking terrors of city life brought a new immediacy to the horror film, one which would persist through the decades. The noir dark metropolis is transformed into a literal urban netherworld in the New York City of *The Seventh Victim* (1943), *Rosemary's Baby* (1968) and *Jacob's Ladder* (1990), the New Orleans of the *Cat People* remake (1982) and *Angel Heart* (1987) and the Los Angeles of *Lord of Illusions* (1995). Horribly decayed cityscapes became emblematic of urban criminality in films like *Wolfen* (1981) and *Se7en* (1995). These nightmarish cities removed the grim urbanism of film noir to a farther circle of Hades.

A fascination with the dark side of human nature is at the heart of both genres. Much of horror and film noir consists of an exploration of extreme psychopathology and homicidal obsession. In *The Wolf Man* the affliction of lycanthropy is described as "a variety of schizophrenia ... it's the technical expression for something very simple: the good and evil in every man's soul." Aside from the supernatural element, there's not much difference between a noir psycho-killer and a lycanthrope who kills by the light of the full moon, except for the killer's M.O. Critic Edmund G. Bansak notes that "a surprising number of noir elements were already present in the horror genre. The noir protagonist, almost always a down-on-his-luck male, was a tragic hero with a tragic flaw, a character usually beset by hasty decisions, obsessive behavior (often entwined by the lure of a *femme fatale*), and well-intentioned ambitions that go awry, a man in a trap of his own making."[5]

As the horror film began to veer away from the supernatural and enter the realm of the psychological, their emphasis shifted to characterization. Film noir has been described as "a horror film in which there is no supernatural element and all the monsters are human," while Bansak notes, "The prototypical film noir is a modified horror film, one which exploits adult concerns and discards the fantastic elements ... both genres are the stuff of nightmares."[6] In other words, noir constitutes a kind of Halloween for grownups, or what could be described as an "adult" variation of the horror film. Noir's schizophrenic psychodrama is amplified in the horror film into a literal transformation of flesh and being in key works like *Dr. Jekyll and Mr. Hyde*, *The Wolf Man* and *Cat People*. In many cases, the primary, or "good" personality suffers from a noir-esque amnesia about the evil deeds of its dark side.

At the nexus of classic horror and film noir was a unique rogue's gallery of colorful and sinister thespians who were admirably suited to the demands of both forms. Alfred Hitchcock once observed about thrillers that "the stronger the evil, the stronger the film," and these two genres have created some of the most memorable villains in screen history. The diminutive, bug-eyed Hungarian actor Peter Lorre, for instance, was equally at home in both genres. Suave Vincent Price utilized his villainous screen persona to provide menace in a number of films noir and horror movies. The portly Laird Cregar played the heavy in both crime melodramas and fear films, while Lon Chaney, Jr., J. Carrol Naish and Claude Rains also made the jump from horror to film noir. Conspicuously absent (for the most part) are 1930s-era horror stars Boris Karloff and Bela Lugosi, whose old world screen personas were not ideally suited to either the emerging urban American horror film or film noir.

Existentialism and the workings of the hellish apparatus of destiny are central themes in both forms. Like the monsters and victims in horror films, the doomed protagonists of classic noirs like *Detour* and *Out of the Past* are caught in a web of fate from which there is no escape. Both genres are highly subversive, positing an out-of-control universe of violence, terror and anarchy that defies all attempts to impose an Apollonian order upon the human condition. Night and fate permeate the dark landscapes of horror and noir.

Hybrid Genres

Film historians tend to classify movies according to specific genres, but in the world of commercial movie-making there has always been a certain cross-pollination between the various genres. Terms like "Western Noir" and "Tech-Noir" describe the synthesis of noir stylistics and thematics with the established cinematic forms of the western and the science fiction movie. The term "Horror Noir" can refer to a similar hybrid melding of noir elements with the genre conventions of the horror film.

Despite the essential realism of the genre, a number of classic noirs contain distinct horror and fantasy motifs. Consider, for example, the postmortem monologues of the deceased William Holden at the beginning and end of *Sunset Boulevard*. Noir icon Edward G. Robinson struggles with the psychic terrors of precognition in *Night Has a Thousand Eyes*, while Bogart is haunted by ghostly visions of the wife he murdered in *Conflict*. Ray Milland is Satan incarnate rubbing shoulders with noir gangsters in *Alias Nick Beal*, while suave mentalist Tyrone Power succumbs to carnival sideshow horrors in *Nightmare Alley*. Peter Lorre portrays a hideously disfigured criminal mastermind in *The Face Behind the Mask*, and Robert Mitchum is the preacher from Hell in *The Night of the Hunter*.

The series of horror features made by producer Val Lewton for RKO during the 1940s have long been recognized as being precisely on the cusp of horror and noir. Working with a talented stable of future film noir directors that included Jacques Tourneur, Robert Wise and Mark Robson, Lewton brought a fresh approach to the horror programmer during the noir formative period of the early 1940s. The urban terrors of Lewton's break-through films, especially *Cat People*, *The Leopard Man* and *The Seventh Victim*, surely exerted a dark influence on the emerging shadow worlds of the film noir universe. But there were suggestions of noir in a number of oddball horror films made during the 1930s, including *Freaks*, *The Mystery of the Wax Museum*, *Dracula's Daughter* and *Supernatural*.

As the '40s progressed, popular radio mystery/horror programs were adapted for the screen. Columbia's *The Whistler* (1944) and its seven sequels, most of which were directed by future horrormeister William Castle, starred Richard Dix in a series of crime melodramas that were presided over by the sardonic title character, a whistling ghostlike entity that was a noir personification of fate itself. Universal's *Inner Sanctum* series, beginning with *Calling Dr. Death* (1943) and continuing in five sequels, featured horror star Lon Chaney, Jr., in a series that combined murder mystery and the supernatural.

The influence of the Lewton films and the radio-inspired mystery/horror films reintroduced gothic and detective fiction motifs into horror movies. Films like *Night Monster* (1942), *The Undying Monster* (1942), *She-Wolf of London* (1946) and *The Beast with Five Fingers* (1946) combined horror with crime melodrama. Offbeat horror/crime melodramas like *Dr. Renault's Secret* (1942) and *The Mask of Diijon* (1946) further reflected a film noir influence. Gothic noirs such as Edgar G. Ulmer's *Bluebeard* (1944), Robert Siodmak's *The Spiral Staircase* (1946) and Joseph L. Mankiewicz's *Dragonwyck* (1946) took both film noir and the psychological horror film in new directions.

As the decades progressed, the horror film began to reach new heights of sophistication in the hands of European directors in such memorable works as Henri-Georges Clouzot's *Diabolique* (1955), Georges Franju's *Eyes Without a Face* (1958) and Michael Powell's *Peeping Tom* (1960). All of these films eschewed the supernatural element and costume melodrama in favor of contempo psychological horror that is much closer to the spirit of noir. This new approach was also evident in American horror noirs like Alfred Hitchcock's *Psycho* (1960), William Wyler's *The Collector* (1965) and Peter Bogdanovich's *Targets* (1968). The urban supernatural thriller would also make a comeback in Roman Polanski's *Rosemary's Baby* (1968), William Friedkin's *The Exorcist* (1973) and Irvin Kershner's *The Eyes of Laura Mars* (1978).

The 1980s produced a number of stylish horrors noir, including Michael Wadleigh's urban update of the werewolf legend, *Wolfen* (1981), Paul Schrader's erotic remake of *Cat People* (1982) and Tony Scott's arty vampire opus *The Hunger* (1983). Alan Parker's *Angel Heart* (1987) deliberately evoked styles and themes from classic film noir within a terror tale of supernatural mystery. The urbane cannibal-murderer Hannibal Lecter, personified by the chillingly dapper Anthony Hopkins in Jonathan Demme's thriller *The Silence of the Lambs* (1991), created the archetype for the horrifying serial killer thrillers to come, and inspired the grisly sequels *Hannibal* (2001) and *Red Dragon* (2002). The supernatural horror noir was represented by William Peter Blatty's *Exorcist III: Legion* (1990) and Clive Barker's *Lord of Illusions* (1996). The Lecter movies inspired a new wave of neo-noir thrillers in which urban detectives pursued horrific serial murderers by descending into the killer's own personal hell in films like *Se7en* (1995), *Fallen* (1998) and *The Bone Collector* (1999).

So the nightmare underworlds of horror and film noir converge into one haunted landscape, an out-of-control universe where alienated antiheros mingle with monstrous femmes, pale gothic heroines and human and inhuman monsters of every ilk, where criminality and terror commingle. Mysteries and murders await in the shadows of the evil in the hearts of men. Are those phantoms real or is it all in your mind? Or is someone trying to drive you insane? As you enter here, be afraid. Be very afraid.

1

Horror and Fantasy Elements in Classic Films Noir

While film noir is generally thought to be a realistic genre, especially in its "neo-realist," phase during the late '40s–early '50s period, noir has another side that occasionally strays into the realm of the fantastic. The era of "classic" film noir is generally regarded as extending (roughly) from 1941 to 1958, with the genre thriving in a black and white, B-movie milieu. Some noirs, while preserving their essential realism, appropriate the trappings and mise-en-scène of the horror film, while others actually incorporate supernatural or paranormal motifs into the plot. Before examining noir elements in films of the horror genre, it's instructive to recognize that some of the most memorable films in the noir canon have a deep affinity with horror.

Chief among these is surely Billy Wilder's masterwork of Hollywood gothic, *Sunset Boulevard* (1950), one of the most acclaimed and compelling works in all of noir. The film opens with a typically noir voice-over narration — except for the fact that the narrator is a corpse. A police motorcade is seen racing down Sunset Boulevard in Los Angeles and turning into the driveway of a palatial but decrepit estate. The dead body of the narrator is floating face down in a swimming pool, shot eerily from below as if suspended somewhere in eternity. The rest of the tale is told by the dead man in an extended flashback.

Our antihero is Joe Gillis (William Holden), a down-on-his-luck Hollywood screenwriter fleeing from creditors who want to repossess his car. One day, while eluding the repo men, Gillis makes a wrong turn off Sunset and into the driveway of a rundown-looking mansion. Concealing his car in a parking structure, Joe decides to have a look around the weird estate when he is ordered into the house by an imperious, bald-headed Germanic man (Erich von Stroheim) who seems to be expecting him. Bemused and more than a bit confused, Gillis is ushered inside the moldering manse and directed up an enormous staircase. "If you need any help with the coffin," the man helpfully offers, "call me."

Gillis is met by the mistress of the house (Gloria Swanson), a haughty middle-aged woman clothed in black who is wearing dark glasses. There's a dead body lying on a table in the room, covered by a blanket, and while the woman rambles on about burying it on the grounds, a hairy arm drops down, revealing the corpse to be that of a dead chimpanzee. Gillis has been mistaken for an undertaker who is scheduled to deliver a child's coffin for the chimp's burial, and he soon learns that his hostess is silent film diva Norma Desmond, and that her faithful retainer is her former husband and silent-era director Max von May-

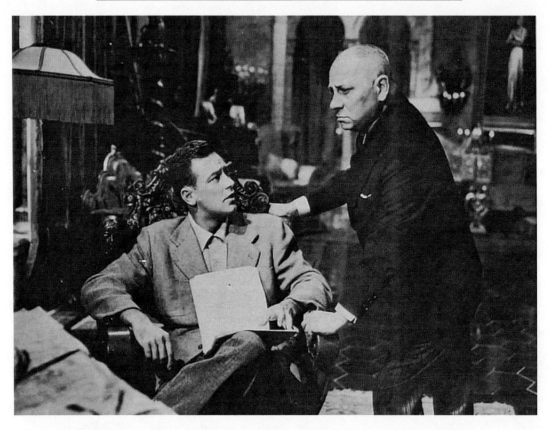

**Joe Gillis (William Holden, left) and Max von Mayerling (Erich von Stroheim) converse inside
Norma Desmond's Hollywood gothic mansion in *Sunset Boulevard* (Paramount, 1950).**

erling. When Norma finds out that Gillis is a screenwriter, he is invited to work on her
script, based on the Biblical story of Salome, and, looking for a way to stay out of sight
for a while, he accepts her offer of interim room and board while he works on the screenplay. That night, from the window of his room, Joe observes rats swarming inside the
empty swimming pool and watches Max and Norma bury the chimp in a macabre moon-
light ceremony.

Of course, it isn't long before Norma has drawn Gillis deep inside her web as he
becomes her lover. He tries to adjust to life inside the "grim Sunset castle" amid the ornate
squalor, but chafes at being Norma's kept man. The aging star seems to feed, vampire-
like, on Joe's very life force while plying him with expensive clothes and gold cigarette
cases. While Norma is a doting, loving mistress, Gillis is appalled by the decaying surroundings and by Norma's fervid self-delusions about making a screen comeback. Becoming more and more dependent upon her largesse, he begins to lose all respect for himself.

Trying to assert himself and break free from Norma's influence, he begins a collaboration with Betty Schaefer (Nancy Olson), a pretty young script reader at Paramount,
on an original screenplay that they hope will propel them onto the studio's A-list. Things
come to a head when Norma forces Joe to reveal his true situation to Betty, but even
though he loves her his lack of self-respect compels him to reject her. In his shame, he

realizes that he has also had enough of being Norma's gigolo and attempts to leave her, whereupon she shoots him in the back, causing him to fall into her swimming pool. In the incredible finale, Gillis's posthumous soliloquy continues, offering sardonic observations on the action. "They fished me out ever so gently," he muses. "Funny how gentle people get with you once you're dead." Norma has suffered a psychotic break in the wake of the murder, and believes that the police and newsreel cameramen assembled to record her being taken into custody are studio cinematographers shooting a scene in *Salome*. Her mind completely divorced from reality, she descends her ornate staircase one last time, her face frozen into a grotesque mask, while uttering one of the most unforgettable lines in the history of cinema: "All right Mr. DeMille, I'm ready for my closeup."

Commenting on the ghoulish qualities of *Sunset Boulevard*, film writer Richard Corliss described the film as being the definitive Hollywood horror movie and compared the Norma Desmond character to Count Dracula. The film inverts the classical gothic formula by making the protagonist a male and the mysterious, powerful figure into a female. While she is not a literal vampire, Norma sucks the life blood out of the hapless Joe Gillis before killing him. Corliss even compared von Stroheim's Max von Mayerling character to Dracula's demented slave, Renfield. The film's set design, featuring enormous, vaulted rooms dominated by an elaborate central stairway down which the monstrous character descends, seems to consciously suggest the monumental castle set built at Uni-

Norma Desmond (Gloria Swanson, center) is ready for her close-up at the conclusion of Billy Wilder's *Sunset Boulevard* (Paramount, 1950).

versal for Bela Lugosi's *Dracula* (1931). The netherworld inside the Desmond estate is contrasted with real-life Los Angeles locations like the famous Schwab's Drugstore, as Joe shuttles back and forth between the two realities.

On a psychological level, Norma and Max suffer from a condition known as "folie à deux," in which two people, usually siblings or a husband and wife, live within a shared delusion. In this situation there is a stronger personality that dominates the weaker, which perfectly describes their relationship. Norma Desmond is not really a *femme fatale*, an evil spider woman in the usual noir sense, but her self-obsession and severe delusions cause her final descent into madness, until, as the dead Joe observes, "The dream she had clung to so desperately had enfolded her."

The film's most macabre element, however, is Joe Gillis's posthumous voice-over. The dead Gillis not only offers ironic commentary on his own murder, but also has omniscient knowledge of events presumably observed in his ghostly state after his demise. This technique adds an eerie, morbid element to the proceedings, although a dead man's off-screen narration had previously been used in Rudolph Maté's *D.O.A.* (1949). As originally shot, *Sunset Boulevard* contained a preface that has come to be known as the "morgue prologue." The film was to begin with Gillis being taken to the L.A. County morgue, where his body is tagged and wheeled into a sterile white room filled with rows of white-sheeted corpses. When the morgue attendants leave, an eerie glow suffuses the place, and the dead begin to converse with one another in voice-over. They mostly speak of the manner of their deaths and offer one another comfort, and when it's Gillis's turn, he begins relating the story in flashback.

This bizarre sequence, probably inspired by a similar gimmick in Thornton Wilder's popular play *Our Town*, wound up on the cutting room floor when preview audiences laughed at it. They reportedly not only laughed, but found it hysterically funny, a reaction which did not jibe with the mood of the rest of the film. Wilder may have meant the scene to be satiric, such as a bit of dialogue in which one of the stiffs asks Gillis about baseball scores, but surviving footage and production stills from the prologue indicate that Wilder was also going for the same horror movie ambience that suffuses the rest of the film.

Wilder would revisit *Sunset Boulevard* in a film he made decades later in Germany, entitled *Fedora* (1978), in which Hildegarde Neff plays the title character, a Norma Desmond–like aging movie queen who creates an illusion of eternal youth through the ruse of being impersonated by her daughter Antonia (Marthe Keller) on and off the screen. *Boulevard*'s Bill Holden plays Dutch Detweiler, a movie director who uncovers Fedora's secret, while Jose Ferrer portrays Dr. Vando, the schizoid plastic surgeon whose unorthodox experimental surgeries were responsible for disfiguring the faded star, and who is now her loyal retainer. As in the previous film, Holden narrates the story in voice-over while the events unfold in flashback. *Fedora* performed poorly during test screenings, and was afforded a severely limited, art-house run in the United States.

The "Spook Racket"

Edmund Goulding's *Nightmare Alley* (1947) is another acclaimed film noir that flirts with the conventions of the horror movie. Glam actor Tyrone Power is cast against type as lowlife carny huckster Stanton Carlisle, who dreams of leaving the carnival life behind

Stan Carlisle (Tyrone Power) shares an intimate moment with Molly (Coleen Gray) as carny strongman Bruno (Mike Mazurki) looks on disapprovingly in *Nightmare Alley* (20th Century–Fox, 1947).

for the big time. "Body of a man — Soul of a beast," a banner at the Hoatley and Henny Carnival proclaims. "Is he the Missing Link?" The advertisement is for the carny attraction known as the geek, a depraved individual whose "performance" consists of biting the heads off of live chickens. Handsome Stan has a strange fascination with the geek. In a fit of presentiment he wonders, "How do you get a guy to be a geek? Is he born that way?" Stan is destined to find out the answer to this awful question.

Stan is part of the carnival's mentalist act, and works alongside the "clairvoyant" Madame Zeena (Joan Blondell) and her husband Pete (Ian Keith), who use simple trickery to simulate ESP while scamming the rubes. Stanton learns that Pete and Zeena have invented a sophisticated code that had once made them a celebrated mind-reading act that they are no longer able to perform because of Pete's severe alcoholism. One night Stan mistakenly gives Pete a bottle of wood alcohol to drink, and when Pete dies of poisoning Stan suffers from enormous guilt yet manages to persuade Zeena to share the code with him. Once he has learned the code, he shunts her aside in favor of the shapely carny doll Molly (Coleen Gray), whom he eventually marries. Oddly, it seems that Zeena has genuine clairvoyant powers and can read the future using a deck of arcane Tarot cards. She foresees the rapid rise and meteoric fall of Stanton Carlisle's fortunes, which are associated with Stan's selection of the card for "The Hanged Man" from the Tarot deck.

Molly and Stan quit the carnival and take their show on the road. Billed as "The Great Stanton," he and Molly perform their telepathy act at ritzy nightclubs in Chicago, where they amaze the urban sophisticates with their carny tricks. During one of their performances he makes the acquaintance of shady psychologist Dr. Lilith Ritter (Helen Walker), and the two con artists conceive a scam wherein Stan will use confidential material gleaned from her files to manipulate wealthy clients. He soon has the ultra-rich industrialist Mr. Grindle (Taylor Holmes) and other Chicago socialites under his sway while he plies his phony spiritualist trade in what he calls "the spook racket." Cynical about religion due to a harsh upbringing, Stanton begins mixing elements of the Christian faith with his spiritualism, bilking Grindle out of 150 thou in cash as a down payment on a "tabernacle" that will never be built. Molly balks at this new development, warning him plainly that "you're going against God," but the irreligious Stan fails to heed her advice.

When Stanton learns that Grindle is obsessed with a lost lover who had died decades earlier, he convinces a reluctant Molly to impersonate the dead girl in a staged vision designed to utterly convince the rich man of his divine powers. That night, as Stanton and Grindle discuss spiritual matters on the rich man's palatial estate, Molly appears as

Molly (Coleen Gray) and Stan (Tyrone Power) work their "spook racket" con on Chicago society in *Nightmare Alley* (20th Century–Fox, 1947).

the ghost, dressed in a white, turn-of-the-century outfit. Grindle is totally spooked by the eerie apparition, but the illusion is completely shattered when Molly can no longer play the game and confesses that she is Stanton's wife. Humiliated by the swindle, Grindle sics the cops on the phony psychic for fraud, while the wily Lilith manages to cheat him out of the money he has already stolen.

Broke and on the lam, Stanton sends Molly back to the carnival while he goes into hiding. In despair and suffering from guilt, he starts hitting the bottle and soon becomes a hopeless drunk. He gravitates back to a carnival, looking to reinsert himself into carny life, but the manager has only one job available — that of geek! Stanton replies with a line he has used throughout the film: "Mister, I was made for it." It isn't long before the horrors of geekdom propel the fallen Stan into the depths of his own personal hell, from which he can only be redeemed by the selfless love of his wife.

Unusual even for the cynical milieu of the film noir, *Nightmare Alley* is rightly revered as one of the classics of the genre. Adapted from a novel by William Lindsay Gresham exposing the seedy side of carnival life by Jules Furthman, *Nightmare Alley*'s blend of carny exploitation, white-collar criminality, obsession, degradation, malevolent psychiatry and the psychic chicanery of the "spook racket" was perfectly realized by director Goulding and cinematographer Lee Garmes. Joan Cohen noted, "The film's subject and the exposition of its milieu through Lee Garmes's low-key photography is strongly expressionistic. From the dark, shadowy world of the second-rate carnival to the moneyed, jeweled rooms of bright nightclubs, Stan is a man trapped by his own cunning fate."[1] Unlike most films noir, there are no murders and minimal violence in the plot, but nonetheless *Nightmare Alley* perfectly typifies the dark noir universe of malevolent destiny, night and madness.

The cast's performances are first-rate, including Joan Blondell as the warm, earthy Madame Zeena and Ian Keith as her pathetically alcoholic husband, while Helen Walker's twisted psychiatrist Dr. Lilith Ritter is as ruthless and smooth as any *femme fatale* in film noir. In retrospect, whereas the unusual casting of leading man Tyrone Power as a carny geek seems inspired, contemporary audiences proved to be less than enthusiastic, and the film failed to score at the box office. Nonetheless, Power's performance as the opportunistic mentalist in this grim rags-to-riches-to-rags story is superb, and arguably the best of his career. *Nightmare Alley* only became available on DVD in 2007, and remains one of the most eminently watchable as well as one of the most unique and fascinating works in the noir canon.

In addition to its noir pedigree, *Nightmare Alley* also trades on a number of the conventions of the horror picture. First and foremost of these is the carnival setting, a motif that goes back to the primordial cinematic terrors of Robert Weine's silent expressionist classic *The Cabinet of Dr. Caligari* (1919). In the late silent–early sound era, American director Tod Browning, who had a taste for carnival grotesquerie, directed a series of horror films in carny settings that included *The Unholy Three* (1925), *The Unknown* (1927) and the infamous *Freaks* (1932). The carnival of terrors continued in genre entries as diverse as *Murders in the Rue Morgue* (1932), *Gorilla at Large* (1952), *Circus of Horrors* (1959), *Carnival of Souls* (1962) and *Something Wicked This Way Comes* (1983). The twilight world of the midway was also evoked for films noir such as Fritz Lang's *Ministry of Fear* (1944), Joseph H. Lewis's *Gun Crazy* (1949) and Alfred Hitchcock's *Strangers on a*

Train (1951). Indeed, some critics believe that the horror film is little more than a "cinema of attractions," an extension of the exhibits of geeks and freaks to be found at a carnival side show.

Like the protagonist of many a horror film, Stanton Carlisle is damned because he has gone "against God," and this spiritual sin of hubris is what eventually brings him to ruination. Once he has committed the sacrilege of claiming that his psychic "powers" come from the Almighty, he is doomed to a fast track on the highway to Hell. The bogus psychic shtick, which is part and parcel of the carny underworld, is further mystified by Madame Zeena's apparently real prescient abilities, and her use of the esoteric deck of Tarot cards to tell fortunes (that come true) add a hint of the supernatural to the proceedings, while the bogus apparition of Grindle's lost love is staged in a suitably haunting cinematic fashion. Stanton's descent into madness, guilt and geekitude, with an assist from demon alcohol that recalls the nightmare hallucinations of delirium tremens in Billy Wilder's *The Lost Weekend* (1945), makes *Nightmare Alley* into a classic of psychological horror.

John Farrow's paranormal thriller *Night Has a Thousand Eyes* (1948) reverses the cynicism of the film noir "spook racket" in a tale in which the protagonist's psychic powers are all too real. Noir icon Edward G. Robinson stars as John Triton, a Stanton Carlisle–like carnival mentalist who begins to experience vivid precognitive visions of events that later come to pass. After predicting several tragic happenings, Triton is devastated when he foresees the death of the girl he loves, Jenny (Virginia Bruce), during childbirth. Devastated by Jenny's imminent death and by the inevitability of his visions, Triton goes into hiding, hoping that his "gift" of prophecy will thereby be nullified. Unfortunately, his psychic powers remain undiminished after twenty years, and when he foresees the death of Jenny's husband, Whitney Courtland (Jerome Cowan), he reveals himself to Jenny and Whitney's daughter, Jean Courtland (Gail Russell).

Jean's fiancé Elliott Carson (John Lund) thinks Triton's powers are bogus, but when her father, now a rich industrialist, dies exactly as Triton predicted, she is so distraught that she attempts to commit suicide by stepping in front of a moving train before being rescued by Elliott. Still not convinced that the seer is on the level, Elliott goes to the cops and Triton is taken into custody by detective Lt. Shawn (William Demarest), but even the hard-boiled police officer is convinced of Triton's weird abilities when he correctly predicts the suicide of a prisoner. Upon release, Triton has an even more disturbing vision: he sees Jean lying dead at the feet of a lion, and knows that she is doomed to die at precisely 11 P.M. that very night. He also stares into a mirror and envisions his own death. In the film's climactic scenes, a criminal associate of Whitney stalks Jean on her father's palatial estate and Triton takes a bullet intended for her and collapses, mortally wounded, at the feet of a stone lion in the garden.

Adapted from a novel by ace mystery writer Cornell Woolrich, this parable of fate, mortality and altered destiny that is unusual because of the supernatural element, is seamlessly woven into the realistic milieu of film noir by scripters Barre Lyndon and Jonathan Latimer, and rendered believable to the audience. Director Farrow, ably assisted by cinematographer John F. Seitz and composer Victor Young, imbues the film with a brooding sense of dread that gives it the creepy ambience of a horror movie. The venerable Edward G. carries the film with his portrayal of the tortured psychic, John Triton, who

The eyes of Edward G. Robinson (right) look out across the fates of John Lund and Gail Russell in the psychic noir thriller *Night Has a Thousand Eyes* (Paramount, 1948).

emerges as a tragic, sympathetic character. Joan Cohen observes that the film "is a psychological thriller with its seer hero poised on the brink of doom. It is precisely this feeling of doom throughout the film that separates it from most mysteries ... *The Night Has a Thousand Eyes* depicts the noir universe at its darkest. The night itself is the enemy, and the stars fatally oversee every misadventure."[2] Farrow also directed the surrealistic noir *The Big Clock* (1948) and the allegorical fantasy noir *Alias Nick Beal* (1949).

ESP was a key feature of Alfred Hitchcock's noir thriller *Shadow of a Doubt* (1943). Joseph Cotten plays Charles Oakley, a psychotic murderer dubbed the "Merry Widow Killer" because he preys on rich, elderly women. On the lam from the cops, he decides to lay low at his sister's digs in the sleepy town of Santa Rosa, California, for awhile. Meanwhile, on the West Coast, Oakley's niece, who is also named Charlie (Teresa Wright), after her uncle, gets a sudden urge to send a telegram to her namesake inviting him to their home. While she is composing the message at the Santa Rosa telegraph office, a telegram from her Uncle Charlie arrives at that very moment announcing his visit. Pleasantly surprised by the synchronicity, she believes the apparent coincidence is due to "mental telepathy." Her uncle soon arrives in town, greeted by his sister, Emma Newton (Patricia Collinge), and her husband, Joseph (Henry Travers), and the rest of the Newton family.

Uncle Charlie soon settles into small-town life at the Newton residence, wowing the Santa Rosans with his cosmopolitan manners and big bank account. His niece, however, detects dark currents beneath the surface via their telepathic link. "I have the feeling that inside you somewhere, there's something nobody knows about," she tells her uncle innocently, "because we're not just an uncle and a niece ... we're sorta like twins." Uncle Charlie presents his niece with a homecoming gift, an ornate emerald ring with someone else's initials engraved inside, and later that evening Charlie seems to pluck the melody of Victor Herbert's "Merry Widow Waltz" from her uncle's mind, which is a clue to his hidden identity. "I think tunes jump from head to head," she declares to the family.

The shadows of doubt begin to darken when Charlie figures out that the initials inside the ring are identical to those of one of the Merry Widow Killer's victims. Things get even dicier when a couple of detectives show up in Santa Rosa looking for Uncle Charlie. When detective Jack Graham (Macdonald Carey) explains that they suspect her uncle of being the serial killer, Charlie still withholds evidence from the police for the sake of the family. She makes it clear to her uncle, however, that he must leave Santa Rosa immediately. Uncle Charlie agrees, but tries to kill his niece by attempting to push her from the train on which he is departing but accidentally slips and falls to his death in front of an oncoming locomotive. Ironically, during Charles Oakley's funeral he is extolled as a pillar of the community, his identity as the Merry Widow Killer obscured.

Hitchcock reportedly considered *Shadow of a Doubt* one of his personal favorites of all his films, and it remains one of his most watchable works today. Joseph Cotten turns in a chilling performance as Uncle Charlie, the first in a long line of Hitch's charming psychopathic murderers, and Teresa Wright is the perfect foil as his innocent, virginal namesake. Unlike many of Hitchcock's other works, there is little in the way of onscreen violence, and the shadows of film noir scarcely intrude into the sunny Santa Rosa setting. Scripted by Thornton Wilder, author of the popular play *Our Town*, along with Sally Benson and Alma Reville (Hitch's wife), *Shadow of a Doubt* serves up a slice of mid–

20th-century Americana that contrasts with the perverse noir universe inhabited by the film's psycho-killer. Writer Gordon McDonell received an Academy Award nomination for best original story for the film.

While Hitchcock reportedly avoided overt supernatural elements in his movies because he believed they detracted from the dramatic impact of the narrative and were too distracting, he occasionally alluded to the occult or the paranormal in several of his works (to be discussed later). Although the ESP angle in *Shadow of a Doubt* is played down, it is essential to the plot, as it is only Charlie's telepathy that reveals the grim truth behind her uncle's genteel façade. The film presents the first significant example of Hitch's fascination with doublings and doppelgangers in his movies. Charlie and Uncle Charlie are paired opposites that represent the good and evil halves of the human psyche.

The double or, in German, *Doppelgänger*, is a folk belief that each person has a kind of psychic twin, and that it is usually a very bad thing for one to be in the same place at the same time as one's double. The doppelganger theme seemed to have a special resonance for Hitchcock, and appears in many of his later films. Hitchcock biographer Donald Spoto notes, "This motif of the double had been an important convention in late Victorian stories.... It is central, for example, to Robert Louis Stevenson's *The Strange Case of Dr. Jekyll and Mr. Hyde* (1886), and to Oscar Wilde's *The Picture of Dorian Gray* (1891) — popular works during Hitchcock's adolescent years."[3] In psychoanalytic terms, the notion of the double was connected to the idea of schizophrenia, popularly referred to as "split personality." The displacement of one personality by another occurs in Hitchcock's *The Wrong Man* (1956), *Vertigo* (1958) and *Psycho* (1960), among others.

Noir Ghosts

In the universe of classic film noir, ghosts are never real in a supernatural sense, but exist only as psychological constructs designed to manipulate victims who may be gullible enough to believe the con. The most memorable example of this occurs in *Vertigo*, in which a hard-boiled San Francisco detective gets lost within a maze of romantic self-delusion when he comes to believe that the woman he loves is a ghost. Of course, she is merely an actress playing the role as part of an elaborate criminal murder scheme, a deadly illusion concocted to deceive the detective's mind.

This type of "ghost" appears in other films noir of the period as well. In *Conflict* (1945), noir mega-icon Humphrey Bogart stars as Richard Mason, who is unhappily married to his rather forbidding spouse, Katherine (Rose Hobart), but secretly covets his wife's younger sister, Evelyn (Alexis Smith). After being injured in a car accident, Richard feigns being crippled as part of a complex plot to murder his wife. He intercepts her car on the misty road to a mountain resort, strangles her (offscreen), re-inserts her body inside the car, and pushes it into a ravine. A pile of logs falls over the auto, hiding it from view beneath a weird-looking, five-sided tangle.

For a while, it seems as if Richard has pulled off the perfect crime. The body and the car remain undiscovered, and he is preparing to make his move on Evelyn when odd events begin to occur. A pickpocket is arrested in downtown L.A. with his wife's cameo ring in his possession, which he claims he pinched which from a lady fitting Katherine's description. At his home, Richard catches the distinctive scent of Katherine's perfume in the air.

Alexis Smith, Sydney Greenstreet, and Humphrey Bogart in *Conflict* (Warner Bros., 1945).

He even receives an envelope addressed in her handwriting. Finally, on a downtown street he spots a woman wearing his wife's dress and pursues the mysterious phantom lady, but is hampered by his bum leg. He manages to track her to an apartment house, where she goes through one of the doors and seemingly vanishes inside a vacant apartment. Confronting the landlady inside the empty flat, Bogart starts to lose his composure. "She's supposed to be murdered," he blurts out. "You put cats in a bag and throw them in the river, but sometimes they get out and they come back."

Becoming unhinged, Richard consults his friend, psychiatrist Dr. Mark Hamilton (Sydney Greenstreeet) about the spooky goings-on. "Funny things happen inside people's heads, don't they," he confides. "I don't believe in ghosts and I don't believe in the supernatural." Dr. Hamilton agrees, dismissing Richard's concerns about the ghostly happenings by offering rationalistic alternative explanations. Not entirely convinced, Richard returns to the scene of the crime to look upon Katherine's corpse with his own eyes. Picking his way through the eerie logjam in the fogbound woods, he finds the wrecked auto empty. Abruptly, Dr. Hamilton and the police show up to take Richard into custody. It seems that the body had been discovered immediately after the killing, and the psychiatrist had suspected Richard from the first. Katherine's "ghost" was an elaborate ploy, an illusion cleverly devised by Hamilton and the police to get Richard to incriminate himself. In the end, Richard seems more relieved that he is not insane or haunted than concerned with being executed for Katherine's murder.

Based on a story by German expressionist director Robert Siodmak, a Hollywood émigré who directed stylish noirs like *Phantom Lady* (1944) and equally arty horror fare such as *Son of Dracula* (1943), *Conflict* explores the psychological effect of guilt upon the criminal mind while adding a whiff of the fantastic. While director Curtis Bernhardt (another German émigré) shoots in a naturalistic style that does not suggest that the pre-ternatural is at work, there are several eerie scenes, including the disappearance of Katherine's "ghost" inside the empty, sterile-looking apartment that so unhinges Bogie, and the denouement at the creepy, fog-bound murder site as the killer seeks his wife's corpse. The screenplay by Arthur T. Horman and Dwight Taylor keeps both Bogie and the audience guessing about the true nature of the mysterious events. *Maltese Falcon* alums Bogart and Greenstreet, with an assist from the charming Alexis Smith, elevate *Conflict* out of the mediocre, and it's fun to watch Bogie's descent into paranoia using the same twitchy nuts-boy routines he would later perfect in *The Treasure of the Sierra Madre* (1948), *In a Lonely Place* (1950) and *The Caine Mutiny* (1954).

Noir ghosts were back to terrify their victims into madness in *The Amazing Mr. X* (a.k.a. *The Spiritualist*, 1948), a neat little thriller from poverty row PRC Studios. Christine Faber (Lynn Bari), a rich widow, lives in a palatial mansion perched on a cliff high above the Pacific, a house that seems to have become haunted after the untimely death of her husband in an automobile accident two years earlier. Troubled by feelings of guilt, she is having second thoughts about her engagement to her new fiancé, Martin (Richard Carlson). Christine hears the voice of her dead husband, Paul, calling her from out of the surf, and while she is walking on the beach she encounters the mysterious personage of Xavier (Turhan Bey). The suave Xavier, Christine learns, is a "psychic consultant" who seems to know a lot about her life history, presumably through paranormal means. He gives her his business card in case she may be in need of his services.

Soon afterward, Christine experiences the terrifying vision wherein she is attacked by the glowing white form of her wedding dress. The luminous specter pursues her around the room until she faints from sheer fright. Alerted by Christine's screams, her sister, Janet Burke (Cathy O'Donnell) bursts into her room to find nothing amiss, but the troubled Christine decides to consult with Xavier concerning her supernatural problems. Mr. X's mysterioso digs come equipped with sliding doors, one-way mirrors, weird statuary, a live raven, closed-circuit TVs, secret panels and other accoutrements of his psychic trade. It isn't long before both Christine and her sister come under the sway of the phony spiritualist, much to the chagrin of Martin. His fears are justified, for Xavier, with his girlfriend/confederate working at Christine's mansion as a maid, has arranged all of the spooky illusions as part of an extortion scheme.

Unexpectedly, however, their plans go awry when Christine's supposedly dead husband, Paul (Donald Curtis), shows up very much alive with criminal plans of his own. After cleverly staging his own "death," he is plotting to murder his wife, have Xavier marry Julie, and control the estate through Xavier. He blackmails the psychic by threatening to expose him, and points out that he can get away with murder because he is thought to be dead and no one will come looking for him as a suspect. Thus intimidated,

Richard Mason (Humphrey Bogart) searches for his murdered wife's corpse in *Conflict* (Warner Bros., 1945).

Mr. X goes along with the scheme for awhile, but ultimately balks at killing Christine and rebels. Tracked to his psychic lair by Paul, Xavier cleverly uses the props and devices of his stagecraft to confuse and disorient the killer during the final shoot-out in which Xavier is wounded and Paul is brought to justice.

This modest PRC suspenser is a minor gem due to the atmospheric treatment of director Bernard Vorhaus and the gorgeously evocative cinematography of ace noir cameraman John Alton. In his book *Death on the Cheap: The Lost B-movies of Film Noir*, author Arthur Lyons states, "Everything in this superior small film is well done, from writing to photography to acting. The original story was penned by talented writer, director, photographer and actor Crane Wilbur, who went on to write the screenplays for the noir films *Phenix City Story* and *I Was a Communist for the F.B.I* and the classic 3-D horror film *House of Wax*."[4] Crane's story deftly combines realistic crime melodrama with the visual trappings of the supernatural ghost story. Alton's use of day-for-night photography in the beach scenes creates a surreal luminous landscape of sky and sea that is perfect for the ghostly goings-on, and his spectral phantom recalls a similar female spirit in Lewis Allen's ghost movie *The Uninvited* (1944).

Considered by horror movie fans to be one of the classiest and most Lewtonesque of Hollywood ghost stories, *The Uninvited* is an above average spook tale in which two female revenants haunt a mansion inhabited by siblings played by Ray Milland and Gail Russell. The film's popularity provoked Paramount into lensing a sequel of sorts, entitled *The Unseen* (1945). Lewis Allen returned to the director's chair and Ms. Russell was contracted to play the female lead, while Ray Milland was replaced by Joel McCrae. Based on the novel *Her Heart in Her Throat* by Ethel Lina White, *The Unseen* was co-scripted by noir patriarch Raymond Chandler and emerged as an intriguing meld of film noir and the ghost story.

Russell plays Elizabeth Howard, a young governess assigned to care for the children of widower David Fielding (Joel McCrae). The two children, Barnaby (Richard Lyon) and Ellen (Nona Griffith), live on Salem Alley, in an older London neighborhood right next door to a creepy old deserted house at Number 11. A series of unsolved murders is plaguing Salem Alley, and Elizabeth comes to believe that the precocious Barnaby has some secret knowledge of the killings. She realizes that Barnaby has come under the sway of his former governess, Maxine (Phyllis Brooks), who is using the child for her own nefarious purposes and Elizabeth secretly observes Barnaby unlocking the front door and admitting a strange man to the house in the middle of the night. To make matters worse, detective Sullivan (Tom Tully) suspects David of being the serial killer, and David's odd behavior also arouses Elizabeth's suspicions as the corpses continue to pile up and the convoluted Chandlerian plot unwinds.

The Unseen suffers greatly in comparison with its progenitor, *The Uninvited*, and illustrates the move away from supernatural plotlines in favor of the realistic detective story, a trend inspired by Val Lewton's ground-breaking horror films in the early 1940s. Although the film is basically a moody whodunnit, the motifs of the new governess, the two precocious siblings and the spooky old house recall Henry James's classic ghost story novella *The Turn of the Screw* (1898). *The Unseen* also has affinities with gothic costume noirs such as *Gaslight* (1944) and *Experiment Perilous* (1944).

Fate and the Devil

American film director John Huston was visiting London in the mid–1930s when he purchased an odd wooden figurine at an antique shop. At a party in his flat, which was attended by Alfred Hitchcock, Huston came up with a story about three strangers sharing a winning sweepstakes ticket in connection with a magical statuette. Hitch expressed an interest in the idea, which prompted Huston to work up a treatment that he sold to Warner Bros. in 1937. The treatment was expanded into a full screenplay by Huston and collaborator Howard Koch, and filmed as *Three Strangers* in 1947. Originally conceived as a semi-sequel to Huston's seminal film noir *The Maltese Falcon* (1942), the film was to be directed by Huston and to star Humphrey Bogart and Mary Astor in the lead roles. Alas, Bogart and Astor were not available and Huston was in the U.S. Army when the film went into production, but *Falcon* cast members Peter Lorre and Sydney Greenstreet did join the party.

On the eve of Chinese New Year in 1938, socialite Crystal Shackelford (Geraldine Fitzgerald) brings two strangers to her London flat and makes them an offer they can't refuse. The strangers are lawyer Jerome K. Arbutny (Greenstreet) and alcoholic petty criminal Johnny West (Lorre). Her apartment contains a shrine to the Chinese goddess of destiny, Kwan Yin, and Crystal explains that there is a legend that if three strangers make a wish together on the stroke of twelve on Chinese New Year's eve, the goddess will open her eyes and grant their wishes. The three strangers, who are all in need of money, agree to jointly purchase a sweepstakes ticket for the Grand National horse race, the English equivalent of the Kentucky Derby. They further agree that if the horse on their ticket is entered in the race, they will not sell it until after the Grand National is run and their horse ultimately wins or loses.

Arbutny desires the money to join the prestigious Barrister's Club, while Crystal wants to buy her husband back and Johnny dreams of purchasing his own bar where he can drink himself into oblivion. They all sign the ticket and place it underneath the statue, and on the stroke of midnight a sudden breeze blows through the window and mysteriously extinguishes the candle lighting the image of Kwan Yin in the film's only moment of outright fantasy. Soon after the men leave, Crystal's husband David (Alan Napier) arrives to inform her that he is divorcing her for another woman, Janet Elliot (Marjorie Riordan), but the vengeful Crystal visits Janet and claims to be pregnant, causing Janet to reconsider the prospect of matrimony.

After the initial meeting, the hapless Johnny is involved in a robbery in which a murder is committed and is on the lam from the law. Cohort Icey Crane (Joan Lorring) tries to hide him from the cops, but Johnny is arrested when the killer, Bertram Fallon (Robert Shayne), fingers him for the murder. Johnny is tried and jailed for the homicide until Fallon is stabbed in jail and clears Johnny with a deathbed confession. In the meantime, barrister Arbutny, who has been playing the stock market with monies he has secretly embezzled from the estate of eccentric rich widow Lady Rhea Beladon (Rosalind Ivan), suffers a catastrophic financial loss when his stocks go belly up. He is thrown into total desperation when Lady Rhea, who believes she can speak with her dead husband in the hereafter, informs him that hubby has ordered an audit of the estate's books. Realizing that he will be ruined if his grand larceny is revealed, Arbunty proposes marriage, but the idea is nixed from the netherworld by the husband. Driven to his ultimate despair, Arbunty is preparing to kill himself when he sees a newspaper article announcing that the horse on their ticket has been selected to run in the Grand National.

The three strangers converge in Crystal's flat once more, where Arbutny, who is desperate for cash, forcefully insists that they sell their shares of the ticket immediately. Johnny also agrees to the arrangement, but when Crystal wants to go through with their original agreement, Arbutny kills her in a fit of rage with the statue of Kwan Yin. Driven insane by his violent actions, Arbutny wanders off, lost in his madness, while Johnny absconds with the ticket. In the final irony, their horse wins the Grand National, but the ticket is now worthless because it bears all three signatures, and if Johnny tries to cash it in, he will be implicated in Crystal's murder. Reflecting on the arbitrary whims of fate while sitting at the bar, a bemused Johnny burns the winning ticket and orders himself another drink.

Similarities to Huston's *The Maltese Falcon* (1941), which he also wrote and directed, are obvious, including the motifs of a haunted, talismanic statuette and the cast of unusual characters surrounding it. The presence of *Falcon* repertory players Lorre and Greenstreet also deliberately invokes the earlier film, along with the shadowy cinematic ambience conjured by director Jean Negulesco. The film also has affinities with W.W. Jacobs's classic ghost story "The Monkey's Paw" (1902), in which a magical mummified monkey's paw from the Orient grants a family three wishes, with disastrous results. In *Three Strangers* the three protagonists' wishes all come true, the result of which is that Crystal is murdered, Arbutny goes mad and Johnny loses a fortune. Huston's script, co-authored with Howard Koch, shows a preoccupation with the workings of destiny that is one of the hallmarks of classic film noir. Greenstreet's portrayal of the unpleasant barrister Arbutny contrasts sharply with Lorre's breezy, comic portrait of perennial loser Johnny West. Lorre and Greenstreet would play opposite each other again in Don Siegel's costume murder mystery *The Verdict* (1946).

After making the supernatural noir thriller *Night Has a Thousand Eyes*, John Farrow directed film noir's version of the Faust legend, *Alias Nick Beal* (1949). Character actor Thomas Mitchell portrays crusading District Attorney Joseph Foster, whose mission is to bring down organized crime figures in his state. Shortly after making an offhand remark that he would give his soul to nail Hanson, the state's big mob boss, he receives a mysterious note directing him to the China Coast Café, a bar in the city's waterfront area. At the café he meets the slick Mr. Nick Beal (Ray Milland), a mysterious, whistling figure who seems to walk out of the fog from nowhere. Beal, who seems to know everything about everyone, takes Foster to a nearby cannery where he breaks into the premises and produces the accounting ledgers that detail Hanson's criminal financial activities. Knowing that the documents have been obtained illegally, Foster compromises his moral principles by presenting it as evidence that sends the mobster to jail while greatly enhancing his professional reputation. This initial indiscretion puts Foster under the influence of Beal, who threatens to expose the D.A.'s illegal actions to scrutiny if Beal's orders aren't carried out.

The unctuous Beal proceeds to insinuate himself into state politics, making backroom political deals designed to get Foster elected to the governorship. Beal also recruits sultry Donna Allen (played by noir goddess Audrey Totter), a woman of questionable virtue, as one of his assistants. He sets Donna up in a lush furnished apartment (which, inexplicably is adorned with weird, Salvador Dalí–esque murals of withered body parts on the walls), and plies her with posh clothes and jewelry, hoping to use her to seduce Foster as the final step in the D.A.'s moral corruption. Becoming more and more beholden to the mysterious stranger after signing a strange "contract," Foster's political star quickly rises toward its zenith, but Beal's unsavory influence is sussed out by his faithful wife,

Donna Allen (Audrey Totter) helps cook up political mischief at the behest of the devilish Nick Beal (Ray Milland) in *Alias Nick Beal* (Paramount, 1949).

Martha (Geraldine Wall) and his pastor, the Reverend Thomas Garfield (George Macready), who are suspicious.

Tempted toward adultery by Donna and implicated in Beal's murder of a bookkeeper (Charles Evans), who had inside knowledge of his illegal activities, Foster is morally conflicted. After winning the governorship, he promptly resigns and reneges on all of his agreements with Beal. Foster has come to believe that Beal is in reality the Devil himself, but in consultations with the Reverend Garfield, he reflects that such superstitious beliefs are more appropriate to the Middle Ages. The reverend, however, explains that the Evil One has adopted more modern methods. "Maybe the Devil knows it's the 20th-century, too, Joseph," he muses. Having broken the terms of his contract with Beal, Foster is told that he will be remanded to a remote isle, "Isla de las Almas Perdidas," which translates from the Spanish: "The Island of Lost Souls," where he will presumably be damned for eternity. Foster, accompanied by the Reverend Garfield, duly shows up at the waterfront to accept his punishment, but when Foster accidentally drops the contract onto the pier, Garfield drops a Bible on top of it. Unable to retrieve the contract, Beal's power is exorcised and he slinks off into the fog, saving Foster from damnation but leaving him to face the music for his misdeeds in this world.

This strange admixture of horror, fantasy and film noir is a prime example of how the supernatural can intersect with the realistic universe of noir. Director Farrow constructs an atmospheric landscape of urban night and fog that plays equally well as horror, fantasy or noir. As he had done in *The Big Clock* and *Night Has a Thousand Eyes*, Farrow enacts his crime melodrama against an unreal, surrealistic backdrop in which the fantastic element predominates. Solid performances by noir regulars Ray Milland as the charming but diabolical Nick Beal and Audrey Totter as the fallen *femme fatale* carry much of the film. The suave Milland seems to pop in and out of reality with preternatural ease, making Beal into a phantom menace who is everywhere and nowhere. Jonathan Latimer's screenplay, derived from a story by Mildred Lord, deftly retells the Faust legend as a modern-day allegory about the nature of societal evil. *Alias Nick Beal* has affinities with William Dieterle's screen adaptation of Stephen Vincent Benét's popular short story, "The Devil and Daniel Webster," entitled *All That Money Can Buy* (1941), as well as more modern incarnations of Satan in *Angel Heart* (1987) and *The Devil's Advocate* (1997).

Two other obscure classic noirs touch on the paranormal. *Destiny* (1944) was originally an episode of Julien Duvuvier's omnibus horror film *Flesh and Fantasy* (1943) that was split off and made into a separate feature with additional footage shot by Reginald Le Borg. Alan Curtis plays bank robber and con man Cliff Banks, who is on the lam after a bank job and flees to the country and takes refuge in the farmhouse of the kindly Clem Broderick (Frank Craven) and his blind daughter, Jane (Gloria Jean). Although blind, Jane possesses strange psychic powers and foresees Cliff's death by drowning in a river, which causes the crook to abandon his evil ways and reform. Duvuvier's original sequence showed Cliff being killed by the police and his body floating in the river as events unfold in flashback in a prescient foreshadowing of the opening scenes of *Sunset Boulevard*, but this was deemed too grim for audience consumption and cut from the feature version of the film.

In Budd Boetticher's *Escape in the Fog* (1945), Navy nurse Eilene Carr (Nina Foch) has a nightmare in which she sees two men trying to kill a third man on a bridge. Later, she meets Navy intelligence officer Barry Malcolm (William Wright) and recognizes him as the victim she has seen in her precognitive dream. While on an espionage mission in San Francisco, enemy spies waylay an unsuspecting Barry and transport him to the bridge (where they intend to kill him and abscond with the secret documents he is carrying), but Eilene happens to be walking over the bridge and recognizes the scene from her dream. Her screams alert Barry to his danger and he drops the papers into the water, but the spies capture the couple and try to kill them in a gas chamber from which they eventually escape.

So the classic film noir universe is populated with bogus ghosts, phony psychics, real psychics, and even the Devil himself. It's time to explore works of horror that have a noir twist: the psychological ghost stories of noirmeister Alfred Hitchcock; the Inner Sanctum Mysteries and other melodramas from radioland; the poetic horror noirs of Val Lewton; the gothic horrors of noir directors like Robert Siodmak, Jacques Tourneur and Edgar G. Ulmer. Darkness fades to a deeper black as horror meets film noir head on.

2

Horror Noir in the 1930s

American horror movies of the 1920s were dominated by actor Lon Chaney, Sr. Known as "The Man of a Thousand Faces," Chaney employed his considerable acting and makeup skills in the most memorable fear films of the decade, including *The Hunchback of Notre Dame* (1923), *The Phantom of the Opera* (1925) and *London After Midnight* (1927). Utilizing his often painful but highly effective makeup creations, Chaney's grotesque characterizations made him a big box-office draw and created a distinctly American brand of horror.

Unlike the contemporaneous German horrors, Chaney's screen terrors eschewed the supernatural in favor of real-world settings and realistic situations. Several of his films were set in the twisted nightworld of the carnival that provided inspiration for director Tod Browning. In Browning's *The Unknown* (1927), for instance, Chaney plays a hapless circus performer who has his limbs amputated in order to woo Joan Crawford, while in *West of Zanzibar* (1928) he was cast as a sadistic, crippled stage magician. Browning also directed him in *The Unholy Three* (1925), in which a trio of circus performers become a team of criminals.

With the advent of talking pictures in the late 1920s, Chaney was poised to become the premier horror star of the coming decade. For his talkie debut, MGM chose to remake *The Unholy Three* in 1930 as a vehicle for this new iteration of Chaney's career at a time when many silent film stars were unable to make the transition to sound. The silent version's screenplay was extensively reworked by J.C. Nugent and Elliott Nugent, while Jack Conway was signed on to direct in place of Browning.

Chaney plays a carnival ventriloquist named Echo, who is weary of the travails of carny existence and decides to pursue a life of crime instead. He persuades midget Tweedledee (Harry Earles, reprising his role in the silent version) and strongman Hercules (Ivan Linow) to join him, and the unholy trinity disappear from the carnival and drop out of sight, along with Echo's squeeze, the larcenous Rosie O'Grady (Lila Lee) and a pet circus gorilla (!), which Echo uses to intimidate the strongman and keep him in line. The trio resurfaces at Mrs. O'Grady's Bird Store, a pet shop where Echo impersonates the elderly Mrs. O'Grady, Tweedledee is disguised as her baby grandson and Hercules becomes her son-in-law. Their new racket consists of selling talking parrots to wealthy customers and casing their high-class digs when the birds are delivered. Echo uses his ventriloquistic skills to make the parrots "talk" so that they are more desirable to their clientele. They hire the unsuspecting Hector McDonald (played by Elliott Nugent, one of the film's scriptwriters) to work as a clerk at the store and present a respectable front.

When one of Mrs. O'Grady's rich customers complains that the parrot they have sold him will not speak, the ventriloquist goes to his mansion, taking Tweedledee along in a baby carriage. While they are visiting the rich man's crib the malignant munchkin spies an expensive ruby necklace being delivered as Echo is once again in the process of making the bird "talk." The Unholy Three plan to rob the necklace on Christmas Eve, but on the night of the robbery Echo, who has become jealous of a relationship that has sprung up between Hector and Rosie, opts to keep an eye on them as Mrs. O'Grady. Meanwhile the strongman and the midget depart to pull off the jewel heist.

Unfortunately, without Echo's moderating influence Hercules and Tweedledee murder the millionaire while committing the robbery (although the actual killing is not shown). When homicide cops investigating the case learn that Mrs. O'Grady and the "baby" visited the mansion on the afternoon of the murder, they start sniffing around the pet shop for clues but find nothing suspicious. The Unholy Three attempt to beat the murder rap by planting the stolen necklace in the home of the hapless Hector, who is framed for the crime when detectives find the evidence. Removing their disguises, the evil trio drop out of sight and hide out in a log cabin in the woods, taking Rosie and the gorilla with them. When Hector is put on trial for the murder, Rosie convinces Echo to intervene, and, suffering a fit of conscience, he agrees to appear in court as Mrs. O'Grady to testify on the defendant's behalf.

Hercules and Tweedledee have a falling out while Echo is away at court when the midget overhears the strongman plotting to murder him and make off with Rosie. In retribution, Tweedledee lets the maddened ape out of its cage and a battle royal ensues between the gorilla and Hercules, during which the strongman is killed while Rosie runs screaming from the cabin. In the meantime, a sudden drop in Echo's vocal pitch during Hector's trial reveals his true identity and exonerates Hector of the murder charge. In the end, Echo gets five years for grand larceny and selflessly allows Rosie to marry her true love, Hector.

Generally considered a film in the horror genre because of Chaney Senior's presence, *The Unholy Three* is, in reality, a bizarre variety of crime melodrama. Apart from a few shots of the unholy trio framed inside their looming shadows (lifted from Tod Browning's silent version), the film is shot in a straight-ahead realistic style without benefit of the German expressionist lighting techniques or unusual camera angles that would soon become hallmarks of the Universal horror movie. Director Conway moves the action along briskly, especially for an early talkie, and makes effective use of the newly invented sound technology. The film's climactic scene, in which Chaney's inadvertent change in voice reveals his true identity during the murder trial, relies on a sound cue for its effectiveness.

Chaney's angular features, shown without his usual macabre makeup, are well-suited for the role of the criminal mastermind/ventriloquist, Echo. His gruff mannerisms and flinty persona perfectly suit the part, and indicate that Chaney, unlike some of his contemporaries, would have made a smooth transition into the era of talking pictures. Co-star Lila Lee is brash and vivacious as Chaney's sweet Rosie O'Grady, while midget actor Harry Earles provides equal measures of grotesquerie and comic relief as the half-pint menace, Tweedledee. Earles, whose German-accented dialogue is nearly incomprehensible, would return to the screen as one of the carnival denizens of Tod Browning's horror show, *Freaks* (1932).

Carny crooks Professor Echo (Lon Chaney) and Rosie O'Grady (Lila Lee) display their ill-gotten gains in *The Unholy Three* (MGM, 1930).

Left to right: Hercules (Ivan Linow), Rosie (Lila Lee), Echo (Lon Chaney), and Tweedledee (Harry Earles) hide from the law in a cabin in the woods in *The Unholy Three* (MGM, 1930).

A study in outlandish criminality, *The Unholy Three* exists within a noir world of larceny, murder, transvestism and identity transference. The notion of dangerous criminals disguised as infants or harmless little old ladies, while fanciful, is nonetheless strange and disturbing. The early scenes at the carnival emphasize the contrast between the straight-laced rubes in the audience and the noir demimonde of the carnival. From the perspective of the carnys, the straights who come to gawk at the unfortunate freaks are the real geeks. "I wouldn't be one of them if I could," opines Rosie, who, in fact, is outwardly normal. Carnival settings would provide a surrealistic backdrop for both horror movies like *Freaks* and noirs such as *Nightmare Alley*. The film's unusual dramatis personae of freakish circus performers presents a template for the grotesque characters that would later populate film noir.

Horror Comes to America

As the Nazi regime came to power in the early 1930s and cast its long shadow over Europe, many European film-makers began to gravitate toward Hollywood. The list included Fritz Lang, Michael Curtiz, Karl Freund, Otto Preminger, Curt and Robert Siodmak and many others who would shape both the horror film and film noir. These Europeans would bring the ghosts and terrors of the old world with them to America. As the worldwide Great Depression took hold, Americans were in the mood for celluloid thrills and escapism. Fantasy genres such as the musical and the horror film became popular in the new era of sound cinema.

For their initial inspiration, film-makers drew upon three 19th-century classics of English literature: Mary Shelley's *Frankenstein*, Bram Stoker's *Dracula* and Robert Louis Stevenson's *The Strange Case of Dr. Jekyll and Mr. Hyde*. Universal Studios led the charge with their screen versions of *Dracula* (1931) and *Frankenstein* (1931), seminal creations that would foster numerous sequels and imitators. The Universal monsters would become synonymous with the horror film during the 1930s, and while the studio was dubbed the "House of Horrors," some of the more interesting and original genre entries were produced by other studios. Paramount's lavish production of *Dr. Jekyll and Mr. Hyde* (1932) was also a critical and box-office success, earning an Academy Award for best actor for the film's star, Fredric March.

Robert Louis Stevenson's novel, a psychological thriller without supernatural overtones, is much closer to the spirit of noir than either *Dracula* or *Frankenstein*. Stevenson's original story is constructed as a mystery that gradually unfolds as it is told by several different narrators. The fact that Jekyll and Hyde are one and the same person is not revealed until the final chapters. In an introduction to the novel, Robert Mighall points out: "Stevenson's tale put the modern city, and specifically London, firmly on the map of Gothic horror. In this it had an immediate influence on writers like Oscar Wilde, Arthur Conan Doyle and Arthur Machen, and is perhaps largely responsible for creating the late–Victorian London of our cinematic imaginations; a foggy, gaslit labyrinth where Mr. Hyde easily metamorphoses into Jack the Ripper, and Sherlock Holmes hails a hansom in pursuit of them both."[1] Thus, Stevenson created the primordial noir city of night, and his novel had a profound influence on the origins of the detective story.

The 1932 version, directed by Rouben Mamoulian, stars Fredric March as the brilliant, well-respected Victorian physician who perceives that the soul of man is "truly two," divided between moral and atavistic impulses, and muses that, if the baser part of our natures could be eliminated, then "how much freer the good in us would be." Explaining his theories to his colleague, Dr. Lanyan (Holmes Herbert), he laments the priggishness of his society. "Can a man dying of thirst forget water?" he asks rhetorically. "Do you know what would happen to that thirst if it were denied water?" Jekyll intends to quench his thirst for knowledge with a potion he has devised that will separate the good and evil sides of his personality.

Upon drinking the formula, the handsome, morally upright Jekyll is transmogrified into his apelike alter ego, Mr. Edward Hyde. "Free, free at last," Hyde exults before the doctor's mirror, as he rails against the "deniers of life." The furry Id-creature luxuriates in his newfound lust for life by making the rounds of Soho dives, where he strikes up a relationship with prostitute "Champagne Ivy" Pearson (Miriam Hopkins), in spite of Jekyll's engagement to his social peer Muriel Carew (Rose Hobart). When Muriel's father, General Carew (Halliwell Hobbes), who disapproves of Jekyll's experiments, breaks off the engagement and whisks her away to Bath on an extended vacation, the Hyde persona begins to emerge more frequently and forcefully, and his relationship with Ivy becomes more sadistic in nature. "I hurt you because I love you," he explains to the terrified woman.

The staid Dr. Jekyll (Fredric March) is tempted by the lascivious Champagne Ivy (Miriam Hopkins) in Rouben Mamoulian's *Dr. Jekyll and Mr. Hyde* (Paramount, 1932).

Upon Muriel's return to London, Jekyll obtains Carew's consent to marry Muriel and attempts to exorcise Hyde. His resolve is further threatened when Ivy pays him a visit and he is confronted with the bruises and marks on her body as evidence of his alter ego's perfidy. After swearing to Ivy that Hyde will never trouble her again, the good doctor sets out on a walk through Hyde Park on his way to his engagement party at the Carew residence, but spontaneously transforms into Hyde when he observes a cat killing a bird. He travels to Ivy's flat instead, and in a fit of animalistic rage, brutally strangles her. "I'll give you a lover now, his name is death, my little bride," he hisses with his hands around her throat. As angry residents converge on Ivy's apartment fearing foul play, Hyde escapes the crowd, but loses his house keys in the melee and is unable to gain entrance to Jekyll's house in order to obtain the formula.

Soon afterward, Dr. Lanyan receives a note in Jekyll's handwriting instructing him to bring the needed chemicals from Jekyll's laboratory to his home, where they will be picked up by Hyde. When Hyde shows up, however, Lanyan, fearing blackmail or worse, pulls a gun on him and demands answers, forcing Hyde to drink the potion and transform into Jekyll in front of the astonished doctor. Lanyan agrees to keep his friend's secret if he

Mr. Hyde (Fredric March) puts the squeeze on Miriam Hopkins in *Dr. Jekyll and Mr. Hyde* (1931).

refrains from drinking the formula, but when Jekyll visits Miriam to formally break off their engagement, he spontaneously reverts back to Hyde once more. General Carew is brutally beaten to death with Hyde's cane while defending his daughter and Hyde flees the scene, but Lanyan leads the police straight to Jekyll's lab, where the doctor has just imbibed his transforming draught. Insisting that he is Dr. Henry Jekyll, he turns back into Hyde once more in front of the baffled group and is shot dead by Lanyan during the violent fracas.

Mamoulian's lush rendering of Stevenson's tale of split personality is a directorial tour de force that remains the best adaptation of this classic work to date. Mamoulian deftly uses subjective camera, moving camera, extended dissolves, overlapping dialogue and optical split screen techniques to craft a film that is highly effective and lively for an early talkie, and is arguably a much finer effort than its two more famous horror stablemates, *Dracula* and *Frankenstein*. Mamoulian famously used color filters and special lighting to make Hyde's features magically appear over Jekyll's face (although more conventional optical superimposition is used for the later transformation scenes). Fredric March earned a well-deserved Oscar for his dual portrayal of the saintly Jekyll and the sinner Hyde. His characterization of the libidinous Hyde is a wonderful creation, a charming rogue who sniffs the air like an animal, leaps about like an ape and twitches spasmodically like a demonic Jerry Lewis. Co-star Miriam Hopkins also turns in a powerful performance as the pathetic whore, Ivy, and manages to generate a great deal of audience sympathy for the character. The pre–Hays Office film contains a highly erotic scene in which Ivy nearly seduces Jekyll that was censored for the movie's re-release in 1936, but which has since been restored to the DVD version.

The screenplay by Samuel Hoffenstein and Percy Heath dispenses with Stevenson's fragmented detective story narrative structure and instead relies on the 1887 stage version of the novel written by Thomas Russell Sullivan. The stage version added the love interest represented by Miriam, and related the story first-hand through Jekyll's viewpoint. The film's most glaring flaw is the Hyde makeup devised by Wally Westmore. Although Stevenson describes the character as being swarthy and apelike, Westmore transforms Hyde into an unlikely-looking troglodyte with protruding canines that cause March to lisp through his lines. As critic Ivan Butler notes, "Hyde's later appearances, however effective as shock, would surely have led to his apprehension even in the foggy streets of late Victorian London, if not to his immurement in the zoological gardens."[2] All this having been said, the Hyde makeup is more consistent with Stevenson's notion that Jekyll's alternate self is an entirely different person. In the novel, Hyde is physically smaller and younger than the doctor. Thus, Mamoulian's concept is closer to this idea than either John Barrymore's 1920 silent version or Spencer Tracy's 1941 remake, in which the actors attempted to portray Hyde using minimal makeup and relying instead on facial expressions to convey the character's moral "wrongness."

Stevenson's parable of good and evil, of twisted criminality hiding behind a veneer of societal respectability, is a classic noir theme. Mamoulian plays with the audiences sympathies by contrasting Hyde's lust for life with Jekyll's constipated, upper-class existence. Change of persona is another standard noir theme in films like *Man in the Dark*, *Vertigo* and *Dark Passage*. Hyde is almost able to get away with murder by hiding behind his secret identity as the doctor. Interestingly, *The Strange Case of Dr. Jekyll and Mr. Hyde* has a connection with one of the most notorious serial killers in history. Jack the Ripper's murder of prostitutes in the lower-class Whitechapel section of London began in September of 1888, two years after the publication of Stevenson's book, and while a theatrical adaptation was popular on the London stage. Although the crimes were never solved, detectives and the press theorized that the Ripper was an upper-class physician who periodically descended into homicidal bestiality in a real-life analog of Stevenson's bipolar character.

The box-office success of *Dracula*, *Frankenstein* and *Dr. Jekyll and Mr. Hyde* made the horror movie a hot ticket in the early 1930s as competing studios rushed to provide product for the emerging genre. Tod Browning, fresh from his triumph on Universal's *Dracula*, returned to his silent movie roots with a macabre tale set in the netherworld of the carnival in MGM's outrageous *Freaks* (1932), in which real circus freaks were used as actors. The film begins with a carny barker giving his spiel at the freak show in front of a crowd of ordinary, middle-class spectators. "But for an accident of birth, you might be even as they are," he proclaims, directing their attention to an enclosure where one of the freaks is on display (though not shown to the movie audience) as he begins to relate a story. "Their code is a law unto themselves," the barker explains. "She was once a beautiful woman." The rest of the twisted tale is told to us in flashback.

Early scenes portray domestic life in a traveling circus. Despite their grotesque appearance, the sideshow freaks are shown to be no different than the non-deformed circus performers, sharing their homely concerns inside their tightly knit community. Trouble starts when midget Hans (Harry Earles from *The Unholy Three*) gets a crush on normal trapeze artist Cleopatra (Olga Baclanova) while spurning his midget lover Frieda

Femme fatale Cleopatra (Olga Baclanova) looks like she wants to devour Hans (Harry Earles) in *Freaks* (MGM, 1932).

(Daisy Earles). At first she merely teases the little guy, but when she learns that Hans is going to inherit a fortune, she plots to marry him and murder him for his money, assisted by her lover, the carnival's strongman Hercules (Henry Victor). The wedding celebration of Hans and Cleopatra is a bizarre affair during which the freaks present Cleopatra with a "loving cup" while chanting, "one of us ... we accept her ... gobble, gobble ... one of us." Horrified, the bride refuses the initiatory drink and orders the freaks to clear out, and when they have gone another demented scene ensues, in which Cleopatra parades a cuckolded and despairing Hans around the empty tables on her shoulders, accompanied by Hercules.

As Hans becomes ill from a slow-acting poison being administered by Cleopatra, the freaks begin to watch their every move. Midgets and dwarves spy on the two plotters from hidden corners, and the freaks soon apprehend the truth and plan their revenge. One night, as the circus is on the move during a raging thunderstorm, the freaks attack Cleopatra and Hercules, their grotesque forms lurching and squirming through the wet mud in pursuit of the evil couple. The strongman is knifed to death, but the fate of Cleopatra is uncertain. Flash forward to the carnival sideshow at the beginning of the film as the camera reveals the handiwork of the freaks. Cleopatra's legs have been ampu-

Olga Baclanova as the "bird woman" at the conclusion of *Freaks* (MGM, 1932).

tated and her face disfigured. Dressed in a grotesque feathered outfit, she squawks hideously in her guise as the "bird woman," as the freaks have truly made her "one of us."

Freaks was considered so over-the-top when it was released that it was banned in many venues and became a major embarrassment for MGM. It nearly ended the career of director Tod Browning, and existed in the special limbo reserved for "cult" or "exploitation" films for decades. Seen today, however, *Freaks* still has the power to shock. One of the film's major flaws is its thin storyline that resembles a brief anecdote or joke, complete with punch line. As horror critic Carlos Clarens observes, "It is the kind of truculent story that might be heard over a beer from any sideshow barker."[3] Adapted from a short story entitled "Spurs" by Willis Goldbeck and Leon Gordon, the storyline is padded out with the scenes of domestic life among the freaks, including the erotic complications of Siamese twins, an armless, legless "human torso" lighting a cigarette and a woman without arms using her feet to hoist a glass to her lips. While these early scenes serve to humanize the freaks and invoke sympathy for their condition, Browning reverses the audience's emotional polarity in the final scenes and turns them into horrifying figures of menace. The wedding sequence and the film's terrifying climax still have a disturbing power to shock, and for sheer terror and strangeness are unrivaled in Browning's work.

The voluptuous Olga Baclanova dominates the film with her portrayal of the vicious *femme fatale* Cleopatra, her nubile figure providing a stark contrast to the deformities of the freaks. She seems to regard little Harry Earles with a wicked, voracious hunger, and is unforgettable in the film's final scene as the horrifying, demented "bird woman." The movie's dark carnival setting would be replicated in films noir such as *Nightmare Alley*, *Strangers on a Train* and *Ministry of Fear* and the film's grotesque characters are just one step removed from the freaks and geeks that populate the universe of noir. *Freaks* is a noir story of lust, murder and revenge in which the deformed exact street justice on the physically "normal" characters in an inversion of our sympathies. Their morality lies outside of societal strictures, illustrating the notion that "their code is a law unto themselves."

Three from 1933

By 1933 the horror movie craze was in full bloom, and that year produced a number of unusual horror noirs, the most memorable of these being Warners' *The Mystery of the Wax Museum*. Directed by the versatile Michael Curtiz, who would later helm classic films noir such as *Mildred Pierce* (1945) and *The Breaking Point* (1950), the film was shot using the early two-color Technicolor process. Curtiz's previous film, the sci-fi thriller *Doctor X* (1932), also utilized this process, and its two stars, British thespian Lionel Atwill and scream queen Fay Wray, were signed on for *Museum*.

The film opens in 1921 London where genius sculptor Ivan Igor (Atwill) operates a wax museum that is losing money because he refuses to display lurid horror figures and concentrates instead on sculpting historical personages such as Napoleon and Joan of Arc. His highbrow tastes are about to pay off, however, because an influential art critic has just agreed to submit Igor's work to the Royal Academy of Art. His hopes are dashed, however, when his business partner, Joe Worth (Edwin Maxwell), arrives to announce that he is going to torch the failed museum for the insurance money. The two men struggle as Worth knocks Igor unconscious and leaves him to die inside the flaming waxworks. When Igor comes to, he watches in horror as his precious sculptures liquefy before his eyes. As the flames close in his fate is uncertain.

Cut to New York City, 1933, where Igor is reopening his wax museum in the Big Apple with great fanfare. Although he has survived the fire, his arms and legs are horribly burned and he is confined to a wheelchair. Unable to sculpt with his damaged hands, he employs Professor Darcy (Arthur Edmund Carewe), a drug addict, and Hugo (Matthew Betz), a deaf mute, as assistants. In the meantime, brash reporterette Florence Dempsey (Glenda Farrell) is assigned to investigate the apparent suicide of famous model Joan Gale (Monica Bannister) by her editor (Frank McHugh). The aggressive Flo begins snooping around and learns that Gale's body was stolen from the morgue, and that eight other corpses have also disappeared from the facility in the last 18 months, including the body of a well-known municipal judge.

Flo's roommate, Charlotte Duncan (Fay Wray), happens to be going out with Ralph Burton (Allen Vincent), an assistant sculptor at the waxworks. Tagging along with Charlotte as she visits Ralph at the museum, Flo notices an eerie resemblance between the sculpture of Joan of Arc and the missing model. While Igor is distracted by Charlotte, who resembles the figure of Marie Antoinette destroyed in the London museum, Flo discovers Gale's morgue tag on the Joan of Arc figure. She also traces Professor Darcy to an old house where a bootlegging operation is being run, and goes to the cops with the info. The police bring Darcy in for questioning, and the weak-willed junkie soon breaks down and confesses the truth: Igor's museum exhibits are not sculptures at all, but corpses covered with a layer of wax. The judge's body became Voltaire and Gale's became Joan of Arc.

In the meantime, Charlotte goes to the museum looking for Ralph, but is lured into the basement by Igor. The madman confesses his misdeeds to her as he rises from his wheelchair, his disability being just a ruse, and tells her that he wishes to immortalize her beauty within his figure of Marie Antoinette. As he grabs at her, she pummels his face with her fists, whereupon it cracks asunder as the wax mask falls away to reveal Igor's horribly scarred visage. Charlotte is placed on a table as a huge vat of molten wax bubbles and froths and Igor pulls out the stops and valves that will engulf her in the liquid. Fortunately, Ralph and Flo show up with the cops in time to prevent Charlotte from getting her legs waxed along with the rest of her body. Igor is shot and falls into the vat, and Flo has her story.

Curtiz's masterful pacing keeps *Mystery of the Wax Museum*'s momentum moving quickly forward. The screenplay, by Don Mullaly and Carl Erickson, adapted from the story, "The Wax Works," by Charles Belden, doesn't take itself too seriously, and adopts a light tone over its melodramatic plotline. Atwill is in fine form as the demented Pygmalion Ivan Igor, but the film's real protagonist is Glenda Farrell's Flo, the liberated, courageous female newshound whose perspicacity ultimately solves the case. Visiting a police station in one scene, she greets one of the officers with the line, "How's your sex life?" Fay Wray provides the cheesecake, and, as usual, acts as perennial monster bait.

Unlike *Frankenstein*, *Dracula* or *Dr. Jekyll and Mr. Hyde*, the action takes place in contemporary 1930s urban America and the plot does not involve the supernatural. The film is set against a noir-esque backdrop of newsrooms, morgues and police stations, and is constructed in the manner of a detective story. Mad sculptor Ivan Igor is a typically obsessive, homicidal noir villain, while Flo's crusading reporter character anticipates similar film noir news reporters in films like *Night Editor* (1946). Two-color Technicolor did not prove as popular as Warner Bros. had hoped, and this would be the last film in this format released by any major studio. The deep shadows of black and white cinematography were perhaps more suited to the '30s-era horror film, as the B&W idiom would prove to be for classic noir in the following decades. *Mystery of the Wax Museum* was thought to be a lost film for many years until a print was discovered in Jack Warner's personal vault and restored by the UCLA film department.

In 1933, Lionel Atwill gave an interview to *Motion Picture* magazine in which he portrayed himself as a kind of Jekyll and Hyde personality: "See, one side of my face is gentle and kind, incapable of anything but love of my fellow man," the actor explained. "The other side, the other profile, is cruel and predatory and evil, incapable of anything but the lusts and dark passions. It all depends on which side of my face is turned toward you — or the camera. It all depends on which side faces the moon at the ebb of the tide."[4] In truth, the versatile Atwill could play heroic roles in films like *Dr. X* (1932) and *Son of Frankenstein* (1939), but also shone in his roles as a heavy in *Mystery of the Wax Museum* and his other horror noir entry of 1933, Paramount's unusual thriller *Murders in the Zoo*.

Atwill plays a Clyde Beatty type "bring-'em-back-alive" zoologist Dr. Eric Gorman, who, in the opening scene, is busy deep in the jungles of Southeast Asia sewing the mouth of one of his colleagues shut. The hapless man, it seems, had tried to steal a kiss from Gorman's spouse, and Gorman exults, "Now he'll never kiss another man's wife." The victim, his face seen in close-up with his mouth sewn with bloody, ragged stitches, is left to die in the jungle as the insanely jealous husband has his revenge.

Returning to the States on the S.S. *Salvador* with a shipload of exotic beasts bound for the Municipal Zoo, Gorman becomes aware that his sultry wife, Evelyn (Kathleen Burke), has become enamored of socialite Roger Hewitt (John Lodge) and once more begins plotting vengeance. The zoo's director, Professor Evans (Harry Beresford), meantime, is having financial troubles keeping the facility open, and hires alcoholic newspaperman Peter Yates (Charlie Ruggles) to provide public relations (and comic relief). Yates hits on the idea of holding a fund-raiser at the zoo's Carnivora House, where wealthy supporters can "eat with lions and tigers," and Evans thinks this is a pretty good idea. The professor's daughter, Jenny, also works in the zoo, where she assists head herpetologist Dr. Jack Woodford (Randolph Scott) in extracting venom from poisonous serpents in order to produce anti-venom. Jenny and Dr. Woodford are excited about creating a new anti-venom from a rare green mamba snake that Gorman has brought back from his expedition.

On the night of the fundraiser Gorman seats Hewitt next to his wife, and as the festivities commence, Hewitt is bitten by a snake and keels over dead. The mamba's cage in Dr. Woodford's lab is found unlatched and the snake missing, presumably through Woodford's negligence. The partygoers are evacuated and the zoo is closed for good in the wake of the accident, but Woodford and Jenny are retained as part of a skeleton crew tasked with taking care of the animals in the interim. Knowing that her husband has somehow murdered Hewitt, Evelyn is determined to leave him, but the obsessive Gorman will not allow it, and slobbers all over the terrified woman in a fit of possessiveness. Later, observing her husband concealing something in his desk drawer, Evelyn pries open the lock and discovers the real murder weapon — the mummified head of a mamba with venom dripping from its fangs. Gorman surprises her while she is absconding with the evidence, and chases his wife through the darkened zoo, hurling her into a pit filled with hungry alligators who voraciously dispose of her body.

When the missing mamba is found and returned to its cage, Woodford measures the width of the animal's fangs and finds that they do not jibe with the bite marks found on Hewitt's leg, indicating that the victim was bitten by another snake. Confronting Gorman about the matter, Gorman dismisses it with the line, "You don't think I sat there with an eight-foot mamba in my pocket, do you?" (or, to paraphrase Mae West, "Is that an eight foot mamba in your pocket, or are you just happy to see me?"). When parts of Evelyn's dress are fished out of the gator pit, Gorman realizes that he must dispose of Woodford, whom he also suspects of having fooled around with his wife. Gorman visits Woodford at his lab and puts the bite on him with the poison snakehead, but Jenny arrives in time to sound the alarm and save the herpetologist's life with the mamba anti-venom they had been developing. As he flees through the zoo at night, pursued by police and guards, Gorman lets the lions and tigers out of the Carnivora House to create havoc while he hides inside one of the animal cages. Unfortunately, he is unaware that the cage contains a humongous constrictor snake, and in the final frames Gorman's strangulated face is seen writhing in the deadly coils of the monstrous serpent.

Part jungle thriller, part crime melodrama and part horror movie, *Murders in the Zoo* is a delightful romp through 30s-era, pre–Hayes Office perversity. A. Edward Sutherland directs the lurid scenario by Philip Wylie and Seton Miller with a great deal of wit and verve. Atwill is deliciously wicked in the main role of the deranged zoologist Dr. Gorman, while Kathleen Burke, who portrayed Lota the panther woman in the sci-fi horror chiller *Island of Lost Souls*, (1933), uses her exotic looks to great advantage as the adulterous Evelyn. Future cowboy star Randolph Scott stands tall as Dr. Woodford, and in one scene the actor is shown actually handling a venomous snake. *Murders in the Zoo* presents a catalogue of unsavory noir motifs, including adultery, sadism, obsession and murder. Like *Freaks*, the film was considered excessive at the time and drew the ire of censorship boards in several states, causing it to be released in a number of re-edited versions in different markets.

The producer/director team of Edward and Victor Halperin, who had lensed the wonderfully atmospheric Bela Lugosi vehicle *White Zombie* (1932), offered another excursion into horror with *Supernatural* (1933). Glam actress Carole Lombard, best known for her roles in the "screwball" comedies of the 1930s such as *My Man Godfrey* (1936), was cast against type as a socialite who becomes possessed by the spirit of a dead murderess. Playing opposite her was the stalwart Randolph Scott, the hero of *Murders in the Zoo*.

Supernatural begins with a dynamic montage sequence depicting the trial and sentencing of notorious female serial killer Ruth Rogen (Vivienne Osborne), described as "one of the most dangerous women in criminal history," a vicious schizophrenic who has been sentenced to the electric chair for strangling three of her former lovers to death with her bare hands. Awaiting execution on death row, she is paid a visit by scientist Dr. Carl Houston (H.B. Warner), who is concerned that her spirit will somehow infect others after her death and cause copycat murders to occur. The histrionic Rogen consents to have her body bombarded with "nitrogenic rays" by the savant after her execution, and laments that she cannot get revenge on her former lover and betrayer, Paul Bavian. "If I could only use my hands, just for a few minutes," she snarls, laughing deliriously as she crushes a metal cup with the enormous strength of her strangler's grip.

Bavian (Alan Dinehart), Ruth's former squeeze, is a phony spiritualist, swindler and murderer with plans of his own. He is plotting to get his hooks into socialite Roma Courtney (Lombard), by pretending to contact recently deceased twin dead brother in the afterlife. Using this ruse, he intends to control Roma's considerable fortune via John's "advice" from beyond the grave. Toward this end, Bavian breaks into a funeral home and makes a wax death mask of John's face from the corpse, which he intends to use to simulate the brother's ghostly presence during a séance. He then contacts Roma and informs her that John is trying to contact her from the netherworld, and sets up a date for a séance at his spooky Greenwich Village digs.

Roma's fiancé, Grant Wilson (Scott), is predictably chagrined by this turn of events, and tries, unsuccessfully, to dissuade Roma from consulting the bogus medium. In the meantime, Rogen pays for her crimes in the chair, and her cadaver is released to Dr. Hammond. An eerie scene ensues in the scientist's lab as he props the dead murderess's corpse into a sitting position and bombards her with energy rays that cause her dead eyes to open involuntarily. During the séance at Bavian's place, Roma goes into a faint while optical effects superimpose Rogen's face over Roma's features, indicating that her body has become possessed by the killer. Roma, her visage now distorted by Rogen's twisted, psychopathic expressions, plots to be alone with Bavian so that the dead woman may exact her revenge from beyond the grave.

One of the first films to deal with the ghostly phenomenon of spirit possession, *Supernatural* was another slam-dunk for the Halperins after *White Zombie*. Genre critic Joe Kane opines, "*Supernatural* unfolds with pre–Code candor and often feels more like a modern movie in a period setting than an actual product of its time."[5] The use of a fast-moving montage sequence for exposition in the film's opening sequence is an innovative, almost experimental technique. Director Victor Halperin sustains the unearthly mood throughout, conjuring the atavistic terrors of the past against a realistic, modern-day backdrop. Carole Lombard's performance in the dual roles of Roma/Rogen carries the film, along with Vivienne Osborne's portrayal of female serial killer Ruth Rogen. Unfortunately, Randolph Scott's limited part as Roma's boyfriend, Grant, offers little opportunity for the actor to show any flash.

Serial strangler Ruth Rogen is an extreme *femme fatale*, yet despite her homicidal psychopathology her femininity makes her into a sympathetic figure. Female serial killers are rare in real life, yet have been the subject of a number of memorable films over the years, from *The Bad Seed* (1956) to *Monster* (2003). The theme of a dead person taking over a living person's body in order to commit murder would be explored in Hitchcock's *Psycho* (1960), while the criminal psychic character represented by Paul Bavian would become a fixture of classic films noir such as *Murder, My Sweet* (1944), *Nightmare Alley* (1947), and *The Amazing Mr. X* (1948).

Vivienne Osborne as the condemned murderess in *Supernatural* (Paramount, 1933).

Psychoanalyzing the Universal Monsters

By the mid–1930s the horror film boom had gone bust, partly due to the financial mismanagement of Universal by head honcho Carl Laemmle and his son Carl Jr. that led to the Laemmles losing control of the studio. Another factor was the burgeoning power of the Production Code authority under Joseph Breen. Breen and his censors had become concerned about depictions of depravity, sadism and torture in horror films like *Island of Lost Souls* (1932), *The Black Cat* (1934) and *The Raven* (1935), and were determined to bring the hammer down on the perceived prurient content of horror movies. As a result, when Universal began developing a sequel to their first horror hit, *Dracula* (1931), entitled *Dracula's Daughter*, the Breen office took a hard look at the project. Several iterations of the screenplay were rejected as unacceptable until a toned-down version of the script by Garrett Fort was greenlighted. That version still contained heavy lesbian overtones.

Dracula's Daughter (1936) begins immediately after the original *Dracula* leaves off, but the time period has inexplicably changed from the late 19th century to the mid–1930s. British police discover vampire hunter Prof. Von Helsing (Edward Van Sloan) just after having driven a stake through the heart of Count Dracula (represented by a briefly glimpsed wax dummy of Lugosi) and arrest him for murder. Scotland Yard inspector Sir Basil Humphrey (Gilbert Emery) is called in to investigate, but Von Helsing insists that vampires are at work. Sir Basil is justifiably skeptical about his supernatural alibi, but the professor insists that one of his former students, the prominent psychologist Dr. Jeffrey Garth (Otto Kruger), be called in as an expert witness to evaluate his sanity. "You're up against stern reality," Sir Basil insists.

In the meantime, a mysterious, black-clad woman makes off with the count's corpse and transports it to a site deep in the forest. She is revealed as Dracula's Daughter (Gloria Holden), a.k.a. the Countess Marya Zaleska, a female vampire who seeks to break free from her father's dread powers. In an eerie midnight ritual, the hooded and cloaked Marya burns Dracula's body on a funeral pyre, while intoning a magical ritual of exorcism. "Unto Adoni and Aseroth, into the keeping of the lords of the flame and lower pits, I consign this body, to be for evermore consumed in this purging fire," she chants. "Be thou exorcized, O Dracula, and thy body long undead, find destruction throughout eternity in the name of thy dark, unholy master."

Marya now believes herself to be delivered from her father's unholy influence, and exults to her servant, Sandor (Irving Pichel), that she is now "free to live as a woman." The sinister Sandor, however, quickly turns her mind back to morbidity and blood drinking as she stalks out into the London fog to claim another victim. Marya's resolve to be free of the curse of the undead is rekindled, however, when she meets Dr. Garth at a society party and feels a strange attraction to the psychologist. Discussing his involvement with the Von Helsing case, Garth holds forth that "sympathetic treatment will release the human mind from any obsession," words that inspire Marya to use psychiatry to combat her vampirism, and she makes an appointment to see Garth professionally.

Garth's fiancée, Janet (Marguerite Churchill), is less than thrilled at the attention that the psychologist is bestowing on the countess. Visiting Marya at her London flat, which is adorned with weird statuary but lacks any mirrors, Dr. Garth diagnoses her affliction as psychological obsession, although the vampiress is vague about the nature of her unsavory urges. He advises her to deliberately tempt herself and use her willpower to overcome her obsession, but Marya conceives of the therapy as something much more personal, as a struggle between Garth and her father's posthumous powers, a conflict of "the strength of the human mind against the powers of darkness."

Taking the doctor's advice to heart, Marya dispatches Sandor to bring a potential victim to her Chelsea studio under the ruse of needing an artist's model. Sandor hits on Lily (Nan Grey), a despondent prostitute who is about to throw herself into the Thames in despair, and persuades her to return with him to the studio. The Countess Zaleska is immediately tempted by Lily's beauty as she eyes the girl hungrily. "You won't object to removing your blouse, will you?" Marya asks coquettishly, and when Lily complies and bares her throat the countess moves in for the blood seduction. Lily is found on the street the next morning, still alive but suffering from a massive loss of blood and having total amnesia about the night's events. Upon examining her, Garth expresses the opinion that she is not suffering from amnesia, but from memory loss caused by "forced hypnosis." Using a machine that induces hypnotism by beaming a strobe light in the patient's face, together with an injection of adrenaline, Dr. Garth brings Lily temporarily out of her trance, whereupon the girl recounts being taken to Marya's mirrorless studio along with the rest of her terrifying ordeal before dying from shock. The detail about the mirrorless room cements Garth's suspicions that the countess is responsible for the recent string of vampiric homicides in London.

When Garth confronts Marya about his suspicions, she does not deny that she suffers from the "curse of the Draculas," and informs him that she is leaving London immediately and returning to her family estate in Transylvania. She begs the doctor to go with her and effect a cure, but when he refuses she kidnaps Janet and escapes to the Continent in an unmarked airplane. Scotland Yard launches a massive dragnet for the missing girl, but when it fails Garth sets out to rescue Janet and is later followed by Von Helsing and Sir Basil. Back at Castle Dracula, Janet has been placed in a catatonic trance as Marya hovers longingly over her prone form. Just as she bends to consummate their unholy union she is interrupted by the arrival of Garth. Marya promptly offers him a bargain: if he will remain and share the eternal life of vampirism with her, she will free Janet. "Let your science save her," she sneers, "or remain here." His medical skills useless, Garth consents to be her consort out of his love for Janet, but Sandor, who has been lurking nearby, realizes that Marya has betrayed her promise of eternal life to him, and kills her with a wooden shaft fired from a crossbow. At that moment Von Helsing and Sir Basil arrive to dispatch Sandor with a bullet, and the aged vampire hunter regards the death mask of the vampire woman, he declares that she is as beautiful as the day she died "a hundred years ago."

Dracula's Daughter languished in development hell for several years before being lensed, the film's screenplay being the major concern. Supposedly based on Bram Stoker's short story "Dracula's Guest," the finished film bears no resemblance to Stoker's work. One early version of the script by John L. Balderston, who had worked on both *Dracula* and *Frankenstein*, portrayed the count's daughter as a sadomasochistic dominatrix who keeps a secret torture chamber stocked with whips and chains. Star Gloria Holden (who reportedly loathed the part) comes off as a commanding screen presence, her statuesque figure giving her the aspect of a polysexual pagan goddess. Instead of playing the role as a menacing lady vampire, however, the film opts to make the countess a sympathetic figure, causing Ms. Holden to adopt a wide-eyed, rather woebegone expression in most scenes. The rest of the cast turn in workmanlike but lackluster performances, even horror vet Edward Van Sloan as perennial vampire hunter "Von" Helsing, with the exception of Nan Grey as the countess's homoerotic victim, Lily. Direction by Universal veteran Lew Landers is tepid and slow-moving, and the film is further marred by several misguided attempts at comic relief in the early reels. The scene in which Lily is brought out of her coma, raves and dies seems to have been lifted for a similar scene in Jacques Tourneur's supernatural thriller *Curse of the Demon* (1957).

The final version of the screenplay by Garrett Fort changes the dynamic of the vampire tale in several significant respects. For the first time in the history of the Universal monsters, the action is set within a 20th-century milieu of electricity, modern medicine and airplanes. Vampirism is portrayed as a voluntary, curable condition, as an exotic variety of psychiatric disorder similar to drug or sexual addiction. The contemporary setting and the shift toward the psychological and away from the supernatural mark the beginning of significant trends in horror cinema, trends that would become accentuated in many genre films made during the 1940s. These trends would also bring the horror genre closer to the universe of American films noir of the same period. Countess Zaleska presents an intriguing variation on the theme of the noir *femme fatale*, while the film's amnesia subplot would become a feature of several classic films noir.

The film's homoerotic content provides a whiff of noir perversity, and is part of a continuum of sapphic vampirism that stretches from Sheridan Le Fanu's seminal vampire novel *Carmilla* to the lesbo-vampirism of 1970s Hammer productions. Atmospheric art direction by Albert S. D'Agostino lends the film a noir visual flair that would later be evidenced when D'Agostino moved to RKO and worked with director Jacques Tourneur on dark tales like *Cat People* (1942) and *Out of the Past* (1947). Critics have likened the relationship between Countess Marya and her slavish servant Sandor to that of Norma Desmond and Max von Mayerling in *Sunset Boulevard* (1950). *Dracula's Daughter* was the inspiration for Michael Almereyda's *Nadja* (1994), with the action moved to Greenwich Village in the '90s, and for novelist Anne Rice's stories of homoerotic vampirism.

Dracula's Daughter would prove to be the last film made during Universal's "golden age" of horror movies that had begun in 1931 with *Dracula* and *Frankenstein*. With the new studio ownership fretting about censorship in America and Britain, horror film production ground to a halt between 1936 and 1938 and did not revive until Universal decided to revive the form with their highly successful production of *Son of Frankenstein* (1939). The so-called "silver age" of Universal horrors emerged in the 1940s, as war clouds threatened to engulf the entire world.

The studio's new horror star was Lon Chaney, Jr., son of the famous "Man of a Thousand Faces," Lon Senior, the star of *The Unholy Three* and many memorable silent movie roles. Despite being touted by the studio as "The Man of a Thousand Characters," Lon Junior was an actor of limited range who nevertheless showed flashes of brilliance in mainstream films like *Of Mice and Men* (1939) and *High Noon* (1952). In contrast to his father's menacing screen persona, Lon Junior projected a sympathetic warmth to audiences even while playing inhuman monsters in heavy makeup. Although known primarily as a horror actor, Chaney also appeared in a number of films noir, as a gangster in the

Bob Hope noir spoof *My Favorite Brunette* (1947), in the '50s remake of *High Sierra*, *I Died a Thousand Times* (1955) and in the prison picture *Big House, U.S.A.* (1955). Chaney brought a distinctive brand of "American-ness" to the horror film that had been lacking in foreign-born actors like Karloff, Lugosi, Lorre and Atwill. The Americanization of the horror film began with Chaney's first major star vehicle, *The Wolf Man* (1941). Universal had previously dabbled in lycanthropy in *The Werewolf of London* (1935), an odd misfire with science fiction overtones that starred English character actor Henry Hull in the title role. Unwilling to recycle material from the earlier film, and lacking a literary source for inspiration, the studio turned to sci-fi/horror writer Curt Siodmak to generate a screenplay.

Brother of noir director Robert Siodmak, who helmed some of the most memorable films noir of the '40s, such as *Phantom Lady* (1944), *The Killers* (1946) and *The File on Thelma Jordan* (1950), Curt Siodmak was known primarily as a science fiction writer who had penned the Euro sci-fi outings *Floating Platform One Does Not Reply* (1933) and *The Tunnel* (1935), and would later author the seminal horror/SF novel *Donovan's Brain* (1943). Siodmak would also produce stories and screenplays for some of the most acclaimed and popular horror films of the period, including *I Walked with a Zombie* (1943), *Frankenstein Meets the Wolf Man* (1943) and *House of Frankenstein* (1944). The brothers Siodmak, who were of Jewish extraction, had fled the Nazi regime in the 1930s and emigrated to Hollywood along with many other luminaries of the German cinema and brought some of the shadows of the Old World with them.

The Wolf Man begins with a book being opened to a page which reads: "Lycanthropy (Werewolfism). A disease of the mind in which human beings imagine they are wolfmen. According to an old legend which persists in certain localities the victim actually assumes the physical characteristics of the animal." The narrative begins as prodigal son Larry Talbot (Chaney) returns to his ancestral estate in Wales after living 18 years in America. Larry is returning to Talbot Castle to console his father, Sir John (Claude Rains), after the death of Larry's older brother, John, in a hunting accident. Sir John, an astronomer, is aristocratic, formal and restrained while his son is open and warm-hearted, but father and son are soon reconciled.

While adjusting Sir John's telescope, Larry uses the instrument to voyeuristically spy on Gwen Conliffe (Evelyn Ankers) in her bedroom above her father's antique shop. Paying a visit to the shop, he comes on wolfishly to Gwen as romantic sparks fly between them. Larry aggressively solicits a date with her that very night, proposing to take her to a gypsy carnival that has just rolled into town. While browsing around the shop, Larry is attracted to a cane adorned with the grotesque head of a wolf crafted in silver, and buys it. Gwen points out that the animal head represents a werewolf, and recites a traditional poem about a "man who is pure in heart" who transforms into a wolf under the influence of the full moon. Back at Talbot Castle, Larry shows the silver-headed cane to his father and asks him about the werewolf legend, but Sir John dismisses it as "the ancient explanation of the dual personality in each of us."

Later that night, Larry arrives to take Gwen to the carnival only to find that she has invited her friend Jenny Williams (Fay Helm) along as a chaperone. While Jenny goes off to have her fortune told, Larry tries to make time with Gwen, and eventually learns that she is engaged. The two lovebirds continue their intense flirtation as Jenny consults the gypsy fortune-teller, Bela (Bela Lugosi), about her future. Bela immediately perceives that all the omens surrounding Jenny are bad as a mystical five-sided star (pentagram) appears on her palm and he curtly dismisses her with a stern warning to leave as quickly as possible. As Jenny flees across the fog-bound moor a wailing howl rings out and is soon followed by the screams of the terrified girl. Rushing to the rescue, Larry finds Jenny being mauled by a huge wolf, which he beats to death with the silver-headed cane. In the aftermath, Larry stumbles home in shock, believing that he has been bitten by the animal.

The incident is investigated by the local constable, Captain Paul Montford (Ralph Bellamy), and town physician, Dr. Lloyd (Warren Williams), who find Jenny's corpse mutilated by an animal and Bela's body with the skull bashed in, along with Larry's wolf-headed cane. Confronting Larry with the evidence, Larry insists that he killed a wolf, not Bela, but when he attempts to show them the beast's bite marks, they have somehow disappeared. Montford and Dr. Lloyd call Larry's sanity into question, believing that he killed Bela in a state of confusion while defending Jenny from the gypsy's attack.

Larry and Gwen, along with Gwen's fiancé, Frank Andrews (Patric Knowles), return to the carnival at the gypsy encampment on the following evening, where Larry gets perturbed when he cannot fire at the tin image of a wolf in a shooting gallery. Racing through the fair, he comes upon Bela's mother, the aged Maleva (Maria Ouspenskaya), who seems to have been waiting for him. The old gypsy woman reveals to him that her son, Bela, was a werewolf, and now that he has been bitten by the beast, Larry is set to become a lycanthrope himself. A whirling montage of images showing Gwen, the pentagram, the wolf's head cane and other images depict Larry's disoriented state of mind as he flees back to Talbot Castle, where he soon transforms into the wolf man, a hairy, fanged creature with the mind of a homicidal maniac. Running wild out on the foggy moor, the werewolf brutally murders an unfortunate gravedigger while roaming through the town cemetery.

Upon waking on the following morning, Larry is consumed by grief and guilt over the creature's actions, and unburdens himself to his father, but Sir John dismisses his talk of werewolvery as evidence that his son has become mentally unbalanced. "I do believe that most anything can happen to a man in his own mind," he opines. Later that day, when Montford and Dr. Lloyd pay a visit, they are equally dismissive of Larry's claims. "I believe that a man lost in the mazes of his mind may imagine he's anything," Dr. Lloyd offers, confiding to Sir John that Larry is "a sick man" who may have to be sent to a mental hospital because of his irrational beliefs. After all, forensic evidence shows that Jenny and the gravedigger have been killed by an animal, and Larry carries no wound upon his body that supports his story about being bitten by Bela the werewolf.

When the full moon rises on the following evening, Larry transforms once more into the wolf man and roams the moors in search of victims when his foot gets caught in a bear trap set by the town's werewolf hunters. Writhing in agony, the creature loses consciousness as Maleva's gypsy wagon rolls out of the fog. The aged crone recites a bit of gypsy poetry over the prone lycanthrope that summarizes his fateful situation. "The way you walked was thorny," Maleva intones, "through no fault of your own, but as the rain enters the soil, the river enters the sea, so tears run to a predestined end." These sorrowful verses have the effect of changing the creature back into Larry, who extricates himself from the trap and hitches a ride back to Talbot Castle inside the gypsy wagon.

Larry and Maleva begin to bond as the old gypsy woman has become a surrogate mother to him because of their shared curse.

In the final act of the tragedy, Larry announces to Sir John that he is leaving and warns Gwen away when he sees the pentagram materialize on her palm and realizes that she is to be his next victim. Sir John, however, insists on one final test of his son's sanity by tying him to a chair in the castle as he goes out to join Montford and the villagers in their hunt for the beast. Unfortunately, when the moon rises, Larry transforms once more and escapes his bonds, attacking Gwen, who has come looking for the man she loves. As fate would have it, Sir John comes to her rescue, killing his son with the same silver-headed cane Larry had used to kill Bela. Sir John watches in stunned amazement as the creature becomes Larry before his eyes and Maleva arrives to recite her mournful poem over his corpse.

Genre critics consider *The Wolf Man* to be the last of Universal's "adult" horror films and the beginning of the "silver age" of the studio's monster movie output. The Wolf Man, a creation of makeup whiz Jack Pierce, is kept offscreen for a good deal of the film, allowing for character development and dramatic interaction that ultimately makes the movie work. Director George Waggner sustains the eerie mood throughout while keeping the action moving along smoothly through Jack Otterson's atmospheric, fog-bound sets, and John Fulton's elaborate time-lapse cinematography enabled the transmogrification of man into werewolf. Chaney's earnest, if plodding, performance as the doomed Larry Talbot brought a sympathetic warmth to the monstrous role that was reminiscent of Karloff's portrayal of Frankenstein's monster.

The rest of the cast turn in workmanlike but not particularly inspired performances, with the exception of Claude Rains, whose portrait of the acerbic, skeptical Sir John burns with the actor's characteristic screen intensity, and Russian-born actress Maria Ouspenskaya in the role of Maleva, the mysterious old gypsy woman. Perhaps the weakest member of the cast is the Wolf Man himself, whose appearance has been described by critics as resembling "a lumbering, shaggy bear," or "a hirsute Cossack," while Ivan Butler observes that Universal's werewolf "might pass among apes, but it bears not the slightest resemblance to any wolf that ever was, would have been disclaimed with horror by the most devoted wolf-mother, and would not have deceived the hunters for any instant."[6] *The Wolf Man* might have been a stronger film if the creature had been kept in the shadows, an approach taken in *Cat People* (1942).

Chaney's acting in *The Wolf Man* is widely regarded as his most memorable horror movie role, and was a major factor in the film's box-office success. Most importantly, Chaney was the first all–American horror star, and he conferred a distinctly New World flavor upon the film's old world proceedings. This brought a new intimacy and taste of American realism to the Germanic horror formula that audiences could relate to. Although *The Wolf Man* is nominally set in a small village in Wales, most of the other leads, notably Ralph Bellamy and Evelyn Ankers, speak unabashedly in American dialect. The film began the axis shift away from the Euro-horrors of the past toward a novel Americanization of the genre that would soon find its fruition in the urban American horror noirs of RKO producer Val Lewton.

The real star of *The Wolf Man*, however, is Curt Siodmak's masterful screenplay, which is arguably the finest horror script ever produced at Universal. Siodmak imbued his scenario with a feeling of high tragedy as an innocent man is compelled to commit murder and a father is fated to unwittingly kill his only surviving son. The German émigré writer claimed that his life experiences under the Nazi regime "forced into a fate I didn't want: a Jew in Germany"[7] provided inspiration for his tragic horror tale. Indeed, the film's gypsy characters are Siodmak's analogues for Jews, another ethnic minority persecuted and murdered in the Nazi holocaust, and the gypsies are drawn with a great deal of sympathy. The cruel machinations of destiny, a classic film noir motif in noirs like *Detour* (1945) and *Out of the Past* (1947), is also central to the plot, and one of the original working titles for *The Wolf Man* was *Destiny*. Presentiments abound as Larry selects the wolf's-head walking stick that will ultimately be used to beat him to death, and views the magical pentagram sign on the palms of his future victims. "Life itself contains the curse of the Wolf Man," Siodmak observed, "sufferings without having been guilty, being subjected to fates which are decided by the pleasure of the gods."[8]

Siodmak's script also emphasizes psychological explanations for lycanthropy as an alternative to invoking the supernatural. The authorities, including Sir John, are constantly insisting that Larry suffers from some form of obsessive mental derangement. His condition is repeatedly described as "a disease of the mind," "a variety of schizophrenia," or "the ancient explanation of the dual personality in each of us." Of course the audience, who has seen Larry transform into his wolfen state, knows that this is just a bunch of psychobabble. Author Jeremy Dyson notes that Siodmak's script sets up "a tension between the rational and the supernatural where some form of insanity is invoked by the voices of reason to account for whatever unusual events are being depicted."[9] This psychological approach to horror would become a feature of many genre films to follow, which would explore the *frisson* between the workings of the mind and concepts of the preternatural. A similar skepticism concerning the value of psychiatry would later emerge in noirs such as *Nightmare Alley* (1947) and *Brainstorm* (1965), which featured malignant, manipulative psychiatrists and portrayed the discipline in a highly negative light.

Personality transformation (or split personality) is another noir theme explored in *The Wolf Man*. Larry Talbot is, in effect, a homicidal maniac who is compelled to kill by the light of the full moon and seems to have partial amnesia about what he does in his werewolf state. Unlike a real wolf or other wild animal in nature, Larry's alter ego is compelled to murder without any rationality or reason, in a manner more similar to a human serial killer. The swirling montage of fearful and libidinous images that precede Larry's initial transformation also appears in both the 1932 and 1941 versions of *Dr. Jekyll and Mr. Hyde*, and in all cases is meant to signify the protagonist's descent into the vortex of the Id-double, the atavistic self-within-a-self that resides in the most primitive regions of the mind.

Unfortunately, the Universal creature feature would go into a decline during the war years, descending into monster rallies like *Frankenstein Meets the Wolf Man* (1943), *House of Frankenstein* (1944) and *House of Dracula* (1945), all of which featured Chaney as Larry Talbot and his lycanthropic alter-ego. But the Hollywood horror film was about to be remade, and in a distinctly noir configuration, over at RKO.

3

The Val Lewton/ Jacques Tourneur Noir Legacy

By 1942, RKO Studios was teetering on the brink of financial ruin. After cranking out a string of popular and memorable features, including *Gunga Din* (1939), *The Hunchback of Notre Dame* (1939) and *Kitty Foyle* (1940), the studio was in a fiscal funk because of *wunderkind* director Orson Welles, whose lavish RKO productions of *Citizen Kane* (1941) and *The Magnificent Ambersons* (1942), although critically acclaimed, were major-league flops at the box office. "In case of an air raid," a wartime Hollywood joke went, "report to RKO studios because they haven't had a hit in years."

A new studio head, Charles Koerner, was brought in to put RKO's financial house in order, and promptly sent Welles and his Mercury Theatre troupe packing. Instead of arty but unpopular A-list movies, Koerner decided to concentrate on producing low-budget, high-profit B-pictures. Since Universal's *The Wolf Man* was doing a brisk business, Koerner decided to create a B-movie unit at RKO to produce a series of modest horror thrillers to compete with the Universal product. His choice for the job was a young producer named Val Lewton.

Lewton had worked as an assistant to famed producer David O. Selznick on such lavish productions as *Anna Karenina* (1935), *The Prisoner of Zenda* (1937), *Gone with the Wind* (1939) and *Rebecca* (1940). Chafing under Selznick's authoritarian shadow, Lewton was amenable to heading up his own production unit on Koerner's terms. Each film was to cost no more than $150,000, running time was not to exceed 75 minutes, and the studio would supply the titles from an "audience tested" list. Outside of these constraints, Lewton was to have complete artistic freedom in all production matters. The first title assigned by Koerner was *Cat People*, meant as RKO's answer to *The Wolf Man*.

A Russian émigré, Lewton was a highly sensitive, deeply literate soul who would put his individual stamp on the series of stylish chillers he would produce, which would take the traditional horror film in new directions. Critics have long recognized Lewton's contribution to the genesis of classic film noir during the early 1940s. Arthur Lyons, for instance, observes, "Orson Welles has been given much critical credit for helping define the RKO look, but Val Lewton's B-unit, given virtual autonomy by the studio, was busy cranking out B-gems that, although billed as horror movies, were in many cases fine psychological thrillers. They would have a great effect on film noir to come."[1] Similarly, Edmund Bansak notes, "The Lewton RKO films have strong associations with early 1940s examples of noir melodrama, which is what sets them apart from the horror fare of the previous decade,"[2] while Eric Somer states, "In fact, standard film noir visuals abound in the Lewton horror cycle with emphasis on darkness, chiaroscuro lighting, entrapping shadows and cage-like imagery. These 'horror films,' I suggest, are equally at home in the film noir genre."[3]

Lewton's chief collaborator on the first three films in the series was French-born director Jacques Tourneur. The son of acclaimed director Maurice Tourneur, Jacques had met Lewton when he was working as a second unit director on Selznick's *A Tale of Two Cities* (1935) for MGM, and Lewton was impressed enough to bring him aboard at the RKO horror unit. Tourneur would lens the best of the Lewton thrillers before going on to direct one of the most visually exquisite of the classic films noir, *Out of the Past* (1947) as well as the gothic noir *Experiment Perilous* (1944). The Lewton/Tourneur artistic symbiosis has caused some confusion about the authorship of the films they made together, which are usually credited to Lewton rather than Tourneur in a reversal of standard auteur theory. A recent documentary about Lewton produced by Martin Scorsese illustrates the conventional wisdom by stating that "the films he [Lewton] produced belonged to him," Scorsese narrates, emphasizing that the producer "pre-directed his films on paper." This reduces Tourneur and Lewton's other directors to mere technicians who simply realized Lewton's visions with their cameras.

A contrary view has been expressed in a recent bio of Tourneur by Chris Fujiwara, who has delineated elements of Tourneur's directorial style that stand apart from his work with Lewton. "The director's narrative and stylistic choices constantly underline absence and distance," Fujiwara observes. "Significant events take place offscreen or before the start of the film; exposition is omitted or, when needed, made empty and incomprehensible, so that the motives of characters, even protagonists, remain mysterious to the audience.... His heroes seem outside themselves, far away, indifferent to what happens to them.... *I Walked with a Zombie, Experiment Perilous,* and *Out of the Past* highlight this strange self-remoteness in a unique way by having characters narrate sections of the action in voice-over and by emphasizing the disjunction between the act of narration and the unity of the represented events."[4] In any case, the Lewton/Tourneur collaboration seemed to bring out the best artistic qualities in both film-makers and inspired some of the most poetic horror films in the history of cinema.

Lewton's first assignment from Koerner was *Cat People* (1942), which was conceived as a low-budget rip-off of Universal's *The Wolf Man*. Working with scriptwriter DeWitt Bodeen, the producer initially intended to adapt a story entitled "Ancient Sorceries" by British horror writer Algernon Blackwood involving witches and cats and set in the typical Old World milieu familiar to fans of the Universal horror product. Somewhere along the way, however, a decision was made that would change the aesthetic of the horror film and set the stage for the emerging stylistic matrix of film noir. According to one account, it was Tourneur who rejected the idea of doing *Cat People* as a formulaic costume movie and instead opting for setting the film in contemporary America. "At first Bodeen wrote *Cat People* as a period thing, but I argued against that," Tourneur recounted. "I said that if you're going to have horror, the audience must be able to identify with the characters in order to be frightened."[5] Bodeen, however, insisted that the notion to set the action in the modern world was Lewton's idea. Thus, the shadows of the horror film were transported to the mean streets of 1940s-era urban America.

Cat People opens in the Central Park zoo, with the skyscrapers of Manhattan looming in the background, where draftsman Oliver Reed (Kent Smith) is enjoying a lunch break. He strikes up a chance flirtation with cute fashion illustrator Irena Dubrovna (Simone Simon), which quickly blossoms into a romance. Irena is a refugee from Serbia who leads a lonely, hermetic existence in the big city, and Oliver is immediately fascinated and attracted to the mysterious Serb and soon proposes marriage. Irena has misgivings about the wedding, citing local legends about "cat people" and witchcraft from her Serbian village that are symbolized by a statuette of King John of Serbia spearing a cat on his sword, but Oliver overcomes her objections by appealing to American level-headedness and dismissing her Old World beliefs as mere fairy tales. "You're Irena," he admonishes her, "you're here in America. You're so normal you're even in love with me, Oliver Reed, a good plain Americano. You're so normal you're going to marry me. And those fairy tales, you can tell them to our children."

During the wedding party at a local restaurant, a striking-looking witchy woman (Elizabeth Russell) rises to address Irena as "her sister" in Serbian before stalking out. On their wedding night Irena is unable to participate in the nuptials, and appeals to Oliver for patience. It soon becomes evident that his wife is sexually frigid and that her aversion to sex is based on a superstitious folk belief that she will transform into a panther if any man attempts to make love to her. "Let me have time," she pleads to her husband, "time to get over that feeling there's something evil in me." Under these emotional stresses, Irena's behavior begins to descend into irrationality. She develops a fixation for a black panther at the zoo, feeding it a pet bird that she has accidentally killed in a fit of catlike aggression, and later steals the key to the panther's cage from a careless zoo worker.

Oliver's patience soon begins to wear thin, and he insists that Irena be treated by a psychiatrist, Dr. Louis Judd (Tom Conway). The urbane Manhattanite shrink places Irena under hypnosis, where he probes into her family history in Serbia and her strange obsession with feline transformation as it relates to her sexual dysfunction. Predictably, the psychiatrist dismisses her superstitious beliefs as "a canker of the mind." In the meantime, Oliver begins to warm to his co-worker at the C.R. Cooper Ship & Barge Construction Co., Alice Moore (Jane Randolph), a warm, open Americano woman who is the antithesis of Irena. Although Irena warns her husband to "never let me feel jealousy or anger," the romance between Oliver and Alice starts to blossom around the water cooler, and their relationship quickly becomes apparent to Irena.

Soon Alice is stalked by an unseen panther that pursues her down a lonely path in Central Park, and, in the film's most terrifying sequence, prowls around a darkened swimming pool as Alice screams for her life until she is rescued. After her first "werecat" transformation, Irena experiences a nightmare that includes images of a whirlpool, an animated sequence featuring black cats, and King John drawing his sword. In the wake of the attacks Irena's erratic behavior comes under increased scrutiny, but her therapy with Dr. Judd is not going well and has descended into a contest of wills between doctor and patient as the psychiatrist attempts to probe deeper into her personality. Judd vows, "I shall discover your secret," as he falls under the erotic spell of the panther woman.

Things come to a head when Oliver confesses to his wife that he loves Alice and wants to divorce her. Concerned about Irena's mental state, he consults Dr. Judd, who recommends that Irena be committed to an asylum. "These hallucinations approach

Cat lady Simone Simon is psychoanalyzed by malicious shrink Tom Conway in Jacques Tourneur's *Cat People* (RKO, 1942).

insanity," he opines. "It's a deterioration of the mind, an escape into fantasy. And it's dangerous." Oliver arranges for Judd to interview Irena prior to committing her, but when she doesn't show up for the interview, Oliver and Alice decide to catch up on their work, while Judd secretly jimmies the lock to Irena's apartment so that he can sneak back in later. In the darkened drafting office illuminated from below by light tables, Irena menaces Alice and Oliver in panther form, but is repulsed when Oliver brandishes a crucifix-like T-square. Irena returns home to find Dr. Judd waiting, and the lecherous shrink takes her in his arms and kisses her, whereupon, to his immense surprise, she transforms into the panther once more and attacks him. Defending himself with his sword cane, Judd manages to impale the beast before being mauled to death, and Irena escapes, mortally wounded by the broken shard of Judd's blade lodged inside her. She returns to the panther cage at the zoo, where she uses the stolen key to unlock the cage, and the animal springs at her to deliver the coup de grâce. The cat is soon killed when it runs out into traffic, and Alice and Oliver arrive to find Irena's corpse.

Lewton and Tourneur's modern tale of supernatural menace would revolutionize the horror film. The Americanization of the genre that had begun with *The Wolf Man* came full circle in *Cat People*, where the terrors of the Old World were transplanted from Transylvania to Manhattan, a realism that gave cinematic horror a new, vital immediacy. Lewton insisted that his characters be shown working at their jobs in prosaic surroundings like the C.R. Cooper Ship & Barge Construction Company or Sally Lund's restaurant. One of the key scenes, in fact, transpires when the were-panther invades Oliver and Alice's workplace at the barge construction company. The injection of supernatural darkness into the workaday world of modern America is the film's most profound achievement.

Tourneur's direction shines in the latter half of the film, especially in the walk through Central Park and the swimming pool sequence, both of which make masterful use of sound. The sudden cessation of Irena's quick footsteps herald her transformation into the cat, while Alice's screams in the swimming pool are echoed in reflected light from the water playing upon the ceiling in abstract patterns. Tourneur's exquisite use of light and shadow is evident in several key scenes that take place in rain, snow and fog, and in the frequent use of zones or "barriers" of darkness within the frame. "I'll tell you a secret," Lewton once explained in an interview, "if you make the screen dark enough, the mind's eye will read anything into it you want! We're great ones for dark patches."[6] It should be pointed out, however, that the use of these "dark patches" was not entirely a matter of aesthetics, but was also driven by economics. Shadows were used to disguise

Simone Simon's feline menace is displayed in this poster for *Cat People* (RKO, 1942).

pre-existing sets from films like Welles's *The Magnificent Ambersons* so that they could be used again, and turning off the arc lights simply saved money on electricity and personnel. Noir icon Robert Mitchum, star of Tourneur's *Out of the Past*, reflected on the use of these techniques in RKO B-movies in typical noir fashion: "Cary Grant and all the big stars got all the lights," the actor recalled. "We lit our sets with cigarette butts."[7]

These low-key lighting techniques created a psychological effect of tension and uncertainty in the viewer. J.P. Tellote observes that Tourneur's use of "dark patches" of screen space "signals a black hole or vacant meaning in the physical realm which, in spite of man's natural desire to fill it with consciousness and significance, persistently and troublingly remains open."[8] This style of lighting was also perfectly suited to the fear-drenched cinematic ambience of film noir. Nicholas Musuraca, Tourneur's director of photography, had shot Boris Ingster's *Stranger on the Third Floor* (1940), an atmospheric crime melodrama that is considered one of the very first films noir. In addition to *Out of the Past*, Musuraca would also provide noir visuals for genre entries such as John Farrow's *Where Danger Lives* (1950), Ida Lupino's *The Hitchhiker* (1953), Fritz Lang's *Clash by Night* (1952) and *The Blue Gardenia* (1953), as well as Robert Siodmak's gothic noir *The Spiral Staircase* (1946).

DeWitt Bodeen's screenplay emphasizes the psychological aspects of the story over its supernatural overtones. Jeremy Dyson observes, "What's interesting about the use of psychiatry in *Cat People* is that it is not just present as a surface detail, but that it actually drives the plot. It creates another layer of conflict for Irena, and in Dr. Judd's behavior we see how it can be at least as amoral, if not immoral, as the dark magic of Irena's ancestors."[9] Similarly, J. Robert Craig and Carrol L. Fry note that "the supernatural clap-trap of the story line is a veneer for yet another story — the gradual deterioration of a woman's psyche into schizophrenic violence. Through patterns of visual symbols and symbolic imagery, Lewton and Tourneur show the story of a girl who is the victim of severe sexual repression and who, because of her repression and jealousy, develops a personality split that ultimately destroys her."[10] Because Irena's shape-shifting is only suggested but never actually seen by the audience, an element of ambiguity is introduced as to whether the were-panther is real or a figment of her imagination and atavistic fears. She is a typically alienated noir character, consumed by a dreadful loneliness and embracing the nighted side of her personality. "I like the dark," she purrs to Oliver during their courtship, "it's friendly." Malignant psychiatry, as represented by Dr. Judd, a character type who would later become a feature of a number of classic films noir.

Simone Simon's Irena is a bipolar, schizoid figure, who is sometimes portrayed in a sympathetic light, but at other times seems to exult in her bestial alternate persona. The actress sports a demented, carnivorous leer in a couple of key scenes. Irena is not exactly a typical noir *femme fatale* à la James M. Cain, but the cat woman does represent a murderous aspect of female sexuality and dangerous sexual repression as a result of jealousy. Her homicidal rages are directed not at her husband, but at her romantic rival, Alice. Simon is suitably exotic as the Serbian panther lady, but her heavy French accent causes her to flub some of her lines and her performance is a bit stiff at times. Kent Smith is perfectly cast as the doltish, clueless Oliver, and Jane Randolph's performance as Alice, "the new kind of other woman," ranges from a cheery optimism to absolute terror and actually carries much of the film.

Cat People hit a chord with contemporary audiences and was credited with reversing the fortunes of RKO with its exceptional box-office performance, grossing $4 million against an investment of less than $135,000. Lewton and Tourneur had delivered one of the landmarks of the American horror film on a shoestring budget and beaten Universal at their own game. The Lewton productions represented a significant shift toward psychological and contemporary horror that would eventually culminate in Hitchcock's *Psycho* (1960), another tale of dual personality, and their influence can also be discerned in '40s-era horror fare from other studios like Universal's *Son of Dracula* (1943) and Paramount's *The Uninvited* (1944). Hitchcock cribbed the idea of using an animated cartoon as part of a dream sequence in *Spellbound* (1945) and later in *Vertigo* (1958), and critics have pointed out resemblances between the plot of *Cat People* and Hitch's *Marnie* (1964), a similar tale of a man who marries a frigid woman with a homicidal past.

Koerner's next assignment for Lewton and Tourneur bore the incredibly lurid but "audience-tested" title *I Walked with a Zombie* (1943). Curt Siodmak, creator of Universal's *The Wolf Man*, which, ironically, was the template for *Cat People*, was brought on board to script. The title was based on an article in *American Weekly* magazine by Inez Wallace entitled, "I Met a Zombie," a non-fiction account of voodoo practices in Haiti. Lewton decided to transform the sensational subject matter into his version of "*Jane Eyre* in the West Indies."

The film begins in Canada, where nurse Betsy Connell (Frances Dee) is dispatched to the Caribbean island of Saint Sebastian by her employment agency to care for the wife of sugar plantation owner Paul Holland (Tom Conway). Arriving at Fort Holland, the Holland estate on the tropical isle, Betsy learns that Paul's wife, Jessica (Christine Gordon), exists in a strange, death-like state after being afflicted with a virulent fever and wanders about the plantation like a wraith in a white, flowing dress. The dour Paul is bitter about his wife's illness, and harbors a barely concealed enmity toward his alcoholic half-brother, Wesley Rand (James Ellison). Betsy eventually learns that a love triangle existed between Paul, Jessica and Wesley before Jessica became ill after hearing the lyrics to an eerie song performed by a local calypso singer (Sir Lancelot). The troubadour's acid lyrics reveal that Jessica was plotting to go away with Wesley before being stopped by Paul, and that the two half-brothers may renew their rivalry over Betsy, the new addition to their household.

Although Betsy falls in love with Paul, she is driven to find a cure for Jessica's condition and arranges for her to have a series of insulin injections designed to shock her body out of the illness. When the insulin treatments fail, Betsy hears about "better doctors," the island's voodoo priests from Alma (Teresa Harris), one of Fort Holland's servants. Desperate for a cure, Betsy leads the spectral Jessica on a walk through the sugar cane fields to the nighttime ceremonies at the Houmfort, the open-air voodoo "church." In the film's most beautiful and terrifying sequence, the two women traverse the dreamlike landscape of the cane fields until they encounter Carrefour (Darby Jones), the towering zombie guardian of the Houmfort, who allows them to pass by the crossroads unharmed.

At the ceremony, Betsy witnesses ecstatic voodoo drumming, the spirit possession of one of the celebrants, and other weird rituals. When Betsy consults Damballah, the voodoo oracle, about Jessica's condition, she is suddenly ushered into a room where she unexpectedly encounters Wesley's mother, Mrs. Rand (Edith Barrett), who is using the "oracle" to dispense Western medical diagnosis and treatment under the guise of super-stition. But while Mrs. Rand is explaining her psychological manipulation of native beliefs to Betsy, the voodoo practitioners, who suspect Jessica of being a zombie, begin to subject the comatose woman to a series of ritual tests that Betsy interrupts to lead Jessica home.

Jessica's appearance at the Houmfort creates a stir among the locals, who demand that she be returned to endure further ritual tests, which leads to a formal legal inquiry from St. Sebastian's administrators. During the proceedings, Mrs. Rand reveals that her involvement in the voodoo cult is deeper than anyone suspected. She relates how, unhappy with the discord Jessica created within the Holland household, she turned to voodoo for a solution and unexpectedly became possessed by the god Damballah during a ceremony. It was she who pronounced the spell that turned Jessica into a zombie. While the author-ities have a hard time believing this, the cultists launch a psychic assault on Ft. Holland designed to return Jessica to the Houmfort. First, Carrefour is sent to abduct her, and when this fails, their magic is used to compel the weak-minded Wesley to murder her. As he flees from Carrefour holding the dead Jessica in his arms, he escapes into the surf, only to drown as the evil lovers are united in death. The film ends as their bodies are returned to Ft. Holland as a solemn native delivers a mournful requiem in voice-over: "The woman was a wicked woman and she was dead in her own lifetime. Yea Lord, dead in the selfishness of her spirit and the man followed her. Her steps led him down to evil, her feet took hold on death."

I Walked with a Zombie is considered the high point of the Lewton/Tourneur col-laboration, and is one of the most poetic and beautiful horror films ever made. Tourneur's use of chiaroscuro is breathtaking as he creates a shadow landscape through which the characters move about like somnambulists in a nightmare. In an article about the film, Michel Perez characterizes the movie's dark cinematic ambience as "an atmosphere whose dominant visual and sound elements—the unyielding and maleficent glare of the moon-light in counterpoint with the overriding background beat of voodoo drums—combine rather to reflect a general psychosexual imbalance comparable in its vertigo to the flounderings of, and the sensations experienced by, a drowning man."[11] In several key scenes the characters seem to glide like specters through the immaterial dreamscape. As in *Cat People*, Tourneur's vivid use of sound greatly enhances the visuals, from the weird moan of the wind and throbbing drums in the walk through the cane field sequence to the scraping whisper of Carrefour's feet as he prowls through Ft. Holland in search of Jessica. In contrast to the suggested, unseen horrors of *Cat People*, *Zombie* has an onscreen monster in Darby Jones's Carrefour, a gaunt, threatening creature who truly seems to be one of the undead and provides the film with a concrete visual menace.

Siodmak's script, co-written by Ardel Wray and overseen by Lewton, plays upon the *frisson* between belief and disbelief in the supernatural, between the Apollonian and Dionysian realms of consciousness. In the film, Paul is skeptical about the voodoo and dismisses it as "cheap mummery," while Wesley takes the opposite tack, declaring that the priests "have charms that can pull a man halfway around the world," and the pivotal figure of Mrs. Rand, a level-headed product of Western society, becomes possessed by a voodoo god. The atavistic voodoo practices of the Islanders are depicted with an anthro-pological detachment that is the result of Lewton and Siodmak's extensive research into voodooism. Tourneur's artistic sensibilities were no doubt stirred by the subject matter because he professed a belief in the occult. "I detest the expression 'horror film,'" the director later confided in an interview. "I make films on the supernatural and I make them because I believe in it."[12] Tourneur's utter conviction helped to make audiences into true believers as well.

Like *Cat People*, the plot of *Zombie* revolves around a romantic triangle that is ultimately resolved by violence and death. Like the earlier film, it is also about a monstrous form of sexual repression. The living/dead Jessica is a necrophiliac sex object who, before her zombification, was a classic *femme fatale* that nearly destroyed the Holland family by seducing her husband's brother. Perez observes, "The burden of sexual frustration which pervades the atmosphere of *I Walked with a Zombie*, as of so many American films, is inherent in the plot; it is assumed as given. The film develops as a tapestry of frustration: the forlorn sexuality which is its determining motif is comparable in its enmeshing weave to the web spun by a spider."[13] A mood of deep melancholy hangs over the production, while the performances of the cast members are highly restrained. Two of the most arresting roles are by the actors portraying the zombies. Christine Gordon as Jessica and Darby Jones as Carrefour are otherworldly figures who command much of the audience's attention in key scenes and conjure the shadows of the supernatural in a most convincing way.

Although it is set in the 1940s, *Zombie* has the ambience of a 19th-century gothic thriller and contains many key motifs culled from the genre. As in *Jane Eyre*, the work on which it is reputedly based, a young woman travels to a crumbling estate where she becomes the servant of a mysterious man whose wife suffers from a form of insanity which presents an obstacle to the protagonist's romantic desires for the master of the house. Fort Holland is a typical gothic manse, outwardly impressive but inwardly crumbling. "There's no beauty here," Paul says of the island paradise of St. Sebastian, "only death and decay." Critics have noted similarities with Hitchcock's *Rebecca* (1940), another contemporary iteration of the gothic formula, which Lewton had worked on during his stint with Selznick just a few years earlier. Like *Rebecca*, *Zombie* features a noiresque voice-over narration by the main character that comments on the action in some future time after the events of the film have taken place.

Zombie also functions as a kind of supernatural mystery story. As Chris Fujiwara notes, "Many Tourneur films—both the fantastic and the realistic ones—share an important feature of another genre, the mystery.... *I Walked with a Zombie* never obliges the viewer to commit to either a natural or supernatural explanation of Jessica Holland's state. By the end of the film, we may still not be convinced that a supernatural causality has determined the events of the narrative. A mystery that never reveals its solution, the film extends mysteriousness to all its levels and characters."[14] As in film noir, shadows of night and dread deepen ambiguity and sustain the mysterious atmosphere.

While contemporary screen notions of zombies as flesh-eating, undead ghouls originated with George Romero's *Night of the Living Dead* (1968), there is a real phenomenon of voodoo and zombies in Haiti. *I Walked with a Zombie,* based on a non-fiction magazine article by Inez Wallace and supplemented by the research of Siodmak and Lewton, accurately reflects certain aspects of these bizarre practices. Laws prohibiting the making of zombies are written into the Haitian penal code, and reports from Haitian doctors in the 1970s concerning individuals who had been pronounced medically dead and later shown up alive provided scientific evidence for the phenomenon. In 1982, ethnobotanist Wade

Davis traveled to Haiti at the behest of the Harvard Botanical Museum to obtain a sample of the "zombie poison," a substance alleged to cause a temporary "voodoo death" prior to the zombification process. As recounted in his non-fiction book *The Serpent and the Rainbow*, Davis actually met real zombies, learned a great deal about the anthropology of voodoo, and finally obtained a sample of the fabled poison.

Analysis showed that the active ingredient in the poison was a substance derived from the liver of a puffer fish called tetrodotoxin, which, although very deadly, can induce a cataleptic state that is indistinguishable from death at certain dosages. The victim is brought in contact with the poison in the form of a powder, which is absorbed through the skin. After the burial, the prospective zombie is then dug up and resuscitated through the use of an antidote. Victims can suffer brain damage from oxygen deprivation during the burial, which explains their zombified mental state. This entire scenario was outlined in Victor Halperin's *White Zombie*, made in 1932 and based on William Seabrook's non-fiction book on Haitian voodoo, *Magic Island*, and *I Walked with a Zombie* also makes mention of the poison. Interestingly, according to Davis's research, only socially undesirable individuals who are perceived to be a threat to the community are subjected to zombification by the voodoo priests. The home-wrecking *femme fatale* Jessica Holland in *I Walked with a Zombie* being turned into a zombie is therefore consistent with actual voodoo practices.

Noir Horrors

Like *Cat People*, *Zombie* was a hit at the box office, establishing Lewton and Tourneur as the most financially successful purveyors of horror movie fare in Hollywood. As the Universal monster factory collapsed into absurdity in a series of inane monster rallies, the RKO B-movie team forged ahead into fresh territory by introducing elements of the crime melodrama into a horror movie milieu while moving away from supernatural themes. Lewton's next assignment was entitled *The Leopard Man* (1943), but instead of being a sequel to *Cat People*, it was derived from a novel by one of the luminaries of literary noir, Cornell Woolrich.

Previously cited as the author of the supernatural film noir *Night Has a Thousand Eyes*, Woolrich is best known as the author whose works were the basis for Robert Siodmak's *Phantom Lady* (1944) and Hitchcock's *Rear Window* (1954). His works are steeped in urban fear and paranoia, and his "black" series of novels from the 1940s (all of which have "black" in the title), are signature works which were made into classic and neo-noir films that include François Truffaut's *The Bride Wore Black* (1967) and Roy William Neill's *The Black Angel* (1946). *The Leopard Man* was based on *The Black Alibi*, a thriller set in a small town in South America where a series of violent killings of women are being committed either by an escaped black jaguar or a human serial murderer. Lewton, Tourneur and screenwriter Ardel Wray relocated the action to Santa Fe, New Mexico, while preserving the episodic narrative structure of Woolrich's novel.

The Leopard Man opens in a Santa Fe nightclub, where publicist Jerry Manning (Dennis O'Keefe) has had a brilliant promotional idea for his client/girlfriend, performer Kiki Walker (Jean Brooks). He has rented a "tame" black panther for Kiki to use as a gimmick in her nightclub act. During her performance that night, Kiki makes a dramatic entrance to the club wearing a stunning black dress while leading the panther on a leash, creating an air of dark fantasy about her. Kiki's entrance displeases rival performer Clo-Clo (Margo), a flamenco dancer, who uses her loudly clicking castanets to agitate the cat, causing it to break from the leash and run out into the desert night. Later that evening a teenaged Mexican girl, Teresa Delgado (Margaret Landry), is sent on an errand to buy cornmeal by her mother (Kate Lawson). In the film's most memorable sequence, the terrified girl encounters the leopard while passing underneath a train trestle and is pursued home by the beast. Senora Delgado ignores her daughter's screams for help as a prank until Teresa's blood runs under the front door.

In the aftermath of the killing, Jerry is not held legally responsible by the authorities while police and hunters scour the area looking for the big cat. Later, at the nightclub, Jerry and Kiki meet Dr. Galbraith (James Bell), an academic who works as the curator of the local museum and is knowledgeable about wildlife, who offers the opinion that, in order to catch the cat, "You'd have to be a leopard and think like a leopard." Referring to a fountain in the nightclub that features a ball suspended in the air by a jet of water, Galbraith offers some curious comments to Jerry: "We know as little about the forces that move us and move the world around us as that empty ball does about the water that pushes it into the air, lets it fall, and catches it again." The mysterious workings of fate are also evoked by the nightclub's resident fortune-teller (Isabel Jewell), who reads in Clo-Clo's cards that "you will meet a rich man and he will give you money." Unfortunately, the flamenco dancer also consistently draws the ace of spades, the death card.

The action shifts across town to the family home of the wealthy young woman Consuelo Contreras (Tula Parma), who is carrying on a secret courtship with her boyfriend, Raoul Belmonte (Richard Martin). That evening, Consuelo conspires to meet Raoul at her father's gravesite in the town cemetery, but he fails to show and she accidentally gets locked inside the graveyard, which is surrounded by a high wall. Calling for help, she hears a man respond to her cries, and he drives off to get help, but before he can return she is attacked and killed by an unseen assailant. Dr. Galbraith and Jerry are called to the scene, where a leopard's claw and black feline hairs are found near the body, but Jerry doubts that the panther is responsible. "It doesn't eat what it kills," he muses, offering that "it might not be a cat this time." While Galbraith and the police are not convinced, the cat's owner, a Native American named Charlie How-Come (Abner Biberman) agrees with Jerry. "My cat didn't kill that girl," he explains, expressing his opinion that the panther would have headed for open country rather than hanging around town.

That night, Clo-Clo meets Mr. Brunton (William Halligan) a kindly older man with whom she shares a drink and her life's woes. Moved by her plight, Brunton gives her a $100 bill out of the goodness of his heart, thus fulfilling the fortune-teller's prophecy. The dancer consults the fortune-teller again, but the cards indicate a dark future for her. "Something black," the seeress proclaims, "something on its way to you." The usually overconfident Clo-Clo is shaken by these words, and is even more upset when, upon returning home that night, she finds the $100 missing. Frantically searching for the money through the gloomy streets, she is approached by someone in the dark and murdered. The leopard is blamed again but Jerry remains skeptical, and his suspicions are confirmed when Charlie How-Come discovers the body of the leopard, which has been dead for several days, in an arroyo which had supposedly been searched by Galbraith. Jerry and Kiki,

A mysterious killer threatens female victims in this poster for Jacques Tourneur's *The Leopard Man* (RKO, 1943).

feeling remorse over their role in the tragedies, decide to forego leaving for Chicago for their next gig. "We're not going to catch a train, darling," she tells him, "we're going to catch a murderer."

Jerry enlists the aid of Consuelo's boyfriend, Raoul, in nailing Galbraith as the serial killer, and the three of them plan to provoke Galbraith into making a confession. When Galbraith returns to the darkened museum that night he is greeted by what sounds like Consuelo's plaintive cries for help and the clicking of Clo-Clo's castanets. Then Kiki arrives, ostensibly to watch the town's annual procession of the Penitentes, a religious/historical pageant that commemorates the slaughter of an innocent Indian tribe during the 17th century and the Spanish priests who did penance for the horrible deed afterwards. As the candlelit procession approaches and the basso chanting of the Penitentes swells louder, Kiki accidentally drops the castanets she was using to imitate Clo-Clo, and Galbraith, realizing the ruse, lunges for her. At this point Jerry and Raoul surge out of the shadows, causing the curator to flee out into the desert and join the procession. Pursued by Jerry and Raoul, Galbraith is collared and begins graphically confessing his crimes, blubbering that he was inspired to kill Consuelo because of the expression of terror on her face. "The eyes full of fear," he moans while reliving the event, "fear, that was it!" This is too much for Raoul, who shoots Galbraith dead in a fit of vengeful passion and is arrested by the police. Their mission accomplished, Jerry and Kiki prepare to depart for Chi-town while Jerry muses that human beings are like pawns of fate who are "pushed around by things bigger than themselves."

Critics have long considered *The Leopard Man* to be the weakest of the Lewton/ Tourneur outings, and its producer and director even disavowed it. Tourneur expressed the opinion that "it was too exotic, it was neither fish nor fowl: a series of vignettes, and it didn't hold together."[15] In his book on Lewton, *The Reality of Terror*, Joel Siegel criticizes the basic storyline (as derived from Woolrich) thus: "*The Leopard Man* is essentially a thin, nasty-minded story.... It amounts, in the long run, to little more than an exercise in sadistic voyeurism — three innocent women dying like trapped animals."[16] While there may be some truth in these criticisms, the film is quite tame by today's gore-splatter standards, as the actual killings all occur offscreen. It should be pointed out, however, that *The Leopard Man* arguably had more of an influence on the evolution of the horror genre than either *Cat People* or *I Walked with a Zombie*. Chris Fujiwara notes that the film foreshadows the Italian *giallo*, a subgenre of the horror film that features episodes of women being sadistically murdered that achieved cult popularity in films like Mario Bava's *Blood and Black Lace* (1964) and Dario Argento's *Deep Red* (1976). Fujiwara further states, "The film also anticipates Michael Powell's *Peeping Tom* (1960) in making the sight of a victim's fear the factor that fascinates the killer and compels him to kill."[17] Perhaps *The Leopard Man*'s most profound influence, however, was on Hitchcock's *Psycho* (1960), which featured a similar episodic structure and abrupt shift of viewpoints between several characters. As in *Psycho*, the murders are solved not by the police but by a couple acting as amateur sleuths, and the killer is a psychopath who has assumed another identity.

While the lack of a central protagonist in the narrative serves to distance the viewer from a deeper emotional involvement in the action, it nevertheless creates a sense of unease and disorientation. When the viewpoint shifts among the various women, who become short-lived protagonists, the audience anticipates their deaths in a way that could not be possible using a conventional, single protagonist storyline. Lewton and Tourneur are at the top of their form, crafting a superior B-horror noir thriller that captures much of Woolrich's paranoid literary style. As in the earlier films, Tourneur's use of sound is highly effective, from the insect-like clicking of Clo-Clo's castanets to the mournful chanting of the Penitentes. The black menace of the panther is actually felt more strongly here than in *Cat People*, where the violence is not so explicit. The film's studio-bound New Mexico setting provides an exotic, mythic backdrop for the unfolding tragedies, much as the island of St. Sebastian had in *Zombie*. Critic Edmund Bansak points to the film's reflection of wartime angst, calling it "a courageous essay in the random nature of death.... Wartime audiences may not have liked *Leopard*'s downbeat message — that the young and the innocent also die — but it was an important one for them to grasp."[18] A mood of deep wartime melancholy pervades every frame of *The Leopard Man*.

With the third film in the RKO Lewton series the emphasis had transitioned away from supernatural horror into the realm of the psychological, and *I Walked with a Zombie* would prove to be the last Lewton film to feature an overtly supernatural element. The "trappings" of the supernatural, however, the dark visual ambience of the horror film, would remain. Tourneur's comment that *The Leopard Man* was "neither fish nor fowl" is actually an indication of the film's genre-bending approach of combining mystery/detective themes with horror movie conventions into a formula that is pure horror noir. Critic Manny Farber observes, "*The Leopard Man* is a cleaner and much less sentimental Lewton, sticking much more to the suspense element and misdirection, using some of his favorite images, people moving in a penitential, sleep-walking manner, episodes threaded together with a dramatic sound. This fairly early peak example of his talent is a nerve-twitching whodunit giving the creepy impression that human beings and 'things' are interchangeable and almost synonymous and that both are pawns of a bizarre and terrible destiny."[19]

The theme of characters caught in a grim web of fate, one of the hallmarks of film noir, is one of *The Leopard Man*'s primary motifs. The implacable, unknowable forces of destiny are represented by the ball suspended on a jet of water in the nightclub's fountain and by the character of the fortune-teller, a world-weary, chain-smoking figure wrapped in a melancholy shawl, and the theme of the card reader whose fortunes come true would recur in *Nightmare Alley*. Set in a Santa Fe that seems nearly as cosmopolitan as 1940s Los Angeles, many of the film's key scenes take place in the noir locale of a nightclub or on city streets. Lewton reportedly dispatched an assistant to photograph locations in Santa Fe that were replicated in the film's set designs. The nighttime streets and alleys of the small New Mexican city, as depicted by Lewton and Tourneur, are more cramped, narrow and claustrophobic than their big city counterparts, lending them an enhanced feeling of menace, especially in the scene in which Clo-Clo is stalked and killed. On the other hand, the filmmakers also exploit the alien landscape of the southwestern desert, with its arroyos and Joshua trees, that would provide the backdrop for classic films noir like *The Hitchhiker* (1953) and *Border Incident* (1949), as well as a plethora of 1950s-era science fiction horror flicks. Noir critic Barry Gifford states, "The Penitente Parade at the end is as weird a procession as anything ever filmed. Lewton and Tourneur knew precisely how to make the innocent and obvious seem strange and unknown."[20] This nightmare surrealism is another distinctly noir element of *The Leopard Man*.

Substantial box-office receipts from the first three Lewton productions caused RKO to break up the Lewton-Tourneur team, reasoning that the two talents could make twice as much money if separated than they could if working together. Tourneur was bumped up to the studio's A-list of directors, but Lewton, whose production savvy had saved RKO from bankruptcy, was not similarly rewarded and remained in the B-horror unit. For his next film, *The Seventh Victim* (1943), Lewton promoted film editor Mark Robson, who had cut the first three entries in the series, to the director's chair.

As the film opens, schoolgirl Mary Gibson (Kim Hunter), a cloistered young lady who is a student at the Highcliffe Academy in upstate New York, is notified that her sister Jacqueline has disappeared, causing Mary to travel to New York City to look for her. Intimidated and bewildered by life in the big city, Mary begins her search at the La Sagesse Cosmetics Company, a business founded and owned by Jacqueline. She learns that her sister has sold the company to her associate, Mrs. Redi (Mary Newton), an aggressive middle-aged woman who claims to have no knowledge of Jacqueline's whereabouts. Mary does get a tip from Frances (Isabel Jewell), a friendly worker at the cosmetics plant, that Jacqueline has recently been seen at the Dante Restaurant, a Greenwich Village hangout for aspiring writers and artists. She finds out from the restaurant's owner that Jacqueline has rented an upstairs room, and prevails upon the owner to unlock it for her. The room turns out to be completely empty except for two objects—a chair and a hangman's noose.

After this ominous discovery, Mary is obliged to visit the Missing Persons Bureau and the city morgue, to no avail, but she does come in contact with attorney Gregory Ward (Hugh Beaumont), who turns out to be secretly married to Jacqueline. Gregory tells Mary that Jacqueline had deep emotional problems and "lived in a world of her own fancy" that compelled her to rent the room with the noose in order to prove that "life wasn't worth living unless one could end it." Puzzled, Mary returns to her residential hotel where she is approached by private investigator Irving August (Lou Lubin), a wizened, Damon Runyonesque character who has heard about her situation at the Missing Persons Bureau and who offers to take the case on a contingency basis.

Checking through city records, August learns that Jacqueline did not sell her business, but ceded ownership of the company outright to Mrs. Redi, and believes that she is being kept against her will in a locked room at the cosmetics company. Mary convinces August to break into La Sagesse that night so that they can see if she is being imprisoned there. That night the two of them enter the premises, and when Mary gets spooked by the silence and the darkness, she sends August on ahead to unlock the hidden room. A few moments later the P.I. walks back through the shadows toward her with a stiff, unnatural gait and then falls down dead. Horrified, Mary flees out of the building and into the subway at 14th Street, where she rides to the end of the line. When the train returns to the 14th Street stop, two men who appear to be inebriated enter the subway car supporting a third man between them, who seems to be dead drunk. The trio sit down across from her, and when the train lurches the third man's hat falls off, revealing him to be the corpse of Irving August. Mary runs through the train to find the conductor, but by that time the two men and their grisly companion have vanished.

Soon afterward, Gregory is paid a visit at his law offices by psychiatrist Dr. Louis Judd (Tom Conway, playing the same urbane psychiatrist character who had been mauled to death by Irena the panther woman in *Cat People*), who claims that Jacqueline is now in his care and currently living at an undisclosed location. Judd solicits money from Gregory for Jacqueline, but refuses to give the lawyer a hint as to his wife's current living arrangements. When Judd visits Mary however, he agrees to take her to the hotel where her sister is staying, but when they arrive at her room she seems to have disappeared once more. When Judd leaves to consult with the hotel staff, Jacqueline (Jean Brooks) suddenly appears at the hallway door like an apparition. She is a striking-looking woman with a mysterioso air about her, who sports an exotic, neo–Egyptian coiffure. After motioning for silence, Jacqueline quickly closes the door, and when Mary opens it again her sister seems to have vanished into thin air like a ghost.

That night, over dinner with Gregory at the Dante restaurant, local poet Jason Hoag (Erford Gage) promises to help Mary find her sister, and does some snooping around at the public library, where he learns that both Mrs. Redi and Dr. Judd have been consulting restricted books on the history of diabolic cults. Hoag finds a paper bearing a strange image inside one of the books, of a triangle enclosed inside a parallelogram that turns out to be the symbol of the Palladists, a dangerous group of devil worshippers connected to La Sagesse, who use the symbol as the cosmetics company's trademark. Soon afterward, Mary is paid a visit by Mrs. Redi, who barges in on her while she is taking a shower. In a brilliant sequence that predates the shower murder in Hitchcock's *Psycho*, Mrs. Redi's head is seen through the shower curtain as a shadow whose angular hat resembles a pair of devilish horns. Mrs. Redi tells Mary that it was Jacqueline who killed Irving August out of sheer fright when he surprised her at La Sagesse, and warns her that her sister will ultimately face charges as a murderess if Mary continues snooping around.

The Palladists, who are revealed as a motley crew of decadent socialites, meet to discuss Jacqueline's fate. Fearing that she has revealed the cult's secrets during her therapy with Dr. Judd, they agree that Jacqueline must die, preferably by her own hand, as have six previous betrayers of the cult (making her the "seventh victim" of the film's title). In the meantime, considering the circumstances, Dr. Judd takes Mary, Gregory and Jason to Jacqueline's current address, where Mary is finally reunited with her sister. She is taken to Mary's room, where Jacqueline reveals that when she tried to break away from the cult they kept her locked up inside the secret room at La Sagesse. Jacqueline also admits to killing August with a pair of scissors when he entered the room at night. Everyone agrees that Jacqueline must go to the authorities and face the music over August's killing, but when Mary leaves her sister in the apartment to go to work the next day, Jacqueline is kidnapped by the Palladists.

She is held against her will at the Greenwich Village apartment that serves as the cult's headquarters while the Palladists use their occult powers of persuasion to make Jacqueline drink a glass containing poison. They fail, however, and allow her to leave, but tell her, "There'll be another decision, today, tomorrow, but we'll find you." Leaving the apartment, Jacqueline is stalked through the darkened streets of the city by one of the cultists who menaces her with a switchblade before she narrowly escapes. In a fit of despair, she returns to the rented room with the noose above the Dante, where she encounters fellow apartment dweller Mimi (Elizabeth Russell), who is terminally ill with a wasting disease. After a morbid conversation with the dying woman, Jacqueline realizes that she, too, has nothing left to live for, and enters the room with the noose. As Mimi leaves to celebrate a final fling, she hears the sound of the chair being kicked away as Jacqueline hangs herself inside the apartment, but passes by without comprehension.

One of the most personally revealing works in the Lewton canon, the film reflects the producer's morbid, tortured nihilism. "In all of his best work," Joel Siegel observes, "one finds Lewton embracing dark, negating forces—suicide, diabolism, witchcraft. *The Seventh Victim* is his most forthright negation, a film in which existence is portrayed as a hellish void from which all souls yearn for the sweet release of death."[21] The film ends with a title displaying a famous epigraph by John Donne that reads, "I run to Death and Death meets me as fast, and all my Pleasures are like Yesterday," that illustrates a profoundly morbid turn of mind that Lewton would revisit in *Isle of the Dead* (1945). As such, *The Seventh Victim* is a cold, emotionally distancing work that expresses an oppressive, unremitting pessimism.

Scripter DeWitt Bodeen constructs an intriguing meld of crime melodrama and horror. The narrative unfolds as a detective story in which the protagonists hunt for a missing person through the maze of a haunted urban landscape. Lewton reportedly directed much of the film on paper by using an extensively annotated shooting script that left nothing to chance. Journeyman Mark Robson delivers a solidly constructed suspenser in his directorial debut, but Tourneur's visual poetry is sorely missed. The principals turn in earnest, convincing performances in this unusual melodrama, in particular Kim Hunter (in her screen debut) as Mary, the naïf in the Big Apple, Elizabeth Russell in a brief but powerful performance as the consumptive Mimi, and the lovely Jean Brooks who steals the picture with her intense, otherworldly portrayal of the ethereal Jacqueline.

The film's overpowering nihilism and dark visual style bring it squarely within the orbit of film noir, making *The Seventh Victim* the most truly noir of the Lewton series. As in *The Leopard Man,* there is no supernatural element in the plot, continuing the trend toward realism and crime melodrama in 1940s-era horror movies. There is more of a sense of the gritty urban environment of New York in this production than in the equally studio-bound metropolitan landscape of *Cat People,* and stock footage of the New York subway inserted into a couple of brief shots provides a touch of documentary verisimilitude. The scene in which Jacqueline is chased through the shadowy streets by a homicidal assailant is pure noir, as is the death of Irving August in the darkened cosmetics factory and the removal of his corpse in plain sight on a subway train. *The Seventh Victim* exploits urban angst and paranoia to the max, and surely had an influence on the newly evolving noir genre. Alfred Hitchcock, who took a keen interest in Lewton's work, most likely cribbed elements of the film's shower scene for the famous bathroom murder in *Psycho.* An equally bland cult of Manhattanite Satan worshippers would provide the villainy for Roman Polanski's horror noir *Rosemary's Baby* (1968) decades later. Director Robson would go on to direct the noir *Edge of Doom* (1950) and the boxing exposé *The Harder They Fall* (1956), starring Humphrey Bogart.

The End of the Lewton Noir Cycle

Unfortunately, *The Seventh Victim* would be the last Lewton production with noir overtones. It was followed by the waterlogged melodrama *The Ghost Ship* (1943), a tepid potboiler of malfeasance and murder on the high seas, and the non-sequel *Curse of the*

Tom Conway (left), Kim Hunter (center) and Jean Brooks are featured in this poster for the Val Lewton/Mark Robson production of *The Seventh Victim* (RKO, 1943).

Cat People (1944), which turned out to be a sensitive portrait of a fantasy-prone little girl but provided little in the way of terror or thrills. After this, Lewton tried his hand at contemporary drama in the socially conscious *Youth Runs Wild* (1944) and historical costume drama with *Madamoiselle Fifi* (1944). None of these four films did any significant business at the box office.

In 1944, Jack Gross, who had been an executive producer on Universal's horror unit, was hired on to supervise Lewton's work at RKO. Gross, whose lavish Universal horror movies had been trumped by Lewton's low-budget thrillers, disagreed with Lewton's approach to the genre, and signed Universal's biggest horror star, Boris Karloff, to a three-picture deal with RKO, ostensibly to make chillers that were more like the Universal product. During production, however, Karloff and Lewton got along famously, but the three movies they made together —*Isle of the Dead* (1945), *The Body Snatcher* (1945) and *Bedlam* (1946)—come off as Karloff vehicles as much as Lewton productions, and only *The Body Snatcher*, lensed by fledgling director Robert Wise, approached the earlier films in quality.

For the three Karloff movies, Lewton turned his back on the contemporary horror film template he had created for *Cat People* and instead reverted to making costume movies, a taste he had acquired from his days working with Selznick and in the making of *Madamoiselle Fifi*. This historical approach to horror lacked the immediacy of the earlier films that took place in a modern setting. Lewton also adopted the curious practice of basing his movies on works of fine art: *Isle of the Dead* was derived from the Boecklin painting of the same name, whereas *Bedlam* was suggested by a work of William Hogarth. This "painterly" direction had an adverse effect on Lewton's films. As Joel Siegel observes, "His pictures became more and more striking in their composition, an aesthetic advance somewhat vitiated by a certain static quality which seemed to creep in at times, robbing his later films of some of the graceful movement of the earlier ones."[22]

Bedlam would be the last feature Lewton would make at the RKO B-unit. By 1946 the bottom had fallen out of the horror movie market and RKO was again in financial trouble. Lewton, a high-strung, sensitive individual who was ill-suited to working in the cutthroat movie business, suffered a heart attack. He moved to Paramount and later to MGM and Universal, where he produced nothing of consequence. In the late '40s he attempted to form an independent production company with his former protégés, directors Mark Robson and Robert Wise, but was ultimately rejected by the younger men, an action that shattered him emotionally and professionally. He suffered a serious heart attack and died in 1951 at the age of forty-six.

Lewton's seminal thrillers not only revolutionized the horror film but had a heavy influence on the development of film noir, which was just emerging as a distinct genre in the early 1940s. Along with Jacques Tourneur, Lewton brought the shadows of expressionist German cinema into a modern American idiom. They were responsible for taking the horror movie out of the realm of the supernatural and into the domain of the psychological. In particular, the urban terrors of *The Leopard Man* and *The Seventh Victim* are practically indistinguishable from films noir of the same period. After parting company with Lewton's B-unit, Tourneur would go on to direct the gothic noir *Experiment Perilous* (1944, see Chapter 6), the exquisite classic noir *Out of the Past* (1947), and noiresque thrillers such as *Circle of Danger* (1951) and *Nightfall* (1957), as well as the supernatural mystery/horror film *Curse of the Demon* (1957).

In his article entitled "The Noir Horror of *Cat People*," Eric Somer writes of Lewton, "All of his films — whether with elements of the horror piece, mystery or period film — are marked by the same visual style and sense of fatalism that was so noteworthy in the noir films, especially during the noir peak from 1946 into the early '50s."[23] The shadow worlds that Lewton and Tourneur created tapped into the same wellspring of urban angst that informed the emerging noir genre, and constitute the most perfect mating of the two forms. In a couple of recent documentary films on Lewton, cinematic and literary luminaries such as Martin Scorsese, William Friedkin, George Romero, Harlan Ellison, Richard Matheson, Ramsey Campbell, John Landis and Guillermo del Toro have attested to the poetry and dark magic of his vision and have helped to make contemporary audiences aware of his unique contribution to both film noir and the horror film.

4

Horror Noir from Radioland

The medium of radio, once one of the cornerstones of American popular culture, has today been relegated to the domains of political talk and commercial music. During its glory days in the 1930s and '40s, however, radio was a vibrant force in everyday life, the equivalent of television in the modern world. Little remains of this vast "empire of the air" today outside of recordings of old programs hawked by nostalgia merchants. Radio offered a vast spectrum of entertainment to its audience, including comedy, soap opera, drama, westerns, detective and horror shows on a weekly basis. Unlike visual media like film or television, radio had a creepy intimacy all its own that was particularly suited to tales of suspense and dread. In a darkened room at night the disembodied voice from within the device stimulated the visionary powers of the "theater of the mind's eye," conjuring hideous monsters and shadow landscapes from the depths of the listener's imagination.

In his non-fiction book *Danse Macabre*, horror maven Stephen King describes listening to a 1950s rebroadcast of a program that originally ran on Arch Oboler's horror show *Lights Out*, an adaptation of a Ray Bradbury short story entitled "Mars Is Heaven!" in which a group of seemingly kind Martians metamorphose into homicidal monsters at the end of the story. "That night I slept in the doorway," King relates, "where the real and rational light of the bathroom bulb could shine in my face. That was the power of radio at its height."[1] King also rhapsodizes about another *Lights Out* episode, "The Chicken Heart That Ate the World," in which runaway protoplasm from a chicken heart being kept alive artificially escapes from the lab and grows to engulf the entire world. Another celebrity victim of Oboler's rampaging chicken heart was comedian Bill Cosby, who, on his 1966 comedy album *Wonderfulness*, describes listening to the program against his parents' wishes while home alone one night. At the end of the bit Cosby's parents come home to find the young Cos hiding in a closet and gibbering in fear about the monstrous chicken heart so vividly etched into his imagination by the show.

There was also a noir connection to radio that is all but forgotten today. A number of popular films noir were later adapted as radio plays, often with the original stars: Bogart in *The Maltese Falcon* and Richard Widmark in *Kiss of Death* are two examples. Noir private eyes continued their exploits on the airwaves in shows featuring Dashiell Hammett's sleuth *Sam Spade*, voiced by Howard Duff, and *The Adventures of Philip Marlowe* as portrayed by Van Heflin. These shows often contained pithy noir dialogue and Chandleresque prose worthy of the original authors. In a couple of cases radio shows became translated into films noir on the screen. *Night Editor* (1946), was adapted from an episode of the radio series of the same name while *Sorry, Wrong Number* (1948) was based on an episode of the crime show *Suspense*. In an interesting reversal of the trend, the forensics expert played by Jack Webb in *He Walked by Night* (1948) became the main character in the police procedural radio series *Dragnet*. Radio is often credited with inspiring the use of voice-over narration and sound effects in films noir. Director/screenwriter Billy Wilder claimed that he cribbed the use of interior monologue from radio for his noir classics *Double Indemnity* and *Sunset Boulevard*.

Crime, suspense and horror shows, like B-noir films of the '40s, were inexpensive to produce as most of them did not need to employ star talent, and as a consequence, they were not as popular as the big comedy shows or the soaps. While shows like *Suspense* or *Dragnet* stuck strictly to a realistic crime melodrama format, the radio medium provided a fertile ground for intermingling noir and horror on shows like *I Love a Mystery* and *The Mysterious Traveler*. Radio, by playing upon the audience's imagination, could conjure up all manner of exotic, fantastic and unlikely scenarios that could bridge the universes of horror and criminality.

One of the most popular shows of the period, and one of the few that is still known to audiences today, is *The Shadow*. The character had started out in 1931 as a narrator/host on a program called *The Blue Coal Radio Revue*, where he read crime stories from *Street & Smith's Detective Story Magazine* on the air. From the first, the character was associated with a maniacal, disembodied laugh that would begin every show, followed by his familiar spiel: *I ... am the Shadow. Conscience is a taskmaster no crook can escape. It is a jeering shadow even in the blackest lives. The Shadow knows.* In the beginning the Shadow merely offered commentary on the criminal goings-on in the radio play, but as the 30s wore on and the show became more popular, Street & Smith decided to create a pulp magazine that would tie into the program, and the character underwent a metamorphosis. The pulp incarnation of the Shadow was the brainchild of stage magician Walter Gibson, writing under the *nom de plume* Maxwell Grant, who reconfigured the radio host as a crimefighting superhero with preternatural powers.

Gibson's Shadow was the alter ego of wealthy man-about-town Lamont Cranston, a world traveler who had acquired the hypnotic power to "cloud men's minds" and render himself invisible from magical adepts in Tibet. As the Shadow, Cranston uses his powers of invisibility to fight crime, stop injustice and right wrongs as his ghostlike attributes and mocking laughter strike terror in the hearts of criminals. As depicted on the covers and interior illustrations in the *Street & Smith* magazine, the Shadow dressed in an operatic black cloak and oversized black hat, a scarf obscuring his lower face with a huge, beaklike nose presiding above it. Unlike the comic book superheroes who followed, who all abrogated their right to bear arms, the Shadow came equipped with two .45 automatics, with which he meted out instant karma to all manner of evildoers. The Shadow was the prototype for the comic book hero Batman, who would come along a few years later, yet he also sported the maniacal laugh of Batman's arch-nemesis, the Joker.

The pulp fiction version of the character was adopted for the radio show, which now began with the Shadow's noir query, *Who knows what evil lurks in the hearts of men? The Shadow knows...* followed by a machine gun burst of maniacal laughter. The announcer would then explain the show's superhero premise: *Cranston is known to the underworld*

The Shadow's alter ego, Lamont Cranston (Victor Jory), investigates the criminal underworld in the Columbia serial *The Shadow* (Columbia, 1940).

as the Shadow. Never seen, only heard, as haunting to superstitious minds as a ghost, as inevitable as a guilty conscience. Cranston has learned the hypnotic power to cloud men's minds so they cannot see him. Cranston's friend and companion, the lovely Margo Lane, is the only person who knows to whom the voice of the invisible Shadow belongs. During the 1937–38 season, the Shadow was voiced by none other than Orson Welles, with Agnes Morehead playing opposite as Margo Lane, although actor Bret Morrison would later take over the role and play the Shadow on the air for 15 years. The show combined crime melodrama with horror and fantasy elements as the invisible avenger squared off against all manner of natural and supernatural foes.

Alas, the character was never able to transition from radio and the pulps to the silver screen. In 1940, Columbia released a serial based on the character, with Victor Jory in the title role as The Shadow/Lamont Cranston and Veda Ann Borg as Margo Lane. Oddly, the Shadow is stripped of his powers of invisibility, which are instead conferred upon the villain, The Black Tiger, a masked baddie who wants to take over the city and dominate the world's financial markets. Jory plays the Shadow with bulging eyes, presumably to indicate his hypnotic powers of mind, and runs around in his Shadow outfit in broad daylight, which tends to compromise the character's aura of dread and mystery. It's the usual Saturday matinee cliffhanger material, replete with fistfights, gun battles and explosions which the Shadow survived on a weekly basis. The titular crimefighter in the serial did not resemble either the pulp or radio version of the crimefighter, and no further serials were forthcoming.

The character did not appear onscreen in a feature film again until 1994, when Alec Baldwin appeared as *The Shadow* in Russell Mulcahy's updated feature film version. Although David Koepp's screenplay is faithful to the pulp and radio versions of the Shadow, the film adopts a cartoonish, tongue-in-cheek ambience that is obviously modeled on Tim Burton's superhero megahit *Batman* (1989). Baldwin is woefully miscast in the title role, playing the part with a distinct lack of sympathy, while the rest of the interesting cast, including Jonathan Winters, Ian McKellan, Tim Curry and Penelope Ann Miller, are simply wasted. The plot revolves around a mystical duel between the Shadow/Cranston and a resuscitated Genghis Khan (John Lone) featuring a pre–Hiroshima prototype atomic bomb that Khan wants to use to blow up New York City. While production values are excellent and Mulcahy, director of the *Highlander* heroic fantasy films, offers some deft visual flourishes, the basic storyline is weak and unfocused. Part of the problem is that the Shadow's maniacal laugh works very well as a radio gimmick, but seems odd and more than a bit out of place as the attribute of a cinematic superhero.

Shadow of the Whistler

The Shadow program provided inspiration for another shady character who was much closer to the spirit of film noir. *The Whistler*, which premiered in 1942 and ran for 23 years thereafter, featured a shadowy figure, a ghostly personification of a criminal's guilty conscience known only as the Whistler. Each program began with an eerie, minor-key theme (actually whistled by a woman named Dorothy Roberts), followed by the voice of announcer Bill Forman playing the title character, who solemnly intoned the show's poetic opening lines: *I am the Whistler and I know many things, for I walk by night. I know many strange tales hidden in the hearts of men and women who have stepped into the shadows. Yes, I know the nameless terrors of which they dare not speak.* In his book *Raised on Radio,* Gerald Nachman relates that "the whistle was accompanied by footsteps on what sounded like a damp street; you couldn't see the hazy glow of a streetlight, but, boy, could you ever hear it."[2]

Unlike *The Shadow* or *I Love a Mystery, The Whistler* was a straight crime show devoid of fantasy elements, except for the creepy presence of the Whistler himself. The Whistler did not interact with the characters in the radio play, but instead provided a sardonic running commentary on their evil activities that were invariably written in the second person. *Yes, you intend to kill your wife, don't you Frank,* the Whistler would gloatingly inform the audience. *But you know it's dangerous and you have to proceed with care. You have to be clever in how you carry out your plan. Step by step, you go over it in your mind. Knowing that one slip and it will be over for you, won't it Frank?* John Stanley writes, "You could almost see the omniscient Whistler hunkering just out of sight, following every step of the nefarious plans being carried out by the characters, and then darting forward to whisper evil designs into the ears of his doomed characters."[3] Predictably, the crooks and murderers would slip up on some small detail, or fate itself (of which the Whistler was a personification) would inflict ironic justice on the villains by the conclusion of each episode.

Like the Shadow before him, the Whistler was incarnated as a movie character during the 1940s in a series of eight feature films made at Columbia between 1944 and 1948. Unlike Columbia's Shadow serial, however, the Whistler movies were not kiddie matinee fare, but serious noir B-pictures. Most of the films in the series were directed by William Castle, who would later become notorious as the producer of schlocky, gimmick-laden horror films like *The Tingler* (1959), *The House on Haunted Hill* (1959) and *13 Ghosts* (1960). All but one of the Whistler films would star Richard Dix, a former silent film and western actor best known for his role in *Cimmaron* (1931).

Working with a minuscule budget of $75,000, about half the budget of one of Val Lewton's cut-rate RKO productions, Castle had his work cut out for him. "I tried every effect I could dream up to create a mood of terror," Castle recalled, "low key lighting, wide-angle lenses to give an eerie feeling, and a hand-held camera in many important scenes to give a sense of reality to the horror." In short, Castle employed the tried and true techniques of film noir in order to create screen tension. His method of working with his star, Richard Dix (who was struggling with alcoholism, hypertension and other health problems at the time), bordered on outright sadism. "To achieve a mood of desperation," Castle related, "I insisted that Dix give up smoking and go on a diet. This made him nervous and irritable, particularly when I gave him early-morning calls and kept him waiting on the set — sometimes for an entire day before using him in a scene. He was constantly off-center, restless, fidgety, and nervous as a cat. When I finally used him in a scene, I'd make him do it over and over again until he was ready to explode. It achieved the desired effect — that of a man haunted by fear and trying to keep himself from being murdered."[4] Like the old saying goes, it's great cinema but it's hell on the actors.

The series opener, *The Whistler* (1944), began with a shot tracking the Whistler's shadow down a darkened city street. It's the shadow of a man wearing a trench coat and hat gliding through the gloom, warbling the same eerie, 13-tone theme from the radio show. Poster art for the film depicts the Whistler as a Shadow-like figure, trench coat collar pulled up and slouch hat pulled down to obscure his features. After the Whistler (voiced by Otto Forest) delivers his standard spiel, the camera shifts to a greasy spoon diner where the film's narrative begins to unfold. Dix plays Earl Conrad, a wealthy industrialist who is so despondent over the death of his wife that he contemplates suicide. Unable to take his own life, he arranges with criminal go-between Lefty Vigran (Don Costello) to have a hit man murder him. Lefty duly sets up the contract with a hitman (J. Carrol Naish), but soon afterward is killed in a confrontation with the police. In the meantime, Conrad learns that his wife is still alive, having been interned on a Pacific island by the Japanese, and is headed home. Having a reason to live again, Conrad frantically tries to stop his own execution, but with Lefty dead he has no way of communicating with the assassin.

The killer relentlessly stalks Conrad through the labyrinth of the city, and at two junctures is saved from death when the hitman actually hears the Whistler's weird music and is unnerved by hearing the song of the avenging phantom. Finally, Conrad's loyal secretary, Alice Walker (Gloria Stuart), brings him to a police station where he is taken into protective custody and ensconced in a jail cell. Desperate to complete his contract, the hitman attempts to shoot Conrad through a window, but is gunned down by the cops.

Castle's radio show spinoff was generally well received by the public and the press alike. *The Whistler* is a tightly constructed B-noir with horror movie overtones. The director establishes an atmosphere of lurking dread using standard noir cinematic techniques, and his unorthodox method of working with star Richard Dix paid big dividends in the actor's twitchy, nerved-out performance. J. Carrol Naish, a frequent player in horror noirs of the 40s such as *Dr. Renault's Secret* (1942), *Calling Dr. Death* (1943) and *The Beast with Five Fingers* (1946), provides just the right touch of menace as the nameless killer, who is himself pursued by the ghostly figure of the Whistler. The plot device of having Naish actually hear the Whistler's eerie tune injects a muted element of the supernatural into the otherwise realistic crime melodrama, but this was the only time that the title character intruded into the proceedings during the series. The basic plotline was lifted (sans Whistler) for the Hammer/Lippert British noir *Paid to Kill* (1954).

The rest of the movies in the *Whistler* series were straight-up films noir. Castle directed the second entry, *Mark of the Whistler* (1944), which was based on the Cornell Woolrich story "Dormant Account." Dix plays a homeless man who is killing time on a park bench when he reads in a newspaper that a bank is seeking to locate heirs for money in inactive accounts that remain unclaimed. He manages to convince the bank officials that he is the missing heir to one of the accounts and is awarded the proceeds of $99,000. Checking into a posh hotel in town, he is stalked by homicidal crooks who have their own claim to the cash. Dix manages to avoid being killed, and is eventually forced to confess his ruse and return the money, which, it turns out, belongs to his homeless beggar friend Limpy (Paul Guilfoyle). The film was critically well received and was a worthy follow-up to the first film.

Despite these successes, Columbia bypassed Castle and assigned the next film in the series, *The Power of the Whistler* (1945), to studio hack Lew Landers. In this installment,

The shadow of the Whistler hangs over Richard Dix in this poster for *The Mark of the Whistler* (Columbia, 1944).

Dix is hit by a car and temporarily loses his memory. Befriended by Jean Landers (Janis Carter), he tries to piece his identity together from the objects he finds in his pockets. When his amnesia abruptly clears, Dix is revealed as a homicidal maniac who has escaped from an asylum and is intent on murdering the head of the asylum and the judge who consigned him to the nuthouse. When Carter tries to dissuade him, Dix comes after her and she is forced to shoot him dead in self defense. Unfortunately, the film's intriguing premise was not fully realized by Landers's plodding direction.

Castle returned to the series to direct the fourth film, *The Voice of the Whistler* (1945), which was based on an episode from the radio program. This time out Dix plays a wealthy industrialist who suffers a physical and mental breakdown. Recovering at a local clinic, he falls in love with his nurse (Lynn Merrick) and woos her away from her doctor fiancé (James Cardwell). Dix proposes to Merrick, offering her all his wealth after he dies of his terminal illness, and she accepts, breaking off her engagement to the doctor and moving into a remote lighthouse with her husband. When Cardwell pays a visit to the couple, the flame with Merrick is rekindled, and things get even more dicey when Dix confesses that his illness is not terminal after all but merely a ruse. Dix and Cardwell plot to murder each other, and Dix succeeds in killing his rival but is discovered by Merrick, and later tried, convicted and executed for the crime, leaving Merrick sadly alone in the brooding lighthouse.

Castle also directed the fifth Whistler film, *Mysterious Intruder* (1946), which many critics judge to be the best of the series. In this one, Dix is a private eye hired by the elderly Swedish proprietor of a music store to find a girl named Alora Lund who lived next door. Curious about the old man's motives, Dix sends a young woman to the music store claiming to be Ms. Lund, and learns that the store owner is holding onto some rare old phonograph records that are worth a cool 200 grand that were given to him for safe-keeping by Lund's mother. Unfortunately, before the proprietor can deliver the records, he is stabbed to death by a silent, hulking killer (played by perennial noir tough guy Mike Mazurki), who is also after the collector's items. When the woman impersonating Lund is found strangled in her apartment, the cops finger Dix as the killer. Returning to the record store, Dix engages in gunplay with the crooks, killing two and locating the records, but he is mistakenly shot to death by the police as the valuable records get broken during the fracas. In his book *The Detective in Hollywood*, Jon Tuska writes, "William Castle in his treatment of the story had certainly been influenced by what Eddie Dmytryk had achieved in *Murder, My Sweet* (RKO, 1944). The settings are musty old shops and a dilapidated house where Mazurki is sleeping off a drunk. All the important action takes place in fitful lighting and heavy shadows."[5] The story, adapted by Eric Taylor from his script for one of the Whistler radio programs, contains ironic plot twists that are typical of the Whistler radio melodramas.

In *The Secret of the Whistler* (1947), directed by George Sherman, Dix plays an artist who is financially dependent on his sick wife (Mary Carrier), who has heart problems. When wifey catches Dix in a compromising position with his model (Leslie Brooks), she threatens to cut him out of her will. Trying to prevent this, Dix attempts to poison her before she can talk to her attorney, but she finds out and records the event in her diary. She then dies of a sudden heart attack, but Dix thinks she succumbed to the poison and has her body cremated. He inherits his wife's fortune and marries Brooks, who is only after the money. Brooks finds the page in the first wife's diary incriminating Dix in her attempted poisoning, and threatens to blackmail him with it, but Dix strangles her instead as the cops arrive to ironically clear him of the murder of wife number one and arrest him for the murder of wife number two.

In *The Thirteenth Hour* (1947) directed by William Clemens, Dix plays the head of a trucking outfit who gets nailed for DUI in a traffic accident and has his license suspended for six months. Unable to drive legally, he undertakes a clandestine run and is ambushed by an unknown assailant, who kills a highway patrolman during the incident, leaving Dix wrongfully accused of the killing. Pursued as a cop killer, Dix must stay one step ahead of the law in order to find the real killer and prove his innocence. *The Thirteenth Hour* would prove to be Dix's last screen appearance, as the actor suffered a massive heart attack in October 1948 and died in the following year.

The last entry in the series was *The Return of the Whistler* (1948), directed by D. Ross Lederman and based on Cornell Woolrich's story entitled, "All at Once, No Alice." Michael Duane plays Theodore Anthony, a man who plans to marry an enigmatic French girl named Alice Dupres Barkley (Lenore Aubert) he has only known for a short time, but when his fiancée disappears, Anthony hires private eye Gaylord Traynor (Richard Lane) to help him find her. The trail leads to an insane asylum, where Barkley is being kept against her will by the family of her previous husband, who are trying to get their hands on the deceased hubby's estate by declaring her insane. When he learns that P.I. Traynor is secretly working for the family, Anthony poses as a mental patient in order to infiltrate the asylum and rescue Barkley. Tuska notes, "The Woolrich story had stressed the impossible, crushing autocracy of asylum administration and its bending medical practice to serve whoever is paying the bill. None of this was in the film, save in the most fleeting insinuations."[6]

Deprived of the guiding talents of William Castle and Richard Dix, the Whistler movie series faded into oblivion, although the radio program would continue to be broadcast until 1965. While all of the films in the series were squarely within the orbit of classic film noir, their horror content was restricted to the presence of the ghostlike title character. As one reviewer put it, "The Whistler may be Fate, or he may be the voice of conscience signaling a warning to a person about to take his first plunge into crime. We see him ... merely as a shadow accompanied by an eerie whistled refrain."[7] Gerald Nachman explains the mysterioso appeal of the character thus: "Just why the Whistler whistled was never explained, nor was there any need to; it was purely to make your hair curl. Clearly, he wasn't calling for his dog."[8] The character, who "knows many things, for I walk by night," added a touch of otherworldly ambience to the otherwise realistic noir melodramas. Because of Columbia's use of hack directors like D. Ross Lederman and William Clemens, the individual films in the series varied widely in quality, but future wannabe Hitchcock William Castle would hone his horror movie-making directorial skills working on the Whistler films.

The Inner Sanctum *Mysteries*

Another radio program that would be translated into a series of B-horror noirs was *The Inner Sanctum*. The brainchild of radio dramatist Himan Brown, each show famously began with the sound of a hideously creaking door (a copyrighted sound effect) opening into a realm of horror. A blast of funereal organ music would follow, accompanied by an intro delivered by the program's host, Raymond (played by Raymond Edward Johnson, and later, by Paul McGrath), who was surely the template for the ghoulish "Vault Keeper" and "Crypt Keeper" characters later featured in the EC line of horror comics. Horror maven John Stanley writes, "While radio's *The Whistler* was to be taken seriously, *Inner Sanctum Mysteries* was another matter entirely, mixing tongue-in-cheek black comedy with over-the-top haunted house thrills. *The Whistler* always dealt with seemingly real people in identifiable situations, while *Inner Sanctum* was purely made up of graveyard humor with devilish twists. A listener never knew if the supernatural or horrific elements of a story were real, or events had been concocted by a character to mislead others. Sometimes it really was a ghost that returned for revenge, other times it was a set-up to trick someone into confessing or revealing the hiding place of the treasure map or the family jewelry."[9] This *frisson* between psychological and supernatural terror is the very essence of horror noir.

The show began life as a radio spin-off of a Simon & Schuster series called the "Inner Sanctum Mysteries." In June of 1943, Universal studios bought the rights to the title for a series of low-budget B-thrillers that were designed as a movie tie-in to both the radio show and the publication. The *Inner Sanctum* film series was conceived as vehicles for Universal's newly minted horror star, Lon Chaney, Jr., who would star in all six films in the series. Unlike the radio series, however, the *Inner Sanctum* movies were basically crime melodramas, some of which had supernatural overtones. In each of the films Chaney plays a man who is accused of committing murder, sometimes during an amnesiac episode, making it unclear if he is the killer both to himself and to the audience. The series was made under the auspices of associate producer Ben Pivar, head of Universal's B-horror movie unit, who cranked out modest chillers like *The Mad Ghoul* (1943), *Captive Wild Woman* (1943) and *She-Wolf of London* (1946). Pivar was reportedly the antithesis of a creative producer like Val Lewton, and showed little interest in the horror dreck he was obliged to churn out. The first three films would be lensed by Reginald LeBorg, a competent, if undistinguished director.

Dispensing with the radio show's famous creaking door and horror host Raymond, most of the *Inner Sanctum* features begin with a shot of a library room with a long table in the center. A crystal ball sits upon the table, inside of which can be seen the shifting, distorted face of character actor David Hoffman glaring at the audience. Then the voice of this "Spirit of the Inner Sanctum" solemnly intones the series intro: *This is the Inner Sanctum. The strange, fantastic world controlled by a mass of living, pulsating flesh: the mind. It destroys, distorts, creates monsters, commits murders. Yes, even you, without knowing, can commit murder.*

In the series opener, *Calling Dr. Death* (1943), Chaney plays neurologist Mark Steele, a highly successful physician who uses hypnosis in his practice. As the film begins, he is shown treating a mentally disturbed girl in his darkened office with tight spotlights and a metronome with a glowing tip. Although he is doing very well professionally, Steele's personal life is in shambles, as his marriage to his beautiful wife, Maria (Ramsay Ames), is on the rocks because of her barely concealed infidelities. The troubled medico spills his guts to the audience in a succession of stage-whispered voice-over narrations that would become one of the hallmarks of the series. Confronting Maria one evening when she returns from one of her late-night dalliances, she tells her husband that she will not grant him a divorce, leaving him only one option to end their marriage. "Murder, doctor?" she asks mockingly. "You haven't the courage." Stung by her words, Steele tries to strangle her, but is interrupted by the harsh cry of their pet cockatoo in a homage to similar squawking bird scenes in *Mad Love* (1935) and *Citizen Kane* (1941).

After this episode, Maria decides to spend a weekend at the Steeles' lodge in the country, presumably to engage in a romantic tryst with a lover. During this time, Dr. Steele experiences an amnesiac episode, and cannot recall anything that occurred during the weekend. Awakened in his office by his loyal nurse and confidante Stella Madden (Patricia Morison) on Monday morning, he is visited by two homicide detectives who inform him that his wife has been found murdered at the lodge, and that he is required to identify the body. At the murder scene Steele's subjective view is shown as he approaches his wife's corpse through a gaggle of cops and reporters. Maria has been killed in a particularly brutal fashion, having been bludgeoned to death and her face disfigured with acid, suggesting a crime of passion. As he looks over the body, Steele finds a button from his jacket apparently overlooked by the police that implicates him in the murder. As he is pocketing the evidence, in walks Inspector Gregg (J. Carrol Naish), who is in charge of the murder investigation and makes no secret about the fact that Steele is the primary suspect in his wife's homicide.

Suffering from amnesia, Steele also has his doubts and is without an alibi for the time in question. Things get even crazier when Maria's lover, Robert Duval (David Bruce), is fingered for the murder. Visiting his romantic rival in jail, Duval tells him that he was in love with Maria, and, like Steele, wanted her to divorce the doctor, but that she also rejected his pleas. Witnesses heard their loud quarreling just before Maria was murdered. The ubiquitous Inspector Gregg, however, continues to express his opinion that Steele murdered his wife and urges him to confess. "Pretty dangerous invading the unknown," Gregg says of the doctor's profession. "You learn strange things."

Obsessed by guilt and yearning to know the truth, Steele instructs Stella to hypnotize him and record the results on a phonograph machine used to record the doctor's hypnosis sessions with his patients. Played back for Gregg, Steele's entranced voice relates how he took a strong sedative and slept the weekend away in his office. Gregg, however, is not convinced of the veracity of the hypnotic process, and questions if it's possible to control one's subconscious in order to avoid punishment. In the meantime, Duval is tried, found guilty of Maria's murder, and sentenced to die in the electric chair, causing Steele to go into intense spasms of guilt. The doctor learns, however, that Duval had gambling debts and was hitting his wife up for money. After a suspicious fire at Steele's office that destroys the physician's financial records, Steele begins to suspect that Stella may be involved. Placing her under hypnosis, we are shown a dream sequence montage of images that reveal that Stella was involved with Duval, giving him money from Steele's account to cover his debts. The flashback also shows Stella murdering Maria and burning her face with acid (discretely in shadow), and the hypnotic session concludes with nightmarish images of buildings collapsing on Stella and the murderess screaming in terror as she is being led to the electric chair for her crimes. When the lights come up, Gregg is there to take her into custody and make a phone call to stop Duval's execution.

The first of the *Inner Sanctum Mysteries* is a neat little B thriller that is greatly enhanced by LeBorg's directorial flourishes. The director uses lighting, unusual angles and moving camera to construct a dark mystery with horror overtones provided by the exotic practice of hypnosis, which was looked upon as something of a quasi-occult nature during the 1940s. There are three sequences in which characters are hypnotized in darkened rooms using trance-inducing paraphernalia, and the film's climax occurs during Stella's hypnotic flashback/dream sequence. LeBorg's use of subjective camera in a key scene predates the utilization of this technique in Robert Montgomery's film noir *The Lady in the Lake* (1946). Chaney is stolid and believable in the lead role, and projects a sympathetic, if hangdog, screen presence. J. Caroll Naish is cheerfully relentless as the Javert-like Inspector Gregg, while the doe-eyed Patricia Morison almost steals the picture as the sultry Stella.

Note that the original screenplay by Edward Dein has a plot that revolves around not one, but two *femmes fatales*: the beautiful but promiscuous wife Maria and the sly, calculating Stella, who masquerades as the "good" woman and is ostensibly Maria's foil until she is finally unmasked as the psycho killer. Stella's psychopathic character is as cold and deadly as any dark lady in film noir, and the act of disfiguring her rival's face with acid is a particularly horrific touch. The film uses (and according to many critics, overuses) the noir technique of voice-over narration in the many scenes in which Chaney ruminates about his troubles in a whispered interior monologue. In an article on the film, Alan Warren writes, "These voice-overs have been repeatedly criticized over the years, but Don G. Smith makes a convincing argument that they embody the concept of the mind as the true inner sanctum, allowing Chaney to provide exposition without resorting to lengthy, drawn-out sequences."[10] Furthermore, these whispered monologues express the protagonist's true thoughts and feelings, and suggest the inner voice of the conscience of a man who believes that he may be a murderer. The amnesia subplot, in which the lead character doesn't know whether or not he committed a murder, is a film noir cliché that figures prominently in the fiction of mystery writer Cornell Woolrich.

Calling Dr. Death and the other entries in the *Inner Sanctum* series are frequently dismissed by Universal horror fans as failed horror films that lack monsters or an overtly supernatural element. These criticisms miss the point that the films are clearly labeled as mysteries while trying to replicate the mingling of supernatural horror and crime melodrama made popular on the *Inner Sanctum* radio program. Warren observes, "In keeping with Chaney's status as Universal's leading horror star, several entries had semi-horrific overtones, but Universal hedged its bets by providing rational explanations that undercut the seemingly supernatural goings-on."[11] As such, the *Inner Sanctum Mysteries* are prime examples of horror noir.

Many horror buffs and "Universalists" consider the second film in the series, *Weird Woman* (1944), to be the best of the *Inner Sanctum* series chiefly because it contains the clearest supernatural plot elements. Reginald LeBorg was back in the director's chair, while the screenplay was adapted from sci-fi/fantasy writer Fritz Lieber, Jr.'s classic witchcraft novel *Conjure Wife* by W. Scott Darling and Brenda Weisberg. In this one, Chaney plays anthropologist Norman Reed, who has just returned to bucolic Monroe College from a field trip to the South Seas with his new wife, Paula (Anne Gwynne), the daughter of a deceased anthropologist who has been raised by her native nurse and is steeped in island traditions of witchcraft and voodoo.

As an academic, Norman is wedded to Western skepticism about the supernatural, and has authored a book entitled *Superstition vs. Reason and Fact* that debunks native magic: "The so-called phenomena of mysticism and sorcery are brought about through fear, fear enslaving countless millions." He is, therefore, sorely chagrined when he discovers his wife performing a voodoo ritual, a spell of protection against his enemies, and forces her to destroy her voodoo paraphernalia. Shorn of her magical protective barriers, Norman's professional life begins to unravel. An old flame, college administrator Ilona (Evelyn Ankers), is stung by Norman's marriage to Paula and begins to actively plot against him. She finds evidence that Norman's rival, Professor Sawtelle (Ralph Morgan), has plagiarized a dead student's thesis for his book and convinces Sawtelle that Reed will ruin him with the knowledge. Plunged into despair, Sawtelle commits suicide, and his wife, Evelyn (Elizabeth Russell), blames Norman for her husband's death. Next, Ilona orchestrates a bogus scandal involving a co-ed research assistant, Maggie (Lois Collier), who claims she was sexually harassed by Norman, and when Maggie's boyfriend, David (Phil Brown), comes gunning for Norman, the student is accidentally killed when his gun goes off while he is grappling with the professor and Norman is accused of murder. As if all of this isn't enough, Ilona begins harassing the superstitious Paula by playing recordings of the eerie Polynesian "death chant" over the telephone.

One night, when the bitter Evelyn is belittling Paula about Norman's role in her husband's suicide, Norman manages to persuade her that it was really Ilona who orchestrated his death. This knowledge transforms Evelyn into an avenging witchy-woman who confronts Ilona with black magic of her own. She tells Ilona that her dead husband came to her and proclaimed, "I am dead because a woman lied. She must confess or she will die." Evelyn then displays a small box containing a voodoo doll with a string wrapped around its neck, telling her that "the woman who lied" must confess or she will die precisely 13 days later at one minute after midnight of the last day. Ilona begins to crack under the pressure of the voodoo curse, which is shown as a clever montage of images as the 13 days count down: a theater poster advertises that the play *The Lady Lies* is in its "Last 7 Days"; Ilona opens a carton to find a card reading "6 Skeins Yarn." Terrified, Ilona confesses to Evelyn that she is indeed the "woman who lied" who drove her husband to suicide and incited David to kill Norman. It is the stroke of midnight on the thirteenth day, and at this point, Norman and college administrators emerge from concealment to reveal that the curse was merely a ruse to make her confess her crimes. Driven over the edge by fear and guilt, Ilona attempts to escape from her tormentors by going out a window and running over a vine arbor, but the structure gives way and she is accidentally strangled when one of the vines wraps around her throat. The time of her death is exactly one minute after midnight.

Horror mavens dismiss *Weird Woman* in the light of Sidney Hayers's excellent supernatural thriller *Burn, Witch, Burn* (1962), which is a much superior screen version of the same source material, Lieber's novel *Conjure Wife*. But while *Burn, Witch, Burn* is clearly a better movie, *Weird Woman* is arguably a better exposition of Lieber's underlying theme: that *all* women are witches who fight secret wars of magic among themselves, of which men are blissfully unaware. In *Weird Woman* there are actually three witchy *femmes fatales*: Paula, the white witch; Ilona, the rejected, spiteful seductress and Evelyn, the avenging harpy. Ilona and Evelyn quickly adopt the voodoo world view and use the tools of magic against each other. Like *Burn, Witch, Burn,* and many of the Lewton films, *Weird Woman* explores the *frisson* between skepticism and the supernatural.

Director LeBorg reportedly had about ten calendar days to prepare for shooting, and this lack of development time shows in the production, which is not as elegant as LeBorg's treatment in *Calling Dr. Death.* Chaney's performance is particularly lackluster, and the script gives him little to do except talk to himself in the usual *Sanctum* stage whisper, as the ladies conduct their supernatural cat fight. *Weird Woman* contains a hilarious flashback set in Polynesia, in which native girls shake their booties to the throbbing drums of a voodoo ceremony to the local deity, "Kahuna-Ana-Ana" and utter lame voodoo chants like, "Malama, Malama, Malama" (English translation: "Protect, Protect, Protect").

On the plus side, the female leads manage to carry the picture. Evelyn Ankers, Chaney's co-star in *The Wolf Man,* is nicely cast against type as the sinister Ilona, but Elizabeth Russell, who had been used to great effect in Lewton's *Cat People* and *The Seventh Victim,* dominates the movie as soon as she begins mouthing dialogue about "the woman who lied," and transforms into the most powerful witch of all. Although it plods through most of its screen time, *Weird Woman* builds to an eerily effective climax, which includes Ilona's nightmarish (and sometimes silly) montage of images as the voodoo curse torments her with guilt during the final 13 days. While there are no murders and little in the way of mystery, the film has the dark visual tone of film noir and explores the noir themes of guilt and fate.

Next in the series was *Dead Man's Eyes* (1944), in which Chaney plays artist Dave Stuart, who is working on a portrait of sultry, exotic-looking Tanya Czoraki (Acquanetta). When Tanya accidentally switches a bottle of Stuart's eyewash with a container of acid, his corneas are burned out and he becomes blind. Unable to paint, Dave becomes "a useless hunk of humanity," and descends into a welter of self-pity and alcoholism despite the support of his close friend, psychiatrist Alan Bittaker (Paul Kelly). He even wants to break off his engagement with socialite Heather Hayden (Jean Parker), but her father, Stanley "Dad" Hayden (Edward Fielding), realizing that Dave will not marry his daughter while he is blind, makes legal arrangements to give his eyes to Dave for a corneal transplant operation in the event of Dad's death.

One evening, Dave muses in typical *Inner Sanctum* whispered voice-over about his desperate condition. "If Dad Hayden were dead..." he whispers to himself, letting the thought trail off into silence. When Heather returns home that night, she is horrified to find her father dead and Dave staggering about with blood on his hands. Dave is accused of homicide, but to Heather's dismay the legal papers signed by her father are binding, and the dead man's eyes must be given to Dave for the corneal transplant operation. Strangely, the canister containing the eyes is stolen and, just as mysteriously, returned just in time to perform the operation. When the bandages come off, though, the corneal grafts are not effective, and David is still blind.

The plot thickens as Dave, free on bail, retrieves a key piece of evidence in the murder, but keeps it hidden from homicide detective Captain Drury (Thomas Gomez), who is investigating the case and considers the blind artist his prime suspect. Then Tanya, who has figured out the identity of the killer, is herself murdered before she can reveal the information. Visiting Dave's apartment/studio, Drury finds that some of the oil paint on Tanya's portrait is still wet, indicating that Dave has recently worked on it. Is Dave feigning blindness? Did he murder Tanya and Dad Hayden? These questions are eventually answered as this neat murder mystery builds to a satisfying climax.

In his third *Inner Sanctum* outing, director LeBorg acquits himself well in this stylish whodunit, which is enlivened by his use of noir shadows and angles. Chaney gives what is arguably his best performance of the series as the tortured artist Dave Stuart. Unfortunately, the same cannot be said of the performance of horror starlet Acquanetta, who would portray the ape maiden she-creature in Universal's *Captive Wild Woman* (1943) and *Jungle Captive* (1944) and is easy on the eyes but delivers her lines in comically wooden fashion. The Tanya character is the film's *femme fatale*, the beautiful object of desire around which the film's action moves, even though she is not evil or sociopathic in this case. The rest of the cast is merely adequate. Although *Dead Man's Eyes* is a straight-ahead murder mystery, the subplot involving corneal transplants provides a touch of sci-fi horror, as the transplantation of body parts from a deceased person is a medical fact in the 21st-century, but was considered a science fictional notion when the film was made.

Fourth in the series was *The Frozen Ghost* (1945), in which LeBorg was replaced by director Harold Young. This time Chaney portrays Alex Gregor, a.k.a. Gregor the Great, a hypnotist who performs in a mentalist act that consists of placing his lovely assistant and fiancée Maura Daniel (Evelyn Ankers) into a trance in which she becomes clairvoyant and telepathic. As the film opens, Alex and Maura are performing the act during a live radio broadcast during which Maura seems to exhibit genuine psychic powers. When a rowdy drunk (Arthur Hohl) starts heckling him, Alex brings the man on stage in an attempt to hypnotize him, but Alex is severely annoyed by the heckler, and confides to Maura that "I could kill him." When Alex tries to place him in a hypnotic trance, the man keels over and dies on stage, causing Alex to believe that "I murdered that man mentally." Even after an autopsy shows that the heckler died of complications from acute alcoholism, Alex is consumed by guilt, cancels his radio show and breaks off his engagement to Maura.

Alex's business manager, George Keene (Milburn Stone), suggests that the hypnotist take a sojourn at the Monet Wax Museum, which is operated by an old friend, Valerie Monet (Tala Birell). Valerie welcomes Alex into her home and place of business, and introduces him to her young niece, Nina (Elena Verdugo), and Dr. Rudi Polden (Martin Kosleck), a former plastic surgeon who now works as the museum's sculptor. "He's a wizard in wax," Valerie explains as they tour the exhibits of famous murderers and villainous historical and literary figures such as the caveman "Stone Age Joe," Attila the Hun, Genghis Khan and Hamlet. Dr. Rudi is none too pleased to have Alex move in, as he sees the mentalist as competition for the affections of Nina, with whom he is in love. After a few weeks, Rudi falsely tells Valerie that Nina and Alex have become lovers, which enrages Valerie, who is beginning to have feelings for Alex herself. When she confronts Alex with the story, he becomes angry and orders her to "be still," whereupon she collapses to the floor. Thinking that he has used his psychic powers to kill again, Alex runs out into the night in a frenzy of guilt.

Believing that he has murdered Valerie, Alex and George return to the wax museum, where it seems that Valerie has vanished and police Inspector Brant (Douglas Dumbrille) is investigating her mysterious disappearance. When Nina discovers Valerie's body disguised as a wax figure of Lady Macbeth, Rudi places her in a state of suspended animation using a formula he has devised. It turns out that Rudi is plotting with George Keene to get Alex declared legally insane before a "psychopathic court," in order to seize the assets of his estate. As the two conspirators plan to dispose of Valerie and Nina in the waxwork's basement furnace, Alex and Maura return to the museum, where Alex places Maura in a hypnotic trance, and the clairvoyant Maura must psychically view the crimes, uncover the plot, and save Nina from being incinerated.

The Frozen Ghost has received a lot of bad press from critics over the years, but it's actually one of the more lively and inventive entries in the Inner Sanctum series. The film's unusual settings, including the radio studio and the wax museum, are novel and very different from the mostly pedestrian sets used in the other movies. Director Young makes fine use of Universal's prop department, peppering the waxworks with all manner of statuary, Egyptian sarcophagi and odd bric-a-brac to create a cluttered, image-rich screen environment that greatly enhances the film's spooky ambience. The screenplay by Bernard Schubert and Luci Ward draws inspiration from Michael Curtiz's seminal thriller, The Mystery of the Wax Museum (1933) in combining horror and mystery elements, and the sequence set in the radio studio that opens the film is a clever reference to the Inner

Left to right: Tala Birell, Milburn Stone, Lon Chaney, Jr., and Martin Kosleck tour the wax museum in the *Inner Sanctum* thriller *The Frozen Ghost* (Universal, 1945).

Sanctum radio program. Chaney presents his usual morose screen persona, and seems more believable in the role of a mentalist than the more intellectual characters he played in *Calling Dr. Death* or *Weird Woman*. Much of the film's charm, however, is provided by the sinister-looking Martin Kosleck, who would reprise his role as a mad sculptor in the Rondo Hatton vehicle *House of Horrors* (1946).

Perhaps the most horror-oriented entry in the series, *The Frozen Ghost* deftly combines wax museum thrills with hypnotism, psychic powers and murder mystery. Unlike the phony clairvoyants who populate films noir such as *Nightmare Alley* and *The Amazing Mr. X*, Alex and Maura's psychic abilities are the real deal, and are ultimately used to solve the crime. The film's gloomy, surrealistic ambience combined with its modern urban setting is typically noir as the plot caroms through a number of unlikely situations. The notion of Alex recuperating within the morbid confines of the wax museum strains credulity, and the mechanics of Rudi's suspended animation procedures are never explained.

The next feature in the series, *Strange Confession* (1945), is perhaps the most atypical of the *Inner Sanctum* thrillers in that it was adapted from the offbeat melodrama *The Man Who Reclaimed His Head* (1934), directed by Edward Ludwig from a popular stage play by Jean Bart, in which Claude Rains played a pacifist writer whose works are exploited by an unscrupulous publisher who drives him to commit decapitation. After the initial release of *Strange Confession*, Bart's estate objected to the film's taking "inordinate dramatic liberties" with the original and got a court order to have the film shelved until 1997, when story rights were renegotiated for the video reissue of the series.

Lon plays idealistic scientist Jeffrey Carter, a chemist who works for a drug outfit run by the ruthless industrialist Roger Graham (J. Carrol Naish), an immoral man who routinely exploits Jeff's research and takes credit for all his discoveries. Jeff, who is working on a new drug with great healing potential, is on the verge of a breakthrough when he chooses to quit Graham's firm rather than continue to be exploited. Blacklisted by Graham, Jeff is reduced to working as a pharmacist at a local drugstore and is excoriated by his wife, Mary (Brenda Joyce), who wants her husband to be more of a breadwinner and less of an altruist. When Graham visits Jeff's home to convince Jeff to return to his old job, Jeff reluctantly accepts after being prodded by Mary, while Graham, meeting Jeff's wife for the first time, is consumed by desire for the scientist's spouse.

Jeff soon realizes that the drug formula he is working on is not effective, and wishes to augment it with material derived from a rare mold that only grows in South America. Graham obliges by dispatching Jeff and his assistant, Dave (Lloyd Bridges), south of the border to conduct extensive research on the mold. His ulterior motive is to make a move on Mary while marketing Jeff's imperfect pharmaceutical, dubbed "Zymurgine," in order to make a quick buck. Unexpectedly, however, Jeff's son, Tommy (Gregory Muradian), becomes gravely ill during an epidemic, and Mary, believing that Zymurgine is Jeff's completed formula, authorizes treatment with the drug and cables Jeff to return home immediately. Unfortunately, Tommy does not respond to the Zymurgine and dies, while Graham chooses this moment to attempt to seduce Mary, inviting her to his digs for a midnight tryst. Mary accepts Graham's invitation that evening, but intends to kill him instead. In the meantime, Jeff arrives to find his son dead and his wife at Graham's house and is pushed beyond his limits. Mary attempts to shoot Graham, but he wrests the gun away from her as the prodigal Jeff shows up to settle the score. Seizing a machete from a nearby wall display, he uses it to render street justice by removing Graham's head from his shoulders.

Arguably the most off-the-wall entry in the *Inner Sanctum* franchise, *Strange Confession* plays more like a drama than a mystery or horror film. The adaptation of Jean Bart's 1932 pacifist play by screenwriter M. Coates Webster places the emphasis on corporate malfeasance and humanitarian social altruism rather than shock and suspense. Director John Hoffman shoots in a flat, uninteresting style that contains little in the way of horror or noir dark atmospheric ambience. The one noir touch is Graham's murder, which, although not directly shown, seems excessively brutal for the 1940s. Chaney delivers an earnest performance as the long-suffering chemist who is driven over the edge by corporate greed, but newcomer Lloyd Bridges steals every scene in which they appear in together. By this time the effects of severe alcoholism were beginning to show on Chaney, whose performance seems oddly sluggish and unfocused. J. Carrol Naish carries much of the film with his portrayal of the suave but ruthless industrialist, Graham.

The final *Sanctum* installment, *Pillow of Death* (1945), stars Chaney as attorney Wayne Fletcher, who is estranged from his wife, Vivian (voice of Victoria Horne), and seeking to divorce her and marry heiress Donna Kincaid (Brenda Joyce). Donna lives in a spooky old house with her uncle Sam (George Cleveland) and aunt Belle (played by Clara Blandrick, the beloved Auntie Em from *The Wizard of Oz*). Belle, the Kincaid family matriarch, disapproves of Donna working as Wayne's secretary, and seeks to break up the relationship. One night when Wayne and Donna are working late at the law office, Vivian is found dead, suffocated in her bed with her pillow. Detective Captain McCracken (Wilton Graff) is on the case, and Wayne is the prime suspect in his wife's murder, but has the alibi of working late with Donna, although she realizes that Wayne arrived at his office that night about 15 minutes later than he told the police. The plot gets weirder when "psychic consultant" Julian Julian (J. Edward Bromberg) arrives on the scene to report that the deceased Vivian was "a perfect medium for the spirit world" and wishes to arrange a séance to contact her at the Kincaid house, to which true believer Belle immediately agrees.

Wayne, invoking habeas corpus, forces the police to free him due to lack of evidence. He joins the Kincaid family and Julian for the séance, during which a woman's voice claiming to be Vivian accuses Wayne of killing her. The veracity of the supernatural manifestation is called into question, however, when Wayne discovers neighbor Bruce Malone (Bernard B. Thomas) concealing himself behind a secret panel. It seems that Bruce is able to slink through the Kincaid mansion via a secret tunnel that runs to his house, and has been keeping an eye on Donna. In the aftermath of the séance Wayne starts hearing Vivian's disembodied voice once more, which lures him out to the local cemetery, to the Fletcher family vault where her body is interred. When the crypt is later unlocked, Vivian's corpse is found to be missing. Soon afterward, Sam and Belle are found suffocated in their beds in a series of so-called "pillow murders," leaving Donna the entire Kincaid fortune.

One night Wayne and Donna are exploring one of the Kincaid mansion's secret passages when they discover Vivian's body. Then Bruce appears and confesses that he has stolen the corpse in order to make Wayne confess to the murder. Returning to the mansion, Wayne starts hearing his dead wife's voice once more. The mysterious voice lures him into a room, taunting him to confess his crimes. Surprisingly, Wayne seems entranced by the voice and starts blurting out details of the three homicides that reveal him to be the psycho killer. McCracken and the cops arrive in time to witness Wayne's confession, but before he can be taken into custody, Vivian's voice speaks to him once more and urges him over to the window, through which he plunges to his death. Earlier in the film, McCraken traded playful jibes with Julian, suggesting that the psychic, who has performed as a theatrical ventriloquist, has used his vocal abilities to snare the killer.

Pillow of Death is a lively send-off to the *Inner Sanctum* series, its fast-moving plot, concocted by scriptwriter George Bricker from an original story by Dwight V. Babcock, keeps the viewer guessing until the last frames with a variety of twists and turns. Direction by studio hack Wallace Fox, who had helmed the Monogram Lugosi horror vehicles *Bowery at Midnight* (1942) and *The Corpse Vanishes* (1942) keeps the action moving along quickly but is not particularly distinguished. Chaney acquits himself well in the lead role, but the screenplay keeps him out of the action for much of the picture. The rest of the cast is merely adequate, with the exception of Clara Blandrick, who brings some of her "Auntie Em" screen persona to the role of the curmudgeonly Kincaid matriarch, Belle.

Like the other *Inner Sanctum* movies, *Pillow of Death* is primarily a murder mystery about a serial killer, but like *Weird Woman* and *The Frozen Ghost*, it contains a genuine supernatural element. It is not clear at the end of the movie whether Wayne was actually hearing the voice of his dead wife (reportedly a medium) from the other world, whether it is the interior voice of his conscience, or whether the supernatural goings-on are merely a trick concocted by the psychic Julian in order to make Wayne confess. The film's ending deliberately invokes this ambiguity between the real and the unreal, which was central to the radio version of *Inner Sanctum*. *Pillow of Death* contains the trappings and settings of a horror film, including a spooky old mansion, a scene in a graveyard, a séance, and a ghostly, disembodied voice.

Unlike the *Whistler* series, The *Inner Sanctum Mystery* franchise has received scant attention from students of film noir. The films are routinely derided by horror film aficionados as inferior and are scarcely afforded any serious analysis. Much of the criticism is directed at the perceived acting faults of the series star, Lon Chaney, Jr. In analyzing the *Inner Sanctum* movies, horror film historian Carlos Clarens declares, "In all of these, Chaney revealed himself as a monotonous actor of rather narrow range, possessing neither the voice and skill of Karloff nor the demonic persuasion of Lugosi, and his rash of films were themselves mechanical, uninventive, and hopelessly serialized in flavor."[12] The films are also mocked for their lack of clear supernatural content by fans of Universal monster movies. This view is expressed by critic Bryan Senn, who writes, "God help those pictures which pass themselves off as horror (as the *Inner Sanctum* series did) but fail to present the devoted genre fan with some kind of monster or preternatural trick or two."[13]

While Chaney certainly had his flaws as a thespian, as noted in Chapter 2, he brought a distinctly American screen presence to the Hollywood horror film, which had hitherto been dominated by Karloff, Lugosi, Lorre, Atwill and other European actors. This "Americanization" of the horror film brought it closer to the orbit of film noir, which was developing into a distinctive form at precisely the time the *Inner Sanctum*s were being made. Chaney's performances in these films were certainly adequate, and superior to many of

Lugosi's camp outings made during the same period. His contributions as an actor are currently being re-evaluated apart from comparisons to Universal's "golden age" horror stars, and he is now frequently referred to as "underrated."

As to the supposed dearth of horror motifs in the series, contemporary viewers tend to forget that audiences of the 1940s, familiar with the unique meld of mystery and horror that was presented in the *Inner Sanctum* radio program every week, found no difficulty with being entertained by the hybrid form. All of the *Inner Sanctum* movies were very profitable for Universal, especially considering their low production costs. Critic Alan Warren notes, "With the exception of the atypical *Strange Confession*, all of the *Inner Sanctum*s climaxed with the exposure of the mystery killer in standard whodunit tradition. Whether or not this provided the sought-after variety, these films were standard mysteries at heart and the juxtaposition of horror and mystery elements throughout the series was an interesting example of 'crisscrossing genres.'" Universal's marketing strategy, casting horror star Chaney in the series, has tended to unfairly ground the films in the horror genre despite their mystery content, and it's arguable that had another actor starred in the franchise these films would unambiguously be considered part of the classic film noir canon.

Recently, however, the series has been re-evaluated in terms of its noir, rather than its horror content. Regardless of any supernatural content, the accent is on psychological horror, as indicated by the introductory spiel made by the bodiless "Spirit of the Inner Sanctum" prior to each episode, who reminds us with great relish that the mind "destroys, distorts, creates monsters, commits murders." Noir themes like sexual jealousy, amnesia, fate, obsession, poisonous women, medical malpractice and corporate malfeasance pervade the series. Michael H. Price and Kerry Grammill note, "For the *Sanctum*s have plenty in common with such acknowledged lesser classics of noir as *Detour* (1946), *The Devil Thumbs a Ride* (1947) and *Behind Locked Doors* (1946)—from their appropriately modest production values, to their combination of random misfortune and calculated manipulation, to the hapless schmoes whose eager-to-please nature strands them somewhere between heroism and antiheroism."[14]

The *Inner Sanctum Mystery* series, in its bold combination of supernatural and psychological horrors in a distinctly American setting, parallels the development of the horror noir form in the Val Lewton thrillers, especially *The Leopard Man* (1943) and *The Seventh Victim* (1943). These urban thrillers utilized many of the same cinematic techniques that were then being incorporated into the noir playbook, including low-key lighting, unusual angles, moving camera, subjective camera, flashbacks, voice-over narration, etc. *The Shadow*, *The Whistler* and the *Inner Sanctum* films are a tribute to the forgotten influence of radio on the development of classic film noir, and are prime examples of how the horror and noir genres intersect.

5

Monster Noir

Monsters are, of course, a staple of the horror film. In fact, one might say that monsters are the *raison d'être* of the genre. Something monstrous is created, via science, sorcery or sociology, and then must be destroyed. Monsters are subversive, a force of chaos; they rend the fabric of society through their insanely violent behavior. They can be inhuman creatures of the night, or they can be, alas, all too human. In either case, they hold a dark mirror up to the human condition so that we may recognize the shadow of the beast that resides within all of us.

As a realistic genre, film noir deals only with abominations of the human variety, which are arguably the most terrifying sort. The homicidal maniac Cody (James Cagney) from Raoul Walsh's acclaimed noir *White Heat* (1949) is just as much of a monster as Frankenstein's creation, and comes to a similar fiery end. Noir has no use for supernatural creatures, and it seems absurd to imagine a noir icon like Bogie or Robert Mitchum chasing a vampire or werewolf around the mean streets of Los Angeles. Yet classic film noir did flirt with supernatural themes from time to time (as discussed in Chapter 1), and there were a number of monster movies made during the 1940s, the early years of classic noir, that reflect noir themes, stylistics and sensibilities. There were also a number of dark crime melodramas that spotlighted human monstrosities and horrific behavior that had affinities with the horror film.

Killer Ape-Men, Werewolves and Vampires

Beginning with Michael Curtiz's *The Walking Dead* in 1936, a number of films were produced that combined crime themes with science-fiction horror. This trend continued with tech-noir thrillers such as *The Man They Could Not Hang* (1939), *Before I Hang* (1940) and *Black Friday* (1940), all of which starred Boris Karloff. The plot formula in these films revolved around an individual who is killed or executed and returns to exact revenge from beyond the grave. In all of these films the posthumous avengers were strictly human, but Paramount took the formula into creature-feature territory with their offbeat meld of crime melodrama and horror, *The Monster and the Girl* (1941).

The film has an unusual narrative structure. It begins with the black-garbed figure of Susan Webster (Ellen Drew) walking out of a bank of fog to look straight into the camera and address the audience directly. "I'm Susan," she narrates, "a bad luck penny. I bought a million dollars worth of trouble for everyone." From there, she walks into a courtroom where her brother Scot (Phillip Terry) is on trial for the murder of a mobster. Other pieces of the story continue to unfold in flashback as the various witnesses to the crime give their testimony. Ellen is a small-town girl who has traveled to the Big City to be "someplace where things are happening." Alone and unable to find work in her new surroundings, Ellen is befriended by the handsome and charming Larry Reed (Robert Paige). After a brief courtship, Reed asks Ellen to marry him and she accepts. The wedding ceremony is an odd, off-kilter affair, and afterward Ellen is whisked off to a wild reception party at a swanky hotel.

Susan awakens alone in her nuptial bed at the hotel the next morning to find herself living in a nightmare. She is being kept prisoner and forced into prostitution by a gang of criminals run by the sinister mob boss Bruhl (Paul Lukas), her marriage to Reed a sham arranged by the crooks to entrap her. When Scot gets wind of this, he comes looking for Susan only to be confronted by Bruhl and his brutal henchmen Sleeper (Marc Lawrence), The Deacon (Joseph Calleia) and Munn (Gerald Mohr), who frame Scot for a murder he did not commit. Flashing forward to Scot's murder trial, Susan gives her testimony in court, hoping to exonerate her brother, but the corrupt D.A. (Onslow Stevens) casts aspersions on her character during cross-examination. "Will you kindly explain to the jury the nature of your, er, occupation, how you live," he taunts, and Susan can only hang her head in shame and silence. Predictably, Scot is found guilty and sentenced to be executed. On the way out of the courtroom, he vows revenge on Bruhl and his mob. "You'll get yours," he snarls, "all of you."

While awaiting execution Scot has a strange visitor, a scientist named Dr. Parry (George Zucco), who is seeking "a strong, healthy brain" for an unspecified experiment, and wishes to persuade Scot to leave his body to science. Struck by the oddness of the request, Scot agrees, laughing, "Help yourself mister, help yourself." After the execution, Scot is whisked away to the mad doctor's laboratory, where his brain will be given new life by being transplanted into the body of a gorilla. "He should be proud when he wakes up with a human brain," Parry exults, but when the ape-man regains full consciousness he wastes no time breaking out of the doctor's digs on his mission of vengeance against the gang who framed him. After briefly visiting the sleeping Susan, the family dog, Skipper, who can somehow sense Scot in his simian form, becomes attached to the gorilla and follows him everywhere.

One by one the members of Bruhl's gang start coming up dead, all of them killed by having every bone in their body broken by the gorilla's enormous strength. While the cops are baffled by the M.O. of the "mangle murderer," the ape-man clambers over the city's rooftops while Skipper the dog fingers the victims on the streets below. After the Deacon, Sleeper and Munn have all had their bones broken by the mangle murderer, Reed and Bruhl kidnap Susan in an act of desperation, believing she knows who is committing the killings. Scot and Skipper trace the mobsters back to Bruhl's hotel room, and when it looks like Susan's life is in danger, the ape-man crashes through a window to rescue her. Street justice is done as Scot goes on the rampage and crushes Bruhl and Reed to death with his gorilla strength, but is mortally wounded by shots from Reed's revolver, to be mourned by Susan and Skipper.

While the film's central premise may seem ludicrous, this grim little tale of urban angst and big city criminality works surprisingly well as a noir tale of murder, social cor-

Left to right: Paul Lukas, Marc Lawrence, Robert Paige, Joseph Calleia, Charles Gemora (in gorilla suit) and Ellen Drew in ***The Monster and the Girl*** (Paramount, 1941).

ruption and revenge. *The Monster and the Girl*'s original screenplay (by Stuart Anthony) deftly combines elements of the crime melodrama and the horror movie, with the emphasis on the former. Made in the same year as *The Maltese Falcon* (1941), the film's use of narration and flashback anticipates the use of these techniques in later noirs. The plot formula of a wronged individual who is killed or executed and later exacts revenge from beyond the grave was used in numerous films over the years, including *Supernatural* (1933), *The Walking Dead* (1936), *Indestructible Man* (1956) and *The Most Dangerous Man Alive* (1960). The prostitution angle was daring by 1940s-era standards, and could barely even be alluded to in the film's script. In one early scene, for instance, a bellhop is shown delivering room service to a prostitute's hotel suite.

Director Stuart Heisler does a fine job of working with this unusual material, as most scenes take place in the shadow-drenched criminal demimonde of Bruhl and his grotesque mobsters. Heisler would go on to lens the acclaimed films noir *Among the Living* (1941), *The Glass Key* (1942) and *I Died a Thousand Times* (1955). Veteran horror thespian George Zucco provides the proper horror movie ambience, while Paul Lukas would later lend his oily European menace to Tourneur's gothic noir *Experiment Perilous* (1944). Director of photography Victor Milner composes shadowy low-key lighting setups that set the mood for the film's horror and crime melodrama components, and would later lend his talents to lensing the classic noirs *Dark City* (1950) and *The Strange Love of Martha Ivers* (1946). The film's murderous ape prowling the rooftops of the big city recalls the urban killer gorillas in *Murders in the Rue Morgue* (1932) and *King Kong* (1933). Movie historian William K. Everson sums up *The Monster and the Girl*'s film historical significance as follows: "It was a *different* kind of horror film, and today has added elements of interest in its foreshadowings of so many of the key elements of classic film noir: the doomed protagonists, the voice-over narration, the contrast of the purity of country life with the depravity of the big city."[1]

The indefatigable George Zucco was back monkeying around with apes and humans the following year in 20th Century–Fox's first entry into the 1940s monster sweepstakes, *Dr. Renault's Secret* (1942). The film opens with American medico Dr. Larry Forbes (John Shepperd) arriving at a small French village outside of Paris on a dark and stormy night. Dr. Forbes is bound for a local chateau to reunite with his fiancée, Madeline (Lynn Roberts), and her scientist uncle, Dr. Robert Renault (Zucco). As a bridge had been washed out, Forbes takes refuge for the night at Le Chat Noir Inn, where two of Dr. Renault's eccentric servants are also spending the night. Hulking ex-con Rogell (Mike Mazurki) is Renault's gardener, while the husky, enigmatic Noel (J. Carrol Naish) serves as the scientist's handyman. After Forbes flashes a wad of cash at the proprietor while paying his bill and retires to his room, he unexpectedly has to change rooms when he discovers a drunken tourist in his bed. That night, the tourist is found strangled to death, and local detective Duval (Arthur Shields) proclaims that "the murderer must have had fingers of steel." Suspicion falls on both Rogell and Noel, but when nothing can be proven Forbes, Rogell and Noel continue on to the chateau the next morning.

Madeline and Dr. Renault greet Forbes at the scientist's sprawling chateau, where the American settles in to prepare for the wedding and review some of Renault's experiments. Curious about the taciturn Noel, Madeline informs him that her uncle brought Noel back from a recent expedition to Java, and that he appears to have trouble understanding language, but is essentially harmless. The normally mild-mannered Noel responds savagely, however, when attacked by a large dog, which he nearly strangles to death. It also becomes clear that the mysterious Java man has a platonic attraction to Madeline, whom he pathetically addresses as "Madamoiselle." When Inspector Duval visits the chateau in order to get Dr. Renault's take on the village murder, he opines that "the criminal mind is like the animal mind. It betrays its savagery very easily." Duval also becomes aware of some shady goings-on between Rogell and Renault's butler, Henri (Jean Del Val), but is unable to pin anything down.

During the night, the dog is found hanged to death in its kennel by its own leash, and Renault blames Noel for the brutal act. Confronting the handyman in the scientist's basement lab, Renault orders him to "stand up like a man — the way I taught you." Dr. Renault's secret then becomes apparent: Noel is a Javanese jungle ape whom the scientist has surgically altered and made into the semblance of a human being through glandular injections and brain surgery. Savagely whipping Noel, Renault locks him in a cage, forbidding him to visit the village for the annual Bastille Day celebration. Noel, however, uses his simian strength to escape from the cage so he can be with "Madamoiselle." At the village celebration two waiters make fun of Noel, and the ape-man clambers over the town's rooftops to stalk and murder both of them in savage retribution. In the wake of these violent incidents Forbes, Madeline and Renault return to the chateau, where Forbes discovers Renault's lab notes about Noel's transformation. While Forbes is confronting the scientist, Noel arrives, knocks Forbes unconscious and strangles Renault to death. In the meantime, Rogell kidnaps Madeline, presumably to hold her for ransom, and transports her to an old water mill, but Noel follows and a battle royal ensues between the ape-man and the giant thug. In spite of being mortally wounded by a bullet from Rogell's gun, Noel manages to overcome the gangster before leaning over to address Madeline with his dying breath. "Everything all right now, Madamoiselle," he says. Fade to black.

Fox's initial foray into the horror market is a neat little thriller that is as much a mystery as it is a horror film. The screenplay by William Bruckner and Robert E. Metzler was inspired by the silent film *The Wizard* (1927), which in turn was based on "Balaoo," a story penned by *Phantom of the Opera* author Gaston Leroux. The story is convincingly updated into a 1940s-era idiom, and there are also plot elements borrowed from H.G. Wells's novel *The Island of Dr. Moreau* and its screen version, *The Island of Lost Souls* (1933). The narrative is basically a variation on the "Beauty and the Beast" theme. Fox's lush production values lend the film an A-picture gloss, and director Harry Lachman conjures the dark shadows and human pathos of this grim horror noir melodrama. Lachman's use of extreme close-ups and low-key lighting is particularly noir-esque.

J. Carroll Naish's portrayal of the half human Noel is one of his finest and most unusual performances, and foreshadows his role as the pathetic hunchback in *House of Frankenstein* (1944). The humble, soft-spoken creature is both sympathetic and monstrous, capable of erupting into violence at any moment, and the film's tag line read, "His animal instinct cannot be tamed!!!" B-movie fixture Naish would go on to co-star in the Chaney *Inner Sanctum* series entries *Calling Doctor Death* (1943) and *Strange Confession* (1945), as well as *The Whistler* (1944) and the gothic noir *The Beast with Five Fingers* (1946). Fans of film noir will appreciate the beefy role played by Mike Mazurki as the ex-con Rogell. Not long afterwards, Mazurki would portray the hulking mobster Moose Molloy in Edward Dmytryk's Chandler adaptation *Murder, My Sweet* (1944). Mazurki would go on to a series of memorable roles in classic films noir such as *Nightmare Alley* (1947), *Abandoned* (1949), *Night and the City* (1950), *Dark City* (1950) and *New York Confidential* (1955).

Fox released *Dr. Renault's Secret* on a double bill with their next horror thriller, *The Undying Monster* (1942). Based on a 1936 novel by Jessie Douglas Kerruish, the story is set around the turn of the century, on the ancient Hammond estate in rural England. The Hammond family, it seems, has been plagued by the "Hammond Curse," thought to have been brought about during the Crusades when one of their ancestors reportedly sold his soul to the devil. A creature known as the "Hammond Monster" is thought to still live in a hidden room inside the mansion and is said to strike "when the stars are bright on a frosty night." The film opens on a frosty evening when a dreadful howling sounds over the moors and the family heir Oliver Hammond (John Howard) is found mauled by a mysterious beast near the still-living body of the latest of the monster's victims, servant girl Kate O'Malley (Virginia Traxler), by Oliver's sister Helga (Heather Angel). The Hammond case comes to the attention of Scotland Yard, and forensic detective Robert Curtis

Helga Hammond (Heather Angel) and Walton (Halliwell Hobbes) search the moors for *The Undying Monster* (20th Century–Fox, 1942).

(James Ellison) and his daffy assistant Cornelia "Christy" Christopher (Heather Thatcher) are dispatched to Hammond Hall to investigate.

Arriving on the scene, the two Scotland Yard detectives begin gathering clues. The stolid Curtis is a pipe-smoking skeptic, while Christy fancies herself a ghostbuster. When the comatose Kate O'Malley dies at Hammond Hall under mysterious circumstances, Curtis suspects the family physician, Dr. Geoffrey Colbert (Bramwell Fletcher) of poisoning her to conceal Hammond family secrets. Curtis suspects that Dr. Colbert may be trying to kill Oliver and marry Helga in order to control the Hammond estate. In one intriguing scene, Curtis performs a spectrographic analysis of animal hairs thought to belong to the monster at a Scotland Yard crime lab, and after getting a positive match with wolf hair, the specimen mysteriously self-destructs. After the detectives pursue a number of red herrings the monster is revealed to be Oliver Hammond, who transforms into a shaggy wolf-man on the next frosty night and kidnaps Helga. Curtis and a squad of policemen pursue the werewolf over the moors and rocky crags, rescue Helga, and shoot Oliver dead (no silver bullet required here). In an epilogue back at Scotland Yard, Curtis and Christie explain that the Hammond males suffered from the brain disorder known as "lycanthrophy," a strange illness that caused them to grow hair, howl at the moon and commit homicide. Case closed.

The Undying Monster can be aptly described as *The Wolf Man* meets *The Hound of the Baskervilles*. Indeed, Fox had produced what is considered the finest version of *Hound* in 1939, the first of the Sherlock Holmes series of films featuring Basil Rathbone in the

Dr. Geoffrey Colbert (Bramwell Fletcher, left) looks in on Kate O'Malley (Virginia Traxler) as Detective Robert Curtis (James Ellison) watches from the shadows in *The Undying Monster* (20th Century–Fox, 1942).

title role. *The Undying Monster* consciously references *Hound* in the opening scenes that feature an enormous dog straight out of the Holmes story. Like *Dr. Renault's Secret*, the film blends mystery and horror, and there are even elements of the police procedural as the forensics experts gather and interpret evidence. German émigré John Brahm, assisted by ace cinematographer Lucien Ballard, imbues the film with gorgeous expressionist shadows and gobs of murky atmosphere. Brahm would go on to direct two of the finest '40s-era gothic noirs for Fox, *The Lodger* (1944) and *Hangover Square* (1945), and the classic noirs *The Brasher Doubloon* (1947) and *The Locket* (1947). The film's main flaw is with the character of Christie, who destroys the mysterioso mood at every turn by providing "comic relief" with her inane chatter about ghosts and the supernatural. Scripters Lillie Hayward and Michael Jacoby apparently thought that this sort of levity was needed to bridge the gap between mystery and horror, but this approach illustrates the difficulty of mixing supernatural monsters with the detective story.

Over at Universal, the trend toward combining mystery and monsters continued with *Night Monster* (1942). The film is set in the sleepy rural town of Hillsdale, where reclusive quadriplegic Curt Ingston (Ralph Morgan) has summoned his former physicians, Dr. Timmons (Frank Reicher), Dr. Phipps (Francis Pierlot) and Dr. King (Lionel Atwill), to his creepy old mansion, Ingston Towers. The three doctors, who are responsible for Ingston's paralyzed condition, have been invited to a demonstration of a revolutionary new medical technique that Ingston has supposedly discovered. Ingston employs a motley crew of eccentric servants on his estate, including a menacing butler, Rolf (Bela

Lugosi), a hulking, lecherous chauffeur Laurie (Leif Ericson) and a mysterious Hindu mystic, Agar Singh (Nils Asther). Adding to the mansion's bad reputation is an unsolved homicide that occurred at Pollard Slew, a fog-bound marshland adjacent to the Ingston estate.

Co-incident with the visit of the three physicians is the arrival of a fourth, psychiatrist Dr. Lynn Harper (Irene Hervey), who has been contacted by Ingston's daughter, Miss Margaret (Faye Helm), to evaluate her mental condition. Thought to be severely neurotic or even insane, Margaret is obsessively looked after by the estate's austere, black-clad housekeeper Sarah Judd (Doris Lloyd). Dr. Harper is accompanied by local writer Dick Baldwin (Don Porter), whose literary specialty is authoring "horror gories." That night, as local girl Millie Carson (Janet Shaw) leaves Ingston Towers and transits the foggy Pollard Slew, she hears the sound of a heavy door creaking open, followed by the complete cessation of all the night sounds of frogs and crickets. The terrified girl is stalked through the sudden silence by something or someone unknown and strangled to death.

Back at the Ingston mansion the guests are treated to a demonstration of the paranormal powers of Agar Singh, who materializes a kneeling skeleton holding a blood-dripping box containing a ruby from an ancient tomb in Thessaly. The skeleton and the box are real material objects, not illusions, and when the yogi is forced to break concentration, the objects quickly de-materialize. After the demo, Ingston explains that "cosmic substance" can be manipulated by yogic practitioners to replace damaged bodily tissues. Over the next couple of nights the three doctors are all found strangled, and the town's sheriff, "Capp" Beggs (Robert Homans), is busy investigating the homicides aided by amateur sleuths Dick and Dr. Harper. Suspicions fall on the sleazy Lawrie and the inscrutable Agar Singh, but neither man's shoe size matches that of the killer's large prints that have been discovered in the mud of Pollard Slew. Lawrie is soon eliminated as a suspect when the big guy comes up dead and is found hanging in a closet. Dick then posits the possibility that Ingston may be faking paralysis, but when they confront the old man he reveals that indeed he is not paralyzed, but is a quadruple amputee without arms or legs.

In the final act Miss Margaret finally goes completely bonkers and locks herself and Judd in a room and sets Ingston Towers on fire. As Dick and Dr. Harper escape the burning blaze and head through Pollard Slew, the door creaks open and the frogs stop croaking. A monstrous figure stalks the couple through the fog, and is revealed as Ingston. As he is in the process of strangling Dick a shot rings out and Ingston falls dead. Agar Singh appears holding a pistol and explains that he was responsible for teaching Ingston the yogic techniques that allowed him to materialize a set of phantom limbs, which he used to murder the doctors he held responsible for his condition. As they watch, Ingston's arms and legs magically fade into insubstantiality.

Considered one of Universal's lesser efforts and remembered today primarily as a film in the Bela Lugosi canon, *Night Monster* is in reality an entirely original and highly effective horror/mystery thriller that has lapsed into an undeserved obscurity. Scripter Clarence Upson Young delivers an offbeat blend of whodunnit, horror and metaphysics that is unlike anything else produced by the Universal monster factory. Producer/director Ford Beebe, best known for his Flash Gordon and Buck Rogers space-opera serials, moves the action along at a gallop while employing evocative lighting and other expressionistic flourishes, reportedly on a shooting schedule of just eleven days. Several scenes, including

Left to right: Dr. Timmons (Frank Reicher), Laurie (Leif Erikson), Kurt Ingstrom (Ralph Morgan), Dr. Phipps (Francis Pierlot), Dr. King (Lionel Atwill), Agor Singh (Nils Asther), Dick Baldwin (Don Porter), and Rolf (Bela Lugosi) prepare for dinner in *Night Monster* (Universal, 1942).

the murder on the moors amid an ominous silence, the materialization of the skeleton and the revelation of Ingston's limbless condition, are chillingly effective.

Despite its gothic trappings and horror movie ambience, the murder mystery element of *Night Monster* predominates. It's basically a noir tale of revenge, serial murder and medical malpractice, and the subplot in which a couple become amateur sleuths in order to solve a murder would later appear in Val Lewton's horror noir thriller *The Leopard Man* (1943). The film has a particularly strong cast that includes Ralph Morgan, Bela Lugosi and Lionel Atwill, but newcomer Leif Ericson steals practically every scene he's in with his portrayal of the menacing, libidinous chauffeur Lawrie. Ericson gets to deliver noir-esque lines of dialogue like, "She's no doctor, she's just a dame," and, "Anything could happen in this morgue and nobody'd be any the wiser." Famed director Alfred Hitchcock reportedly viewed the film during his stint at Universal and signed actress Janet Shaw for a small part as a waitress in his crime thriller *Shadow of a Doubt*.

After Lon Chaney, Jr., Universal's "Man of a Thousand Characters," had taken his turn playing Frankenstein's monster in *The Ghost of Frankenstein* (1942) and the Mummy in *The Mummy's Tomb* (1942), he was cast as the titular vampire in *Son of Dracula* (1943). Curt Siodmak, who had penned the breakthrough Chaney vehicle *The Wolf Man* (1941), was assigned to write the screenplay, while his older brother, Robert, was signed on to direct. After unsuccessful stints as a B-movie director at Paramount and Fox, Robert Siodmak had found a home at Universal, where he would later direct his most memorable films noir such as *Phantom Lady* (1944), *The Killers* (1946) and *Criss Cross* (1949). Unfortunately for his younger brother, Robert's deep sibling rivalry motivated him to have the studio remove Curt from the project, and the screenplay was generated by Eric Taylor. Nevertheless, *Son of Dracula* would prove to be the only screen collaboration between the brothers Siodmak since the acclaimed 1929 German documentary *Menschem am Sonntag* (*People on Sunday*).

The action has been relocated from Europe to the American South during the mid–20th century, where Kay Caldwell (Louise Allbritton) awaits the imminent arrival of a certain Count Alucard (spell it backwards), a Euro-nobleman she had met on a recent trip to Budapest. The Count has been invited for a stay at the Caldwell plantation, aptly named Dark Oaks. Kay is an elegant-looking young woman with a mordant turn of mind who has become preoccupied with death and matters of the occult. When her guest does not arrive by train that day, Kay, guided by some telepathic instinct, runs out into the mangrove swamp to seek guidance from fortune teller Madame Zimba (Adeline DeWalt Reynolds). The aged seeress reveals Kay's bleak future thus: "I see you marrying a corpse ... living in a grave." Suddenly a vicious bat flies into the witch's hut to put the bite on the old woman as Kay flees back to Dark Oaks.

At a reception party for the Count, who fails to arrive, Kay hints to her fiancé, Frank Stanley (Robert Paige), that she is preparing to carry out a bizarre plan involving Alucard, but gives him no details. During the party Alucard (Chaney) arrives to stealthily murder the family patriarch, Colonel Caldwell (George Irving). In addition to transforming himself into a bat, the Count can also de-materialize into a swirling mist in order to remain undetected. When the Colonel's will is read, Kay inherits only the plantation while the rest of the estate goes to her sister, Clair (Evelyn Ankers), but the inheritance is another part of Kay's master plan. In one of the film's most memorable moments, Kay witnesses Alucard materializing atop his coffin as it glides through the swamp toward her. After seemingly being romantically swept off her feet by the supernatural nobleman's dark embrace, Kay and the Count are secretly married by the town's justice of the peace.

In a jealous rage, Frank visits Dark Oaks to confront Kay, but instead winds up tussling with her new husband. Driven to murder, Frank pulls out a revolver and shoots Alucard, but the bullets pass harmlessly through the undead Count and kill Kay instead. Mentally unhinged by the episode, the distraught Frank confesses the murder to the town's physician, Dr. Brewster (Frank Craven), but the doctor is baffled when he visits the plantation that night to find Kay seemingly very much alive, albeit pale as a ghost. Frank, however, still insists she is dead, and the next day the local authorities return to Dark Oaks to investigate. This time Kay is found dead and lying in a coffin and Frank is thrown into jail pending a legal hearing. That night Kay seeps into his room as a mist and appears before him to explain her plan. She has merely used Alucard to attain immortality as a

Count Alucard (Lon Chaney, Jr., left) menaces Frank Stanley (Robert Paige) in Robert Siodmak's *Son of Dracula* (Universal, 1943).

vampire, and now wants Frank to eliminate the Count and join her among the undead, where "we will spend eternity together." Kay hands Frank the keys to his cell and a gun, which he uses to break out of jail. Having been told where to find Alucard's coffin, he invades the Count's lair and sets his coffin afire. Alucard is destroyed when the sun comes up before he can extinguish the flames that are consuming his resting place. In the tragic ending, Frank incinerates Kay in her coffin to free his beloved from the curse of the undead.

Son of Dracula is an unusual entry in the Universal monster movie canon. Curt Siodmak's story, fleshed out by Eric Taylor, brought the Dracula character to America for the first time, while the casting of Chaney in the lead role completed the Americanization of the role. The morbid, necrophobic Kay is a particularly twisted variety of *femme fatale*, who plots to attain immortality from her vampiric husband and then murder him. While the film is nominally set in the deep South, there's nary a Southern accent to be heard, but the midnight swamp ambience, with clumps of Spanish moss festooned among the twisted mangrove trees, is eerily effective. Siodmak translated the story into American gothic in which the Dark Oaks plantation is transformed into the typical haunted gothic estate, while the Count becomes the mysterious beloved who is cloaked in a strange and terrible secret.

The film's execution, however, is pure Robert Siodmak, with the director's signature expressionist lighting and moving camera very much in evidence. Most of the key scenes take place at night, in a claustrophobic world of shadows that anticipates Siodmak's later work in the noir idiom, and the horror movie visuals are greatly enhanced by the camerawork of ace Universal cinematographer George Robinson. The transition from horror film stylistics in *Son of Dracula* to Siodmak's later films noir, especially *Phantom Lady* (1944) and *The Spiral Staircase* (1946), is clearly evident. Many critics have pointed out a resemblance between Siodmak's style and that of Jacques Tourneur in the contemporaneous Val Lewton thrillers like *Cat People* (1942) and *I Walked with a Zombie* (1943)

While Chaney makes for a somewhat unlikely Count Dracula in comparison with Bela Lugosi's classic portrayal in *Dracula* (1931), the beefy young actor does manage to add some menacing heft to the role. The Count is kept offscreen for much of the proceedings, which adds to the remote, mysterious qualities of the character. Co-stars Robert Paige (who had played the oily crook in *The Monster and the Girl*) and Louise Allbritton provide most of the dramatic fireworks. Paige's performance is particularly intense as one of the victims of the vampire woman's macabre designs, while Allbritton's elegant vampiress provides the film's real menace. For the first time special effects were used to show the vampire's onscreen transitions into bat and fog, and *Son of Dracula* is today regarded as having liberated the character from the stage-bound conventions of previous incarnations. Siodmak's vampires are curiously ghostly and insubstantial, fading into invisibility or into their misty forms during key scenes and presenting a very different take on vampirism than the fleshy incarnation portrayed in the Hammer horror films decades later. The bleak noir-esque narrative is atypical of the Universal product, and film writer Bruce Dettman notes, "If for no other reason, the downbeat nature of *Son of Dracula* makes it unique in Universal horror film annals. A leaden sort of gloominess presides throughout the proceedings and, given the content and character development, there is really no room for a happy ending, as was usually the case in such films."[2]

Columbia's *Return of the Vampire* (1944) was another unusual, contemporary take on the vampire theme. The film takes place in wartime London, where the vampire Armand Tesla (Bela Lugosi) is revived from the dead when a Nazi bomb disturbs his grave. The resurrected Tesla is on a mission of vengeance against his former nemesis Dr. Jane Ainsley (Frieda Inescort), who had foiled the vampire's evil designs back in 1918. Andreas (Matt Willis), Tesla's erstwhile werewolf slave, who has allegedly been cured of his lycanthrophy and, reformed by Dr. Ainsley, is called back into service by the vampire. A string of murders follows as Tesla slakes his thirst while carrying out his plan to turn Jane's daughter, Niki (Nina Foch), into a vampire.

Tesla assumes the identity of scientist Hugo Bruckner, who has supposedly escaped the Nazis and fled to England, but who has secretly been killed by Andreas. Jane, however, becomes suspicious, and enlists the aid of Scotland Yard Commissioner Sir Frederick Fleet (Miles Mander), who is skeptical but assigns detectives Lynch (Leslie Denison) and Gannett (William Austin) to stake out "Bruckner" and Andreas. Gannett and Lynch attempt to collar Andreas, whom they find slinking around an alleyway, but he reverts to his lycanthropic form and escapes. The policemen report to a disbelieving Sir Fredrick

Werewolf in a business suit (Matt Willis) gets instructions from Armand Tesla (Bela Lugosi) in *The Return of the Vampire* (Columbia, 1943).

that "he turned into a wolf sir, right before our eyes," but they provide specimens of hair that are analyzed by forensics experts and identified as those of a wolf. The Scotland Yard boys are similarly baffled in their attempts to tail Tesla, who (via a clever bit of editing) vanishes as he exits to the street through a hotel door. Dr. Ainsley, who becomes a sort of female Van Helsing, strives in a battle of wills with Tesla to protect Niki, but the vampire has Andreas abduct her and transport her to his secret gravesite. As Tesla prepares to vampirize Niki inside the ruins of a bombed-out church, German planes arrive on their bombing run, and Andreas is wounded in the explosion. When Tesla refuses to help him, the werewolf turns away from the dark side and attacks his master, dragging the vampire into the sunlight that has been let in by the bombers and driving a stake through his heart before expiring.

While it is a standard-variety horror film, *Return of the Vampire* is unique because of its nihilistic admixture of vampires and werewolves with the horrors of World War II, as the Universal-type monsters commit their evil deeds against the backdrop of the Blitz, blackout curtains, air-raid sirens, skies full of bombers and streets strewn with rubble. The scenes in which the Scotland Yard detectives stalk the vampire and werewolf are played largely for comic relief, and illustrate why film noir and movie monsters don't mix. The intriguing story idea was conceived by Nathan Juran, who would later direct a number of memorable creature features during the 1950s. Veteran horror director Lew Landers, who had worked with Lugosi and Karloff on Universal's *The Raven* (1935), delivers an old-fashioned horror flick that seems more like a product of the 1930s than the '40s.

The Coming of the Creeper

In the mid–1940s, Universal "discovered" another horror star: Rondo Hatton, billed as "the ugliest man in the world," who reportedly portrayed his macabre roles without benefit of makeup. Hatton, who had been a handsome man in his youth, suffered from a disorder of the pituitary gland called acromegaly, a disease that severely disfigured his face and would ultimately kill him in 1946. The studio created a bogus P.R. story about how Hatton had become uglified through exposure to mustard gas while serving in the Army during World War I in order to hide their exploitation of his illness. Hatton had made his screen debut in Henry King's *Hell Harbor* (1930), and went on to perform uncredited bit parts in a number of Hollywood features, including *The Hunchback of Notre Dame* (1939), *The Ox-Bow Incident* (1943) and *The Lodger* (1944). His big break came with his portrayal of a character called "the Hoxton Creeper," a brutish homicidal maniac in Universal's *The Pearl of Death* (1944), one of the studio's Sherlock Holmes thrillers starring Basil Rathbone. Hatton was assigned to Ben Pivar's horror movie B-unit to star in a horror series based on the Creeper character. The Creeper was a kind of urban Frankenstein's monster, a hulking yet stealthy serial murderer who used his super-human strength to dispatch his victims, yet at times exhibited a hint of pathos. Dressed in a dark overcoat and signature slouch hat, the Creeper crept through a tangle of noir cityscapes on his nefarious missions of mayhem.

House of Horrors (1946), the first film in the series, co-starred character actor Martin Kosleck as down-and-out New York sculptor Marcel de Lange. As the movie opens, de Lange is waiting in his studio, amid pieces of his tortured statuary that consist of twisted limbs and body parts, for a buyer for one of his pieces. Before the deal can be consummated, however, influential art critic F. Holmes Harmon (Alan Napier) arrives with the prospective client only to severely criticize de Lange's work, leading the buyer to cancel the sale. Despondent over his wretched condition and contemplating suicide, the failed sculptor slinks to the city's waterfront, where he spots a figure struggling in the dark waters of the river, which turns out to be (who else?) the Creeper (Hatton), a notorious killer already wanted by the police. De Lange fishes the big man out of the drink and takes him home to nurse him back to health as a bond forms between the two social misfits. The demented sculptor is artistically inspired by the Creeper's extreme ugliness, and begins to sculpt a larger-than-lifesize bust of the murderer's head.

Before long the Creeper is skulking around the city's rougher neighborhoods murdering prostitutes in back alleys. The cops are baffled by the killer's M.O. because the Creeper has snapped his victims spines with his enormous strength. Then de Lange gets the bright idea to send the Creeper out to exact vengeance on F. Holmes Harmon for dissing his art. That night, before the Creeper arrives, Harmon receives a visit at his newspaper office from a fellow art critic named Joan Medford (Virginia Grey), who is there because Harmon has written a negative review of her boyfriend's artwork. Her beau, Steve Morrow (Robert Lowery), paints girlie pin-up pictures, and Joan pleads with Harmon and even comes on to him to get him to change his review. Thinking she has won a tactical victory, Joan leaves as the Creeper arrives soon afterward to snap Harmon's spine. Unfortunately, Steve gets nailed for the crime when another searing review of his work is found in the critic's typewriter.

The police finger Steve, who had publicly railed against Harmon for his scathing art criticism, for the crime. His alibi, however, proves to be solid and he is soon released. Mulling over Harmon's art reviews leads Joan to suspect that de Lange may be involved in the killings, so she pays a visit to the sculptor's Greenwich Village digs to sniff out clues. As the Creeper hides himself from view, Joan confronts de Lange, but the artist professes his innocence and intimates that he will blame the Creeper for the crimes if push comes to shove. Hearing this betrayal, the Creeper emerges to kill de Lange and goes after Joan, but before her spine can be snapped Steve and the cops arrive in time to break down the door and shoot the Creeper dead.

Director Jean Yarbrough packs a whole lot of murder, dark atmosphere and suspense into the film's brief running time of 65 minutes. Unusual lighting playing over Rondo Hatton's twisted features exploits the actor's fearsome appearance. While Hatton is an indifferent thespian he projects an extraordinarily malevolent screen presence, but the film's real acting grit is provided by B-movie veteran Martin Kosleck. Kosleck, whose dark aristocratic features caused him to be cast as a Nazi in a number of wartime melodramas such as *Nazi Agent* (1942) and *Berlin Correspondent* (1942), had played a similar role in the *Inner Sanctum* mystery *The Frozen Ghost* (1945).

House of Horrors was a grotesque anomaly even by Universal horror movie standards. The screenplay by George Bricker contains vivid strains of homosexuality and misogyny by contrasting the male-to-male relationship between social outcasts de Lange and the Creeper, with the "normal" heterosexual relationship between Joan and Steve. De Lange's decrepit art studio is filled with demented sculptures of twisted, disembodied limbs, while Steve's lush studio is populated by curvaceous models and girlie pictures. No rationale is provided for the Creeper's brutality against women, except that he is upset when they scream at the sight of him (who wouldn't?). In his book on film noir, *The Devil Thumbs a Ride*,

Rondo Hatton as his screen persona, "The Creeper."

Barry Gifford observes, "The use of shifting shadows and sudden dark-to-light maneuvers similar to Edgar G. Ulmer's *Detour* are effective tricks that create an appropriately moody black-and-white rhythm.... *House* is Rondo Hatton's greatest performance; his strange shape and countenance are unlike anything on the screen this side of Tod Browning's *Freaks*, or the traveling carny sideshow wagon in Hitchcock's *Saboteur*. The Creeper's problem with women is right on the surface, unquestioned; no hokey psychologizing in this one."[3]

Universal followed *House of Horrors* with *The Brute Man* (1946) the next film in the Hatton series, with Jean Yarbrough directing again. Hatton returned once more as the Creeper, seemingly none the worse for wear after having been drilled full of lead at the conclusion of *House*. The Creeper stalks out of a thick fog on the grounds of Hampton University to confront a woman named Joan Bemis (Janelle Johnson Dolenz). In the wake of Joan's murder, the daily papers scream lurid headlines about the bizarre "Back Breaker" murderer. On the run from the law, the Creeper climbs up the fire escape of a waterfront tenement building, where he hears piano music wafting out of a window. Climbing into the apartment he finds blind girl Helen Paige (Jane Adams) tickling the ivories. In a scene obviously lifted from the scene between the Monster and the Blind Hermit in *The Bride of Frankenstein* (1935), the virginal Helen forms an instant bond with the hulking psychopath, claiming to be able to "see" his nobler qualities, and hides him from a police dragnet. "I haven't seen anyone," she informs the cops rather disingenuously.

After his escape, the Creeper hides out in a storage bin on the waterfront, but when he is obliged to break the back of a snoopy grocery delivery boy in order to remain concealed, detective Lieutenant Gates (Peter Whitney) tracks him to his waterfront lair and discovers an old newspaper photograph about a football hero at Hampton University dating from the 1930s. The detective then turns his attention to Clifford Scott (*Detour*'s Tom Neal with a mustache), who is now a dean at Hampton U., and his wife Virginia (Jan Wiley), who recognize the person in the photo as former student Hal Moffet. Clifford relates how Moffet, who was competing with him for Virginia's attentions, lost his cool over losing Virginia while handling chemicals in the chem lab and was horribly disfigured by the acrid fumes. This leads Gates to believe that the Creeper was formerly Moffet, who bears a grudge against Clifford and Virginia, and he places a police guard at the couple's home in case the Creeper decides to drop in.

The Creeper continues to visit Helen, and snaps the spine of a pawnbroker to steal a butterfly brooch to give to her. When he learns that Helen needs two or three thou for an eye operation to cure her blindness, he decides to hit Clifford up for the dough. Eluding the police bodyguard, he creeps into the Scott residence to confront Clifford and demands Virginia's jewels from the family wall safe. Clifford gives him the jewels but pulls out a concealed pistol and wounds the Creeper, but the homicidal maniac survives the shots, murders Clifford and manages to escape. Helen receives the jewels from the Creeper's heist, but when she takes them to be appraised the jeweler tips off the cops. Gates uses the blind girl to lure the Creeper into a trap when newspapers print a story that Helen has betrayed him. When he arrives to murder her the police are ready to take him down.

This variation on the "Beauty and the Beast" theme is definitely a step down from the heady surrealistic ambience and deliciously abnormal psychology of *House of Horrors*.

Another problem is that Hatton was largely mute in *House* whereas in *The Brute Man* he has a fair amount of dialogue in his tender scenes with the blind girl, which emphasize Hatton's raspy speaking voice and minimal acting talent. It's hard to elicit pathos for the homicidal Creeper who smiles as he brutally murders the poor grocery boy, yet this is what the film attempts. There are too many repetitive scenes of the Creeper climbing up and down fire escapes and holding conversations with his blind friend. Apart from Hatton's performance, noir icon Tom Neal breezes through his role as academic administrator Clifford Scott, and appears as a younger varsity version of himself in flashbacks.

Unfortunately, Rondo Hatton died from a heart attack related to his glandular condition before either of his two star vehicles could be released. Universal became so ashamed of their exploitation of Hatton that they sold the rights to the films to the poverty-row studio PRC for release. The Creeper, however, retains his power as a noir menace as he stealthily slinks through tenements and creeps across rooftops on his murderous tasks, an urban ghostlike figure of dread with monstrous features and the power to snap spinal columns in two. Director Yarbrough later lensed a thriller entitled *The Creeper*, which was released in 1948, but it had nothing to do with Hatton's Creeper character.

Masks of Noir

The Hungarian-born actor Peter Lorre is an iconic figure who was equally at home in the worlds of both film noir and the horror film. The diminutive, bug-eyed Lorre seemed born to play unusual screen characters, beginning with his first starring role as the tormented child murderer in Fritz Lang's expressionist crime melodrama *M* (1931). His first English-speaking part was his breezy portrayal of a terrorist gang leader in Alfred Hitchcock's thriller *The Man Who Knew Too Much* (1934), and he made his Hollywood debut playing the demented, bald-headed surgeon in Karl Freund's tech-noir horror film *Mad Love* (1935). In 1940 he portrayed a psycho-killer in Boris Ingster's *The Stranger on the Third Floor*, a work that is considered one of the very first examples of film noir. He would appear as the effete criminal Joel Cairo in John Huston's seminal noir *The Maltese Falcon* (1941) in the following year, and would also star in Robert Florey's horror noir B-movie *The Face Behind the Mask* (1941).

Lorre plays European immigrant Janos Szaby, a bright-eyed innocent who is initially full of enthusiasm for his adopted country when he first arrives in New York. A watchmaker by trade, he is soon plunged into despair when he cannot find a job and is reduced to begging for work on the streets. Things get even blacker when Janos escapes from a fire in his rat-trap hotel with his face so horribly burned that the doctor's nurse screams in horror as his bandages are removed, and in the aftermath he begins to wear a mask that resembles his own features. Janos is befriended by tubercular petty thief Dinky (George E. Stone), who initiates him into the city's criminal underworld when Dinky is too sick to participate in a heist and Janos takes part in the robbery in his stead. Soon Janos is using his watchmaking precision to orchestrate a series of complex robberies and becomes the indispensable brains of the mob.

Janos meets a blind girl, Helen Williams (Evelyn Keyes), who is undeterred by his disfigurement and able to perceive the better angels of Janos's character without seeing

Peter Lorre as the disfigured criminal mastermind Janos Szaby in Robert Florey's *The Face Behind the Mask* (Columbia, 1941).

his physical ugliness. When Dinky suggests that he could have plastic surgery to restore his fire-scarred face, Janos is motivated to obtain enough money for an operation and then plans to abandon the mob to marry Helen. Unfortunately the gang has other ideas as they murder Helen with a car bomb in order to hold on to their meal ticket. Janos is plunged into a suicidal devastation by Helen's killing, and the former watchmaker begins to plot a meticulous revenge against the gangsters. He charters an airplane as part of a complex caper and deliberately sabotages the plane so that it crash-lands in a remote desert area, stranding the crooks without food or water. The masked Janos is lashed to one of the plane's landing struts and left to die as he watches the mobsters wander out into the wasteland to certain death.

Directed by French émigré Robert Florey, whose expressionist style had been evidenced in Universal's *Murders in the Rue Morgue* (1932), *The Face Behind the Mask* (1941) is arguably the director's finest work. The realism of the film's early scenes depicting the plight of the struggling immigrant contrast with the dark film noir stylistics of the later scenes set against the backdrop of the criminal underworld. Columbia insisted on an abbreviated shooting schedule, so Florey was obliged to complete the picture in two weeks while working on the detective flick *Meet Boston Blackie* at the same time. Based on a radio play by Thomas Edward O'Connell, the film was devised by screenwriters Allen Vincent and Paul Jarrico as a story of one man's descent into despair and suicide. The downbeat, unhappy ending was atypical of the Hollywood product of the early 1940s, but is pure noir. Made during the period when film noir was just beginning to emerge as a cinematic genre, *The Face Behind the Mask* adroitly mixes elements of the horror film and crime melodrama into a perfect horror noir blend.

Lorre's performance is superb as his portrayal of the innocent, good-natured Janos is transformed into that of the cold criminal mastermind. The actor reportedly simulated wearing a mask through the application of white powder on his face along with two strips of tape, a technique which demanded that Lorre keep his face completely immobile and express emotions solely through his eyes during shooting. Lorre would go on to become a fixture of film noir in movies like *The Mask of Dimitrios* (1944), *Black Angel* (1946) and *Three Strangers* (1946, see Chapter 1), and would again team with Florey for the gothic noir *The Beast with Five Fingers* (1946).

Billed as "the man you love to hate," Austrian actor and former film director Erich von Stroheim starred as the title character in PRC's *The Mask of Diijon* (1946). Diijon (von Stroheim), a washed-up stage magician, flounders in poverty in a ratty boarding house as he plans a comeback. He is treated to the convincing illusion of a beheading by guillotine at a nearby theatrical magic supply shop run by Mr. Sheffield (Edward Van Sloan), but Diijon is no longer interested in creating stage illusions and has developed a keen interest in hypnotism instead. His young wife and assistant, Vicky (Jeanne Bates), is loving and supportive, but Diijon treats her like dirt. When an old flame, piano player Tony Holliday (William Wright), hits town Vicky gravitates toward the younger man, which makes Diijon insanely jealous. Trying to be helpful, Tony sets up a gig for Diijon and Vicky at a local nightclub, but the magician, who is severely out of practice, clumsily botches an illusion and is booed off the stage. Humiliated, the illusionist blames Tony, accusing the pianist of trying "to make small of me in front of my wife."

Devastated, Diijon wanders through the city's fog-swept streets until stopping in a greasy spoon joint for a cup of java. When a crook drops in to hold the place up, the magician decides to test his hypnotic powers. Shining the reflection of a watch into the thief's eyes, he places the man in a trance, takes away his gun and orders him out of the restaurant. Next, Diijon tests his powers on an unsuspecting newsboy, convincing him that the morning paper is the evening edition. The ultimate test comes when he gives one of his friends, Danton (Maurice Hugo), a post-hypnotic command to write a suicide note and then jump in the ocean. When Danton comes up dead, an apparent suicide, Vicky decides she has had enough of Diijon and leaves her husband to stay with a friend pending a divorce. She begins singing in a nightclub act with Tony accompanying her on piano.

Driven over the edge by jealousy, the homicidal hypnotist places Vicky in a trance and commands her to go to Sheffield's magic store to retrieve a theatrical pistol that Diijon has loaded with live ammo, bring the gun to the nightclub and shoot Tony to death. That night Diijon goes to the club to watch his wife perform with his rival, as he squirms in anticipation as the appointed time approaches. Vicky suddenly stops singing, draws the gun and fires, but she has taken a gun loaded with blanks by mistake and Tony is unharmed. Fleeing from the cops, Diijon takes refuge in Sheffield's magic store where a shootout ensues. Wounded and debilitated by tear gas, he gets his head caught in the guillotine, whereupon Sheffield's pet cat (who is apparently unfazed by the commotion and in a playful mood), pulls a string that activates the device and accidentally beheads the mad magician.

A product of poverty-row studio PRC, *The Mask of Diijon* nevertheless manages to transcend its humble origins primarily through the star power of von Stroheim. An actor of limited range who delivers his lines with a flat lack of inflection, his maleficent screen presence adds an aura of palpable menace to the role of Diijon. Von Stroheim had played a similar part as a performer involved in jealousy and a love triangle in noir director Anthony Mann's *The Great Flamarion* (1945), and he would go on to film noir glory in Billy Wilder's *Sunset Boulevard* (1950, see Chapter 1). Edward Van Sloan, who had portrayed vampire hunter Van Helsing in Universal's *Dracula* (1931), has a throwaway part as the proprietor of the magic shop. Director Lew Landers, who had previously lensed horror fare such as *The Raven* (1935) and *Return of the Vampire* (1944), conjures the proper dark ambience for this twisted tale of hypnosis, murder and revenge. Hypnotism, which was something of a quasi-occult fringe practice in the 1940s, was also featured in a number of horror noir films that include *Dracula's Daughter* (1936), *Cat People* (1942), *Calling Dr. Death* (1943) and *The Frozen Ghost* (1945). Although it's a minor cinematic effort, *The Mask of Diijon* stands precisely on the cusp of film noir and the horror film, and is frequently assigned to either one of these genres by film critics.

Horror Femmes: Bat Girl and She Wolf

As the 1940s horror cycle started to wind down after the conclusion of World War II in 1945, horror films began to appropriate elements of the mystery genre as a novelty, a trend that had started with films like *Night Monster* (1942) and *The Undying Monster* (1942). Typical of this approach was another PRC effort, Frank Wisbar's *Devil Bat's Daughter* (1946). It's allegedly a sequel to PRC's *The Devil Bat* (1941), a low-budget sci-fi horror thriller in which Bela Lugosi plays Dr. Paul Carruthers, a scientist who creates a gigantic bat and trains it to eliminate extraneous characters from the plot.

Devil Bat's Daughter begins with the mysterious appearance of a young woman who has recently arrived at Wardsley, a small town in Westchester County, New York, from abroad. Her identification indicates that she is Nina MacCarron (Rosemary La Planche), but the unfortunate girl is in an amnesiac coma after having been found near the old abandoned Carruthers lab. Local physician Dr. Elliot (Nolan Leary) feels that Nina's condition is above his level of expertise and refers the case to Dr. Clifton Morris (Michael Hale), a wealthy New York psychiatrist who has recently moved to Wardsley with his wife, Ellen (Mollie Lamont). Dr. Morris's bedside manner has a beneficial effect upon Nina, who is soon coaxed out of her coma by the headshrinker. Suffering from intense nightmares about gigantic bats, Dr. Morris permits Nina to recuperate at his estate, where Ellen takes the disturbed girl under her wing.

In the meantime, Dr. Elliot and the town Sheriff (Edward Cassidy) have been nosing around the old Carruthers place and find evidence that Nina is the scientist's offspring, or, more dramatically put, "the Devil Bat's daughter." One day Ellen's son, Ted Masters

(John James), who has just been discharged from the Army, arrives at Wardsley. There is tension between Ted and Dr. Morris, who is Ted's stepfather, and it is revealed that Morris is having an affair with Myra Arnold (Monica Mars), and the psychiatrist maintains an apartment in New York which he uses as a love shack where he can tryst with his mistress. Myra demands that Morris divorce his wife to be with her, but he balks because he is unwilling to separate himself from Ellen's money.

While living under the same roof Ted and Nina hit it off until his parents insist Ted leave for Boston because they do not want him to form an attachment with the troubled girl. After Ted's departure Nina's condition promptly gets worse. Her nightmares intensify and she begins to believe she is an evil vampire possessed by the spirit of her father. Dr. Morris starts upping her meds, giving her pills and a special "tonic" to drink, but she continues her slide into mental instability. Finally, Ellen is brutally murdered with a pair of scissors and Nina awakens with the murder weapon in her hand and no memory of anything that has transpired. Nonetheless, she admits to committing the crime as newspaper headlines blare "Devil Bat's Daughter Confesses," and she is soon to be put on trial for Ellen's murder. Ted, however, is still convinced of her innocence and begins to suspect that his stepfather is responsible for his mother's murder. He finds Dr. Carruthers's missing scientific papers in Morris's possession, along with a letter to Myra stating that he is planning to elope to Cuba with her, and a "dream stimulant" pill used to sedate Nina so that she could not have committed the murder. Ted, Dr. Elliot and the Sheriff accuse Morris of murdering Ellen in order to inherit her money and go off with Myra, whereupon Morris tries to escape and is shot to death in a gunfight. Nina is declared innocent of all charges and is free to marry Ted.

Director/producer Wisbar, who is best remembered for the atmospheric ghost story *The Strangler of the Swamp* (1945), brings his German expressionistic vision to this minor-key horror/mystery thriller. The pacing is slow, however, and camera setups are mostly static and uninteresting. Griffin Jay's screenplay, from a story by Wisbar and Ernst Jaeger, recalls the psychological orientation of Lewton's *Cat People* but without a clear supernatural element in the mix. Dialogue is sometimes ludicrous, with lines like, "Who would be interested in learning the secret of enlarging bats?" Who indeed. The plot of *Devil Bat's Daughter* clearly illustrates the trend away from monsters and toward psychological horror at the end of the '40s horror film cycle. Stripped of its associations with *The Devil Bat*, the film is a recognizably noir tale of adultery, mental illness and murder, and the psychiatric angle is a frequent theme in films noir of the period, while the "drive her insane" subplot appeared in '40s gothic noirs like *Gaslight* (1944) and *Experiment Perilous* (1944). Star Rosemary La Planche, who also starred in *Strangler*, delivers a convincing portrayal of a woman teetering on the edge of madness without overacting, while co-star Michael Hale provides the proper touch of villainy as the malicious psychiatrist.

In a similar vein was another non-monster monster movie, Universal's *She-Wolf of London* (1946). Set in London at the turn of the 19th century, the story follows heiress Phyllis Allenby (June Lockhart), who believes she has inherited the "Allenby Curse" of lycanthropy from her ancestors. Her fears crystallize when a brutal murder occurs in a London park near the Allenby estate that has allegedly been perpetrated by a female werewolf who has ferociously mutilated the corpse. Phyllis's fiancé, Barry Lanfield (Don Porter), scoffs at the werewolf notion, calling it, "The sort of thing one reads in penny dreadfuls." The Allenby estate is managed by live-in housekeeper Martha Winthrop (Sara Haden) and her daughter Carol (Jan Wiley), who are a couple of strange characters. The intrigue deepens as a mysterious, hooded female figure is seen leaving the Allenby mansion late at night. When a boy is found horribly mauled to death at the park, Phyllis finds mud on her slippers and blood on her clothes that indicate that she is the marauding "She-Wolf." A few nights later Scotland Yard detective Latham (Lloyd Corrigan) visits the Allenby home on a routine house call and later has his throat ripped open by the female lycanthrope. A claw-like bloody garden implement is discovered in Phyllis's room the next day.

With his fiancée's sanity hanging in the balance, Barry decides to do some amateur sleuthing and stakes out the Allenby place. He observes a woman leaving the estate and follows her out into the fog-bound park, but it turns out to be Carol, who is going to a secret meeting with her boyfriend, Dwight Severn (Martin Kosleck). The real She-Wolf turns out to be Martha, who is trying to drive Phyllis insane so that she will not marry Barry and she and Carol would inherit the estate. Martha drugs Phyllis and plans to kill her with a kitchen knife before her sanity can be medically questioned, but snoopy maid Hannah (Eily Malyon) overhears her. Pursuing Hannah with the knife, Martha trips while running down a flight of stairs and is impaled upon the blade, and, with the mystery solved, Phyllis and Barry are free to marry.

Arguably the worst monster movie ever cranked out by the Universal horror factory, *She-Wolf of London* again illustrates the trend away from creature features in favor of mystery narratives. Heavily influenced by Fox's *The Undying Monster* (1942), the film is basically a period whodunnit with no lycanthrope in sight. Horror B-movie vet Jean Yarbrough, who had directed the Creeper films, delivers a tepid, uninspired product. There's little in the way of dark atmosphere provided, with many key sequences occurring in bright sunlight. Doe-eyed ingénue June Lockhart is dreadfully miscast in the lead role, while Sara Haden dominates the movie as the real psychopathic murderer whose mask slips in the final scenes. Character actor Martin Kosleck has a minuscule part as Carol's boyfriend, Dwight.

Most film historians list *House of Dracula* (1945) as the final film in the monster movie cycle that had begun with Lugosi's 1931 *Dracula*, but *She-Wolf of London*, released in 1946, was actually the last film in the Universal horror film series. The end of World War II heralded the demise of the horror movie, and the genre would not revive until the dawn of the sci-fi horror boom of the 1950s. Disillusioned at the end of the war, movie audiences turned away from fantasy and toward the realistic terrors presented by film noir.

6

Gothic and Costume Noir

Gothic — the term conjures visions of ruined castles, hereditary curses, haunted heroines and depraved noblemen. Gothic literature, which emerged in the late 18th-century, had a profound influence on the development of both the horror and mystery genres. Beginning with novels such as Horace Walpole's *The Castle of Otranto* (1764), Anne Radcliffe's *The Mysteries of Udolpho* (1794) and Matthew Gregory Lewis's *The Monk* (1796), gothic thrillers captured the public imagination with lurid tales of haunted houses, debauched clergy, mysterious plots and other dark, or noir, aspects of human nature. As the 19th-century progressed, gothic literature rose to greater prominence with popular and enduring romances like Charlotte Brontë's *Jane Eyre* (1847) and Emily Brontë's *Wuthering Heights* (1847). A distinctly American gothic sensibility was expressed in the works of Edgar Allan Poe, most notably in stories like "The Fall of the House of Usher" (1839) and "The Pit and the Pendulum" (1842) and in Nathaniel Hawthorne's novel *The House of the Seven* Gables (1851). Gothic literature came into its own during the Victorian era with provocative works such as Robert Louis Stevenson's *The Strange Case of Dr. Jekyll and Mr. Hyde* (1886), Oscar Wilde's *The Picture of Dorian Gray* (1891) and Bram Stoker's *Dracula* (1897).

The gothic plot formula (sometimes referred to as "female gothic") revolved around a naïve young woman from the lower classes who comes to live in the decaying mansion of a degenerate nobleman who harbors a mysterious secret. Ghosts, murders, ancestral curses, insanity and other seemingly preternatural goings-on are frequently involved in the narrative. The protagonists are usually virtuous women, while men assume the role of "Byronic heroes," after the 19th-century poet Lord Byron, who was once described by a contemporary as "mad, bad and dangerous to know," a variety of *homme fatal*. Male lust toward *femmes fatales* as a primary motivation for the masculine characters in film noir is replaced by the feminine protagonist's attraction to the Byronic hero's extensive real estate holdings and elevated social status. The diabolical *homme fatal*, typified by such mysterioso characters as Henry Jekyll/Edward Hyde, Dorian Gray and Count Dracula, wielded great wealth and power in the service of their dark and murderous obsessions The influence of gothic literature is evident in both horror films like *I Walked with a Zombie* and films noir such as *Sunset Boulevard*.

During the 20th century gothic literature received a boost from Daphne du Maurier's seminal novel *Rebecca* (1938), which redefined the gothic formula in a modern idiom. Du Maurier's spooky tale of a nameless heroine who marries an enigmatic wealthy man with a homicidal secret and moves to his palatial estate which is haunted by the persona of his dead wife was an enormous popular success and made into an Oscar-winning film by Alfred Hitchcock two years later. The modern haunted mansion has electricity, telephones and automobiles, and the apparitions and clanking chains that characterized gothic ghosts have been replaced by purely psychological, unseen revenants. The commercial and critical success of *Rebecca* inspired a cinematic female gothic revival that was evidenced in the prestigious, A-list productions of George Cukor's *Gaslight* (1944), Jacques Tourneur's *Experiment Perilous* (1944), Joseph L. Mankiewicz's *Dragonwyck* (1946) and Robert Siodmak's *The Spiral Staircase* (1946).

A related development was the emergence of what can be called "costume noir," that is, noir-oriented mystery thrillers set in the 19th century that departed from the female gothic formula. These films revolved around the exploits of male psycho-killer Byronic antiheroes while exploring their homicidal mania firsthand, and are somewhat closer to the spirit of classic film noir. Kicking off the costume noir sub-genre was MGM's 1941 remake of *Dr. Jekyll and Mr. Hyde*, which was followed by Edgar G. Ulmer's *Bluebeard* (1944), John Brahm's *The Lodger* (1944) and *Hangover Square* (1945) and Albert Lewin's *The Picture of Dorian Gray* (1945). These films transposed the universe of '40s-era noir into a 19th-century setting, with remarkable results.

Female Gothics

The film that started the female gothic revival was MGM's lavish production of *Gaslight* (1944). Set in Victorian-era London, the film begins with the brutal strangulation murder of famed operatic diva Alice Alquist at No. 9 Thornton Square in a tony section of the city. The only witness to the crime is young Paula Alquist (Ingrid Bergman), the singer's niece, who has been raised by her aunt Alice after the death of Paula's parents. Traumatized by the killing, the girl is sent away to Italy to study music and hopefully to become a great opera singer like her illustrious aunt. Cut to Italy ten years after the murder, where Paula, now in her twenties, realizes that she does not have her aunt's talent but has fallen in love with her piano accompanist, Gregory Anton (Charles Boyer), a suave continental type, and marries him after a whirlwind courtship. After Gregory expresses a desire to relocate to London, Paula reluctantly consents to move back to the "house of horrors" at No. 9 Thornton Square (which she has inherited from her aunt) in order to please her new husband and allow him to work on his musical compositions.

Haunted by lingering fears of the murder, Paula has grave misgivings about moving back to the house, which has been vacant for the ten years since the killing occurred. "The whole place seems to smell of death," she comments, leading Gregory to suggest that all of her aunt's things be moved up to the third floor attic and the door boarded up. Before this can happen, however, Paula discovers a letter written to her aunt by an admirer named "Sergius Bauer" dated two days before the murder suggesting a meeting. She is startled and confused when Gregory reacts violently and snatches the letter away from her. Once they have refurnished their new home, Gregory begins to isolate his wife from the outside world, claiming she is "highly strung" and needs rest. They stop going out and seeing visitors at home as Paula becomes a virtual prisoner. Gregory hires a saucy cockney maid, Nancy Oliver (Angela Lansbury, in her screen debut), and begins to humiliate Paula in front of the serving girl.

Paula's mental condition seems to worsen when she seemingly becomes forgetful, loses things and performs other irrational acts that are mercilessly criticized by her husband. Claiming that he cannot compose at Thornton Square, Gregory rents a room in order to work on his sonatas, and while he is out ostensibly working at night, Paula begins to hear ghostly footsteps in the empty attic overhead and observes the gaslight lamp periodically dimming. These strange goings-on cause her to doubt her sanity as she is overcome with fear and stifled by the lurking shadows of the murder house. During a rare outing to see the crown jewels, Paula is seen by Scotland Yard Inspector Brian Cameron (Joseph Cotten), who wonders at her resemblance to her aunt Alice, whom he had met briefly years earlier. His curiosity piqued, Cameron begins to investigate the oddness at No. 9 Thornton Square and reopens the cold case file on Alice Alquist, where he learns that the murderer's motive was probably the theft of a set of fabulous jewels given to the diva by a foreign head of state and found missing in the aftermath of the murder.

Staking out the residence, Cameron observes Gregory depart on his night-time jaunts and disappear into an adjacent building and theorizes that he is gaining access to No. 9 via a skylight on the rooftop. Forcing himself inside Paula's house, Cameron confronts her with evidence that her husband strangled Alice Alquist while searching for the jewels and is trying to drive her insane by dimming the gaslights and walking around seeking the gems in the supposedly boarded-up attic. His motive is to have Paula declared insane so that he can legally confiscate her assets. As they are speaking Gregory finally discovers the jewels hidden in plain sight among faux gems sewn into one of Alice's old stage costumes. When Gregory returns home Cameron confronts him with his crimes, whereupon he tries to bolt but is subdued by police. Tied to a chair, Paula excoriates her tormentor, even threatening him with a knife before he is led off to jail.

Lensed by "woman's director" George Cukor, who was also adept at directing costume movies, *Gaslight* proved to be a popular and critical success, and along with Hitchcock's *Rebecca*, assured the commercial viability of the female gothic formula. Not known for his use of chiaroscuro or other fear-inducing cinematic techniques, Cukor nevertheless employs low-key lighting, fluid camera movements and gorgeous compositions to establish a mood of fear and tension in this mystery thriller. Lavish MGM production values re-create the eerie fog-bound streets of Victorian London that they had conjured up three years earlier for *Dr. Jekyll and Mr. Hyde* (1941). Nominated for seven Academy Awards, *Gaslight* garnered two, including a Best Actress Oscar for Ingrid Bergman's bravura performance as a wife caught in her husband's web of deceit, fear-induced insanity and homicidal treachery. Charles Boyer, cast against type as the film's *homme fatal*, plays his role of the jewel-obsessed pianist with continental charm mixed with understated menace that garnered him a Best Actor nomination. Angela Lansbury, in her screen debut at seventeen years old, received a Best Supporting Actress Oscar nod for her portrayal of the cheeky maid Nancy. Other nominations included Best B&W Cinematography for D.P. Joseph Ruttenberg and a win for Best B&W Art Direction for Cedric Gibbons, William Ferrari, Edwin B. Willis and Paul Huldschinsky.

The film was based on a 1938 London stage play by Patrick Hamilton and a 1940 British film version directed by Thorold Dickinson starring Anton Walbrook and Diana

Wynyard. The American version was written by John Van Druten, Walter Reisch and John L. Balderston, who also received an Oscar nomination. Made during the formative period of film noir, *Gaslight* demonstrated the portability of the noir genre into the realm of the costume picture, and its theme of a persecuted wife vs. a murderous husband was replicated in '40s-era films noir such as William Castle's *Betrayed* (1944), Vincente Minnelli's *Undercurrent* (1946) and Richard Whorf's *Love from a Stranger* (1947). The term "gaslighting," denoting one individual psychologically tormenting another, came into popular usage after the film's release.

Director Jacques Tourneur, liberated from Val Lewton's horror movie B-unit at RKO, moved onto the A-list with his essay in female gothic *Experiment Perilous* (1944). Adapted from a novel by Margaret Carpenter by producer/screenwriter Warren Duff, the novel's contemporary setting was changed to 1903 to create a more convincing backdrop for the film's leading lady, Viennese actress Hedy Lamarr, who played the part of a cloistered wife that seemed more appropriate to a turn-of-the-century backdrop. Had the film been shot in its original setting it would have been a standard film noir, but lensed as a costume movie it acquired an element of fantasy.

Experiment Perilous opens on a train hurtling through a stormy night toward New York City, where psychiatrist Dr. Huntington Bailey (George Brent) makes a chance acquaintance with Cissie Bederaux (Olive Blakeney), who is returning home after a long illness to be reunited with her younger brother, Nick (Paul Lukas). With his professional eye, Bailey notes a certain "terror in her eyes" as she discusses her brother and his beautiful young wife, Allida (Lamarr), which piques his curiosity about the Bedereaux household. Arriving in New York, Bailey's luggage gets mixed up with Cissie's and he accidentally comes into possession of Cissie's handbag containing her diary and a biographical account of Nick she has been writing. While attending a party with his sculptor friend Clag (Albert Dekker), Bailey learns that Cissie has died suddenly of an apparent heart attack at Nick's home that very night.

Out of curiosity Bailey accompanies Clag to a reception at Nick's palatial home in the exclusive Murry Hill district, where he is introduced to Nick's trophy wife, Allida, with whom he instantly falls in love. When introduced to Nick, however, the psychiatrist is startled to learn that her husband thinks Allida is showing signs of mental instability. In a subsequent meeting Nick confides that he is concerned that his wife may harm their young son Alec (Billy Ward) and makes Bailey an offer he can't refuse to have the doctor treat Allida as a patient. Bailey accepts but says nothing about his chance meeting with Cissie on the train. He sees nothing to indicate that Allida is mentally ill, but he does notice a mysterious man who is shadowing her and soon finds himself under surveillance as well. The psychiatrist begins reading through Cissie's papers where he finds out about an incident in which a young writer, Alec Gregory (George N. Neise), with whom Allida may have had a tryst, sent Nick into a jealous rage. Alec was later killed in a mysterious traffic accident, and Bailey theorizes that Nick may have murdered his rival and killed Cissie when she suspected him of the crime.

Visiting the Bedereaux house, Bailey finds further evidence that Nick is trying to gaslight his wife. Snooping through the mansion's dark, forbidding rooms, he clandestinely observes Nick deliberately frightening little Alec by telling him his mother is a witch. When Cissie's papers are stolen from Bailey's apartment he knows that Nick is on

Turn-of-the-century psychiatrist Dr. Huntington Bailey (George Brent) attempts to psychoanalyze Allida (Hedy Lamarr) in Jacques Tourneur's *Experiment Perilous* (RKO, 1944).

to him. Surprisingly, though, Nick suddenly announces that he is leaving Allida, but fakes his suicide at sea in order to exact his revenge on his unfaithful wife and her new lover. In Nick's absence, Bailey rushes to the Bederaux house, where Nick gets the drop on him, holding him at gunpoint while he explains his belief that his son was fathered by Alec Gregory, which is why he forced Allida to name him Alec. He has been punishing his wife for her infidelity by trying to drive her mad and tormenting her son and announces he has locked them in a room and turned on the gas jets to asphyxiate them. The wily Bailey keeps his cool and manages to turn the tables on Nick, disarming him and knocking him unconscious. He rescues Allida and Alec before the gas causes an explosion that kills Nick and destroys the Bederaux mansion in a fiery conflagration.

Unlike the films he made for Val Lewton, Tourneur's gothic noir has fallen into an undeserved obscurity. *Experiment Perilous* is a competently made thriller that shows occasional flashes of Tourneur's visual brilliance but suffers from a lack of dramatic focus and indifferent acting, especially in comparison to the similarly themed *Gaslight* released earlier that year. The stolid George Brent displays little in the way of emotion, while the urbane Paul Lukas fails to project much in the way of villainy until the film's final scenes.

Nick (Paul Lukas) menaces his trophy wife, Allida (Hedy Lamarr), in *Experiment Perilous* (RKO, 1944).

Similarly, European actress Hedy Lamarr, playing a young lady from Vermont, strains credulity. Ms. Lamarr's masklike features do not register the fear she is supposedly experiencing at the hands of her sadistic husband, in contrast to Ingrid Bergman's tortured portrayal in *Gaslight*. Still, Tourneur's use of dark atmosphere, ably assisted by Oscar-nominated art direction of Albert S. D'Agostino and Jack Okey elevate *Experiment Perilous* above mediocrity. The film makes exquisite use of statuary in several key scenes in which the sculpted images seem to silently brood over the unfolding events, establishing a surrealistic, unearthly mood. The gothic Bederaux house of dark shadows, replete with large illuminated aquaria "like something out of Jules Verne," is particularly fear-inducing.

Warren Duff's screenplay contains several narrative techniques common in film noir, including multiple flashbacks, voice-over monologue, and Bailey hearing snippets of the other characters' dialogue inside his head. The scenario inverts the standard female gothic formula as established in *Rebecca* and *Gaslight* by making the film's viewpoint character a man instead of using a female protagonist. Allida's character can be considered a *femme fatale* (she is described in one scene as being "fateful") like the titular heroines of the classic noirs *Laura* (1944) and *Gilda* (1946), who are not themselves evil but whose intrinsic sexual desirability elicits homicidal behavior in the men who surround them. *Experiment Perilous* also reflects a noir fascination with psychiatry as evidenced in films like *Conflict* and *Nightmare Alley* and Tourneur's horror thriller *Cat People*. Producer Duff, director Tourneur and art director D'Agostino would soon join forces once more for the stylish noir *Out of the Past* (1947).

After directing the classic film noir *Phantom Lady* (1944) for RKO, Robert Siodmak tackled the female gothic in *The Spiral Staircase* (1946). Set in a small New England town in the early years of the 20th century, the film's protagonist is Helen Capel (Dorothy McGuire), a young woman who has been rendered mute by a traumatic incident in her past. As the film opens she is watching a silent movie being shown in the village hotel one afternoon, while upstairs an unseen assailant stalks a lame woman in the room directly above. The killer's maniacal eye is shown in extreme close-up before he emerges from a clothes closet to strangle her. The commotion causes the movie to be interrupted and the lame girl's body to be discovered, the third such murder to have occurred in the town in the last several weeks. All of the victims have been young women who are physically or mentally disfigured in some fashion.

In the aftermath Helen must walk home through the gathering darkness of a stormy night while being pursued by a shadowy figure. Helen is employed as a servant in the Warren house, a big, gloomy mansion on the outskirts of town. The Warren family consists of the staid, middle-aged professor Albert Warren (Paul Brent from *Experiment Perilous*), his younger half-brother Steven (Gordon Oliver) and Steven's aged, infirm mother, Mrs. Warren (Ethel Barrymore), who is bedridden. Steven has recently returned from abroad, which sets off a rivalry between the two brothers bordering on hatred that partly arises over their competition for the affections of Albert's pretty, young live-in secretary, Blanche (Rhonda Fleming). The unseen figure who has followed Helen into the Warren home is seen watching her from the shadows, his insanely staring eye bizarrely seeing her without a mouth on her face.

Mrs. Warren, who seems to have some special knowledge of the killings, repeatedly warns Helen to leave the Warren house immediately. The cranky old lady sleeps with a revolver by her bedside for unspecified reasons. The new physician in town, Dr. Parry (*Cat People*'s Kent Smith), who is treating Mrs. Warren, also wants to help Helen overcome her affliction. Knowing that her inability to speak stems from seeing her mother and father burned to death in a fire, he convinces Helen to go to a special clinic in Boston for treatment. While she is preparing to leave that night, the feud between the professor and Steven intensifies, causing many members of their staff to depart. As Blanche is retrieving her suitcase in the house's gloomy cellar, she is strangled by the lurking serial killer. Helen discovers the body and, thinking Steven is the killer, locks him in the cellar, but the real murderer is soon revealed to be the professor, who stalks her through the mansion. Because she is mute she cannot use the telephone to call for help, or alert the town constable who stops by on routine business. As the professor pursues his quarry up the spiral staircase from the basement, he explains that he is motivated to eliminate the weak and disabled because "there's no room in the whole world for imperfection." Suddenly, Mrs. Warren appears at the head of the stairs with her revolver and shoots the professor dead. Helen screams as the counter-shock abruptly cures her of her affliction, and, in the film's final scene, she speaks into the telephone to call for help.

Often described by the adjective "Hitchcockian," Siodmak's intense serial killer thriller seems to have exerted an influence on Hitchcock's later works. An overhead shot looking down the film's titular spiral staircase are echoed in a similar shot of the interior of the bell tower in *Vertigo* (1958), while the close-ups of the murderer's eye watching his prey would be repeated in *Psycho* (1960). Siodmak establishes an exquisite atmosphere of lurking fear using drifting camera movements, expressionist lighting and Wellesian deep focus that accentuates the menace of the enormous house with its myriad of hiding places. The influence of the Lewton psychological horror films, which were also being made at RKO at the time, can also be discerned. Cinematographer Nicholas Musuraca, whose deft touch at creating noir shadow worlds, enlivened Tourneur's *Cat People* and *Out of the Past*, and a number of classic films noir including Boris Ingster's *Stranger on the Third Floor* (1940), Ida Lupino's *The Hitchhiker* (1953) and John Farrow's *Where Danger Lives* (1950), provides the film's wonderfully eerie atmosphere.

Adapted from the novel *Some Must Watch* by Ethel Lina White by scripter Mel Dinelli, *The Spiral Staircase* lags a bit with a number of talky sequences in the second act, and the action is so time-condensed that the busy serial killer murders two women in a single day and is going for the trifecta by attempting to kill Helen. Siodmak coaxes fine, nuanced performances from an above-average cast. Paul Brent's psycho-killer is hidden beneath an icy reserve for most of the picture, while Dorothy McGuire is perfectly cast as the mute heroine and delivers a sensitive portrayal. The redoubtable Ethel Barrymore received an Academy Award nomination for her role as the crotchety Mrs. Warren. All in all, *The Spiral Staircase* remains a wonderfully stylish female gothic noir in which all the individual filmic elements combine to create a highly satisfying whole.

After 17 years as a Hollywood writer, including his co-authorship of the screenplay for the American film classic *Citizen Kane* (1941), Joseph L. Mankiewicz made his directorial debut with the gothic noir *Dragonwyck* (1946). Glamour actress Gene Tierney stars as Miranda Wells, a simple farm girl residing in Greenwich, Connecticut, in 1848. One day Miranda's father, Ephraim (Walter Huston), receives a curious letter from a distant relation, Nicholas Van Ryn (Vincent Price). The missive requests that one of his daughters come to his palatial estate, called Dragonwyck, in the Hudson Valley of New York, for employment as a governess to Nicholas's eight-year-old daughter, Katrine. Van Ryn is a *patroon*, a rich landowner of Dutch descent who lords over the tenant farmers on his extensive landholdings who are obliged to pay him rent and tribute. Ephraim, who is a stern, religious man, travels to New York with Miranda to meet Nicholas face to face. While they are waiting for their cousin to arrive, they start reciting Bible verses that read, "I will set no wicked thing before my eyes/I will not know a wicked person," when Nicholas strolls in. Despite this dire foreshadowing, Ephraim is charmed by the urbane patroon and allows Miranda to accompany Van Ryn to Dragonwyck.

The Van Ryn mansion turns out to be a dark, forbidding place, very different from what she imagined. Nicholas's wife Johanna (Vivienne Osborne) is a glutton and hypochondriac who seems more concerned with chowing down on napoleons and honey puffs than attending to the emotional needs of her daughter, Katrine (Connie Marshall). Miranda finds her young charge emotionally detached from her parents and psychologically isolated. There's more family weirdness on display in the form of the Van Ryn matriarch, their great-grandmother, who committed suicide after bearing the elder Van Ryn a son. Her portrait presides over the parlor and her ghost is said to sing and play the harpsichord in the middle of the night. Creepy maidservant Magda (Spring Byington) also tries to warn Miranda off the premises, uttering the prophecy, "You'll wish with all your heart you never came to Dragonwyck." The master of the house seems to spend much of his time sequestered in the mansion's tower room doing God knows what. The only normality is provided by Dr. Jeff Turner (Glenn Langan), the handsome young country doctor who is treating Johanna's series of petty illnesses.

While presiding over a harvest festival during which he traditionally collects rents from his tenant farmers, the aristocratic patroon confronts angry farmers who dispute his authority. The revolt suggests that the old-time patroon system's days are numbered in a newly emerging populist America. During a grand ball at Dragonwyck, Nicholas waltzes with Miranda, exhibiting a romantic attachment to his cousin that is plain for all to see. That night, Nicholas moves a plant bearing his "favorite oleander" flowers into Johanna's room, and the next morning his wife is found dead from unknown causes. Miranda learns that Nicholas had despised and rejected Johanna because she became unable to have children after Katrine's birth and, therefore, cannot bear him a son and heir. It isn't long before Nicholas proposes to Miranda, and she accepts, having fallen in love with her cousin.

To her horror, Miranda soon finds her husband to be a godless man who unashamedly proclaims his contempt for the Christian faith. "I believe in myself and I am answerable to myself," he tells her. "I will not live by ordinary standards. The couple is somewhat reconciled when Miranda becomes pregnant, but their joy is short-lived when their son is born with a malformed heart and dies soon after birth. Nicholas suffers a mental breakdown in the aftermath and starts spending more and more time alone in the tower room, and when Miranda enters his sanctum sanctorum to confront him, her husband reveals that he has become a drug addict. In the meantime Miranda's personal maid, Peggy (Jessica Tandy), goes to Dr. Turner to express her suspicions about Nicholas's malicious treatment of his wife. When Turner learns that Nicholas's "favorite oleander"

Nicholas Van Ryn (Vincent Price) admires the classic beauty of Miranda Wells (Gene Tierney) in Joseph L. Mankiewicz's gothic noir, *Dragonwyck* (20th Century–Fox, 1946).

has been moved into Miranda's room and she has taken ill, the doctor puts two and two together and theorizes that the plant contains a slow-acting poison and that her husband is attempting to murder her because he fears she cannot bear him a viable heir. After Dr. Turner rescues Miranda from Dragonwyck, the crazed patroon is shot to death during a confrontation with local farmers.

Mankiewicz (who also scripted) imbues *Dragonwyck* with an intelligent, measured treatment that elevates the film out of the realm of mere melodrama. Adapted from a popular gothic novel by Anya Seton, Mankiewicz creates a fine period feeling despite relying on painted backdrops and model work in some key scenes. Unfortunately, the film's religious moralizing and left-leaning social consciousness do not jibe with its horror/gothic sensibilities. Spooky interludes inside the haunted castle must contend with realistic scenes of class struggle between the democratic Yankees and the aristocratic patroon system as gothic chills clash with the historical backdrop of the 1839–1846 Anti-rent War of the period. The film's eerie sequences set inside the shadowed halls of Dragonwyck are well handled, however.

Price and Tierney, who had starred opposite each other in Otto Preminger's classic film noir *Laura* (1944), deliver standout performances supported by a fine cast. Price's portrayal of the decadent Byronic *homme fatal* Nicholas Van Ryn drives the picture and presages his aristocratic horror roles in Roger Corman's series of Edgar Allan Poe adaptations of the 1960s such as *House of Usher* (1960) and *The Pit and the Pendulum* (1961). At its core, *Dragonwyck* is a twisted noir tale of obsession, murder, mental illness and drug addiction set in an exotic historical period.

The female gothic noirs were all A-pictures, partly because it's difficult to produce a decent costume movie on a B-budget. They were all made at the major studios by some of Hollywood's most gifted directors, including Hitchcock, Cukor, Siodmak, Tourneur and Mankiewicz, as well as the industry's top acting talents. Many of these productions garnered Academy Award nominations, including a Best Picture win for *Rebecca* and a Best Actress award for *Gaslight*'s Ingrid Bergman. Art direction, cinematography and production values in general were also of the highest quality.

Contemporaneous gothic novels, rather than original screenplays, provided the inspiration for these horror noir thrillers. Even though ghosts were part of the landscape of *Rebecca* and *Dragonwyck*, they were psychological and not supernatural in nature. The gothic noirs instead dealt with crime, murder, madness, obsession and fate, all of which are typical film noir themes. They also employed the expressionist visual style of noir and all are fundamentally mystery stories in which the beleaguered heroine stands in for a police detective or private investigator to solve the crimes. The female gothic faded into obscurity, along with horror movies in general, after 1946, but elements of the form would resurface in later films such as *Rosemary's Baby* (1968).

Costume Noir

What may be termed "costume noir" emerged with the 1941 MGM version of *Dr. Jekyll and Mr. Hyde*. Like the female gothics, costume noirs were set in the 19th century and revolved around the actions of *hommes fatals*, but they departed from the gothic formula by offering male antiheroes as protagonists rather than the procession of terrified, haunted femmes that populated the gothics. The costume noirs dispensed with the crumbling, ghost-infested real estate holdings like Manderley and Dragonwyck that dominated the female gothics, and were set instead in the horror noir urban landscapes of London and Paris, where the psychological examination of homicidal male psychosis took center stage.

MGM's production of *Jekyll and Hyde*, made by the family-friendly studio that eschewed the morbid and morally decadent qualities of the horror film, strove to be a class act. Dramatic film star Spencer Tracy was cast in the lead roles opposite leading ladies Ingrid Bergman and Lana Turner. Tracy, unlike his arch-rival Fredric March in the 1932 Paramount version, announced that he would employ his acting skills and minimal makeup to depict the transition from the saintly Henry Jekyll to the twisted Mr. Hyde. The able Victor Fleming, best known for helming the screen classics *The Wizard of Oz* (1939) and *Gone with the Wind* (1939), was slated to direct.

The remake begins with a swell of choral hymns on the soundtrack as the camera pans down to a London church where Dr. Jekyll is attending Sunday services along with his fiancée Beatrix Emery (Lana Turner) and her father, Sir Charles (Donald Crisp). The pastor's sermon is interrupted by the jeering and heckling of parishioner Sam Higgins (Barton MacLane), who has recently suffered a serious work injury that seems to have disabled his moral compass. Dr. Henry Jekyll (Tracy) intervenes when a policeman arrives to collar the rowdy Higgins, suggesting that the heckler suffers from an emotional disturbance and should be sent to the doctor's clinic for treatment instead of to jail. This unnerving episode foreshadows the emergence of Jekyll's crazed alter ego, Mr. Hyde.

One night while strolling through the London streets with his physician friend Dr. John Lanyon (Ian Hunter), Jekyll rescues a Cockney barmaid, Ivy Peterson (Ingrid Bergman) from an assailant. The two gentlemen escort Ivy back to her East-end flat, where, overcome with gratitude, she attempts to seduce her rescuer, but the pure-hearted Jekyll is already spoken for and demurs. Jekyll immerses himself in his pharmacological attempts at "separating the facets of the brain," but when Higgins dies from the effects of his treatments, he is left with no choice but to test the experimental potion on himself. After quaffing the bubbling brew, Jekyll begins the histrionic transmogrification into his alternate self. These transformations are accompanied by a swirling montage of abstract Freudian imagery that includes breaking ocean waves, popping champagne corks, explosions and, most bizarrely, the depiction of Jekyll sadistically whipping Ivy and Beatrix as if they are tandem horses pulling his chariot.

Hyde's features differ from Jekyll's in that his hair is unkempt, his eyebrows more bushy and the crow's feet wrinkles on the outer edges of his eyes are more pronounced. In place of the doctor's perpetually serene expression, Hyde sports a maniacal, Joker-like grin. Hyde's first appearance is cut short when he is interrupted by Jekyll's manservant, Poole (Peter Godfrey), forcing him to become the doctor once more. Another complication arises when Beatrix has a dire premonition that night and rushes to her fiancé's home expecting the worst. Unfortunately, Sir Charles follows her, and, appalled by his daughter's behavior, breaks off the engagement and announces that he is taking Beatrix abroad.

Jekyll goes into a funk in Beatrix's absence and begins to obsess about Ivy and the potion. He eventually gives in to temptation, imbibing the strange brew once more and changing into Hyde. Visiting the Palace of Frivolities, the lavish music hall tavern where

Ivy works as a barmaid, Hyde muscles his way into her life by causing a ruckus and then paying off her boss to have her fired. Hyde then moves in and forces himself on the hapless woman, assuming the role of sugar daddy and setting her up in an upscale apartment. In a strange anticipation of *Gaslight* (also an MGM production), Hyde terrorizes and sequesters Ivy (Bergman) in the domicile, forbidding her to go out or see other people.

During Beatrix's absence the Hyde persona has been dominant, but when she and Sir Charles return to London, the doctor manifests himself again. Sir Charles has become reconciled to his prospective son-in-law, and the wedding is on again. Jekyll is unexpectedly confronted with his sins when Ivy pays him a visit and he can see the scars that he has cruelly inflicted. Shamed, he swears to her that Hyde will never trouble her again, and Ivy is elated. Her joy is short lived, however, when Jekyll is unable to prevent himself from spontaneously turning into Hyde without using the formula. He returns to her flat in a rage, and taunts her with snippets of the conversation she has had with Jekyll (whom he lambastes as a "smug, hypocritical coward") as he strangles the pathetic creature to death and then escapes.

With the evil personality dominant, Hyde is unable to obtain the drugs from his lab to affect the transformation back to Jekyll and is forced to approach Dr. Lanyon in order to obtain them. Holding Hyde at gunpoint while he drinks the formula, Lanyan watches as he transforms back into Jekyll and now knows the secret of his friend's dual personality. Realizing that he can never marry, Jekyll confronts Beatrix and breaks off the engagement, leaving his former fiancée in tears. He returns a few moments later, however — as Hyde. As Beatrix struggles in the embrace of the lecherous psychopath, Sir Charles arrives to save his daughter from being raped but is savagely beaten to death with Hyde's walking stick. Lanyon arrives on the scene with the police, and, recognizing his friend's cane, leads them to Jekyll's laboratory, where Hyde has taken the potion and transformed once more. "I'm Doctor Jekyll," he insists when confronted by Lanyon and the police, "I've done nothing," but as they watch he changes back to Hyde again. Hyde lashes out like a cornered rat, menacing the officers with a knife before being shot dead. As he becomes Jekyll one last time, hymns sung on the soundtrack suggest that Jekyll has found some measure of redemption in death.

Except for the prelude at the church, Fleming's remake closely follows the script of the 1932 Mamoulian version. Indeed, MGM purchased the rights to the earlier film from Paramount and salted it away in a vault for decades so as to discourage comparisons between their product and Fredric March's Oscar-winning performance. The Fleming iteration is marred by MGM's pious "quality picture" approach that tames and softens the film's mordant thematics, especially in comparison to the pre–Hays Code verve and experimental cinematic techniques of the Mamoulian *Jekyll and Hyde*. Eschewing the expressionist shadows of the horror film (except in a few key scenes), Fleming shoots in a flat, naturalistic style that is not appropriate to the film's sordid and horrific subject matter. The big-budget production tends to emphasize the lush, monumental set designs of Edwin B. Willis and the art direction of Cedric Gibbons, lending the film more of the flavor of a costume movie than a psychological horror tale. Poster art depicted Tracy stroking his chin, trying to decide between the charms of Turner and Bergman with the tag line, "A good woman — A bad woman — He needed the love of both," marketing the film as a costume romance instead of a melodrama. On the plus side, the Oscar-nominated cinematography of Joseph Ruttenberg beautifully evokes the menacing, fog-shrouded streets of Victorian London and Franz Waxman's rousing score provides a stirring musical backdrop.

Another point of critical contention is Spencer Tracy's performance in the dual roles. As Jekyll, Tracy is merely dull, his face masklike and his manner hesitant. As Hyde, the actor's features are frozen in a grimace of lust and violence that is equally masklike. While Fredric March's apelike version of Mr. Hyde strains credulity, Tracy's minimalist makeup by Jack Dawn is merely uninteresting. Tracy's thespian pride was stung when famed British writer Somerset Maugham visited the set of *Jekyll and Hyde* and watched the actor's performance, inquiring, "Which one is he playing now?" Throwing himself into the part with renewed fervor, Tracy shines in the murder scenes, particularly when he strangles Ivy while sadistically taunting her. Leading ladies Bergman and Turner reportedly exchanged roles, casting each other against type. Turner is photogenic but merely adequate in her role as Jekyll's staid fiancée, Beatrix, while Bergman lacks the sensuality of Miriam Hopkins's portrayal of Ivy in the 1932 version. Bergman's overall performance as Hyde's tormented mistress is superb, however, and full of raw pathos. She later would win an Oscar for her similar portrayal of the tortured, dominated heroine in *Gaslight*.

As *Rebecca* had inspired the female gothic revival, the '41 *Jekyll and Hyde* led to a series of costume horror noirs in which tortured madmen stalked their victims through the shadowy streets of 19th-century European cities of night. Like the female gothics, the majority of these films were produced between 1944 and 1946, during the formative period of classic film noir, and represent an exotic variation of the genre. The costume noirs focused more on mystery, police procedural and the abnormal psychology of invariably male mass-murderers in an urban setting.

Cult film-maker Edgar G. Ulmer, best known to aficionados of film noir for his low-rent nihilistic melodrama *Detour* (1945), directed films in a number of different genres during his illustrious career, including Universal's first Karloff/Lugosi pairing, *The Black Cat* (1934). Ulmer's contribution to costume noir was *Bluebeard* (1944), made during Ulmer's stint at the poverty-row Producer's Releasing Corporation (PRC) studio. Starring in the title role as the notorious lady killer was the eccentric character actor John Carradine, whose thespic talents had graced prestige productions like John Ford's *The Grapes of Wrath* (1940).

The film is set in Paris in the year 1855, where policemen are seen fishing the corpse of a young woman out of the Siene. Warnings to the citizens of Paris are posted all over the city, cautioning them, "A murderer is in your midst! A criminal who strangles young women!" The enigmatic serial killer, dubbed "Bluebeard" by the populace, remains elusive as three potential victims, Lucille (Jean Parker), Bebette (Patti McCarty) and Constance (Carrie Devan) attend a puppet show production of *Faust* in a public park. The operatic marionettes are voiced and operated by puppet master Gaston Morrell (Carradine), his girlfriend Renee (Sonia Sorel) and his assistant Soldat (Emmett Lynn). After the show Gaston speaks with Lucille and arranges for her to create costumes for his puppets as Lucille finds herself strangely attracted to the Byronic figure with a hint of tragedy in his past.

That night, when Renee jealously protests the attention he has paid to Lucille, Gaston coldly strangles her and disposes of her body through a secret passage leading to the river.

When Bluebeard's latest victim is discovered by the gendarmes, police inspector Lefevre (Nils Asther, the mystic swami from Universal's *Night Monster*) goes into high gear to find the killer. Lefevre gets a break in the case when the painting of a young woman, recently acquired and displayed in public by a duke, is identified as Bluebeard's fourth victim. The anonymous painting is traced to shady art dealer Lamarte (Ludwig Stossel), who feigns ignorance about the painter, but in reality Gaston is the artist. Lamarte knows that Gaston is Bluebeard and is shielding him from the police while surreptitiously selling his paintings for a large profit.

Lefevre decides to set a trap for Bluebeard by having middle-aged police inspector Deschamps (Henry Kolker) pretend to be a rich South American friend of the duke's who approaches Lamarte about having the anonymous artist paint a portrait of his "daughter," Francine (Teala Loring), who is in reality Lucille's sister and Lefevre's fiancée. Offering Lamarte 150 thousand francs to complete the portrait, the greedy art dealer persuades Gaston to accept the assignment. Lamarte's studio, where the picture is to be painted, is surrounded by Lefevre and his gendarmes as Deschamps and Francine arrive for the portraiture session, where Gaston has stipulated that he will only paint her using a mirror, his identity concealed behind a barrier. Unfortunately, when Gaston emerges from his hiding-place to pose Francine, she recognizes him from a visit to her sister's and he is obliged to strangle her. In the meantime, the greedy Lamarte knocks out Deschamps and is trying to sneak away with the 150 thousand francs when he is intercepted by Gaston and added to the strangulated victim roster. As the cops break down the door, Bluebeard escapes through a secret passage to the sewers with the secret of his identity intact.

In the finale Lucille recognizes a tie used as Bluebeard's murder weapon that Lefevre shows her as belonging to Gaston and knows that he has killed her sister. Dressed in her black mourning clothes, she pays a visit to Gaston in his spooky studio, which is festooned with the eerie shadows of marionettes hanging like lost souls, to confront him. Gaston professes his love for Lucille and reveals the reason for his violence. In a flashback, Gaston relates how, when he was a starving young artist, he found a girl named Jeanette (Anne Sterling) half-dead on the streets, took her home and slowly nursed her back to health. Gaston fell in love with her during her long convalescence and painted a portrait of her as Joan of Arc, after which she disappeared. Gaston's portrait received a prize and was selected to hang in the Louvre, but when he located Jeanette to tell her the news he found her cavorting with men like a common strumpet. Enraged, he had strangled her and gone on to paint and strangle a series of his models. As he confesses he approaches Lucille and gets his hands around her throat as Lefevre, who has followed her to Gaston's digs, breaks in. The gendarmes pursue Bluebeard over the rooftops of Paris before he falls in the Siene and drowns.

Reportedly shot in six days on a minuscule budget (especially for a costume picture), *Bluebeard* is a remarkable achievement. While it suffers from PRC's modest production values, the film rises to overcome them by Ulmer's deft use of light and shadow, his feeling for period detail and his ability to keep the notoriously hammy Carradine on a short leash. *Bluebeard* is also enhanced by the contributions of the great German émigré cinematographer Eugen Schufftan, who actually shot the movie but only received credit for Production Design. He had invented the "Schufftan process" (a means of enlarging and projecting backdrops using mirrors so that the images could be combined with live actors), for Fritz Lang's science-fiction epic *Metropolis* (1926). In one scene Schufftan projects an image of Paris's Notre Dame Cathedral onto a two-shot of Carradine and Jean Parker to create a gorgeous romantic illusion. Naturally, Carradine's uncharacteristically restrained performance as the artistic psycho-killer dominates the film. Attired in an operatic black cape and top hat and sporting long hair coiffed into a baroque hairdo, Carradine cuts a Byronic figure whose propensities for misogynistic violence smolders just beneath the surface. Jean Parker and a fine cast of character actors provide ample support for the film's star. On the minus side, the film is saddled with a ubiquitous "original" musical score by Leon Erdody that liberally borrows themes from Mussorgsky's *Pictures at an Exhibition* and which seems inappropriate to *Bluebeard*'s dark mood during some scenes.

Like MGM's *Jekyll and Hyde*, *Bluebeard* presents a homicidal protagonist who leads a double life as a seemingly meek puppeteer and Bluebeard the lady killer. The fictional character of Bluebeard was created by Charles Perrault in his 1697 gothic fairy tale "La Barbe Bleue," which in turn is thought to derive from the real-life exploits of the notorious serial child killer Gilles de Rais, a comrade-in-arms of Joan of Arc who was rumored to dabble in the occult and human sacrifice and was executed in 1440. *Bluebeard*'s screenplay, written by Pierre Gendron from an original story by Arnold Phillips and Werner H. Furst, picks up on the gothic elements of Perrault's tale but turns the psychopath into the central character, thereby converting it from female gothic to costume noir. Ulmer's noir vision of Paris, with its clustered rooftops, darkened artist's garrets and sewer labyrinths recalls the urban netherworld of the City of Lights depicted in Lon Chaney, Sr.'s *The Phantom of the Opera* (1925) and Robert Florey's Lugosi vehicle *Murders in the Rue Morgue* (1932).

After the modest financial success of 20th Century–Fox's *Dr. Renault's Secret* and *The Undying Monster*, the studio continued its foray into horror territory with its Jack the Ripper thriller *The Lodger* (1944). Based on a 1913 novel by Marie Belloc Lowndes that had previously been filmed in 1926 by Alfred Hitchcock, the film would attempt to flesh out the exploits of the Ripper, who had disemboweled five prostitutes in London's seedy Whitechapel district in 1888. The actor chosen to flesh out the legend of the famous murderer had plenty of flesh to offer movie audiences. Laird Cregar, who stood 6'3" tall and weighed 260 pounds, had played a variety of screen heavies on the Fox lot, including the effete bullfighting critic in Rouben Mamoulian's *Blood and Sand* (1941) and Lucifer himself in Ernst Lubitsch's afterlife comedy *Heaven Can Wait* (1943). Cregar also added his villainous heft to early films noir such as Frank Tuttle's *This Gun for Hire* (1942), in which he played the decadent, epicurean nightclub owner who hires Alan Ladd to commit murder. His most memorable noir performance, however, was in H. Bruce Humberstone's seminal crime melodrama *I Wake Up Screaming* (1941), in which he towered over the towering "big man" Victor Mature with his portrayal of a homicide detective obsessed with a dead woman. *The Lodger* was conceived as a vehicle for Cregar as a new horror star who would rival Karloff or Lugosi at the box office.

The Lodger opens on the foggy streets of London's Whitechapel one night in 1888. In a series of beautifully executed high-angle crane/dolly shots orchestrated by ace cinematographer Lucien Ballard, the camera follows a drunken floozy down the cobblestone streets, past bobbies on patrol and street vigilantes out looking for the Ripper, until she turns a dark corner and a terrible scream rips through the night. As the police and morbid onlookers flock to the site of the latest Whitechapel murder, the figure of a very large man emerges from the swirling fog in the tony district of Montague Square. The man inquires at #18 about a room for rent at the home of down-on-his-luck aristocrat Sir Robert Burton (Sir Cedric Hardwicke), whose reduced financial circumstances have caused him to advertise for a lodger. The applicant gives his name as Slade (Cregar), and is given a tour of the premises by Sir Robert's wife Ellen (Sara Allgood). Slade, who claims to be a pathologist conducting arcane scientific experiments, settles on an attic room where he will not be disturbed. An early indication of Slade's mental instability comes when he orders portraits of famous actresses that adorn the walls of the apartment removed while spouting misogynistic Bible verses such as, "Behold, there met him a woman subtle of heart." The Burtons have their misgivings about their new lodger, but Slade pays the much-needed rent a month in advance.

Slade's hatred of women is further exacerbated by Burton's pretty live-in niece, Kitty Langley (Merle Oberon), who is an up-and-coming chanteuse in a "very saucy" music hall revue. Having shown his unease around Kitty, Slade declines the offer to watch her perform, opting instead to stalk out into the nighted London streets. Primping up in her dressing room before the show, Kitty is visited by a former actress, Annie Rowley (Helena Pickard), who comes to wish her luck. While Kitty performs her risqué dance routine in a skimpy costume on the stage of the Piccadilly Theatre, the Ripper claims poor Annie as his latest victim. After the performance, Kitty is visited by Scotland Yard detective John Warwick (George Sanders) and told about Annie's murder. Warwick reveals that all of the Ripper's victims were actresses, that the killer appears to have medical knowledge

The Ripper (Laird Cregar) stalks Annie Rowley (Helena Pickard) through the London fog in *The Lodger* (20th Century–Fox, 1944).

and has been seen carrying a physician's black bag. Later on, Kitty catches Slade burning a similar-looking black satchel and his bloodstained clothing, which he claims was contaminated in his pathology work.

Another odd episode makes the Burtons suspicious when Slade shows Ellen "something more beautiful than a beautiful woman," which turns out to be a weird-looking miniature self-portrait of his dead brother, whom Slade idolizes as a genius. With more than a hint of homosexual incest, Slade rhapsodizes over his sibling's picture, cooing, "Isn't that a marvelous piece of work to come from the hands of a man ... a young man?" There is a hint of madness in the portrait, however, as Slade explains, "He had strange eyes ... he was a strange man." It is later revealed that the brother met his ruination at the hands of a beautiful *femme fatale*. In the meantime, romantic sparks begin to fly between Kitty and Inspector Warwick when she visits him at Scotland Yard's infamous Black Museum, where he comes on to her amid a display of hangman's nooses, death masks and other grisly mementos of violent crimes. When Warwick visits the Burton household, Sir Robert and Ellen confess their suspicions about Slade's unorthodox habits.

On the night when Kitty is to perform again, Slade is persuaded to attend and while he is out of the house Sir Robert provides the inspector with a sample of Slade's fingerprints, which turn out to match those of the Ripper's. While Kitty performs her "Parisian Trot" can-can dance accompanied by a bevy of leggy dancers in frilly lingerie, Warwick arrives at the theater with a squad of policemen. He has located another piece of evidence from the Black Museum, a second portrait of Slade's brother, this one looking more depraved than the first, that was found at the site of the Ripper's first murder. Meanwhile, Slade is in the audience leering at the ever-so-saucy spectacle, his mouth hanging slack in a perfect expression of unrequited lust, and when Kitty retires to her dressing-room during a break, Slade emerges from a dark corner and locks the door from the inside. Alone with the object of his desire, the Ripper expresses his feelings to her thusly: "You corrupt and destroy men like my brother was destroyed," he snarls. "I love you and I hate the evil in you." As Slade prepares to destroy the beauty that so troubles him, Kitty finally finds her voice and screams, bringing Warwick and the bobbies crashing through the dressing room door. Wounded but still dangerous, Slade climbs up to the rafters of the theater, where he is trapped like a rat in front of a large attic window. Knife in hand, the Ripper holds his foes at bay as the camera glides in on Slade's twisted, fearful expression. Finally, with a cry of anguish, the Ripper launches himself through the window, choosing death in the dark waters of the Thames to capture.

Possibly the best Jack the Ripper movie ever made, *The Lodger* proved to be a stylistic masterwork for director Brahm and an acting triumph for star Cregar. Brahm and director of photography Lucien Ballard (who had worked together on *The Undying Monster*) transformed part of the enormous set for the 1937 Fox production *In Old Chicago* into London's downscale Whitechapel district, the glistening brickwork, wet cobblestones and patches of mysterioso fog reflecting light in fear-inducing patterns that provide the perfect backdrop for the Ripper's homicidal deeds. High-angle moving camera shots are employed to frame the action scenes, while low angles are used to magnify Cregar's vast bulk into a looming, malevolent giant. Subjective camera is used to wonderful effect in a scene where the Ripper murders Jennie (Doris Lloyd) in her apartment, the murderer's POV revealing the pathetically twisted features of the terrified woman. The sophisticated

Sir Robert Burton (Sir Cedric Hardwicke), Kitty Langley (Merle Oberon), and Ellen (Sara All-good) prepare for a night at the theater in *The Lodger* (20th Century–Fox, 1944).

screenplay by Barre Lyndon injects subtle but daring hints of homosexuality and incest to the plot of the Lowndes novel. Composer Hugo Friedhofer's rousing score effectively punctuates the melodrama's dark tensions.

It is Cregar's magnetic performance as the tormented, misogynistic Slade, however, that dominates the film. Cregar towers over the other actors like a colossus of dread, his superbly expressive features reflecting various phases of the character's torment. Ironically, the film's homosexual subplot was reflected in the actor's real-life torments as a closeted gay man struggling with his sexual identity in 1940s Hollywood, a dimension that adds a tragic poignancy to Cregar's superlative performance. Co-star Merle Oberon contributes some Parisian ooh-la-la to the proceedings but is oddly demure while not exhibiting her feminine charms on stage, while British thesps George Sanders and Sir Cedric Handwicke add a touch of European class.

One of the supreme examples of 1940s-era horror noir, *The Lodger* perfectly straddles the two genres. Cregar's Slade is the perfect example of the horror noir *homme fatal*, a sex-obsessed homicidal maniac with some unspeakable secret in his past. For all her exhibitionistic tendencies, Kitty is not "a woman subtle of heart" seeking to exploit Slade; instead it is Slade who is the misogynistic lady killer. In his book *Hollywood Cauldron*, film historian Gregory Mank perceptively notes that *The Lodger* "was a pioneering horror film, paving the way for sexual neuroses in the cinema of terror. The sight of Cregar's face, twisting and leering as Merle Oberon flaunted her lacy panties and seamed opera hosiery and kicked the can-can, was much more sensational to 1944 audiences than a man growing a face full of special effects hair."[1] This powerful scene possibly inspired a similar sequence in the classic horror noir *The Night of the Hunter* (1955), in which psychotic woman murderer Robert Mitchum squirms grotesquely while watching a strip show. Like film noir, *The Lodger* takes place in an intensely urban environment populated by a variety of eccentric characters. The two portraits of Cregar's deceased brother in the film, the later one more decrepit and depraved, seems to have been lifted from Oscar Wilde's *The Picture of Dorian Gray* (filmed by MGM and released the following year), while plot elements of *The Lodger* appear to have been cribbed for Ulmer's *Bluebeard*.

The Lodger proved to be such a monster hit that Fox execs quickly planned another Cregar vehicle to exploit their horror star's newfound popularity. They settled on *Hangover Square*, a suspense novel written by Patrick Hamilton, author of the MGM hit *Gaslight*. Brahm would again direct and Barre Lyndon was assigned to write the screenplay adaptation of Hamilton's novel, which was a Cornell Woolrich–like story of amnesia and murder set in 1937 London. Lyndon would eventually change the time period to 1903 to tie in with the Victorian setting of *The Lodger*. Co-star George Sanders returned, playing practically the same role as a Scotland Yard inspector. The great film composer Bernard Herrmann, whose magnificent music would later provide the perfect sonic synergy with Alfred Hitchcock's greatest thrillers, *Vertigo* (1958), *North by Northwest* (1959) and *Psycho* (1960), would generate the "Concerto Macabre" score for the picture.

Hangover Square begins with the brutal murder of an elderly antiques dealer (Francis

George Harvey Bone (Laird Cregar, center) gazes longingly at femme fatale Netta Langdon (Linda Darnell) in *Hangover Square* (20th Century–Fox, 1945).

Ford) by a demented killer, who turns out to be composer George Harvey Bone (Cregar). The normally mild-mannered Bone suffers from periodic amnesiac blackouts during which he is transformed into a demented Hyde-like murderer. The fits are triggered by loud discordant sounds such as the raucous music being played on a street celebration outside the shop. Bone accidentally knocks over a lamp and starts a raging fire at the murder scene as he staggers out into the street in an amnesiac fugue state. When his mind finally clears, he returns home to find his girlfriend, Barbara (Faye Marlowe), playing his latest composition to her father, the distinguished conductor Sir Henry Chapman (Alan Napier), who is so smitten with the music that he insists on conducting a performance of Bone's concerto at his own home once it is completed.

In spite of his triumph, Bone is troubled by his missing time episodes and haunted by vague memories of the violent events. He decides to consult Scotland Yard alienist Dr. Allen Middleton (Sanders), and asks him if he would be likely to do anything criminal under these moods. Middleton takes Bone's inquiry seriously, taking blood and fiber samples for comparison with those at the murder site and placing him under police surveillance, but Bone is exonerated when the forensic evidence doesn't match up. The composer is relieved, but the psychologist points out that his affliction might cause Bone "to do strange things, dangerous things" and even elicit, "an urge to destroy anything that stands in his way." Middleton suggests that the composer take a hiatus from the stress of completing his concerto and take some much-needed R&R.

Taking the doctor's advice, Bone goes to a London music hall where he watches risqué songstress Netta Langdon (Linda Darnell) perform and is smitten with her beauty. After the performance, he offers to write music for her to sing, and the wily, amoral Netta is eager to exploit his talents. Soon Bone is diluting his genius by converting musical themes from his concerto into popular songs for Netta's repertoire, but Netta is dismissive of the staid composer stating, "George bores me sick." One night when she is obliged to dine with Bone at a fancy restaurant, Netta is introduced to handsome music impresario Eddie Carstairs (Glenn Langan), and gives him the brush-off in order to perform her act for the producer, and even contrives to milk Bone for another tune. When Bone catches Netta sneaking out of her apartment with his sheet music under her arm that night, he is understandably chagrined and will have no more to do with her.

The stress in his personal life has taken its toll on Bone, and when a load of plumber's pipes accidentally falls off a wagon, it produces a discordant noise that triggers his homicidal transformation. Taking a curtain cord from his home, he attempts to strangle Barbara but does not consummate the deed. A while later, when he comes out of the fugue state, he visits Barbara with no memory of the attack and assures her that he is going back to work on his concerto. Netta, however, has other ideas, and having advanced her career through her association with Carstairs, she needs a new song for a major show he is producing entitled, "I'm a Bad Girlie." In order to get another song out of the composer, she offers herself in marriage. "You could get me," she coos seductively. "There's not a thing I wouldn't do, couldn't do." After giving her the fruits of his genius once more, however, he learns that she has become engaged to Carstairs, and is emotionally shattered. Returning home, Bone tosses the box containing the engagement ring away in disgust, knocking over a gaggle of violins in his studio, creating the discordant sounds that trigger his murderous rage once more. Using the thugee cord, he visits Netta's flat and strangles his betrayer to death and disposes of her corpse on a roaring Guy Fawkes Day celebration bonfire and later forgets everything.

All of this homicidal mayhem has not affected the composer's musical inspiration, however, and rid of Netta's influence he speedily completes his concerto, which is to be performed at a grand premiere at Sir Henry's palatial home. On the night of the performance he receives a visit from Dr. Middleton, who now believes that Bone is guilty of murdering both Netta and the antiques dealer. Desperate to have his concerto performed, Bone locks Middleton in a downtown cellar and rushes to Sir Henry's where he begins his performance at the piano, but while he is playing he suddenly acquires total recall about the murders, mentally reliving them in distorted flashback images. Overcome by guilt and his own macabre music, he collapses as Barbara takes over on the piano and is led away by Middleton and the police to another room, but Bone cannot be restrained and throws a lamp at the policemen, causing a fire. As the conflagration spreads, Bone escapes in the confusion and insists on finishing the concerto as the audience flees in terror for their lives. The mad composer is last seen wreathed in smoke and flame, his face set in an expression of unimaginable ecstasy, as if he is playing his infernal music in Hell for Lucifer.

Compared with *The Lodger*, *Hangover Square* seems more like a 1950s-vintage movie, which is primarily due to Herrmann's more contempo musical score. Herrmann's modernist and experimental "Concerto Macabre" seems to anticipate his later work on *Vertigo* and *Psycho*. In particular, the composer's use of a dissonant piccolo lietmotif to indicate

Mad composer George Harvey Bone (Laird Cregar) contemplates the strangulation of Barbara Chapman (Faye Marlowe) in *Hangover Square* (20th Century–Fox, 1945).

Bone's homicidal change of personality prefigures the jarring string themes that suggest the violent workings of the schizophrenic mind in *Psycho*. Because the plot revolves around music the scoring becomes a more important element, and Herrmann's soaring accompaniment provides the perfect aural counterpoint to Brahm's expressionist visuals. Clocking in at a brisk 77 minutes, Brahm moves *Hangover Square* along at a breakneck pace from the film's first frames. As in *The Lodger*, Fox's attention to Victorian period detail is superb, and Brahm shoots several key scenes of Cregar walking in the distance like a black angel through London's twisted urban landscape in extreme long shot. Fire plays a role in several key scenes, including the infamous Guy Fawkes bonfire sequence and the film's climax, and is possibly a metaphor for Harvey Bone's smoldering mental state. Cameraman Joseph LaShelle's photography might not be as flashy as Lucien Ballard's, but he superbly captures the dark ambience of the central character's psychotic world.

Part of the morbid fascination of watching *Hangover Square* is in observing the transformation of the film's star, Laird Cregar, who was trying to escape being typecast as a perennial villain and had embarked on a severe makeover program during which he lost about 100 pounds from the time he was working on *The Lodger*. As a result, Cregar looks noticeably thin and drawn in comparison to his ox-like appearance in the earlier film. His role in *Hangover Square* again paralleled the actor's offscreen travails. He was reportedly trying to change his sexual orientation while transforming himself into a leading man type. He had been terribly disappointed to lose the part of Waldo Lydecker in *Laura* (1944) because he was too obviously sinister, and was similarly chagrined over being denied the role played by George Sanders in *The Picture of Dorian Gray*. Alas, the extreme effort cost Cregar his life, as he died of a heart attack a few days after having a routine stomach operation at the tender age of 31. He never lived to see his haunting performance as the schizoid composer of *Hangover Square*, which many critics consider his finest work. Cregar's death left a great void in both the horror and film noir genres, and movie buffs can only mourn for the juicy parts this enormously talented character actor might have played had he lived.

Hangover Square is perhaps closer to the conventions of '40s-era film noir than any of the other gothic or costume pieces. For once there is a *femme fatale* in the person of Linda Darnell's Netta that corrupts and leads the male protagonist astray with her sexual allures in time-honored noir fashion. The sultry Darnell is the perfect foil playing opposite Cregar's typical noir chump, and plays the part to the hilt. Darnell would later play a similar *femme fatale* part in Otto Preminger's follow-up to *Laura*, *Fallen Angel* (1946) and later starred in Preminger's remake of Henri-Georges Clouzot's thriller *Le Corbeau*, *The Thirteenth Letter* (1951). *Hangover Square* is also graced with the droll performance of George Sanders, whose part was reportedly cut severely in the final print by Fox mogul Darryl F. Zanuck in retribution for the actor's unprofessional behavior on the set. The core of the plot revolves around the classic noir theme of Bone's schizophrenic dual identity, and the film's title is a reference to the phenomenon of "Korsakov's Psychosis," or alcohol-induced amnesia even though the Bone character doesn't drink.

MGM, which had not produced a horror flick since the '41 version of *Dr. Jekyll and Mr. Hyde*, revisited the genre with their lavish screen version of Oscar Wilde's Victorian gothic novel *The Picture of Dorian Gray* (1945). Like the earlier production, the Wilde adaptation was based on a famous literary classic and would receive the "prestige picture" treatment. With a final cost of nearly $2 million (in 1945 dollars), it would prove to be the most expensive horror film produced by any studio during the entire decade.

The film opens in London in 1886, where the distinguished painter Sir Basil Hallward (Lowell Gilmore) is being paid a visit by his friend Sir Henry Wotton (George Sanders) at his palatial studio. Sir Basil is just putting the finishing touches on his greatest work, a lifelike portrait of a handsome young man. As Sir Henry admires the painting, the portrait's subject drops in, who is an upstanding young nobleman named Dorian Gray (Hurd Hatfield). After listening to an eloquent speech by Sir Henry extolling the virtues of youth and hedonism, Dorian is moved to exclaim, "As I grow old, this picture will remain always young.... If only the picture could change and I could be always what I am now. For that I would give anything. Yes, there is nothing in the whole world I would not give. I would give my soul for that." Unknowingly, Dorian has voiced his wish in the presence of an ancient statuette of a cat, one of the 73 great gods of Egypt, which Sir Basil has included in the portrait and has magically granted his wish. For a moment the portrait glows in Technicolor, providing a jarring note in this black and white film.

Songstress Sybil Vane (Angela Lansbury) meets Dorian Gray (Hurd Hatfield) in *The Picture of Dorian Gray* (MGM, 1945).

After their initial meeting Dorian comes under the Mephistophelean tutelage of Sir Henry, whose amoral philosophy and mordant cynicism prompt the young man into sociopathic behavior. Dorian begins slumming in lower-class dives, where he meets songbird Sybil Vane (Angela Lansbury) performing her gig at a pub called the Two Turtles. He becomes infatuated with the young lady, and even suggests marriage to her although she does not even know his name. Sybil's older brother James (Richard Fraser) disapproves of their relationship but is a merchant seaman who is about to ship out to Australia. As Dorian is about to propose, Sir Henry suggests that he test his bride-to-be's virtue by suggesting that he should invite Sybil to stay the night and observe her reaction. If she leaves, Sir Henry infers, "I'd believe her to be as good as she is beautiful and beg her forgiveness and marry her."

Taking Sir Henry's advice, Dorian tempts Sybil with this devil's bargain, and although the poor girl is shattered by his suggestion, her desperate love for Dorian prevails and she surrenders her virginity to him. After this chicanery Dorian writes Sybil a letter expressing his loathing for her and sends money along with the letter as if she is nothing but a common whore whose favors he has enjoyed. Even worse, he proclaims, "Henceforth I shall live only for pleasure ... and if this leads to the destruction of my soul, then it is only you who are responsible." The next day Sir Henry arrives bringing the news that Sybil has committed suicide and that the police are searching for the gentleman involved in her death. "So I have murdered Sybil Vane as surely as if I'd cut her throat," Dorian muses, but Sir Henry counters, "It's tragic of course, but you mustn't let yourself brood over it.... You should look upon this tragedy as an episode in the wonderful spectacle of life." Dorian heeds his advice and with a complete lack of remorse goes to the opera with Sir Henry, but the next day he notices a subtle change in his portrait. The expression has changed to an evil-looking leer, prompting Dorian to move the painting to his childhood attic room and lock it away from sight. As he had never revealed his name to Sybil or her family, he remains unconnected to the inquiry into Sybil's death and has literally gotten away with murder.

In the wake of this incident Dorian descends into an amoral life of drugs and debauchery, although this can only be suggested rather than shown in this '40s-era MGM production. Dorian is shown visiting a seedy bar in London's Bluegate Field, where a secret door opens and a surly dwarf emerges to admit Dorian to a realm of decadent delights that can only be imagined. Over the next twenty years Dorian, who is "filled with an insatiable madness for pleasure" (according to the film's offscreen narration as voiced by Sir Cedric Hardwicke), indulges in his every whim of debauchery and acquires an evil reputation among upright London society in the process. The young man's appearance shows no sign of his moral degradation while only the portrait shows evidence of Dorian's moral transgressions, which assumes the horrific aspect of a moldering corpse.

Sir Basil's niece, Gladys (Donna Reed), has grown up to be a striking young woman who is in love with Dorian, while she, in turn, is being pursued by young aristocrat David Stone (Peter Lawford). The pair is invited to attend a party at Dorian's one night when Gladys has resolved to ask Dorian to marry her, much to the chagrin of David. At the party that night the guests are entertained by an exotic oriental dancer and Dorian, oddly, refuses Gladys's offer of marriage, which he claims would lead to "a terrible wickedness." One evening Dorian encounters Sir Basil by chance on a foggy London street, and his old friend peppers him with questions about disturbing rumors that have been leveled at Dorian. Dorian fluffs off his concerns, but Sir Basil, who is about to catch a train for Paris, demands to see his portrait. Strangely, Dorian agrees and reveals the transformed painting to its creator, which is shown in all its macabre glory in Technicolor "as if some moral leprosy was eating the thing away," as the narrator observes. Sir Basil is overwhelmed before the evil image, and falls on his knees to pray for Dorian's soul, whereupon Dorian attacks the artist and brutally kills him with a knife. He then compels a friend (and presumably a former lover), Allen Campbell (Douglas Walton), a scientist, to dispose of the body and other evidence using blackmail. Once again Dorian Gray has gotten away with murder.

One night, while visiting Bluegate Field on one of his nocturnal sojourns, Dorian is recognized by Sybil's brother, James Vane (Richard Fraser), who has recently returned from down under and is seeking revenge on the nobleman who ruined his sister. Gray protests that he is too young to be the man involved, but James has his doubts. Shortly afterward, while out hunting with friends on his country estate, one of his guests accidentally shoots a man to death, and Dorian recognizes the corpse as Vane, who has been stalking him with a pistol in his pocket. Gray has escaped punishment yet again, but his conscience is beginning to catch up with him. Scotland Yard has also taken an interest in Dorian in connection with the disappearance of Sir Basil and the recent suicide of Allen Campbell, but there is no hard evidence against him. In the meantime, David has gained access to Gray's residence and has seen Dorian's secret. As David, Gladys and Sir Henry rush to Dorian's house, Gray finally repudiates his evil self by plunging a dagger into the heart of the painting, whereupon his friends arrive to find him dead, his corpse transformed into the vision of sin in the painting, while the portrait has miraculously reverted back to his image as an innocent young man.

Wilde's horror noir allegory has much in common with Stevenson's *Dr. Jekyll and Mr. Hyde*. Both stories feature a central character whose moral transgressions are disguised behind a front of bland Victorian respectability by means of a fantastic plot device, be it potion or painting. They both address the Apollonian/Dionysian split within the human personality and are variations on the theme of the monstrous doppelganger, which is a familiar noir theme. Both are urban tales of madness, murder and drug addiction hidden behind a façade of normalcy.

Director Albert Lewin, who also scripted, delivers one of the most faithful adaptations of a novel in screen history. Although some minor alterations have been made to Wilde's story, Lewin lovingly renders both the spirit and the letter of *The Picture of Dorian Gray* into first-class cinema. Lewin transforms Wilde's epigrammatic prose into sparkling movie dialogue, transposing some passages verbatim in order to capture the flavor of Wilde's philosophy, which is expressed by George Sanders's Sir Henry character. Lewin reportedly had *carte blanche* on production matters, even insisting on shooting the film in sequence, which is a very time-consuming and uneconomical method. Filming dragged on for 127 days and the budget would balloon to nearly $2 million, but MGM would spare no expense on this prestige product. The picture did very good business at the box-office despite its controversial subject matter and mixed critical reviews, but would finish slightly in the red due to its huge production costs. Ironically, the puritan mores of MGM in the 1940s were remarkably similar to those of Wilde's Victorian England as the movie's

Gladys (Donna Reed) is romanced by forever-young Dorian Gray (Hurd Hatfield) in ***The Picture of Dorian Gray*** (MGM, 1945).

notions of sinfulness must be conveyed to the audience indirectly or by innuendo. Wilde's "love that dare not speak its name" remained silent and locked in the closet.

Strong performances by a distinguished cast elevate *The Picture of Dorian Gray* into film classic status. Hurd Hatfield plays the lead role with enormous restraint, his handsome but drawn, skull-like features only hinting at the evil concealed behind the mask of social respectability. Horror noir veteran George Sanders is at the very top of his form mouthing Wilde's sardonic aphorisms as Dorian's acid-tongued mentor, Sir Henry. One of the film's strongest performances is provided by Angela Lansbury as the doomed songstress Sybil Vane, which garnered her second Oscar nomination in two years, after her screen debut in 1944's *Gaslight.* Lansbury's portrayal of the pathetic Sybil, forced to choose between love and honor in a nobleman's cynical game of entrapment, is heart-wrenching. Cinematographer Harry Stradling won an Academy Award for his black and white camerawork which had to integrate brief sequences in color. Another Oscar nomination went to the exquisite interior design of Cedric Gibbons, Hans Peters, Edwin B. Willis, John Bonar and Hugh Hunt, who skillfully decorated the lavish sets with all manner of antiquarian and exotic statuary to provide a fantastic backdrop to the proceedings.

Thematically, *The Picture of Dorian Gray* is a horror noir tale of murder, lust, obses-sion and, ultimately, redemption. Like a number of noir protagonists, the title character possesses a schizophrenic dual personality that embodies both good and evil. A number of films noir feature a strange or unusual portrait in the plot, including *Laura* (1944), *The Woman in the Window* (1944), *Scarlet Street* (1945) and *The Two Mrs. Carrolls* (1947), as well as the gothic noirs *Rebecca* (1940) and *Dragonwyck* (1946). The film's most noir-esque scene is the murder of Sir Basil, whose butchered body casts shadows reflected from a swinging ceiling lamp over Dorian in a manner that prefigures a similar sequence at the climax of Hitchcock's *Psycho* (1960). The film's portrait of the ambivalence between good and evil in the human soul is the very essence of noir.

One could make the case that Robert Florey's horror/mystery thriller *The Beast with Five Fingers* (1946) represents the last quality work made during the 1940s horror movie cycle. The story takes place in the small Italian village of San Stefano at the turn of the century, where the wealthy but dour old pianist, Francis Ingram (Victor Francen), broods over his paralysis at his gloomy ancestral estate at the Villa Francesca. Attended by his faithful live-in nurse, Julie Holden (Andrea King), Ingram practices left-handed Bach transcriptions with his five remaining functioning digits. The aging pianist has acquired an unnatural obsession with Julie, claiming that the young woman has provided him with artistic inspiration. Ingram's wealth and eccentricities have attracted a number of hangers-on, including petty con man Bruce Conrad (Robert Alda) and quirky astrologer Hillary Cummins (Peter Lorre). Perennial houseguest Hillary has spent the last few years searching for "the law that changes the conception of unknown fate into very predictable fact" in Ingram's extensive library of antiquarian books on astrology.

When Hillary eavesdrops on Julie and Bruce, who have fallen in love and are planning to leave the villa, he duly reports this to Ingram, who nearly strangles the astrologer in a fit of anger. The pianist leaves marks on Hillary's throat with his strong musician's fingers. Later that night Ingram awakens and searches through the darkened rooms for Julie in his wheelchair and falls or is pushed down a flight of stairs to his death. In the aftermath Ingram's relatives, brother-in-law Raymond Arlington (Charles Dingle) and nephew Don (John Alvin) arrive at the villa for the reading of the will and Hillary is ter-ribly vexed to learn that they intend to sell all of his beloved astrology books and throw him out into the street. When the will is read everyone is shocked to learn that Ingram has left his entire estate to Julie. However, Ingram's relatives decide to remain at the villa while they contest the will. San Stefano's Commissario of Police, Ovidio Castanio (J. Car-rol Naish), suspects foul play may be involved in Ingram's death and begins a formal investigation.

One night a mysterious light is seen glowing in Ingram's mausoleum and upon inves-tigation it appears that the corpse has amputated its own left hand. Handprints found at the scene seem to indicate that the severed hand has crawled away and is still creeping around the villa. Ingram's Bach arpeggios can soon be heard coming from the grand piano in the middle of the night, presumably played by Ingram's ghostly digits although nothing is ever seen. Then Ingram's former lawyer Duprex (David Hoffman) is found choked to death with the marks of the killer's fingers on his strangulated throat, and soon afterward the Commissario himself witnesses Don being attacked by the hand and nearly killed.

The mystery begins to unravel when Hillary is shown reading his astrology books when the severed hand emerges from a box on his desk. As Hillary watches in scenery-chewing horror, the hand scuttles like a monstrous spider toward him to claim Ingram's ruby ring. Hillary shoves the offending digits into a desk drawer, but it escapes and is later found hiding behind some books. Trying to immobilize the hand, Hillary nails it to a board and proclaims to Julie, "I caught it. I locked it up. I nailed it down so it could not kill again." When Hillary starts hearing the ghostly piano music once more while Julie does not, she realizes that he has lost his mind and is responsible for the crimes, but Hillary continues to insist, "It was the hand." As he menaces her with a switchblade, she cunningly convinces him that he must destroy the evil hand. In a finely rendered, special effects-laden climax, Hillary watches the amputated hand furiously playing the piano before grabbing it and throwing it into a fire. The undead hand is not so easily dissuaded, however, and crawls out of the fire to strangle Hillary as the schizophrenic astrologer writhes and grimaces in his death throes. In the aftermath it is revealed that Hillary, wishing to leave the astrology library intact, had stolen the hand from Ingram's corpse and committed the murders, but had become the victim of his own mordant obsession. The ghostly strains of Bach were simulated by using a concealed gramophone cylinder recording of Ingram's playing, conveniently activated by a string mechanism. The film ends on a comic note when the Commissario addresses the audience directly and is seemingly menaced by the hand once more but finds it to be his own. "How do you like-a that?" the Italian sleuth chuckles. "My own hand."

A surreal blend of horror, mystery and comedy, *The Beast with Five Fingers* combines gothic chills with murder mystery and a whiff of the supernatural. Scripted by horror noir patriarch Curt Siodmak from a story by William Fryer Harvey, the film sets up an intriguing whodunnit and finally takes the audience inside the subjective world of a schizophrenic. Florey, who had previously directed Lorre in *The Face Behind the Mask*, coaxes what is perhaps the actor's finest seriocomic performance from his star. Once Lorre starts mouthing off about "the hand," the movie is all his. His eyes, gleaming with an unholy light of madness, bulge out of their sockets as Lorre twists his expressive face into demonic grimaces at the imagined supernatural terrors. It's hilarious and horrifying at the same time and a far cry from the ultra-subdued character Lorre portrayed in *The Face Behind the Mask*. Lorre had also played a hand-transplanting mad doctor in MGM's remake of *The Hands of Orlac*, entitled *Mad Love* (1935). The rest of the cast deliver undistinguished performances, with the exception of J. Carroll Naish's police inspector, who periodically provides some additional comic relief with his vaudevillian Italian accent. Max Steiner's florid score provides a dark gothic aural backdrop.

Florey, along with cinematographer Wesley Anderson, beautifully evokes gothic dark atmosphere in the scenes set at the haunted villa, where expressionist shadows, low angles and moving camera bring the mysterious tale to life. The plot of *The Beast with Five Fingers* examines the noir themes of obsession, madness, murder and the enigmatic workings of fate. Hillary the mad astrologer is the film's *homme fatal*, although not exactly its protagonist, his mordant fascinations driving the film's grim events. The movie is at its most effective when depicting the madman's hallucinatory inner world.

The plot of *Beast* clearly shows the ascendancy of mystery over supernatural themes at the end of the horror cycle. All of the movie's seemingly occult events turn out to have a rational explanation as the terrors of the night melt into low comedy. As horror film historian Carlos Clarens observes, *The Beast with Five Fingers* "turned out to be a belated funeral march for the genre.... Caught in the interregnum between the gothic period and the age of science fiction, the horror movie could hardly match the newsreel reality of the day, far more impressive than any special effect and far more terrifying than anything the art of the makeup man could devise."[2] After 1946, few horror movies came out of Hollywood until the early 1950s. Film noir, on the other hand, flourished in the same milieu of postwar cynicism that destroyed the horror genre.

The gothic and costume noirs of the 1940s successfully recapitulated the expressionistic look and preoccupation with crime, mystery and abnormal psychology that characterized the classic noirs set in '40s-era America. For the most part the melodrama played out against a backdrop of an urban city of night, on the joyless demimondes of London, Paris and New York. Many of them play upon a Victorian erotic hysteria that is even more sexually repressive than that of mid–20th-century American culture. These films transposed the world of film noir into the past in a manner analogous to the way science fiction oriented tech-noir movies took the noir universe into the future, again displaying the portability of the noir genre's conventions.

The *hommes fatals* portrayed in these movies constitute a memorable rogues gallery of noir villains that were brought to vibrant life by some of Hollywood's most accomplished actors: Spencer Tracy in *Dr. Jekyll and Mr. Hyde*, John Carradine in *Bluebeard*, Hurd Hatfield in *The Picture of Dorian Gray* and George Sanders in *Rebecca*, *The Lodger*, *Hangover Square* and *The Picture of Dorian Gray* are examples. Noir stalwarts Vincent Price (*Dragonwyck*), Peter Lorre (*The Beast with Five Fingers*) and Laird Cregar (*The Lodger* and *Hangover Square*) neatly bridge the horror and noir genres. Academy Award nominations for Angela Lansbury (for *Gaslight* and *The Picture of Dorian Gray*), an Oscar win for Ingrid Bergman (for *Gaslight*) as well as first-class dramatic portrayals by Joan Fontaine and Judith Anderson in *Rebecca*, Linda Darnell in *Hangover Square* and Dorothy McGuire in *The Spiral Staircase* showcased the talents of prominent actresses in these costume melodramas.

All of these films (with the exception of *Bluebeard*) were A-list pictures with decent budgets produced at major studios like MGM, Fox and Warners. They were made by some of Tinseltown's most prominent directors: Alfred Hitchcock (*Rebecca*), Victor Fleming (*Dr. Jekyll and Mr. Hyde*), George Cukor (*Gaslight*), with *Rebecca* receiving the Best Picture Oscar for 1940. More importantly, the gothic and costume noirs were the work of some of the master directors of film noir: Edgar G. Ulmer (*Bluebeard*), Jacques Tourneur (*Experiment Perilous*) and Robert Siodmak (*The Spiral Staircase*). These talented film-makers enlivened and enriched the shadow worlds of these gothic/horror/noir hybrids that were haunted by human monsters like Edward Hyde, Bluebeard, Dorian Gray and Jack the Ripper.

7

Horror Noir in the 1950s

During the early postwar years between 1946 and 1950 the Hollywood horror movie went into deep decline. Very few genre entries were produced in this interregnum as the American movie business went through profound changes for a variety of reasons. In 1948 the U.S. Supreme Court decided the antitrust case *United States v. Paramount, et al.* against the studios, breaking up a booking monopoly that had been controlled by the "big five" studios for decades. As a result of the Court's ruling, the Hollywood moguls were forced to sell off their theater chains, causing a profound shift in distribution patterns. Another factor affecting the film biz was the emerging medium of television, a technological marvel that brought entertainment right into the American living room for free, causing movie attendance to fall off sharply. Postwar demographic shifts from metropolitan areas to suburbs also had a profoundly negative effect on box-office revenues.

Hollywood devised a number of strategies to deal with their loss of market share. They concentrated on producing a much smaller number of high-end features while focusing on expensive and novel gimmicks such as 3-D, CinemaScope and Technicolor, that offered audiences big screen thrills that could not be obtained from their television sets. This left a dearth of B-movies in American theaters as exhibitors scrambled to find product to keep their doors open. Independent studios like American International, Allied Artists and Britain's Hammer Films stepped into the fray to crank out low-end features to meet the huge demand. B-units at the majors continued to produce a steady stream of product until late in the decade, when various factors conspired to make low-budget B&W film-making no longer financially viable. This coincided with the demise of classic film noir, which many genre critics date to Orson Welles's *Touch of Evil* (1958).

The horror film underwent profound changes during the 1950s that can be attributed to the techno-angst of the period engendered by nuclear weapons, the Cold War and the curious phenomenon of flying saucers. These socio-cultural phenomena focused '50s-era anxieties on the perceived depredations of dark technologies that could lead to atomic apocalypse or the invasion of our world by creatures from outer space. The shambling Universal monsters of yesteryear were replaced by a succession of Martians, mutants and giant bugs as the horror movie moved into a science fiction phase and the supernaturally-themed fear film faded. This situation would prevail until Britain's Hammer Studios re-invigorated the supernatural horror film with their color retreads of the Universal monsters that commenced with the American release of *The Curse of Frankenstein* in

1957. Gothic and supernatural horror films continued to soldier on throughout the decade, but in the early '50s they had largely become passé. Weak genre entries such as the Karloff costume vehicles *The Strange Door* (1951) and *The Black Castle* (1951) were typical of the horror film's decline during this period, while producers dabbled in using the novelty of 3-D in *House of Wax* (1953) and *The Creature from the Black Lagoon* (1954) to try and scare movie audiences, with mixed results.

Film noir was still going strong during most of the 1950s, when it had entered its "social realism" phase. Postwar advances in cinema technology had produced lightweight portable cameras that could be used outside of the studio, lending these late-period noirs a documentary feeling. Like the horror film, noir would exist in a B-movie, black and white venue for the rest of the decade. The advent of color technology boded ill for film noir, as its unique visual style and mood relied on the chiaroscuro of B&W for its effect and did not translate easily to a color medium. In addition, the demographic shift away from the inner cities to the suburbs removed '50s-era audiences from the immediacy of the urban problems and settings that had been an essential ingredient of most classic noir.

Raymond Burr Meets a Hollywood Gorilla

A new film noir personality that emerged during the late '40s and early 1950s was actor Raymond Burr, a broad-shouldered giant who would lend his heft to playing a succession of noir heavies in crime melodramas like *Desperate* (1947), *Raw Deal* (1948) *Abandoned* (1949) and *The Blue Gardenia* (1953). During this time the mesomorphic Burr was cast opposite killer apes in a couple of oddball horror/mystery thrillers, *Bride of the Gorilla* (1951) and *Gorilla at Large* (1954). *Bride* was written by and was the directorial debut of the redoubtable Curt Siodmak and co-starred Lon Chaney, Jr., who had starred in the veteran screenwriter's greatest commercial success, *The Wolf Man*.

The film begins in a small community on a tributary of the "Amazonas River" in an unnamed Latin American country. After a flurry of stock footage of monkeys, snakes and panthers in their natural habitat, Chaney begins a voice-over in a typically noir off-screen narration. "This is the jungle," the actor intones, "as young as day, as old as time ... venomous, deadly." As the camera pans slowly over the ruins of a rubber plantation in a scene that recalls the opening of Hitchcock's *Rebecca*, Chaney's voice-over muses about the events waiting to unfold, reflecting about the time that "the jungle itself took the law into its own hands," as the film fades into flashback to prior events.

Fade in to the sight of sultry Dina Van Gelder (Barbara Payton), the beautiful young wife of wealthy rubber plantation owner Klass Van Gelder (Paul Cavanaugh), dancing to Latin rhythms on the phonograph. Enter work boss Barney Chavez (Raymond Burr), who looks longingly at Dina and is obviously enamored of his boss's wife. Barney proposes that she leave her husband and go away with him, observing that the jungle is no place for a beautiful woman and pleads, " Life runs away too fast if you don't hold onto it with both hands." Dina demurs, but when her Klass returns he announces he is firing Barney for incompetence. The two men continue their confrontation in a field outside the plantation, where they come to blows and Barney knocks Klass into the path of a venomous snake and ignores his pleas for help. As Barney watches Klass die from the snakebite he is observed by witchy-woman Ah Long (Gisela Werbsek) and after he leaves the scene of the crime she casts a spell upon him using the forbidden "peduan" plant that enables witchcraft. "Cursed shall be the murderer these eyes have seen," she intones. "He shall be an animal ... an animal!"

After a brief inquest conducted by Police Commissioner Taro (Chaney) and local physician Dr. Viet (Tom Conway), Klass's death is ruled accidental and Barney and Dina are free to marry. On their wedding night, however, Barney alone observes his hand changing as he tries to sign a post-nuptial agreement in which Dina cedes the plantation to him, but Dr. Viet examines him and can find nothing wrong. Later, just as he is about to consummate the marriage, Barney becomes distracted by the nocturnal sounds outside and runs out into the jungle, leaving his new wife to spend their wedding night alone. The next day he is found unconscious and in a confused mental state as he is taken back to the plantation while Commissioner Taro reads dire native portents into these events. Invoking local legends about the "Succarath," an avenging jungle demon who punishes evildoers, he tells Dr. Viet, "Barney Chavez will be brought to justice. The jungle will see to it."

Barney continues his nocturnal sojourns as his fascination with the jungle overwhelms his mind and he continues to ignore his wife sexually. Farm animals in the area are found slain as natives report sightings of the Succarath creature. One night Barney glances in a mirror and sees the image of a gorilla reflected back at him, causing him to break the glass. He continues to roam the jungle at night until Dina discovers him the next day with his foot stuck in an animal trap set to snare the Succarath (in an homage to a similar scene in *The Wolf Man*). Even this ignominy cannot shake Barney's animalistic obsession, but the next time he decamps into the jungle Dina follows him while the pair is unknowingly being followed by Taro and Dr. Viet. The doctor has found evidence that Ah Long has been poisoning Barney with the dread peduan plant that has compromised his sanity. As Barney in his gorilla form menaces Dina, Taro and Viet fire blindly into the bushes and accidentally kill both of them as the jungle exacts its vengeance.

Writer/director Siodmak cannibalizes plot elements from his own prior scripts, notably *The Wolf Man* and *I Walked with a Zombie* to create this pastiche. These elements include a deadly love triangle in the jungle, an old witchy-woman connected to a magical curse and human/animal shapeshifting. Associations with these earlier films is further suggested by the presence of alumni Lon Chaney, Jr., and Tom Conway. Ostensibly set somewhere in Latin America, *Bride of the Gorilla* suffers from an indistinct sense of place, which is further exacerbated by the presence of a gorilla, as no apes of any kind reside on the South American continent. As in *The Wolf Man*, Siodmak was obliged to create bogus folklore about the mythical "Succarath" out of whole cloth, but his invented mythology is not as satisfying the second time around.

As a director, Siodmak's performance leaves much to be desired. He shoots flat two- and three-shots of the actors that lack verve and makes no attempt to create mood or atmosphere using lighting, unusual angles or distorted closeups. There is also an over reliance on stock footage of jungle animals culled from film vaults. To be fair, though, some of these faults are due to the fact that Siodmak was working on a shoestring budget and lensed the movie on a seven-day shooting schedule. Apart from these shortcomings, however, principals Raymond Burr and Barbara Payton are figures straight out of '50s-era film noir in this weird tropical morality play. Burr in particular portrays a typical noir heel, an *homme fatal* who descends into obsession, impotence and homicide, and the actor delivers a credible performance while tackling such unusual material, while co-star Barbara Payton exudes noir sexuality in this steamy rumble in the jungle. Lon Chaney, well into his professional decline and in the throes of acute alcoholism, gives an earnest performance in which he delivers the film's noir-esque framing voice-overs, while his Police Commissioner character delivers fateful commentary on the destinies of the melodrama's doomed protagonists. Siodmak would later direct a similar tale of a marauding South American man-beast, *Curucu, Beast of the Amazon* (1956).

It wasn't long before Burr was tangling with a murderous ape once again, in the horror noir *Gorilla at Large* (1954). Shot in widescreen, Technicolor and 3-D by independent studio Panoramic Productions and released through Fox, this lavish production employed a high power cast that included (in addition to Burr) Anne Bancroft, Cameron Mitchell, Lee J. Cobb and Lee Marvin. Burr plays Cy Miller, owner of an amusement park whose main attraction is the Garden of Evil, a caged grotto that is home to Goliath the monstrous gorilla. Every night Cy's wife, trapeze artist Laverne (Anne Bancroft), performs an aerial beauty and the beast act by swinging low over the ape's head while flaunting her feminine charms at Goliath. The rubes are eating it up but Cy wants to take the act to the next level. He recruits carnival barker Joey Matthews (Cameron Mitchell), a soldier recently returned from the Korean War, to wear a gorilla suit and secretly replace Goliath at the act's climactic moment when the ape will appear to grab the woman in his hairy arms. During a rehearsal of the act the sultry and promiscuous Laverne comes on to Joey, but he is engaged to Audrey Baxter (Charlotte Austin) and resists her advances.

Things start to get crazy when Cy sacks one of the carny workers and soon thereafter the man's body is discovered by Joey and Audrey with his neck broken and his corpse impaled on spikes near Goliath's cage by someone or something with great strength. Detective Sergeant Garrison (Lee J. Cobb) is assigned to the case and considers Cy and Joey suspects, along with Goliath's handler, the cagey gorilla wrangler Kovacs (Peter Whitney). In particular, Garrison is suspicious of Joey, who, he theorizes, may have impersonated Goliath disguised in his ape suit, and his hypothesis seems to be confirmed when the gorilla costume is found to be missing. "There's a couple of gorillas around here and one of them's a killer," the hard-boiled, cigar-chomping homicide cop growls. As if to underscore the detective's concerns, an individual wearing the ape suit knocks out police officer Shaughnessy (Lee Marvin), who is keeping an eye on the murder site, and opens the door to Goliath's cage.

Soon afterward Goliath stalks Audrey through a fun house mirror maze that recalls a similar scene in Welles's *The Lady from Shanghai* (1948). Carnival P.R. guy Owens (Charles Tannen) is killed by the person in the monkey suit while trying to rescue her while Kovacs arrives to hustle Goliath away through a secret passage in the maze and escorts the ape back to his cage. Unexpectedly, Cy confesses to the killings and the park is allowed to reopen, but Joey demonstrates that Cy cannot be the killer due to an old arm injury and has confessed for some other reason. Preparing to impersonate Goliath at the Garden of Evil that night, Joey finds pieces of acrobat's tape inside the ape suit and realizes that Laverne must be the killer. As the new act is performed, Kovacs refuses to call Goliath off the stage and has rigged the trapeze so that the gorilla can reach her because "she's got it coming to her." Goliath plucks the damsel from her perch and goes rampaging through the park before being shot to death on top of the roller coaster and Laverne is taken into custody for the homicides.

This wonderfully nutty exercise in mystery, homicide and 3-D carny monkeyshines is a hilarious misfire but highly entertaining in spite of itself. Director Harmon Jones and screenwriters Leonard Praskins and Barney Slater devise an absurdist whodunnit with an overly intricate plot that attempts to combine elements of film noir with *King Kong*. Shot at Nu Pike Amusement Park in Long Beach, California, the film's setting recalls the dark carnivals of *The Unholy Three* and *Nightmare Alley*. Filmed in lush Technicolor by director Jones, *Gorilla at Large* demonstrates why this color process was inimical to the visual aesthetic of film noir, as expressionist shadows are trumped by the film's highly saturated pastel hues. The scene inside the mirror maze is a self-conscious homage to the climax of the classic noir *The Lady from Shanghai*.

The case could be made that never in the history of cinema has such a distinguished cast of thespians been wasted on such a filmic trifle. Oscar nominees Cameron Mitchell, Anne Bancroft and Lee J. Cobb contribute their considerable talents to this wacky pastiche of crime melodrama, circus movie, horror and unintentional humor. The film was particularly embarrassing for Bancroft, who would later win an Academy Award for Best Supporting Actress for *The Miracle Worker* (1962), but her performance as the trashy trapeze artist cum *femme fatale* in *Gorilla at Large* is surprisingly effective and very different from her roles in noirs like *New York Confidential* (1955) and *Nightfall* (1957) in which she played more conventional leading ladies. Although he does not receive star billing, noir regular Raymond Burr has a substantial but subdued role, his hulking presence providing one of the film's many red herrings. Noir stalwarts Lee J. Cobb and Lee Marvin lend a patina of the dark genre to the proceedings, with Cobb providing the grit while Marvin is wasted on comic relief.

Shapeshifting *Femme fatale*

The Val Lewton/Jacques Tourneur supernatural thriller *Cat People* was reformulated for the 1950s in Universal's *Cult of the Cobra* (1955). The film begins somewhere in east Asia in 1945, where six American airmen are enjoying some leave time in an exotic eastern city prior to being demobilized and sent back to the States at the end of World War II. Looking for some local excitement, the flyboys hook up with snake charmer Daru (Leonard Strong), who claims to be a member of a snake cult called the "Lamians." For a hundred American dollars Daru agrees to sneak the servicemen into a forbidden Lamian ceremony where they will behold the spectacle of "she who is a snake and yet a woman." Clad in cowled robes, the airmen are escorted into the Lamian temple to watch a bizarre ritual that features a woman dancing in an elaborate cobra costume. During the ceremony one of the Americans, Nick (James Dobson), takes a photograph and the presence of the interlopers is discovered. The airmen fight their way out of the temple and escape, but that night Nick is mysteriously bitten by a cobra and dies.

Returning to New York, the five remaining friends settle in Greenwich Village, where Tom Markel (Marshall Thompson) and Paul Able (Richard Long) share an apartment. An exotic, mysterious woman named Lisa Moya (Faith Domergue) moves into the apart-

Tom Markel (Marshall Thompson) is smitten by cobra woman Lisa Moya (Faith Domergue) in *Cult of the Cobra* (Universal, 1955).

ment next door and Tom is immediately smitten with her sultry beauty. The enigmatic Lisa, who dresses in black and has large, expressive eyes, insinuates herself into the group of friends while learning their habits and whereabouts. She is in reality a *lamia* who can shapeshift into a cobra and she is stalking the men to exact the vengeance of the snake cult upon them. Assuming her serpentine form, she slithers into the car of Rico Nardi (David Janssen) to put the bite on him, causing him to lose control of his vehicle, then drives Carl Turner (Jack Kelly) out of his apartment window to his death. The police suspect nothing and rule the deaths accidental, but Paul, who has an academic background, begins to suspect that Lisa is a *lamia* who is killing the members of the group one by one.

Paul's suspicions are reinforced when third member Pete Norton (William Reynolds) comes up dead and his amateur detective work is vindicated when a lethal dose of cobra venom is found during an autopsy of Pete's body. In the meantime, Lisa begins to fall in love with Tom, who refuses to believe that she has had any part in the strange deaths. Despite her beauty, however, Lisa is apparently frigid and cannot respond to her beau's sexual advances. Tom escorts her to a theater to watch a performance of a play in which Paul's fiancée Julia (Kathleen Hughes) has a part, but when Tom is called away for a phone call, Lisa stalks away into Julia's dressing room. As Lisa transforms into the cobra before the horrified Julia, the actress's screams bring Tom running to the rescue. Using the hook on a coat rack, he manages to wrangle the venomous reptile out of the dressing room window to its death on the street below, where it transforms one last time into the inert form of Lisa.

Director Francis D. Lyon and screenwriters Jerry Davis, Cecil Maiden and Richard Collins construct a sincere homage to the Lewton/Tourneur classic, evoking the mysterious feminine terrors stalking the nighted metropolis of New York in the original updated to a 1950s milieu. During the cobra attacks Lyon films the victims from the cobra's point of view framed inside a shimmering oval, a technique he borrowed from Jack Arnold's *It Came from Outer Space* (1953), where it was used to simulate a one-eyed alien's field of vision. D.P. Russell Metty contributes some nicely atmospheric cinematography, but overall the film lacks the poetic terror and fear-drenched ambience that characterized *Cat People*. Part of the problem is that the audience feels little sympathy for the cobra woman's victims, who are portrayed as a band of lecherous dopes whose lack of cultural sensitivity brings disaster down upon their heads.

Faith Domergue's performance as the cobra murderess easily dominates the film. Clad in a succession of slinky black dresses, Ms. Domergue's *lamia* presents an intriguing variation of the *femme fatale*. Domergue's portrayal of the homicidal snake woman, however, projects a certain demure vulnerability that sometimes tends to compromise the character's aura of inhuman menace and makes her seem more like an ingénue lost in the big city. The film's plot, in which a woman in black exacts homicidal revenge on a group of men one by one has affinities with Cornell Woolrich's noir novel *The Bride Wore Black*, which was filmed by François Truffaut in 1967. Note that the body count in *Cult of the Cobra* is much higher than that of the shapeshifting murderess in *Cat People* by a factor of four to one, and as in *Cat People*, murderous female tendencies are associated with sexual frigidity. Shot on a Hollywood backlot, the film's New York locale nonetheless manages to convey the urban terrors that pervade the landscape of classic film noir, which was still a viable genre in the mid–1950s.

In a similar derivative vein was the British production *Cat Girl* (1957), in which Barbara Shelley plays Leonora, heiress to the Brandt family estate. As the movie begins, Leonora has been summoned to the Brandt ancestral mansion by her eccentric uncle Edmund (Ernest Milton). Traveling with her are newly married hubby Richard (Jack May) and their friends Allan (John Lee) and Cathy (Patricia Webster), who are out for a holiday in the country. All is not marital bliss between the newlyweds, though, as Leonora is terribly chagrined by Richard's wandering eye. Her troubles magnify exponentially that evening when she is brought to a secret meeting with Uncle Edmund in the middle of the night. He explains to her that the Brandt family has been under a terrible curse for centuries. In each generation the persona of the family heir becomes mentally linked with that of a leopard and partakes of the beast's bloodlust. "The love of darkness, the craving for warm flesh and blood," he raves, "it is my legacy to you, passed from generation to generation of our family for 700 years!" Upon hearing this news, Leonora runs away in horror while Edmund releases a leopard from its cage which promptly mauls him to death, thereby activating the curse.

The next day Leonora catches Richard making love to Cathy in a clearing in the woods and flies into a jealous rage, after which the leopard appears and Richard is killed by the big cat while Cathy escapes during the struggle. Leonora confesses to killing Richard but the police think she is merely delusional and remand her to the custody of local psychiatrist Dr. Brian Marlowe (Robert Ayres), who happens to be an old flame of hers. Skeptical of Leonora's paranormal claims that she can telepathically control the actions of the leopard, Dr. Marlowe places her under observation at the county hospital where she experiences an hallucination of transforming into a female were-leopard. She is unsuccessful when she tries to demonstrate her shapeshifting to the psychiatrist, who decides that his patient would benefit from moving into his home and being attended to by his wife, Dorothy (Kay Callard). Predictably, Leonora's murderous feline instincts are aroused by close contact with her rival for Marlowe's affections, and, as night comes on, she reverts to form. First, she makes a quick snack of the family parakeet, then lies about a phone call from Marlowe and directs Dorothy to meet her husband on a street in a rundown, crime-ridden part of town instead. As the cat woman follows Dorothy down the mean streets the leopard arrives to stalk her as well, but Marlowe arrives in a motorcar looking for his wife and fortuitously runs over the cat, and Leonora is found dead nearby.

A shameless reworking of the Lewton/Tourneur classic, *Cat Girl* is a dull, minor effort that is remembered today chiefly for an early appearance by future Hammer Films scream queen Barbara Shelley. Alfred Shaughnessy's direction is static and stagey and fails to generate sufficient dramatic tension, while Lou Rosoff's screenplay not only rips off *Cat People* but also incorporates plot elements culled from *The Undying Monster* and *Devil Bat's Daughter* as well. This modest British black and white production was completely overwhelmed by Hammer's color reworking of Universal's monster product, *The Curse of Frankenstein*, which was released in the same year.

Like its predecessor, *Cat Girl* is a study in female psychosexual pathology. At the film's beginning Leonora is a timid, sexually repressed wife who is the victim of her husband's rampant philandering. As her feline side emerges, she is transformed into an assertive, homicidal *femme fatale* whose bestial instincts compel her to murder her husband and any other romantic rivals. Note that Leonora does not actually transform into a leopard, but the notion of a psychic link between humans and animals is a folkloric concept that anthropologists refer to as the "power animal" or "totem animal," which is a creature that acts as an animal guardian who protects an individual with its power. Like many other films noir and horror films, *Cat Girl* explores abnormal psychiatry and features a psychiatrist as one of its principal characters.

Human Monsters

Beginning in the 1950s independent theater owners began importing horror films made in Europe for the exploitation movie market in the United States. These Euro-horrors, which were unrestrained by American movie censorship codes, were frequently more lurid and daring than their American counterparts. Films like Georges Franju's *Eyes Without a Face* and Michael Powell's *Peeping Tom* would eventually migrate to our shores, but the first big horror hit from abroad was French director/screenwriter Henri-Georges Clouzot's *Les Diaboliques* (*The Devils*), released in America as *Diabolique* (1955).

The film is set in the "Institution Delasalle," a dreary, run-down provincial boys' school somewhere outside Paris, where the sadistic principal, Michel Delasalle (Paul Meurisse), openly lords it over both his sick, mousy wife, Cristina (Vera Clouzot), and his urbane blonde mistress, Nicole Horner (Simone Signoret), who is a teacher at the school. The two victims of Michel's petty tyranny commiserate together and begin to plot against him as Nicole soon comes up with a plan to murder their tormentor by drugging him into unconsciousness and then drowning him in a bathtub. At first Cristina, who is a pious former nun and has a severe heart condition, cannot contemplate such an act, but is soon goaded into the murder plot by Michel's extreme cruelty and agrees to Nicole's plan.

During the school's vacation period Nicole returns to her home in the small village of Niort, which is some distance from the school, and takes Cristina with her. Cristina then telephones Michel and tells him she wants a divorce and that, since she is the legal owner of the Institution Delasalle, will be turning him out. Enraged, he catches a train to Niort as Nicole spikes a bottle of expensive Scotch with a powerful sedative. As Miguel arrives, Nicole pays a visit to the upstairs neighbors as a distraction, while Cristina discusses their impending divorce as she pours him several glasses of the soporific liquor. Soon he is unconscious and, when Nicole returns to her apartment, the two women carry out their plan. They drown Michel in the tub, weighting the body down with a heavy statuette, then wrap it in a plastic tablecloth and conceal it inside a large wicker trunk. After a long drive back to the school, Michel's body is dumped into the school's scuzzy swimming pool where he will presumably have drowned.

The two women's tensions mount as they await the discovery of the body in the filthy water, but when Nicole accidentally drops the school keys into the pool, one of the students dives in to retrieve them and also finds Michel's cigarette lighter on the murky bottom. When the pool is finally drained, the body is missing, and soon other odd events begin to occur. The suit that Michel was murdered in is returned from the dry cleaners; one of the students claims that he saw Michel, who confiscated the boy's slingshot for breaking a window; Michel's face mysteriously appears in a window when a photographer takes the class portrait. Nicole thinks that some unknown third party removed Michel's corpse from the pool and is trying to blackmail them but the religious Cristina is consumed with guilt and thinks they may be subject to supernatural retribution for their crimes.

When an unidentified man's body is discovered in the Seine, Cristina visits a Paris morgue to identify the corpse, but it turns out not to be Michel. Her inquiry, however, arouses the interest of retired police commissioner Alfred Fichet (Charles Vanel), who forcefully injects himself into the case as a private investigator tasked with locating her husband. Intimidated by the former detective and not wishing to arouse suspicion, she is unable to prevent the Lieutenant Colombo–like sleuth from snooping around the school and involving himself in her affairs. In the meantime Nicole thinks it prudent that she resign her teaching post at the school, leaving Cristina without any emotional support. Soon afterward, Cristina awakens in her bedroom to find Fichet confronting her. After he asks her some pointed questions, Cristina is entirely consumed by guilt and confesses everything to the detective, but Fichet brushes aside her confession, expressing the belief that her husband is still alive.

Later that night Cristina awakens to hear stealthy movements near her bedroom as the camera reveals doors opening and shows closeups of a hand on the stair banister. Rising to investigate, she is drawn down the darkened hallway by the clacking sound of a manual typewriter. When she enters the room she finds a sheet of paper with her husband's name typed over and over. Panicked, she tries to take refuge in the bathroom, where she is confronted with her ultimate horror: Michel's corpse submerged in the bathtub. Even worse, the dead man rises from the tub as Cristina's terror triggers a heart attack that causes her to literally die of fright. Once she is dead, the ghostly avenger is shown to be a very much alive Michel, who is soon joined by a joyous Nicole. The lovers ghoulishly embrace and kiss while Cristina's corpse, its face contorted by the terror of death, lies on the floor. Their conversation reveals that the entire episode was a plot to murder Cristina in order to obtain ownership of the school when his wife expires of "natural causes." The conspirators' happiness is short-lived, however, as Fichet intrudes upon this tender scene to nail the two murderers. In a weird epilogue, the same little boy who allegedly had his slingshot confiscated by Michel now claims the toy was returned by Cristina, which suggests that there may now be a real ghost at the school.

Clouzot's white-knuckle mystery/horror thriller is one of the supreme examples of horror noir and had an enormous influence on Alfred Hitchcock's *Psycho*. Both films feature a brutal murder in a bathroom involving water, and afterward the incriminating evidence is disposed of in water. Both are crime melodramas that explore the noir underside of human psychopathology while invoking the gothic ghostliness of supernatural horror. Finally, Clouzot, like his fellow Roman Catholic Hitchcock, employs the identical technique of "transference of guilt," wherein the audience is manipulated into rooting for the evil-doers to succeed. For instance, when the flimsy wicker chest containing Michel's "corpse" becomes partly unlatched while being loaded onto the rear of Cristina's car, our nerves are on edge until the murder is concealed once more. In this way the filmmaker makes the audience complicit in the crime. The source material for *Diabolique* was a novel by Pierre Boileau and Thomas Narcejac entitled *Celle qui n'était plus*, and the same authors would later provide the inspiration for Hitchcock's *Vertigo* with their novel *Entre les morts*. As in *Diabolique*, the plot of *Vertigo* revolves around a husband's elaborate plot to murder his wife using a bogus ghost.

The director's style fluidly moves from documentarian to expressionistic, the realistic early scenes depicting the sleazy goings-on at the grotty boys' school are contrasted with the later scenes that take place in the dark shadows of a haunted house. Clouzot masterfully shifts between these stylistic polarities while leading the viewer along through Cristina's subjective narrative viewpoint. The ghoulish events unfold from her naïve, superstitious point of view rather than that of the cold-blooded killers in order to tinge the story with mystery by withholding information from the viewer. Alternating between noir-esque crime melodrama and horror, *Diabolique* brilliantly exploits the *frisson* between human depravity and the trappings of the supernatural. Sound is used to great effect to build a mood of psychological tension; dripping water, the clicking of typewriter keys and even the chant-like voices of the students reciting their lessons provide a chilling backdrop for the enigmatic events. The director's wife, Vera Clouzot, gives a gut-wrenching performance in the scene in which she is scared to death by the apparition of her dead husband, her face twitching and warping in spasms of terror and death. Paul Meurisse exudes sadomasochistic menace as the homicidal school principal, while Simone Signoret plays the film's *femme fatale* with cool Gallic sexuality. The film has affinities with costume noirs like *Gaslight* and *Experiment Perilous* in its plotline about a husband trying to deliberately frighten his wife into a fatal madness. In addition to its influence on the Hitchcock films, *Diabolique* was remade as a neo-noir in 1996 starring Sharon Stone in the role of Nicole.

The year 1955 also saw the release of another riveting study of horror noir psychopathology, *The Night of the Hunter*, directed by the acclaimed British actor Charles Laughton. Adapted from Davis Grubb's haunting novel by *African Queen* co-scripter James Agee, the film starred noir icon Robert Mitchum in what is surely his most villainous role as a psychotic lady killer disguised as an itinerant preacher. Set in West Virginia during the lean Depression years of the 1930s, the film opens with a spectacular aerial shot of a rural house, where some kids are playing hide and seek. As the camera moves in we see that one of the boys has discovered the corpse of a middle-aged woman partially concealed behind a cellar door.

Cut to another aerial shot moving in on a speeding car being driven by the black-clad, black-hatted murderer Harry Powell (Mitchum), fleeing from the murder scene in a stolen car as the audience eavesdrops on the evil preacher's one-way discourse with his God. "Well now, what's it to be Lord?" Harry asks, "Another widow? How many has it been? Six? Twelve?... The widow with a little wad of bills hid away in a sugar bowl." "Lord, I am tired," Harry complains to the deity about his thieving and homicidal exertions as he seeks guidance for his next caper from the Almighty. At the next town down the road the sleazy preacher attends a striptease show and as a dancer takes it off onstage the blade of a switchblade cuts through Harry's jacket pocket in an obscene parody of an erection that illustrates Harry's sexual impotence and his murderous misogyny in a single image. The preacher's reverie is suddenly broken by a trooper who arrives to arrest him for the theft of the automobile, and Harry is convicted and sentenced to a 30-day stretch at the Moundsville Penitentiary.

Another aerial shot shows a farm in the West Virginia countryside as the camera zeroes in on two children, nine-year-old John (Billy Chapin), and his four-year-old sister, Pearl (Sally Jane Bruce), playing in the yard. Suddenly a car pulls up and their father, Ben Harper (Peter Graves), jumps out. Wounded in a bank heist carried out by a father desperately trying to provide for his family during the poverty of the Depression, Harper has killed two people making his escape. Hearing the police sirens approaching, he stashes the ten thousand dollars from the robbery in Pearl's rag doll. As the cops arrive Harper makes John swear that he will "take care of little Pearl" and "never tell about the money," and John solemnly swears to do these things as Harper is subdued and hog-tied in front of his horrified children.

Sentenced to hang for his crimes, Harper winds up sharing a cell at Moundsville with Harry Powell while awaiting execution. Knowing that the ten thousand dollars from the robbery is still missing, Harry tries every trick to find a clue about where the money is hidden from Harper, but the condemned man takes the secret to the grave with him as Harry prays, "Lord, you sure knowed what You was doin' when You put me in this very cell at this very time. A man with $10,000 hid somewhere and a widow in the makin'." When his 30-day sentence is up, Harry travels to the rural town of Cresap's Landing on the Ohio River, where he claims to be the prison chaplain who attended Harper's execution and insinuates himself into the life of Harper's widow, Willa (Shelley Winters). Willa is put under intense pressure to remarry by townsfolk Icey Spoon (Evelyn Varden) and

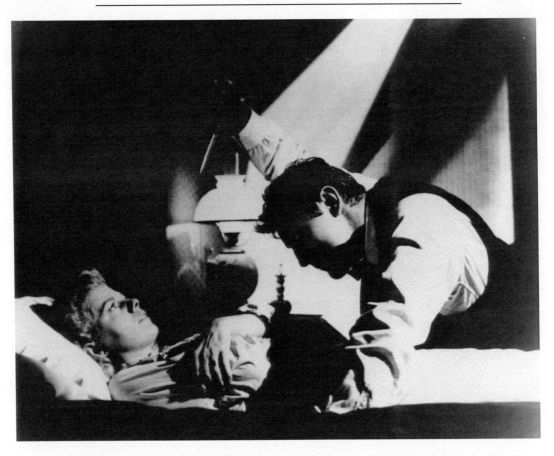

Psycho preacher Harry Powell (Robert Mitchum) prepares to consummate his unholy marriage to Willa (Shelley Winters) in *The Night of the Hunter* (United Artists, 1955).

her husband, Walt (Don Beddoe), proprietors of an ice cream shop where Willa works. When the preacher shows up he wows the townsfolk with his spiel about "the story of life," which features a struggle between Harry's right hand, tattooed with the word L-O-V-E versus his left, inscribed with H-A-T-E as he arm wrestles himself to an inevitable victory for the forces of L-O-V-E.

Charmed by the charismatic man of the cloth, Willa allows herself to be wooed by Harry, although she has some lingering doubts about his sincerity. While Harry courts Willa at a town picnic, Icey delivers a chilling monologue that illustrates the toxic cultural prudery that has contributed to Harry's demonic attitudes toward sex. Referring to sex obliquely as "that," she states, "When you been married to a man forty years, you know all *that* don't amount to a hill o' beans. I been married to my Walt that long and I swear, in all that time, I just lay there thinkin' about my canning.... A woman's a fool to marry for *that*. *That*'s somethin' for a man. The good Lord never meant for a decent woman to want *that*, not really want it. It's all just a fake and a pipe dream." The children do not warm to their prospective new father and have kept the secret of the hidden loot to themselves, but John inadvertently reveals to Harry that he knows where the money's hidden.

Before long Willa and Harry are married and on their wedding night the preacher shames his bride by declaring, "You thought, Willa, that the moment you walked in that door, I'd start to paw at you in that abominable way that men are supposed to do on their weddin' night." Marriage is "the blending of two spirits in the sight of Heaven." He will not touch "the flesh of Eve that man since Adam has profaned," and turns around to go to sleep. Under the preacher's malignant influence the pliant Willa is made to despise herself by assuming the guilt for her husband's crimes at town revival meetings. At the same time Harry intensifies his search for the money and when Willa accidentally overhears him threatening Pearl, she knows that her marriage is a sham. That night in a strange ritual of death, Harry slits Willa's throat while she lies resigned and passive in their bed, then ties her body to the family car and sinks them in the river. He devises a cover story that Willa has left him with the children to live with some distant relatives. John's only remaining friend is the grizzled, alcoholic river rat, Uncle Birdie (James Gleason), who lives on a shanty houseboat on the river and tries to give some solace to the child. Unfortunately, while out fishing Uncle Birdie accidentally discovers Willa's body lying at the bottom of the river like a sleeping water nymph with "her hair wavin' soft and lazy like meadowgrass under floodwater."

Now unrestrained by Willa's presence, the psychotic preacher tightens the noose around the children's necks, taking them into the fruit cellar and threatening John with a knife if he doesn't tell. "I'll cut your throat and leave you to drip like a hog at butchering time," he snarls to the terrified kids. This is too much for Pearl, who blurts out that the money is in her doll, but before Harry can get his hands on it the children manage to escape and lock him in the cellar. Fleeing to Uncle Birdie's houseboat, John finds his friend dead drunk and semi-conscious in the wake of his grisly discovery, so the kids cast off in a boat while being pursued by Harry, who almost catches them before they are borne away in the swiftly flowing waters of the Ohio River. John and Pearl drift downriver, pursued by Harry and his eerie baritone rendition of the traditional hymn, "Leaning On the Everlasting Arms."

The children eventually drift into the care of Miss Rachael Cooper (played by silent film star Lillian Gish), a stern, middle-aged Christian woman who selflessly adopts homeless kids and gives them a home. Harry meets his match in the feisty protector of the children when he shows up at her home and is wounded by a shotgun blast and runs screaming into her barn. The police are called and soon arrive to arrest Harry for Willa's murder, and as the preacher is being subdued, John flashes back to the day of his father's arrest and begins beating Harry with Pearl's doll, revealing where the money is hidden as the bills begin to pour forth. Harry Powell is convicted of multiple murders in a raucous trial where he is called "Bluebeard" and comes very close to being lynched by an angry mob on his way to being executed. The film ends on a happy note as John and Pearl celebrate Christmas with Mrs. Cooper in their new home.

Directing a film for the first and only time, the great screen actor Charles Laughton's admixture of expressionism, film noir, American gothic, child's fantasy, religious allegory and social commentary is today considered one of the timeless classics of American cinema and continues to resonate with modern audiences. Laughton had previously directed stage productions and knew well how to work with actors, but he also brought a keen pictorial sense to the film's visuals. He frequently employs vertically oriented sets with Caligari-esque diagonals and dark borders which gives a sense of the characters being

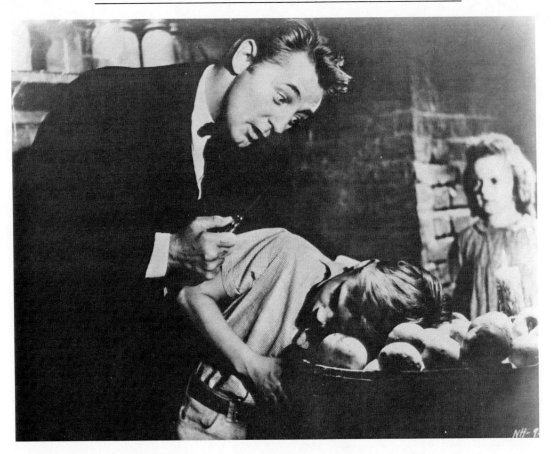

"Where's the money hid?" Harry Powell (Robert Mitchum) threatens John (Billy Chapin) and Pearl (Sally Jane Bruce) in *The Night of the Hunter* (United Artists, 1955).

trapped within the frame by a dark destiny and surrounded by shadows. At other times, minimalist, abstract set backdrops, such as a line of hills in the dim distance, create a dreamlike, surrealistic feeling. Aerial photography is used to great effect for naturalistic establishing shots early in the film and also seems to function as the "Eye of God" that swoops down from above to observe the characters and events. Many of *The Night of the Hunter*'s images are unforgettable, such as the sight of the submerged corpse of Shelley Winters with her hair waving in the weeds. Cinematographer Stanley Cortez, who had shot Orson Welles's *The Magnificent Ambersons* (1942), perfectly realized the director's dark vision with his superbly expressionist black and white photography. Laughton also reportedly did a good deal of work on the film's screenplay and dialogue but claimed no screen credit.

Robert Mitchum's portrayal of the black-clad, lady-killing psycho-preacher Harry Powell is one of the finest of his entire career and prefigures his similar role as a sadistic night-stalking killer in the neo-noir *Cape Fear* (1962). The character's constant one-way conversations with "the Lord" allow the audience first-hand glimpses into the bogus clergyman's misogynistic and homicidal motivations. While Mitchum's noir preacher exudes menace and religious insanity, he leavens the character with occasional flourishes of humorous cowardice. Co-star Shelley Winters is perfectly cast as the passive, victimized wife of two violent men, and silent screen actress Lilian Gish shines in her role as the protector of little children whose true Christian faith contrasts with the evil preacher's false religiosity. The rest of the distinguished cast turn in fine supporting performances, in particular, child actor Billy Chapin's portrayal of a young boy who must assume the grim responsibilities of an adult is particularly strong and memorable. Unfortunately *The Night of the Hunter,* released in standard-format black and white at a time when color and widescreen movies were all the rage in Hollywood, was a critical and commercial failure at the time of its release, but has since been recognized as one of the finest works of American cinema and a classic of film noir.

Davis Grubb's novel was based on the real-life case of mass-murderer Harry Powers, dubbed the "Bluebeard of Quiet Dell," a town near Clarksburg, West Virginia, where Grubb grew up. Powers was convicted of killing local widow Asta B. Eicher and her three children and another widow, Dorothy Lemke of Massachusetts, and also confessed to the murder of traveling salesman Dudley C. White. Unlike his screen counterpart, Powers was an otherwise normal citizen, a grocer and a married man. His trial made national headlines and was conducted in a special courtroom set up in the Clarksburg opera house. It took the jury only two hours to reach a guilty verdict and Powers, like *The Night of the Hunter*'s mass-murderer, was hanged at Moundsville Penitentiary on March 18, 1932.

Psychotic killers come in all shapes and sizes, as was illustrated in another acclaimed exercise in horror noir involving children, *The Bad Seed* (1956), based on a popular Broadway play by Maxwell Anderson. The action revolves around what appears to be a typical Ozzie and Harriet–type 1950s American family living happily in a small town. As the film opens, Air Force colonel Kenneth Penmark (William Hopper) is departing for a temporary duty assignment in Washington, D.C., leaving his wife Christine (Nancy Kelly) in an agitated state. Her anxieties center around her daughter, Rhoda (Patty McCormack), an oddly precocious child who, on the surface, is a "perfect little girl" with blonde pigtails who wears frilly, feminine dresses. Taking Rhoda to a picnic at her private school, Christine confesses her misgivings to the principal, Miss Fern (Joan Croydon), that "there's a mature quality about her that's disturbing in a child." Miss Fern assures her that Rhoda appears to be normal in every way, but later that afternoon one of the boys at the picnic, Claude Daigle, is found drowned near a pier and several witnesses saw Rhoda playing with him just before the "accident" occurred.

Upon returning home, Rhoda seems strangely unaffected by the traumatic event and more concerned about a penmanship

Patty McCormack plays a psychopathic child in *The Bad Seed* (Warner Bros., 1956).

medal that had been awarded to the dead child which she felt she deserved. "I thought it was exciting," Rhoda tells her mother, "I don't feel any way at all." Puzzled about Rhoda's reaction to the traumatic event, Christine is visited by Miss Fern, who provides additional details about the boy's death that seem to implicate Rhoda, and then by Claude's drunken mother, Hortense (Eileen Heckart), who mentions that the penmanship medal was not found on the child's body and that her son had also received some anomalous bruises and wounds about the head and hands. While Christine struggles with the notion that her child may be a murderer, Rhoda continues to charm their landlady, Monica Breedlove (Evelyn Varden), who has become like a grandmother to the little girl. The scuzzy apartment building janitor, Leroy (Henry Jones), however, is a different matter and seems to instinctively know that there is something very wrong with Rhoda and is extremely confrontational in his dealings with the child.

Christine is rocked to the core when she accidentally discovers the penmanship medal among her daughter's things, but does not reveal this to the authorities. Confronting Rhoda with the evidence, the girl simply fluffs off the questions and provides dubious answers about Claude's death while manipulating Christine's maternal instincts with her daughterly charms. Her mother's worst fears are confirmed, however, when she catches Rhoda trying to dispose of her metal-heeled shoes and realizes that the shoes were used to inflict the unusual wounds found on Claude's body. In the light of this incontrovertible evidence, Rhoda goes into a tantrum and confesses that she beat the child on the head and on the hands when he tried to hold onto the pier. She also reveals that she murdered an old lady at their previous home in Wichita, Kansas, by pushing her down a flight of stairs in order to obtain a crystal bauble promised to Rhoda by the woman in the event of her death. Christine again becomes complicit in her daughter's crimes when she orders her to dispose of the murder weapon by tossing it in the incinerator.

As if all this wasn't enough, in a conversation with her father, crime journalist Richard Bravo (Jesse White), Christine learns that she is not his child, but is the adopted daughter of the infamous criminal and female serial killer Bessie Denker, who was "the most amazing woman in all the annals of homicide." Her father, who is considered an expert on criminology, dismisses the idea that Rhoda is a "bad seed" who is "doomed to commit murder after murder" because of her twisted brain chemistry, stating his opinion that it is nurture, not nature, that determines human behavior. His theories are repudiated when Christine catches Rhoda stealing matches just before Leroy is locked in the cellar and burned to death when his mattress is set on fire and the child plays "Clair de Lune" on the piano at a manic pace in order to drown out the man's screams. Rhoda later confides to her mother that she set the fire because the janitor had retrieved the shoes from the incinerator. Convinced that her daughter is a genetic serial killer, Christine decides there is only one way out. Trying to spare her child from what will surely be a grim future, she gives Rhoda a fatal dose of sleeping pills and then shoots herself. In the ironic aftermath her shot brings help that saves the lives of both mother and daughter and the film ends when the psychotic child is vaporized by a lightning bolt while looking for the penmanship medal that Christine threw into the water near the pier where Claude was drowned.

Veteran director Mervyn LeRoy crafts an unusual, electrifying horror noir thriller with a fine cast largely imported from the hit Broadway show. The film's theatrical origins are both a positive and negative virtue. On the minus side, most of the action plays out in the confining screen space of the Penmark domicile, lending the film a stagebound quality. Doorbells and telephones ring at dramatically opportune times that emphasize their artificiality. On the plus side, this same confining quality allows the audience to experience an enhanced, close-up and personal intimacy with the characters. LeRoy coaxes riveting, Oscar-nominated performances from actresses Nancy Kelly, Patty McCormack and Eileen Heckart. Kelly is superb as the film's tortured protagonist who makes the ultimate heart-wrenching decision to kill her own child, while Patty McCormack's portrayal of the psychopathic kid is both surrealistic and chillingly convincing. Supporting players Eileen Heckart, Henry Jones and Evelyn Varden (who had appeared as the acid-tongued Icey Spoon in *Night of the Hunter*) also turn in strong performances that add to the film's overall dramatic tension in exchanges of theatrical dialogue.

Like much of film noir, *The Bad Seed* rips away the façade of 1950s-era normalcy to reveal the dark side of the American psyche beneath. Although several key scenes take place at night, most of the action is staged in brightly lit, homey surroundings that suggest the bland quasi-reality of TV sitcoms instead of the expressionist shadows of horror or noir. Director of photography Harold Rosson, whose high-key lighting setups garnered an Oscar nomination for black and white cinematography, creates a cotton-candy atmosphere of sweetness and light as a backdrop for the film's horrific events. Like *Night of the Hunter*, released in the previous year, *The Bad Seed* explores the enigma of the psychopathic personality, those warped individuals who, in the film's parlance, are "born blind" without a moral compass and act only on their own emotional impulses. Patty McCormack's pigtailed serial killer Rhoda is one of the most chilling psychopaths in screen history, a homicidal brat who thinks nothing of committing murder simply to obtain a childish trifle. The sociopathic little girl indeed represents one of the most unusual *femmes fatales* in the universe of noir.

LeRoy was forced to alter the downbeat ending of Maxwell Anderson's play (which in turn was derived from William March's 1954 novel), wherein Rhoda survives and Christine dies, by the Hollywood censorship office because of the rule that criminals could not be shown getting away with their crimes. Scriptwriter John Lee Mahin was obliged to concoct an alternative ending in which Christine survives and the psychotic evil is destroyed by an act of God. *The Bad Seed* would ultimately provide the inspiration for the monstrous little blonde girls in Mario Bava's *Operation Fear* (1966) and the Fellini episode of *Spirits of the Dead* (1969) as well as the homicidal children in *The Other* (1972) and *The Omen* (1976).

One of the most offbeat and idiosyncratic horror films of the 1950s was Albert Band's *I Bury the Living* (1958), starring the craggy-faced Richard Boone, best known for his role as Paladin, the gunfighter for hire in the TV Western series *Have Gun Will Travel*. Our story takes place in the New England town of Medford, where department store magnate Robert Kraft (Boone) is forced to accept an offer he can't refuse. Local tradition dictates that he is obliged to assume the post of administrator of the town cemetery, Immortal Hills, a duty that periodically passes among the town council members. Accepting the post reluctantly, Kraft visits Immortal Hills, where he encounters Scotsman Andy McKee (played by folksinger Theodore Bikel with the most egregious Scottish accent this side of James "Scottie" Doohan on *Star Trek*), who has been the graveyard's caretaker for 40 years. Kraft's first act as administrator is to pink slip McKee while generously paying him a pension at full salary for his years of service.

The amiable Scot then shows Kraft around the caretaker's cottage, the central feature of which is an elaborate map of Immortal Hills which shows detail "down to the wee-est speck a' dust," as McKee colorfully puts it. The individual grave plots are clearly marked, with empty plots indicated by white pins and occupied ones with black pins. This strange-looking map gives the vague impression of two eyes staring back at the viewer. Just then two of Kraft's friends drive by, newlyweds Stuart Drexel (Glen Vernon) and his bride, Beth (Lynette Bernay), who are checking on their plots as per a condition specified in the will of Drexel's father. After joking about the morbid "wedding gift" with his friends for awhile, the couple drive off to their honeymoon and Kraft duly inserts pins in their plots but mistakenly uses black pins instead of white. Soon afterward he receives word that Stuart and Beth have been killed in an automobile accident.

In a conversation with his fiancée, Annie (Peggy Maurer), Kraft confesses that this weird event "made me feel a little eerie," as if he had somehow caused the couple's death by using the wrong color pins. In order to rid himself of his obsession he changes pins on one of the grave plots he selects at random and is horrified when the man suddenly dies of natural causes. Shaken, Kraft calls a meeting of the town council to discuss the deaths, but his uncle, businessman George Kraft (Howard Smith), thinks it's all in his nephew's mind. George insists that they conduct a test by switching the pins on one Henry Trowbridge (Russ Bender), and Kraft is forced to go along with the majority. Later that night Kraft keeps a lonely vigil at the graveyard cottage before calling Trowbridge, only to be informed by his wife that their experimental subject has died in his sleep. His sanity beginning to fray, he calls the police about the strange goings-on with the map and his case is investigated by homicide detective Clayborne (Robert Osterloh), but the gumshoe can't find any evidence of foul play. Local reporter Jess Jessup (Herbert Anderson) helpfully suggests to Kraft that "maybe somebody's trying to scare you."

In order to settle the matter once and for all, George and the other two council members order Kraft to switch the pins on all three of them. Forced to comply, Kraft nervously awaits word that they have survived, his deteriorating mental state pictured in a P.O.V. shot of the room rippling around him as if he is underwater. His worst fears are realized when he is informed of the deaths of the two councilmen and he later finds his uncle dead in a car on the cemetery grounds. Once more Clayborne can find no hint of homicide in the natural deaths, but proposes a final test: that he switch pins on townsman Jacob Mittel, who is currently visiting Paris, in order to exclude any local factors in the deaths. Again Kraft is forced to comply and awaits the result that night in the caretaker's cottage.

Kraft's ruminations about his seeming powers of life and death cause him to have a brainstorm. He decides to switch the black pins for the seven people who have already died with white ones and awaits the result. Fear gnaws at his mind until he begins to hallucinate in a series of surrealistic images conjured by the famous Hollywood montage master E. Vorkapich. Outside in the cemetery the dirt is disturbed as if the dead are rising from their graves. Kraft is at the point of putting a gun to his head to commit suicide when the phone rings. Clayborne is on the line to inform him that Jacob Mittel has been found dead in Paris. Stunned, Kraft runs through the cemetery to find the graves of his

Robert Kraft (Richard Boone) tries to pin down the cause of mysterious deaths in *I Bury the Living* (United Artists, 1958).

"victims" are all dug up and empty. Returning to the cottage, Kraft finds not the living dead but McKee covered in fresh grave dirt, pointing a gun at him. The deranged Scot reveals that he has been responsible for murdering all seven of the map's "black pin victims" (although just how he has simulated their "natural" deaths is unclear) and has orchestrated other apparently supernatural events in order to compromise Kraft's sanity. But McKee's mental health is also on the borderline, as Kraft somehow uses the power of suggestion to frighten the Scotsman to death. McKee expires under the accursed map as Clayborne and the cops arrive to neatly tie up all loose ends, like the Paris death, which is revealed as a police ruse.

The film is a neat, effective horror thriller right up to the last few minutes of runtime, after which it collapses into a heap of ridiculous absurdities. Scriptwriter Lewis Garfinkle, who would later receive an Oscar nomination for *The Deer Hunter* (1978), concocted the eccentric plotline from his original story. *I Bury the Living* seems to have been modeled after the *Inner Sanctum Mystery* series of the 1940s in which there is ambiguity about mysterious events that can either be supernatural or arranged to seem so in order to "gaslight" the protagonist into madness. Producer/director Band moves the action along nicely and builds a fine sense of morbid atmosphere and mystery that is greatly assisted by Vorkapich's surrealistic imagery in the montage sequences that depict Kraft's subjective descent into insanity. The stolid Richard Boone, who had appeared in noirs like *The Big*

Knife (1955) and *The Garment Jungle* (1957), dominates the film with his understated performance as the film's tormented protagonist, while folksinger-turned-actor Theodore Bikel alternates between menace and comic relief. Composer Gerald Fried, best known for writing the theme music for TV's *Star Trek*, contributes a jarring, aggressive score played on brass and woodwinds that greatly enhances the film's unsettling mood. *I Bury the Living* has a gritty 50s-era noir ambience that is well grounded in realism despite the film's fantastic premise. The hapless Kraft is cast as an *homme fatal* who seemingly wields the power of life and death over the inhabitants of the cemetery. Events conspire to weave the characters into a noir web of mystery, death and destiny.

The Haunted Strangler

Beginning in the late '50s a number of exceptional horror films were produced at European studios for American release following the success of Hammer's *The Curse of Frankenstein* (1957) and *Horror of Dracula* (1958). One of the most intriguing of these Euro-horrors was *The Haunted Strangler* (1958), a product of the fledgling British studio Gordon Films. Boris Karloff stars as James Rankin, a 19th-century socially conscious writer who becomes obsessed with the case of Edward Styles, dubbed the "Haymarket Strangler," a serial killer who was hanged for murdering five women via strangulation and stabbing in London 20 years earlier. Rankin believes that Styles, who maintained his innocence throughout his trial, was truly innocent, and that the real murderer may have been a physician, Dr. Richard Tenant, who performed the autopsies on the Strangler's victims and seemed to have a strangely intimate knowledge of the crimes.

The writer persuades his friend, Police Superintendent Burk (Anthony Dawson), to allow him to examine the cold case files on the Strangler murders, where he finds information on Tenant. He learns that the doctor had suffered a mental breakdown in the wake of Styles's execution during which he experienced hallucinations, amnesia, and partial paralysis of one arm. After staying only a few days, Tenant mysteriously disappeared along with one of the hospital's nurses. Rankin manages to locate the doctor's medical gear in a hospital storeroom and finds that the surgeon's knife is missing from the kit. He theorizes that Tenant may have concealed the knife in Styles's coffin, where it was buried with him. Tracing the doctor to the Judas Hole, a bawdy music hall frequented by Tenant, Rankin interviews the proprietress, Cora Seth (Jean Kent), who had identified Styles as the Strangler but finds her eyewitness testimony specious.

Rankin's wife, Barbara (Elizabeth Allan), is highly perturbed by her husband's morbid pursuits and begs him to stop his investigation, but the crusading writer is undeterred, motivated by a desire to ensure equal justice and legal representation for poor criminal defendants. If he can prove that Styles was wrongfully executed because he could not afford a lawyer it will greatly advance his cause. Denied permission to exhume Styles's remains by the authorities at Newgate Prison, Rankin resorts to bribing the prison Turnkey (Max Brimmel) to allow him to visit the prison cemetery at night with no questions asked. He digs up the coffin and after disturbing the skeleton manages to find Tenant's surgical knife, but when this happens a strange transformation occurs: Rankin's face distorts grotesquely and one of his arms appears to atrophy. The transformed Rankin pays a visit to the Judas Hole, where he slinks into the backstage area and strangles and rips one of the dancers to death. When Cora catches a glimpse of the killer leaving the scene of the crime, she declares it was the same man she had seen twenty years earlier, leading to the conclusion that the Haymarket Strangler has returned from the dead.

Police are baffled by the weird events, but Rankin, who has partial amnesia about the murder, is beginning to suspect the strange truth. He voices his fears to Barbara, who confirms his darkest suspicions that he is really the murderer. Barbara relates that she fell in love with Tenant during his hospital stay and went away with the amnesiac to help him start a new life. Rankin emerged as a second personality with no conscious knowledge of his previous existence as Tenant. As memories of his former life began to surface, Rankin became obsessed with investigating his old identity

Boris Karloff as *The Haunted Strangler* (Anglo Amalgamated/MGM, 1958).

and his reversion to his former self has somehow been triggered by getting hold of the murderer's knife. While they are conversing, Rankin transforms into the Strangler once more and brutally murders his wife. The next day he confesses his crimes to Superintendent Burk, but no one believes him. The Rankins' maid, an eyewitness at the scene of Barbara's murder, fails to ID him as the killer and the Turnkey, who will not admit he took a bribe, denies that he allowed Rankin access to the prison graveyard. Frustrated by this state of affairs, Rankin becomes violent and is committed to a padded cell in an insane asylum, but the Strangler manages to escape and is tracked by the police and shot to death on top of Styles's gravestone.

Directed by Robert Day from a screenplay by John C. Cooper and Jan Read, *The Haunted Strangler* is a deft reworking of *Dr. Jekyll and Mr. Hyde* that also invokes John Brahm's *The Lodger* and Val Lewton's *Bedlam*. Director Day delivers a finely wrought costume melodrama enlivened by a worthy British cast and the crisp black and white photography of Lionel Banes. The great Karloff gives one of his better 1950s-era performances, with the high point being his first transformation into the Strangler, his features twisting and his arm withering in the moonlit graveyard. The film's most intriguing aspect consists of the noir-esque aspects of the plot involving amnesia and double identity. The plotline in which an amnesiac investigates a murder where he himself may be the killer is a staple of noir works as diverse as *Black Angel* (1946) and *Tough Guys Don't Dance* (1987) and is a central theme in Alan Parker's gritty horror noir *Angel Heart* (1987). The film never explains, however, why the kindly Rankin becomes "possessed" by the homicidal Tenant personality once he retrieves the doctor's murder weapon.

By the end of the 1950s the era of both classic film noir and the black and white horror film were over. The chiaroscuro nightworlds of their shadow realms faded into obscurity before the new and dazzling universe of cinema writ large in Technicolor and

Cinemascope. There were still great black and white horror films to come: *Psycho* and *Eyes Without a Face,* for instance, but by the mid–'60s Hammer's lurid color gothic remakes and American International's lush Edgar Allan Poe series had transmogrified the horror film into a new visual modality. It was the twilight of the B&W worlds of crime melodrama and horror that had existed for decades, and new permutations of these genres were poised to emerge.

8

Hitchcock's Psychological Ghosts and Doppelgangers

"Do you think the dead come back and watch the living?... Sometimes I wonder if she doesn't come back to Manderley to watch you and Mr. De Winter together."

— Judith Anderson to Joan Fontaine in *Rebecca*

"Scottie, do you believe that someone out of the past, someone dead, can enter and take possession of a living being?"

— Tom Helmore to Jimmy Stewart in *Vertigo*

"Well, if the woman up there is Mrs. Bates, then who's that woman buried out at Greenlawn cemetery?"

— John McIntire to Vera Miles and John Gavin in *Psycho*

The acclaimed director Alfred Hitchcock has an oblique historical relationship to both film noir and the horror film. Because of their A-picture gloss and Hitchcock's world-class director status his films seem to transcend the gritty B-picture milieu of much of the noir genre, and aficionados of film noir tend to exclude the director's thrillers from consideration as works of noir. Many of Hitchcock's finest films fall squarely within the noir genre, however, most notably *Shadow of a Doubt, The Wrong Man, Strangers on a Train* and *Rear Window*. Hitchcock pioneered the use of color in film noir in *Rear Window* and *Vertigo* and introduced movie audiences to the psychotic killer in *Shadow of a Doubt*, a trend that would eventually culminate in *Psycho*.

Hitchcock's relationship to the horror film is likewise unclear. His only out-and-out essays in the genre are *Psycho* and *The Birds,* both of which were made late in his career. He was reportedly of the opinion that the presence of the supernatural in a movie plot detracted from a film's dramaturgic focus. *Psycho*, of course, is a seminal masterpiece of psychological horror, but with the possible exception of *The Birds*, Hitchcock never ventured into the realm of the supernatural horror film in any of his features.

Or did he? Three of the director's most compelling works, *Rebecca, Vertigo* and *Psycho* all contain the "trappings" of the supernatural, and all are, in essence, ghost stories where the ghosts are not specters composed of ectoplasm but are psychological constructs within the human mind where the dead haunt the living and the past obscures the present. All of these films also deal with the themes of the possession of the living by the dead and with the notion of the alternative self, the "double" or doppelganger, and all of them are, in some sense, noir.

The idea of the doppelganger is a folk belief found in many cultures throughout the world and from many historical eras. According to this belief everyone is thought to have a double, an identical second self that is often the antithesis of one's original identity. Modern psychological theory may equate the double with the unconscious mind or with schizophrenia or multiple personality disorder, but in pre-industrial societies the double is thought to be a real entity. Folkloric beliefs are curiously consistent on one point: it is dangerous or even fatal to be in the same place and the same time as one's double. In Scottish folklore, for instance, the double is referred to as the *fetch*, an identical twin that arrives at the moment of one's death. More recently, anthropologist Carlos Castaneda has chronicled similar beliefs among 20th-century Yaqui Indians in Mexico, for whom the double represents the dream self.

European literature in particular contains many works on this theme by famous writers, a list that includes German ghost story writer E.T.A. Hoffmann's tales "The Doubles" and "Fräulein von Scuderi" and his novel *The Devil's Elixir*, Dostoyevski's "The Double" and de Maupassant's short stories "The Horla" and "Peter and John." During the Victorian period, the double came to symbolize the conflict between the good and evil impulses in the human psyche as in Robert Louis Stevenson's *The Strange Case of Dr. Jekyll and Mr. Hyde* and Oscar Wilde's *The Picture of Dorian Gray*. In describing the nature of the doppelganger, Hoffmann wrote, "I imagine my ego as being viewed through a lens: all the forms which move about me are egos; and whatever they do, or leave undone, vexes me."[1]

The concept of the ghostly doppelganger has also been the subject of a number of memorable films. In the German silent film *The Student of Prague* (1913), a poor university student, Baldwin (Paul Wegener), signs away his mirror image to the Devil in exchange for money and power to woo a wealthy maiden. The Devil makes good on his promise, but Baldwin is haunted by his demonic reflection, who begins to follow him around and even kills a man in a duel on his behalf. He finally lures his doppelganger to a deserted spot where he kills him with a pistol, whereupon a mirror breaks and Baldwin falls dead. Directed by Danish filmmaker Stellan Rye from a screenplay by German horror writer Hanns Heinz Ewers in the pre-expressionist days of German cinema, it was handsomely remade during the Weimar period by Henrik Galeen in 1926 with Conrad Veidt in the title role and Dr. Caligari himself, Werner Krauss, playing the devil. In Louis Malle's short film "William Windom," adapted from a short story by Edgar Allan Poe for the omnibus horror feature *Spirits of the Dead* (1969), French heartthrob Alain Delon stars as a sadistic Austrian student who is haunted by his exact double. *The Man Who Haunted Himself* (1970), a British film directed by Basil Dearden, features future James Bond Roger Moore as a man who undergoes a near-death experience during surgery following an auto accident and afterward finds he has a double who is trying to take over his identity.

In film noir the doppelganger frequently takes the form of two characters who are in diametric moral opposition to each other, yet who share a common bond. In her noir novel *Strangers on a Train*, Patricia Highsmith eloquently expresses this concept thusly: "All things have opposites close by, every decision a reason against it, every animal an animal that destroys it.... Nothing could be without its opposite that was bound up with it.... Each was what the other had not chosen to be, the cast-off self, what he thought he hated but perhaps in reality loved ... there was that duality permeating nature.... Two people in each person. There's also a person exactly the opposite of you, like the unseen part of you, somewhere in the world, and he waits in ambush."[2] In noir, the ghostly double is manifested as an evil twin or counterpart of the protagonist. Stuart Heisler's seminal noir *Among the Living* (1941), for instance, stars Albert Dekker as a man who discovers he has a homicidal twin brother and winds up nearly getting lynched for his sibling's crimes. In Robert Siodmak's *The Dark Mirror* (1946), Olivia De Havilland plays a pair of identical twins who are polar opposites, one of whom has committed a murder.

Critics have long noted the doppelganger theme in many of Hitchcock's key works. Hitch's chief biographer, Donald Spoto, observes, "This motif of the double had been an important convention in late Victorian stories.... The double had been taught to Hitchcock in school, and it was reinforced in his moral education.... The resurgent Gothicism in late Victorian literature and the suddenly abundant stories of dual personality were the modes for exploring the dark underside of human nature that led inevitably to the work of Sigmund Freud at the very end of the Victorian era."[3] The theme first appears in his film noir *Shadow of a Doubt* (1943), in which young Charlie (Teresa Wright) and Uncle Charlie (Joseph Cotten) are paired opposites, one a virginal ingénue and the other a psychopathic ladykiller united by a telepathic link because "we're sorta like twins."

The doppelganger motif appears in many of Hitchcock's other works as well. In *Strangers on a Train* (1951), co-scripted by Raymond Chandler, a chance meeting leads clean-cut tennis pro Farley Granger to "exchange murders" with demented psychopath Robert Walker. After Walker murders Granger's wife, the killer stalks Granger through the surreal landscape of Washington, D.C., like an evil, avenging double. Spoto notes, "Walker is Granger's 'shadow,' activating what Granger wants, bringing out the dark underside of Granger's potentially murderous desires."[4] Another take on the double theme, *The Wrong Man* (1957), stars Henry Fonda in a fact-based story about a New York musician whose unfortunate resemblance to an armed robber causes him to be arrested for the crime. In the film's most remarkable sequence, the director uses a slow, lingering dissolve on a tight closeup of Fonda's face as the features of his criminal double are superimposed over his own.

Hitchcock also drew upon doppelganger folklore in a 1955 episode of his TV show, *Alfred Hitchcock Presents*, entitled "The Case of Mr. Pelham," one of a handful of teleplays he personally directed. Comic actor Tom Ewell played the hapless Mr. Pelham, a staid businessman who finds that an exact double is impersonating him and slowly assuming his identity. In order to differentiate himself from his rival, Pelham starts changing his manners and wardrobe, but in doing so cedes his persona to his doppelganger as he is no longer recognizable to anyone around him, and is carted off to a lunatic asylum. Despite its dark comic touch, the teleplay has a serious undertone, as Spoto points out, "'The Case of Mr. Pelham' fuses the established Hitchcock theme of the double with the terror of madness and enclosure as the inevitable result of the loss of security."[5]

Another theme that is related to the doppelganger is that of identity transference, in which one person's identity is subsumed by that of another. In *Spellbound* (1945) Gregory Peck portrays an amnesiac mental patient who assumes the identity of a psychiatrist whom he suspects he may have murdered, and only comes to retrieve his real self through intensive psychoanalysis. Hitchcock's comic spy thriller *North by Northwest* (1959) stars Cary Grant as a mild-mannered New York advertising executive Roger O. Thornhill (initials: R.O.T.) who is drawn out of his humdrum life and into a web of adventure, espionage and intrigue when he pretends to be the fictitious secret agent "George Kaplan," a made-up identity that becomes more real than Thornhill's bland persona. Posing as "Kaplan," Grant is framed for the murder of an official at the United Nations and goes on the run from the authorities and the spies who are out to get him. The identity transference theme is actually close to the concept of possession, in which one's personality is subsumed by a stronger one.

Three of Hitchcock's most acclaimed films— *Rebecca*, *Vertigo* and *Psycho*—are all, in essence, ghost stories that also involve the doppelganger, possession by the dead and necrophilia. In these films the dead hand of the past intrudes on and overshadows the present, which is a classic gothic theme. In all three cases the ghosts are psychological in nature, kept alive by the unholy love that living persons hold for the dead.

The Unseen Doppelganger

As briefly discussed in Chapter 6, British writer Daphne du Maurier's 1938 novel *Rebecca* was a runaway hit that led to a revival of female gothic books and films. *Rebecca* brought the gothicism of the past into the present in its tale of a naïve, humbly born heroine who marries a headstrong *homme fatal* with a terrible secret, a haunted mansion with a forbidden room and a vengeful ghost. These elements were skillfully updated into the 20th-century by du Maurier with an emphasis on psychology instead of the supernatural, but this is merely a modern gloss upon these time-honored gothic motifs. The lavish David O. Selznick production of the novel was Hitchcock's first American picture, and he was constrained by the producer's insistence that the plot of the movie conform strictly to the book. As a result, *Rebecca* (1940) is a somewhat atypical entry in the Hitchcock canon that lacks much of the director's signature mordant humor but this in no way detracts from the film's effectiveness. The oddest thing about both the film and the novel is that the name of the protagonist is never revealed, as if she has no identity of her own but is only defined by her relationship to the dead titular character.

Like du Maurier's novel, Hitchcock's *Rebecca* begins with an eerie dream sequence accompanied by a noir-esque voiceover by the film's nameless heroine (played by Joan Fontaine). "Last night, I dreamed I went to Manderley again," her voice solemnly recites as the dreamer's eye drifts through the gate and up the drive to introduce one of the film's three main characters: the gothic mansion Manderley, ancestral estate of the British de Winter family. The once-elegant Manderley lies in ruins, but as moonlight plays over the structure, ghostly lights seem to shine through the windows for a moment, but this illusion quickly fades. The narrator laments that she can never go back to Manderley again, then the narrative begins to unfold in noir-style flashback.

Cut to a cliff overlooking the sea in Monte Carlo years earlier, where a distinguished-looking English gentleman, Maxim de Winter (Sir Laurence Olivier), is standing close to the edge of the precipice as if contemplating suicide when he is called back from the brink by a cry from our heroine. She is serving as a paid companion to a wealthy dowager who is staying at a local hotel, but the rich and imperious Max sweeps her off her feet in a whirlwind courtship. The brooding Max de Winter is said to be grieving for his wife, Rebecca, who died in a boating accident a year earlier, and the girl is hoping to be a medicine for his melancholy. The two are quickly wed and after a brief and happy honeymoon Max takes his bride back to Manderley. The new Mrs. de Winter, a shy unassuming soul, is intimidated by this venerable piece of real estate and by the dread presence of the mansion's chief housekeeper, Mrs. Danvers (Judith Anderson). Clad in a long black dress and sporting a grim attitude, the vampire-like housekeeper cuts a forbidding figure who seems to hold a special animus for the new mistress of Manderley.

Max has ordered a new wing of the house to be hastily redecorated to serve as the couple's living quarters. "It was never used much except for occasional visitors," Mrs. Danvers informs her, while Rebecca's room, "the most beautiful room in the house," remains locked, as if still inhabited by her spirit. The new wife feels her predecessor's suffocating presence everywhere in Manderley as she is surrounded by the dead woman's monogrammed linen and stationery and is constantly being compared to the fabulously beautiful, charming Rebecca by everyone, especially Mrs. Danvers. She even comes to feel that Max can never truly love her because he will always be in love with Rebecca. As the humble, mousey woman's personality begins to become subsumed by Rebecca's more charismatic persona, she enters Rebecca's sanctum sanctorum for the first time and is given a guided tour by Mrs. Danvers. Rebecca's lair is palatial, much grander than the humble chamber of Manderley assigned to the new Mrs. de Winter. Danvers has lovingly preserved everything the way it was on the day of Rebecca's death as she rhapsodizes about Rebecca's furs, clothes, embroidered pillows and lingerie hand-woven by nuns in a convent to her despairing mistress. The necrophiliac housekeeper asks if the new wife can detect the unseen presence of her rival. "Do you think the dead come back to watch the living?" Danvers asks. "Sometimes when I walk along the corridor I fancy I hear her behind me, a quick light step. Sometimes I wonder if she doesn't come back to Manderley to watch you and Mr. de Winter together."

Attempting to reassert her personality, the new Mrs. de Winter gets Max to agree to hold a costume ball at Manderley. Searching for an outfit to wear, Mrs. Danvers suggests that she copy the elaborate dress from an oil painting of one of Max's ancestors, the lady Caroline. When Max sees her thus attired on the night of the ball he is horrified because Rebecca had worn an identical outfit at the previous year's ball. Fleeing in tears to confront Mrs. Danvers in Rebecca's room, the housekeeper mercilessly exploits the poor woman's vulnerabilities. "She's too strong for you," Danvers exults. "You thought you could be Mrs. de Winter, take the things that were hers. He doesn't love you, he wants to be alone with her." She even tempts her mistress to throw herself to her death from the window of Rebecca's room and nearly succeeds, but at that moment an alarm is sounded. A ship has run aground in a nearby cove as their guests hurry to the rescue, but what has really happened is that Rebecca has returned from the dead.

During the rescue effort a diver discovers Rebecca's boat sunk on the bottom with her skeleton still inside. Max confesses to his wife that he hated Rebecca, who was in reality a sociopathic, promiscuous woman. During an argument at her boat house Rebecca had taunted Max about being pregnant with someone else's child, whereupon he struck and killed her when she accidentally hit her head on some boating equipment. Fearing that no one would believe that he had not murdered her, Max placed her body in the boat

Max de Winter (Laurence Olivier) and his bride (Joan Fontaine) are haunted by the ghost of his dead wife in the gothic halls of Manderley in *Rebecca* (Selznick, 1940).

and deliberately scuttled it. During an inquest into Rebecca's death a shipwright testifies that the boat was sunk on purpose, and at the same time Rebecca's former lover, ne'er-do-well Jack Favell (George Sanders), surfaces with a potentially incriminating letter written by Rebecca on the day of her death that seems to indicate that she was pregnant with his child that he tries to use to blackmail Max. When Max refuses, Favell goes to the authorities with the letter, but the investigation eventually finds that Rebecca was terminally ill, not pregnant, and her death is ruled a suicide. With Rebecca defeated at last Mrs. Danvers goes insane and sets Manderley on fire and is consumed in the fiery conflagration.

Although it was an American production, *Rebecca*, with a British director and a distinguished cast of English thespians, has a distinctly British flavor. The master is in fine form, eliciting strong performances from principals Joan Fontaine as the drama's nameless heroine and Laurence Olivier as the tormented husband, but Judith Anderson nearly steals the movie in her role as the vampire-like dragon lady Mrs. Danvers. Hitchcock does not neglect the visual aspect of the story and subtly imbues Manderley with the gothic shadows of the haunted house. The imposing estate, with its locked room, resident ghost and dark secrets, was one of the film's central characters. The much-touted "Selznick Touch" imbues the handsome production with a stately elegance and an A-list budget.

Playwright Robert E. Sherwood and co-writer Joan Harrison fashioned a screenplay that was extremely faithful to du Maurier's novel (at Selznick's insistence) and subtly improved the dramatic impact of certain key scenes. The Hollywood censorship office, however, ordered that the story be changed so that Max kills Rebecca accidentally, whereas in the novel he kills her in a fit of rage. This change was made in order to avoid showing Max getting away with murdering his wife, which was considered impermissible.

Rebecca led the way for the female gothic revival of the 1940s, and although it's primarily a "woman's picture," it also contains elements of both film noir and the ghost story. While there are many scenes that focus on the class resentment and comedy of manners aspects of the story, the underlying narrative is constructed as a psychological thriller and a murder mystery. Maxim de Winter is the typical brooding *homme fatal* of femme gothic, an enigmatic male with a strange and terrible secret that seems destined to destroy the couple's happiness, but *Rebecca* may be unique in that the movie's *femme fatale* is a dead woman who contrives to ruin her husband from beyond the grave. The film also deals with the noir themes of identity transference, psychological transformation and erotic obsession. The thinly veiled necro-lesbian yearnings of Mrs. Danvers for the dead Rebecca, for instance, is one of the film's perversely dark fascinations. Dame Judith Anderson's portrayal of the ghost-like, black-clad character seems to echo Gloria Holden's vampiric portrait of *Dracula's Daughter*, made just four years earlier. Hitchcock made the housekeeper appear suddenly in the frame as if she had materialized out of thin air to terrify her nemesis.

In spite of the fact that *Rebecca* takes place in the modern world and not during centuries past, it revolves around the gothic horror motifs of ghosts and possession by the dead. The heroine of both the novel and the movie is a nameless person, an introverted young woman whose weak personality becomes absorbed by that of her dead rival. Rebecca's ghostly presence is depicted solely through the use of synecdoche, as a series of visual leitmotifs. The second Mrs. de Winter has her identity assaulted by the ubiquitous profusion of Rebecca's accoutrements: the dead woman's clothes, furniture, bric-à-brac and monogrammed items are everywhere. The final image in the film is a closeup of Rebecca's monogrammed pillow catching fire, a symbol of her persona being exorcised by the cleansing flames. In addition, composer Franz Waxman creates a spectral five-note musical theme that suggests the presence of Rebecca's ghost.

The dynamic between the two women's personalities is illustrated by the contrast between their domains in Manderley. Rebecca's bedroom, described as "the most beautiful room in the house," is grandiose, with enormous windows and lavish furnishings, while the second Mrs. de Winter is consigned to the house's humble guest quarters. This use of cinematic space and contrasting room sets to define the relationship between a dominant personality and a recessive one inside the geography of a haunted house would later be replicated in *Psycho*. Rebecca's ghost is kept alive by the necrophiliac emotions of Mrs. Danvers, Max's guilty musings and by the charismatic power of Rebecca herself that has left its imprint upon Manderley. Another visual metaphor for the subsuming of the second Mrs. de Winter's personality by that of Rebecca is in the costume ball scene where she puts on Rebecca's costume, as if she is changing clothes and identities with the other woman. The theme of a living person cross-dressing with a dead one reappears in both *Vertigo* and *Psycho* as a symptom of personality displacement.

Among the Dead

Vertigo (1958), considered one of Hitchcock's masterpieces, combines the disparate elements of mystery, suspense, romance, film noir — and the ghost story. It was based on the novel *D'entre les morts* (*Among the Dead*) by the French authors Pierre Boileau and Thomas Narcejac, who had written the novel upon which Clouzot's *Diabolique* was based. Like *Diabolique*, the film has a complex plot that features a phony "ghost" that is part of a murder scheme.

James Stewart stars as John "Scottie" Ferguson, a San Francisco detective who has acquired an intense fear of heights after a rooftop accident in which a policeman fell to his death and has retired from the force. He is contacted by an old college chum, Gavin Elster (Tom Helmore), who has married into money and is now the head of a San Francisco shipbuilding firm. Elster has read about Scottie's predicament in the newspaper, and wants to engage his services as a private investigator. He wants Scottie to follow his wife, Madeleine, but not because he suspects her of infidelity. "I'm afraid some harm may come to her," Elster confides. "From whom?" Scottie asks. "From someone dead," Elster replies. "Scottie, do you believe that someone out of the past, someone dead, can enter and take possession of a living being?" Elster fears that his wife is either possessed or has deep mental problems. The hard-headed former detective is skeptical, but Elster prevails upon Scottie to take the case as a personal favor to him.

Scottie begins to tail Madeleine Elster (Kim Novak) around San Francisco and watches as she buys a corsage and travels to Mission Dolores, where she enters the church graveyard and places the flowers on the grave of a woman named Carlotta Valdes who died in the 19th century. He observes her driving to the art museum at the Palace of the Legion of Honor, where she sits immobile staring at a painting of Carlotta as Scottie notes that Madeleine's hair is done up in the same style as Carlotta's in the portrait. He shadows her as she travels to the McKittrick Hotel in the Western Addition, where he learns that Madeleine has rented a room as Carlotta Valdes, where she comes occasionally merely to stare out the window for hours. Assisted by ex-girlfriend Midge (Barbara Bel Geddes), Scottie does some historical research and finds that Carlotta was a cabaret singer who became the mistress of a wealthy man who built the building that is now the McKittrick Hotel as a gift for her. After Carlotta bore him a child, her rich benefactor turned her out in the street but kept the child, which caused her to lose her sanity and commit suicide. Another detail: Carlotta was Madeleine Elster's great-grandmother. "The idea is that beautiful mad Carlotta's come back from the dead," Midge muses, "and taken possession of Elster's wife."

He duly reports this information to Elster, who now thinks Madeleine may suffer from congenital insanity and her obsession with her ancestor may motivate her to take her own life. Shadowing Madeleine as she drives to Fort Point, underneath the Golden Gate Bridge, Scottie is horrified when she jumps into the bay and dives in to rescue her. He takes her home to dry out and when she awakens she explains that she has fits of amnesia and doesn't remember much of anything that happened. As Madeleine is leaving Scottie's apartment Midge, who still has feelings for Scottie, drives by and sees this. "Well now, Johnny-O," she commiserates to herself. "Was it a ghost? Was it fun?"

When Madeleine shows up at Scottie's the next day to deliver a thank-you note (not

John "Scottie" Ferguson (James Stewart) saves the "possessed" Madeleine (Kim Novak) from drowning beneath the Golden Gate Bridge in *Vertigo* (Paramount, 1958).

knowing that he is a detective hired to follow her), they decide to spend the day together and wind up visiting a sequoia forest. While Scottie marvels at the enormous trees, Madeleine slips into a morbid depression. Looking at the cross-section of one of the felled trees showing historical events over its hundreds of years of growth, Madeleine points to one of the tree rings and declares, "Somewhere in here I was born, and there I died." She seems to be slipping more deeply under Carlotta's baleful influence. "There's someone within me and she says I must die," she tells Scottie as he takes her in his arms and kisses her passionately. He has desperately fallen in love with this haunted, vulnerable woman and wants to protect her from the vengeful ghost that strives to dominate and destroy her.

Madeleine shows up at Scottie's early one morning obsessed with a nightmare about an old Spanish church, which he recognizes as the Mission of San Juan Batista, just north of the city. Thinking that confronting her worst fears may be therapeutic, they drive up to the mission, where Scottie tries to talk some sense into her. "There's an answer for everything," he declares. "No one possesses you, you're safe with me." Madeleine, however, breaks away from his logic and from his embrace. "There's something I must do," she pleads. "Let me go into the church alone." When she fails to come out, Scottie enters the church and finds Madeleine climbing the bell tower. As he pursues her his vertigo kicks in and he is unable to reach the top as he helplessly watches Madeleine through a window as she plunges to her death.

At Madeleine's post-mortem inquest her death is ruled a suicide while Scottie is reproached by the authorities for his failure to save her life. Elster, however, is more philosophical. "You and I know who killed Madeleine," he tells the disgraced detective while announcing that he is leaving San Francisco for Europe in order to forget the whole affair. Consumed by guilt and grieving for his lost love, Scottie suffers a mental break-down. He has a nightmare in which he sees Carlotta and stands before her open grave and then watches himself fall to his death from a great height. The faithful Midge takes Scottie under her wing and tries to cure him of his obsessional guilt, but her well-meaning efforts fail as he drifts into an acute melancholia.

One day Scottie is wandering about downtown and sees a girl in the street who bears a striking resemblance to Madeleine and follows her to her room at the Essex Hotel. He barges in on her and begins asking questions of the woman, whose name is Judy Barton. Judy shows him her driver's license and other proof of identity and claims that she works as a clerk for Magnin's department store and has been living in the city for three years. "You wanna check my thumb prints, are you satisfied?" she asks, and Scottie accepts her bona fides. Moved by Scottie's desperation, she makes a dinner date with him, but after he leaves the audience is shown the truth: Judy has played the role of Madeleine in her husband's scheme to murder the real Madeleine Elster. Gambling that Scottie's vertigo would render him unable to scale the bell tower, Elster threw his identically attired wife from the tower to make Scottie believe he had witnessed her suicide. She was Elster's mistress and was subsequently dumped by him after being well paid for being an accessory to murder. Judy's first instinct is to bolt, but she has fallen for Scottie and lingers to try and reconcile with him.

Scottie takes Judy out on a few dates, but something is missing. He begs her to change her hair color, hair style, makeup and wardrobe to look like Madeleine again. Judy resists changing her appearance, pleading, "Couldn't you like me, just me, the way I am?" Scottie will not be deterred, however, and she reluctantly agrees to undergo his personality-changing extreme makeover. When she appears before him in full Madeleine Elster drag, bathed in an ethereal green light from the hotel's neon sign, Scottie is ecstatic and the lovers embrace. His ecstasy is short-lived, however, when he notices Judy wearing Madeleine's necklace, a replica of the one Carlotta Valdes wears in the painting and per-ceives the truth. Suddenly possessed of a quiet rage, he drives back out to San Juan Batista with her. The couple arrive at twilight and Scottie confronts her with her crimes while trying to exorcize his own personal demons. "I'll be free of the past," he tells her. "I want to stop being haunted." He forces Judy to climb up the tower with him to the scene of the crime, his vertigo in sudden remission. "You were a very apt pupil," he spits, but, "You shouldn't keep souvenirs of a killing." Judy confesses her crimes and that she loves Scottie, but he rebuffs her and at that moment a nun's shadowy form moves toward them through the gloom and Judy, thinking it is Madeleine's ghost, falls from the same tower where her doppelganger was murdered and Scottie is cured of his phobic affliction.

Underappreciated by critics at the time of its initial release, one of whom assailed the film's complex plot as a "Hitchcock and bull story," *Vertigo* is now considered one of the director's finest works, in which romance, mystery and suspense are seamlessly

10344-11

Doppelgangers: Kim Novak as Madeleine Elster (left) and Judy Barton (right) in *Vertigo* (Paramount, 1958).

blended into a satisfying whole. *Vertigo* is the director's most romantic film, the drama centering around Scottie's erotic and necrophiliac obsession with an elusive, mysterious woman who does not actually exist, yet claims to be possessed by a ghost. Hitchcock's use of color is superb, the bright, naturalistic scenes shot on the streets of San Francisco contrasting with the eerie hues and shadows of fantasy and death. A nightmarish dream sequence utilizes cartoon animation to great effect. The film's dreamlike ambience is sustained throughout *Vertigo*'s more than two-hour length and is grandly supported by composer Bernard Herrmann's magnificent score, considered by critics to be some of the finest music ever composed for the cinema. Donald Spoto observes, "The music and the sound effects are elusive and lonely, fragile and ghostly — a ship's horn in the fog of San Francisco Bay, whispers and muffled conversations as background in public places, hollow footsteps on a cemetery garden path."[6] Principals Jimmy Stewart and Kim Novak give some of the finest performances of their careers, and they would soon be paired once more in another tale of an everyday Joe in pursuit of a mysterious, beautiful woman in the supernatural comedy *Bell, Book and Candle* (1958).

It can be argued that *Vertigo* represents the first fully realized film noir in color and widescreen. Although the director had used this format for *Rear Window* (1954), his use of color here is more stylish and experimental. While Hitchcock's TechniColor, VistaVision, A-list venue may seem a long way from the gritty black and white studio-bound B-movie ambience of most classic films noir, and while his visual style may be very different from the conventional noir chiaroscuro, in terms of thematics *Vertigo* is squarely in the noir tradition. The film contains many noir themes, plot elements and characters, including the intensely urban setting, the private detective, the *femme fatale*, the doomed lovers, murder, mystery, deceit, cynicism, obsessive sexual desire, identity confusion and an unhappy ending. Scottie is a typical noir protagonist, a private investigator and streetwise ex-cop who is led into morally questionable behavior by a beautiful woman. As portrayed by the affable Jimmy Stewart, Scottie is a likeable sort who allows himself to be seduced by a woman whom he believes to be his friend's (and employer's) wife and over whom he is supposedly watching. He is also the victim of his own necrophiliac obsession for an erotic ideal that does not exist.

Vertigo's *femme fatale* exists within a maze of doppelgangers and faux revenants as the composite Carlotta/Madeleine/Judy entity. Judy Barton assumes the false identity of Madeleine Elster, who in turn has supposedly assumed the personality of Carlotta Valdes. For most of the movie Judy's persona is subsumed by that of "Madeleine," who is a fictional creation of Gavin Elster's. Scottie falls in love with this false personality, who does not even exist, and on top of this, "Madeleine's" character is "possessed" by the dead Carlotta, and it's almost as if Judy is possessed by both women. Little is shown of Judy's existence: she is portrayed as a *naïf* who has come to the big city from Salina, Kansas, a lower-class working girl with gauche tastes who is the stylistic antithesis of her upper-class alter ego. Scottie utterly rejects her as she is and insists she assume the role of a dead woman who is playing a dead woman. Lost in all of this maze of personalities is the real Madeleine Elster, who is only glimpsed from afar while falling from the bell tower and lying dead on the mission's roof. She is a total cypher who nevertheless presumably provides a template for Judy's impersonation. As in *Rebecca* and *Psycho*, a living person dresses up as a dead person as one persona replaces another. There is one last "ghost" in *Vertigo*, the nun in the final scene whose shadowy form Judy mistakes for Madeleine's avenging spirit emerging from the dark that causes her to fall to her death, thereby replicating the fate of the real Madeleine.

While all of the film's ghosts are eventually explained away as the machinations of a clever murder plot, the narrative unfolds mostly through the prism of Scottie's haunted viewpoint. He falls in love with the false Madeleine precisely because she embodies a mysterioso element of the fantastic, while rejecting the more prosaic Midge, whose line,

"Well now, Johnny-O, was she a ghost?" encapsulates Scottie's demand for fantasy over reality. In the key scene in which Judy is completely transformed into "Madeleine," she emerges into his sight bathed in the eerie neon glow of the hotel sign, an ethereal, ghostly figure that represents Scottie's otherworldly and necrophiliac desires. Boileau and Narcejac's nasty tale of unholy lust, murder and possession from beyond the grave, as rendered by scenarists Alec Coppel and Samuel Taylor, deliberately evokes the supernatural terrors of the horror film by mixing ghosts, possession, premeditated killing and abnormal psychology and combines them with elements of film noir.

"She Just Goes a Little Mad Sometimes"

The clearest example of Hitchcock's obsession with the ghost/possession/doppelganger theme is, of course, *Psycho* (1960). Widely considered the Master's greatest work, and the one with the widest cultural resonance, *Psycho* is implicated in both the demise of the classic film noir cycle and the transformation of the horror film. Like both *Rebecca* and *Vertigo*, *Psycho* explores the motifs of obsession, necrophilia, cross-dressing with the dead, and possession in a context of noiresque murder mystery and crime melodrama.

This Phoenix city story begins late one Friday afternoon, as the camera pans over the city's skyline and glides through the window of a sleazy (and very noir) fleabag hotel, where Sam Loomis (John Gavin) and Marion Crane (Janet Leigh) are lying *hors de combat* after a bout of lunch-hour lovemaking. Marion carps about her dissatisfaction with this arrangement, but they cannot marry because Sam is suffering financial woes because of alimony payments he must make to his first wife. Returning to her office, Marion's boss entrusts her with $40,000 in cash from a real estate deal that she is supposed to deposit in the bank, but on a sudden whim she decides to abscond with the money, which she hopes will enable her to set up house with Sam. Driving aimlessly out of town with no destination in mind, on her second night of flight she is forced to take refuge

Marion Crane (Janet Leigh) and Sam Loomis (John Gavin) meet for a noontime tryst in *Psycho* (Paramount, 1960).

at the deserted Bates Motel during a heavy downpour. The motel's low-lying bungalows are overshadowed by a creepy old gingerbread gothic house that rises behind the cabins, where Marion spies the form of an old woman passing in front of a distant lighted window.

The motel's proprietor, Norman Bates (Anthony Perkins), soon shows up to check her in. Norman is a charming fellow with boyish mannerisms and youthful good looks that Marion finds endearing. After he gallantly offers to bring her something to eat after her long journey, Marion overhears Norman arguing with his domineering mother, who expresses her acid-tongued displeasure at his entertaining a female guest on the premises. When he arrives with a tray of sandwiches, Marion somewhat seductively suggests that they eat in her room, but Norman demurs, insisting that they take the meal in the motel's office instead. After a heartfelt conversation with the young man, during which Marion convinces herself to return the money, she settles in her room for the night while Norman secretly watches her undress through a peephole. Shortly afterward, Marion is senselessly killed in the shower by the figure of an old woman wielding a knife, and afterward Norman arrives to methodically cover up all traces of the brutal murder that has been committed by his homicidal mother. He wraps Marion's nude form in the plastic shower curtain, stows it in the trunk of her car and sinks all of the evidence in a nearby bog, where it vanishes without a trace.

A week later, back in Phoenix, Marion's sister Lila (Vera Miles) contacts Sam Loomis at his hardware emporium to discuss Marion's whereabouts, about which Sam hasn't a clue. Lila has been followed to Sam's by a private detective Milton Arbogast (Martin Balsam), who has been hired to find Marion and the 40 thou. Sam and Lila join forces with Arbogast in an effort to locate Marion as the P.I. burns up a lot of shoe leather tracking down leads until he finds himself at the Bates Motel. After skillfully grilling Norman, Arbogast finds evidence that Marion had registered at the motel as "Marie Samuels," but is not satisfied with Norman's story that she simply left the next day. "If it doesn't gel, it isn't aspic," the detective tells a nerved-out Norman, "and this ain't gelling." Fearing further revelations Norman clams up, but Arbogast phones Lila and Sam that he intends to question Norman's mother, whom he believes he has seen standing at the window of the old house. As the gumshoe is snooping around the house he is attacked and killed by the same old woman who dispatched Marion, and in the wake of the second killing Norman confines his mother to the fruit cellar.

Puzzled by Arbogast's disappearance, Sam and Lila decide to take the investigation into their own hands. They consult with Sheriff Chambers (John McIntire), the law enforcement officer for the nearby town of Fairvale, who tells them a strange story. Norman and his mother led an isolated existence until ten years earlier, when Norman's mother became romantically involved with another man. Shortly thereafter Norman discovered the couple in bed, poisoned to death in an apparent double suicide. When Lila and Sam protest that Arbogast saw a woman's form standing at the window of the Bates house, the sheriff responds, "Well, if the woman up there is Mrs. Bates, then who's that woman buried out at Greenlawn cemetery?"

Lila and Sam decide to pay a visit to the motel and register as husband and wife so that they can snoop around for clues. They soon find proof that Marion had been to the motel and resolve to talk to Mrs. Bates, whomever she may prove to be. While Sam con-

Private investigator Arbogast (Martin Balsam, left) grills Norman Bates (Anthony Perkins) about the disappearance of Marion Crane in *Psycho* (Paramount, 1960).

fronts Norman in the office as a distraction, Lila explores the gloomy old house looking for the elderly woman. She finds that Ma Bates has a large, sumptuously appointed bedroom replete with fine furniture, mirrors, statuary and bric-à-brac, while Norman's room is a child's den that contains toys, stuffed animals, a rumpled children's bed — and a bound volume of pornography. Meanwhile, back at the motel office, Norman smells a rat and grapples with Sam, knocking him unconscious. Lila continues her search and discovers what appears to be an old woman seated in a chair in the fruit cellar, but when she taps the woman on the shoulder the chair swivels around to reveal the skeletal face of Mrs. Bates's mummified corpse. As Lila shrieks in horror at the macabre sight, Norman, wearing his mother's dress and wig, runs in wielding a knife but is subdued by Sam.

In the aftermath Norman is taken into custody at the county courthouse while psychiatrist Dr. Richmond (Simon Oakland) expounds at length about Norman's schizophrenic psychology. He explains that he has obtained the full story from Mrs. Bates, because, "Norman Bates no longer exists. He only half existed to begin with, and now the other half has taken over, probably for all time." Norman's incestuous desire for his mother led him to poison her and her lover but guilt over the matricide obsessed him and prompted him to dig up her corpse and preserve it using his taxidermic skills. "He had to erase the crime, at least in his own mind," Dr. Richmond elucidates, so Norman had to create the illusion of his mother being alive, to give her half his life. "He was never all Norman, but he was often only mother, and now the dominant personality has won." Mrs. Bates has also implicated Norman in the murders of two young girls listed as missing persons in the Fairvale area.

The audience is given a final glimpse of Norman in his jail cell speaking in "Mother's" voice-over internal monologue. "It's sad when a mother has to speak the words that condemn her own son," she grouses while blaming all the murders on Norman. She, however, is innocent and harmless and must prove this to the police and doctors who are watching her. Observing a fly crawling on her hand, she says, "I'm not even going to swat that fly, and they'll say, she wouldn't even harm a fly." As the camera moves into a tight close-up of Norman's wickedly smiling face, Mother's grinning skull is briefly superimposed over it. The final shot shows Marion's car (and her corpse) being dragged out of the mucky bog. Fade to black.

Hitch's twisted tale of a mother-obsessed serial killer proved to be a seminal horror film that changed the conventions of the genre forever. *Psycho* was single-handedly responsible for launching the "slasher film" sub-genre of horror, which would later be picked up and amplified in later movies from *The Texas Chainsaw Massacre* (1974) and *Halloween* (1978) to *Scream* (1996) and beyond. The film was also instrumental in moving the genre away from supernatural concepts in favor of purely psychological horror. Adapted from Robert Bloch's novel by screenwriter Joseph Stefano, the film was based on the real-life exploits of serial murderer Ed Gein, a crazed farm boy from Plainfield, Wisconsin, who was arrested for homicide on November 16, 1957, and found to have raided the local graveyard for body parts that he made into bizarre anatomical keepsakes. Gein, who was a transvestite, liked to dress up in a "woman suit" made from preserved human skin. In addition to *Psycho* and *Texas Chainsaw*, Gein also provided the inspiration for the "Buffalo Bill" serial killer in *The Silence of the Lambs* (1991). Gein, who died in 1984, has become something of a cult figure in American pop culture in the internet age.

An enormous hit with movie audiences at the time of its release, *Psycho* played the audience like a violin by deliberately violating their expectations. After the abrupt murder of viewpoint character Marion Crane in the first half of the movie, viewers did not know what to expect and were plunged into a state of fear and anxiety in anticipation of further murders. Many talents contributed to the film's success: the fine performances of stars Janet Leigh and Tony Perkins, the brilliant editing of George Tomasini (especially in the infamous shower murder sequence), the elegant storyboarding of Saul Bass and the eerie, doom-laden score of the great Bernard Herrmann combined to transform Hitchcock's vision into a classic of American cinema. A gaggle of inferior and unnecessary sequels would eventually follow, including *Psycho II* (1983), *Psycho III* (1986) and *Psycho IV: The Beginning* (1990) as well as a 1998 scene-for-scene color remake directed by Gus Van Sant.

Like many B-noirs, *Psycho* was shot in black and white on a tight budget with a cast of relative unknowns. Cinematographer John L. Russell's expressionistic lighting and camerawork brilliantly evokes the brooding American gothic atmosphere that had enlivened *Sunset Boulevard*, a similarly themed tale of a dominant, homicidal older woman ensconced in a haunted house. Made shortly after the demise of classic film noir in 1958, *Psycho* employs dark noir visuals and contains a number of noir motifs: sleazy sex in seedy hotels, impetuous larceny, murder mystery, a crime of passion, psychiatry, obsession, a private investigator and identity transference. The early scenes of Marion Crane's anxiety-ridden drive into oblivion recall the similar screen environment of noir road movies like *Detour* and *The Hitchhiker*. Like *Rebecca*, *Psycho* is a modern gothic that features a haunted mansion, a charming *homme fatal*, a ghost, a family mystery and an insane relative who is confined to a secret room. As previously mentioned, *Psycho* has affinities with the Val Lewton/Jacques Tourneur classic horror noir *The Leopard Man* in its episodic plot structure that shifts between various viewpoint characters, multiple murders perpetrated by a psycho-killer pretending to be something else, and the homicides being solved not by the police but by a couple who assume the roles of amateur sleuths. *Psycho*'s shower scene may have been inspired by a similar one in the Lewton production of *The Seventh Victim*.

In his seminal book *Dark City: The Lost World of Film Noir*, noir scholar Eddie Muller fingers *Psycho* as "the film that brought down the curtain on that now-lost world." According to Muller, the film's stylistic and thematic excesses prompted film-makers to reject cinematic artistry in favor of slasher sensationalism and manipulative film technique. *Psycho* is described as a "freak carny attraction" that "loosened all the bearings, shattered all the preconceived notions of how things worked, and ushered us into a strange new American fear-scape where suspicion replaced complacency as the pervasive national backdrop.... *Psycho*'s sensational power spawned a legion of imitators—copycat killers, if you will. They've taken many of the dark themes once emblematic of classic film noir and steadily pushed them toward vulgar excess, all in the hope of garnering attention in a market saturated with noise and violence."[7]

Like *Rebecca* and *Vertigo*, *Psycho* is a psychological ghost story involving necrophilia and possession of a weaker personality by that of a dominant dead person. The creepy Bates house, with its secret room inhabited by the family ghost, is the equivalent of the gothic mansion Manderley in *Rebecca*. Both films utilize a contrast in rooms to illustrate the dominant/submissive relationship between the conflicting personalities. Rebecca's bedroom, like that of Mrs. Bates, is large and lavish, while the second Mrs. de Winter's, like Norman's, is correspondingly small, an indication of the dead person's domination of the living. Does the psychiatrist's glib spiel at the end of *Psycho* really explain anything rationally? Norman Bates is possessed by the persona of his mother as surely as if her spirit had risen from the grave and invaded his body. Hitchcock suggests this in the final shot of Norman's features with his mother's skull-face briefly superimposed. Although *Psycho* ostensibly relies on psychological theories of personality development to explain Norman's condition, it's also possible to read its text as a supernatural ghost story involving incest, necrophilia, the doppelganger, and possession by the dead. It is perhaps this disquieting, irrational undertow lurking in the background that lends the work some of its effectiveness as a horror film.

Hitchcock's Other Ghosts

Beyond *Rebecca*, *Vertigo* and *Psycho*, Hitchcock featured a real ghost on a half-hour episode of his CBS television series *Alfred Hitchcock Presents*, entitled "Banquo's Chair." The episode, which first aired on May 3, 1959 (around the time that *Psycho* was going into production), featured John Williams as Scotland Yard inspector William Brent (reprising a similar role he had played in Hitch's *Dial M for Murder*) who is vexed by the unsolved murder of London dowager Miss Ferguson. The main suspect is her nephew, John Bedford (Kenneth Haigh), but despite the inspector's best efforts, Bedford has not confessed to the crime. Brent comes up with an unusual idea designed to make the killer confess. He invites Bedford to a dinner party at Mrs. Ferguson's home which will also be attended by an actress (Mae Thorpe) playing the "ghost" of the deceased aunt, hoping that the sight of the apparition will loosen Bedford's tongue. At the appointed time the actress arrives to impersonate Miss Ferguson and the sight of the ghostly figure has the desired effect upon Bedford. Brent pretends not to see the phantom as Bedford breaks down and confesses to the murder, and as he is taken into custody the actress suddenly arrives, explaining she was unavoidably delayed on her way to the performance, indicating that the specter of Miss Ferguson was the real deal, a ghost who has exacted revenge on her murderer from beyond the grave.

The teleplay was derived from a 1930 short story and play by mystery writer Rupert Croft-Cooke that had been adapted as a radio play many times and provided the basis for the 1945 film *The Fatal Witness*. "Banquo's Chair" is the only Hitchcock film to feature an overtly supernatural element. The title is a reference to the murdered character in Shakespeare's *Macbeth* who appears as an apparition and embodiment of Macbeth's guilt at a dinner party. It's basically a crime story with a supernatural twist at the end. The apparition of Miss Ferguson's ghost is thought by the audience to be nothing more than an actress playing a part, and although it is eerie, it is not perceived as a ghostly visitation. The supernatural element merely providing a typical *Alfred Hitchcock Presents*–type trick ending. It does, however, illustrate Hitch's affinity for the ghost story.

This attraction was also evidenced in two of Hitchcock's unrealized film projects. After the completion of Hitch's *Notorious* in 1946, producer David O. Selznick was proposing a number of projects for the director, whom he still had under contract for one more picture. One of these projects was an adaptation of Henry James's classic ghost story *The Turn of the Screw*, to star Joan Fontaine. While this proposal was soon rejected in favor of *The Parradine Case* (1947), it's intriguing to imagine what Hitchcock might have done with James's work, which is considered to be the finest ghost story in the English language. *The Turn of the Screw* was later filmed by Jack Clayton as *The Innocents* (1961), which turned out to be one of the most haunting horror films ever made.

Hitchcock's great unrealized production, however, was *Mary Rose,* his planned screen version of the play by J.M. Barrie, author of *Peter Pan.* The title character in Barrie's play is an otherworldly young woman who mysteriously disappears on a remote Scottish island and returns to her loved ones 25 years later without having aged a day. Disturbed by the changes time has wrought, Mary dies from grief and comes back as a ghost to have a final conversation with her husband before stepping back into the netherworld, accompanied by a choir of celestial voices. Although the director acknowledged that *Mary Rose* was "not really Hitchcock material," he tried unsuccessfully to make the film over a period of 40 years, envisioning it as a vehicle for his protégées Grace Kelly and Tippi Hedren. Biographer Donald Spoto notes that Barrie's gentle fantasy appealed to Hitchcock's romantic instincts. "The play's doomed, dreary, ghost haunted characters perfectly matched his own ideal," Spoto writes, "the central action — the changelessness of love and the beloved, the meeting and union of time and memory —conformed to his own spirit."[8]

In an interview with director François Truffaut, Hitchcock described the cinematic techniques he would have used to render the spectral Mary Rose on the screen. "What bothers me is the ghost. If I were to make the film, I would put the girl in a dark-gray dress and I would put a neon tube of light inside, around the bottom of the dress, so that the light would only hit the heroine. Whenever she moved, there would be no shadow on the wall, only a blue light. You'd have to create the impression of photographing a presence rather than a body. At times she would appear very small in the image, at times very big. She wouldn't be a solid lump, you see, but rather like a sensation. In this way you lose the feeling of real space and time. You should be feeling that you are in the presence of an ephemeral thing, you see."[9] If Hitchcock had made *Turn of the Screw* or *Mary Rose* he might have turned out some of the most visually stylish ghost stories in cinema history.

Hitchcock's strange fascination with ghosts, identity transference and doppelgangers shows a preternatural sensibility lurking just beneath the surface of the director's avowed realism. There is, therefore, a touch of the otherworldly that pervades many of Hitch's works in the noir genre. Three of the director's most acclaimed works, *Rebecca, Vertigo* and *Psycho,* effectively combine film noir themes with gothic and supernatural motifs and are perhaps the finest classics of horror noir.

9

Modern Horror Noir in the 1960s

By the end of the 1950s the sci-fi horror boom that had taken hold during that post-atomic decade was over. The world had not ended in nuclear war, the Earth had not been invaded by extraterrestrials or menaced by humongous mutant insects or mollusks. As these science fiction themes lost their urgency, film-makers reverted to the gothic themes that had characterized the horror films of decades past. The last of the Universal monsters, the amphibious mutant Gill Man who first crawled out of the primordial slime in *The Creature from the Black Lagoon* (1954) was consigned to oblivion by the end of the decade, and for the most part the major studios got out of the horror business. Of course, the mega-success of *Psycho* would spawn a legion of imitators with titles derived from pop-psychological jargon, including *Homicidal* (1961), *Psychomania* (1963) and *Dementia 13* (1963). There was a revival of a particularly macabre strain of contemporary neo-gothic in thrillers like Robert Aldrich's *What Ever Happened to Baby Jane?* (1962) and *Hush, Hush, Sweet Charlotte* (1964). Hitchcock wannabe William Castle, the *auteur* behind many of the *Whistler* horror noirs, dominated much of the home-grown product during the decade with his gimmick-laden excursions into the genre.

The American horror pictures were replaced by a new spate of horror movies produced overseas, especially in England and Italy, where production costs were much lower than they were in Hollywood. Britain's Hammer Studios purchased the rights to the Universal monsters from the studio and was busy cranking out gory color retreads of the classic creature features of the 30s and 40s starring newly minted horror stars Peter Cushing and Christopher Lee. Other British studios like Amicus and Tigon would soon emerge as Hammer's competitors in the market. American International Pictures (AIP) launched a series of lavish horror movie adaptations of the works of Edgar Allan Poe starring Vincent Price under the able direction of *Wunderkind* Roger Corman, beginning with *House of Usher* (1960) and *The Pit and the Pendulum* (1961). In Italy, the works of horrormeisters Ricardo Freda and Mario Bava would lead to a revival of continental horror.

In the universe of noir, the cycle of classic film noir had come to an end in 1958 with Orson Welles's *Touch of Evil* and had officially entered the phase of "neo-noir," which has extended to the present day. Neo-noir refined and updated the genre into a more modern idiom in films like *Blast of Silence* (1961), *Cape Fear* (1962), *The Manchurian Candidate* (1962) and *The Naked Kiss* (1964), and transitioned the form into color later in the decade in *Point Blank* (1967), *Madigan* (1968) and *Marlowe* (1969). The overall number of films noir produced in America declined precipitously during this period, however. Many of the classic noir conventions had become dated by the '60s and the genre needed time to reconstitute and reconfigure itself. The demise of the black and white idiom in favor of color also provided significant aesthetic hurdles for the genre to overcome.

When Doves Fly

Two significant works of European horror noir were released in 1960. Georges Franju's *Eyes Without a Face* (*Les Yeux sans visage*) transformed one of the most banal sci-fi horror plots into a stylistic masterwork of terror. Based on a novel by Jean Redon, the screenplay was adapted by Pierre Boileau and Thomas Narcejac, the writing team previously responsible for Clouzot's *Diabolique* and Hitchcock's *Vertigo*. Franju would render this gruesome tale of mad science and stolen identity into a haunting, poetic vision.

As *Eyes Without a Face* opens, a sinister middle-aged nurse, Louise (Alida Valli), drives through the darkened streets of Paris with an immobile, trench-coated figure sitting upright in the back seat, its features obscured by a wide-brimmed hat and the action punctuated by Maurice Jarré's haunting waltz theme. Parking near the Siene, Louise hauls out the passenger, which turns out to be the corpse of a young girl who is naked under the coat. Her limp body is dragged to the river and thrown in, after which Louise departs, having done her night's work.

The next day the brilliant plastic surgeon Dr. Génessier (Pierre Brasseur) is summoned to the Paris morgue to identify the body of a young woman found in the river that they suspect may be that of his missing daughter, Christiane. In spite of the fact that the corpse's face has been mutilated, Génessier unhesitatingly pronounces that it is Christiane. Police Inspector Parot (Alexandre Rignault), however, feels that there is something odd about the missing person case. After the burial of the body in the family crypt it is revealed that Christiane (Edith Scob) is in reality still alive and living in seclusion on Génessier's estate after surviving a car accident that has left her face horribly disfigured. Her father has become obsessed with grafting an entire new face onto Christiane, and he and Louise have been kidnapping young girls to use as unwilling subjects in his macabre plastic surgery experiments, aided by his "secretary" Louise.

Génessier's gothic mansion contains a private operating room in the basement and a kennel where he houses the stray dogs he rounds up for his skin grafting experiments. Christiane, her deformed features obscured by a sorrowful-looking mask, drifts through this unnerving landscape like a wraith. In need of another "volunteer" for a full face lift, the doctor dispatches the wicked Louise to find another victim. Stalking the streets of Paris, Louise hits on university student Edna Gruber (Juliette Mayniel), offering her a room at very reasonable rates. The young woman is nervous on the long drive to Génessier's, and her fears are justified when the doctor promptly chloroforms her and drags her away to the operating room. In the film's most horrifying sequence the skin of Edna's face is surgically removed, the ghastly scene revealed by the camera's unblinking eye and in almost complete silence. The facial graft seems to take well on Christiane's face but Edna, kept confined on the doctor's estate with her head swathed in bandages,

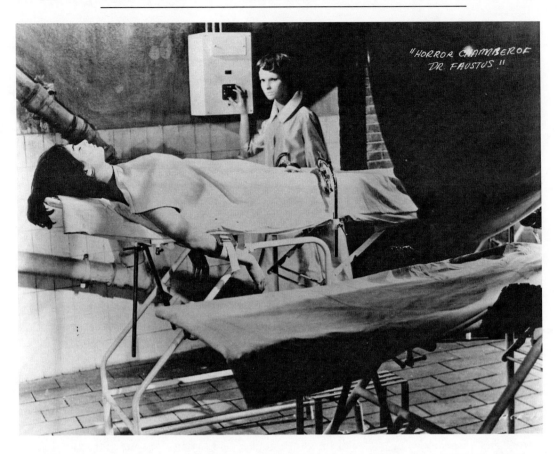

"HORROR CHAMBER OF DR. FAUSTUS"

Christine (Edith Scob, right) examines face donor Edna Gruber (Juliette Mayniel) in *Eyes Without a Face* (a.k.a. *The Horror Chamber of Dr. Faustus*) (Lopert, 1959).

suffers a mental breakdown, gets free and kills herself, and her body is summarily disposed of in the Génessier family crypt.

Christiane's latest graft appears to be doing well, and she can now dispense with wearing the mask while planning to assume "a new face, a new identity." Unfortunately, however, this graft, like the others, does not take and her face begins to degenerate once more. Becoming mentally unhinged, Christiane takes to phoning her former fiancé, Jacques Vernon (François Guérin), and even speaks his name aloud. Recognizing the voice of his "dead" fiancée on the line, Jacques goes to the police where he confesses his suspicions to Inspector Parot, and the detective conceives a plan to entrap Génessier using Paulette Merodon (Beatrice Altariba), a young woman arrested for shoplifting who is persuaded by the police to act as a decoy.

Paulette is sent to the doctor's clinic with a phony ailment and is soon kidnapped by Louise and delivered to Génessier's clinic. As the face transplant operation commences, Parot arrives to question Génessier, and Christiane, who has gone mad from the awful proceedings, enters the operating room and stabs Louise in the neck with a scalpel and frees Paulette. Then she lets the dogs loose from the kennel and frees a cage full of white doves. When Génessier returns to complete the transplant he is viciously attacked and killed by the dogs as Christiane, her mind gone, wanders away into the night surrounded by the flock of doves.

Franju's daring meld of gothic and mad science themes stands as one of the most hauntingly poetic essays in horror in screen history. In an article on the film, French critic Raymond Durgnat observes, "We are launched into a fantasy realm which is only the dark lining of our routine world. Photography becomes a medium in the spiritualist sense — this world speaks to us from beyond the grave, the grave of our belief that the everyday isn't eerie."[1] The director's fantastic visions were executed by the great German cinematographer Eugene Schufftan, whose work had so enlivened Ulmer's costume noir *Bluebeard*. After seeing a dubbed version of the film, luridly retitled *The Horror Chamber of Dr. Faustus* for its American release, the influential critic Pauline Kael opined, "Even dubbed, *Eyes Without a Face* ... is austere and elegant ... even though I thought its intellectual pretensions silly, I couldn't shake off the exquisite, dread images."[2] Franju's camera is cold, clinical, recording the gruesome medical operations with unrelenting clarity and in near-silence. The film combines images of lyrical mythopoetic beauty with ghastly visions of death and disfigurement into a highly disturbing whole.

Scenarists Boileau and Narcejac, of *Diabolique* and *Vertigo* fame, construct a tight thriller that incorporates elements of police procedural into the fantastic proceedings as the Parisian police pursue the serial murderers of young women who are the victims of the mad doctor's unholy experiments. The potentially clichéd sci-fi plot is enlivened by an emphasis on characterization. Edith Scob's ethereal, masked Christiane is the film's most memorable character, the actress's underplayed performance being mostly conveyed by her enormous, incredibly expressive eyes that convey a sense of lost hope and madness. Pierre Brasseur portrays Dr. Génessier as an ice-cold bourgeois, but most of the film's villainy is provided by Alida Valli as the surgeon's enabler, Louise, who functions as a kind of *femme fatale* in the piece, her creepy screen presence evident as she ogles young girls for Génessier's transplants with Sapphic intensity. Maurice Jarré's haunting waltz theme augments the horrific mood of the visuals and the eerie music lingers in the mind's ear long after the film has been viewed.

Eyes Without a Face explores the noir theme of identity, which is frequently expressed through the theme of plastic surgery in classic noirs like *Dark Passage* (1947) and *Man in the Dark* (1953), and more recently in John Woo's neo-noir thriller *Face/Off* (1997). There are also echoes of Peter Lorre's masked, doomed protagonist in *The Face Behind the Mask*. Stripped of its sci-fi element, the film unfolds like a police procedural, with documentary-style scenes following the detective's efforts to crack the multiple murder case. Sinister physicians with criminal motives are a noir staple, and the psychopathic Génessier is portrayed with proper cynicism as a pillar of the community. The motifs of homicide, madness, obsession, medical malpractice and a twisted gothic heroine combine into a masterwork of horror and noir.

Man with a Movie Camera

British director Michael Powell's *Peeping Tom* (1960) would prove to be one of the most infamous films in the history of British cinema. It is the story of Mark Lewis (Carl Boehm), a young man tragically obsessed by fear, movies and murder. The film opens on a very noir-looking deserted street in London's seedy Soho district one night, where Mark picks up a hard-bitten prostitute and surreptitiously films her with a hidden camera, recording her terrified face as he brutally murders her. Later on he is seen watching the developed footage and seemingly has an orgasm while watching the killing.

Mark is employed at London's Tipperfield studio as a menial camera focus puller but he moonlights doing girlie photo shoots for a local pornographer who operates a studio upstairs from his newsagent's shop. Mark owns an apartment house where he maintains extensive darkroom facilities, various types of camera equipment and a projection room where he watches his homicidal "home movies." Obsessed by a camera fetish, he carries his trusty spring-loaded Bell & Howell with him wherever he goes, filming parts of the police investigation of the prostitute's death as part of some demented "documentary." His downstairs boarder Helen Stephens (Anna Massey) becomes intrigued by the shy, enigmatic young man as the two become involved in a budding romantic relationship. Helen soon learns that the primary reason for Mark's oddness is due to being subjected to sadistic experiments conducted by his father, a famous psychologist who was obsessed with the physiology of fear. Mark shows her the films his father made of him when he was a child reacting to having a lizard thrown in his bed or being forced to touch the dead body of his mother.

Under the pretext of making an independent movie of his own, Mark convinces studio stand-in actress Vivian (Moira Shearer) to appear in his production. He commandeers an unused set at night, which he uses as a backdrop for his killing of Vivian with a knife attached to the camera tripod. Afterward he conceals her body in a prop trunk but it is soon discovered during a subsequent movie shoot and Inspector Gregg (Jack Watson) and Sgt. Miller (Nigel Davenport) arrive at the studio to investigate, noting that Vivian's face is contorted in fear in a manner similar to the features of the dead prostitute, leading them to believe they are dealing with a serial killer. In the meantime Helen and Mark are growing closer and Helen, who has written a children's book about a boy with a magic camera, proposes that Mark provide the photos for her book and he agrees, noting cryptically that "there are some things I photograph for nothing."

As the investigation progresses, the detectives become suspicious of Mark and his omnipresent camera, and their suspicions are confirmed when they learn that Mark has been talking to police psychologist Dr. Rosan (Martin Miller), brought on the set to evaluate the cast and crew, about his father's work on voyeurism, or "the morbid urge to gaze." They put a tail on their suspect and track him to the porno news shop, but are unable to prevent Mark from killing one of the models, Milly (Pamela Green), in the usual manner during a photo shoot. Upon finding Milly's body, the detectives race to prevent Mark from murdering Helen and from arranging the ultimate culmination of the murderer's documentary film project.

Michael Powell, who formerly enjoyed a reputation as one of Britain's most acclaimed film-makers as the director (along with collaborator Emeric Pressburger) of prestige productions such as *Black Narcissus* (1947) and *The Red Shoes* (1948), had his career and reputation destroyed by this controversial exploration of murder, pornography and voyeurism. The film's original screenplay was written by Leo Marks, an enigmatic individual who was a onetime antiquarian bookseller and wartime cryptographer and claims to have based the film on his World War II experiences in British espionage and code-breaking. In truth, *Peeping Tom* is a difficult film to watch, especially given the orgasmic nature of the killings. Like Fritz Lang's *M* (1931), the movie attempts to make a deranged psycho-killer into a sympathetic character and only partially succeeds. Powell's personal connection to the film's theme was underscored by the fact that he appeared as Mark's coldly sadistic father and cast his own son, Columba, as the victim of the psychologist's experiments in terror. Some critics were turned off by Pamela Green's nude scene, the first in the history of British cinema, although it is extremely tame by today's jaded standards of screen nudity, and by the film's exploration of Britain's emerging pornography industry. Perhaps one of the most unpleasant things about *Peeping Tom* is that it reminds the audience that the cinema is potentially the most horrific of all the arts, as it has the potential to capture murderous, sadistic documentary images of real death and torture as evidenced in reports of homicidal "snuff" films and graphic beheading videos made by terrorists.

In the years since its original release, *Peeping Tom* has attained the status of a cult film, largely as a result of the efforts of Martin Scorsese during the 1970s, that have forced a critical re-evaluation of the film. Today it is acknowledged as an important work in the history of British cinema, and critics who once despised it have now flocked to its defense. Smoothly directed by Powell in naturalistic Eastmancolor, *Peeping Tom* is emotionally riveting despite its unpleasant subject matter. Leo Marks's screenplay contains no wasted scenes and maintains tension throughout the film in its intricate construction and frank exploration of its unusual and unpleasant subject matter. Carl Boehm's characterization of the shy, soft-spoken, clean-cut serial killer Mark is wonderfully engaging, but perhaps strains credulity as a real-world personality type. Composer Brian Easdale slyly uses silent film–style solo piano accompaniment as an aural counterpoint to Mark's obscene home movies.

Although it's not immediately obvious, *Peeping Tom* is a variation on the gothic formula with its charming *homme fatal* who possesses a deadly secret and the house with the mysterious hidden room. The shadows of Mark's private theater provide a suitably noir expressionistic environment for instilling fear in the audience, while the director also makes fine use of London street locations for purposes of documentary verisimilitude. Mark is a typically twisted noir protagonist, a tormented, homicidal loner living inside his morbid fantasies, and may have provided inspiration for the similarly perverse character of Travis Bickle (Robert De Niro) in Scorsese's *Taxi Driver* (1976). Many critics have pointed out resemblances to Hitchcock's *Rear Window* (1954) and *Psycho* (1960), both of which deal with the psychological perils of voyeurism. The English porno news shop recalls a similar facility in Howard Hawks's classic noir *The Big Sleep* (1946). Snuff films subsequently made an appearance in the Argentinean hoax movie *Snuff* (1976), and was featured in the plots of David Cronenberg's scifi-noir *Videodrome* (1983) and Michael Mann's stylish crime thriller *Manhunter* (1986).

More Euro-Horror Noir

Britain's Hammer Studios, whose gory color remakes of Universal's Frankenstein, Dracula and Mummy monster franchises, also produced a number of modest black and white non–creature feature horror thrillers that bordered on noir. *Scream of Fear* (British title *Taste of Fear*, 1961) was written and produced by Hammer horror maven Jimmy Sangster and directed by Seth Holt and stars Susan Strasberg (the daughter of famed "method" acting coach Lee Strasberg). Strasberg plays paraplegic heiress Penny Appelby, who has been invited to visit her father's house on the French Riviera after a traumatic incident in which Penny's best friend drowned. Penny has not seen her father since the riding accident that left her a cripple ten years earlier. Meeting her at the airport is her father's brawny chauffeur, Bob (Ronald Lewis), who is assigned to tend to her and carry her around.

At the house Penny meets her stepmother, Judy (Ann Todd), for the first time. Judy appears to be a solicitous middle-aged woman who is genuinely concerned with her step-daughter's welfare. Despite the importance of her visit, Penny is informed that her father is currently away on an important business trip, but later that night she is awakened by a loud sound and observes a strange light in the window of the summer house. Wheeling herself out to investigate, she finds her father's corpse seated upright in a chair, his eyes gleaming in the flickering candlelight. She flees in terror and accidentally falls into the swimming pool and nearly drowns, but after the incident the summer house is found to have been locked and no trace of her father's body can be found.

After experiencing other spectral happenings and sightings of her dad's corpse in the gothic mansion that are witnessed only by her, Penny's sanity is called into question. Judy introduces her to the cadaverous Dr. Gerrard (played by Hammer horror star Christopher Lee sporting the most egregious French accent this side of Steve Martin in the *Pink Panther* remakes), who seems eager to medically examine Penny and have her declared legally insane. The feisty Penny, however, resists, realizing that Judy will inherit the entire estate if she is sent to the asylum. She enlists the aid of her confidante, Bob, whom she sends out to gather evidence that she is not going mad and is the victim of a plot to deprive her of her inheritance.

In the end, no one is who or what they seem in Sangster's cleverly plotted horror noir thriller, which takes a number of surprising turns before reaching its *denouement*. While *Scream of Fear* borrows liberally from *Gaslight* and *Diabolique*, it manipulates these plot elements in a way that is not overly derivative and keeps the audience guessing up to the last. Seth Holt's direction does full justice to the twists and turns of Sangster's screenplay and provides shadowy, atmospheric visuals for this modern gothic, and he is aided by the considerable talents of cinematographer Douglas Slocombe on the camera. Ms. Strasberg portrays the supposedly helpless Penny as being very much in command of all situations, her icy demeanor and indomitable spirit contrasting with her crippled body. Hammer horror star Christopher Lee, the film's other name actor, has a throwaway role as the sinister Dr. Gerrard, his ridiculous French accent providing a distracting and unintentional dose of self-parody. Gothic and mystery motifs are elegantly recombined into a work that is a crime melodrama with expressionistic horror movie overtones.

In the early 1960s, American International Pictures had begun producing a series of horror films in widescreen and Technicolor based on the works of Edgar Allan Poe as directed by Hollywood's "King of the B's," Roger Corman. For budgetary reasons, AIP had moved its production unit for the Poe films to England, where production costs were much lower. The success of Corman's *House of Usher* (1960) and *The Pit and the Pendulum* (1961), both of which starred horrormeister Vincent Price, inspired writer/producer

Robert E. Kent to adapt two short stories by French writer Guy de Maupassant into a similar color/widescreen Price vehicle for AIP entitled *Diary of a Madman* (1962). Brought in to direct was veteran Universal B-movie director Reginald LeBorg, who had lensed three of the *Inner Sanctum* series horror noirs during the 1940s.

Diary of a Madman opens with the funeral of Judge Magistrate Simon Cordier (Price), in which the deceased has made a peculiar request to art gallery owner Andre D'Arville (Edward Colmans) and his daughter Jeanne (Elaine Devry) that a letter and his diary be read aloud to parish priest Father Raymonde (Lewis Martin) and police Captain Robert Rennedon (Stephen Roberts) after the ceremony. "I speak to you from beyond the grave," the letter begins, as Price's voice-over narrates the events in the diary and the film's narrative unfolds in flashback. Magistrate Cordier, a wealthy, well-respected official is still consumed with grief and guilt over the accidental death of his son and the subsequent suicide of his wife twelve years earlier. One day Cordier receives an odd request from prisoner Louis Girot (Harvey Stephens), a serial killer who will soon pay for his crimes on the guillotine, for a final meeting with the judge who condemned him to die before he is executed. Thinking Girot is finally about to confess to the murders, Cordier agrees as part of his "endless studies of the criminal mind," but instead the killer continues to insist that he was the victim of an entity that "lives on evil," who "took my body and made me murder." As Cordier listens to the prisoner's lament a strange green light shines in Girot's eyes as the man suddenly attacks him. The two grapple briefly and the Magistrate violently throws Girot to the floor, somehow killing the prisoner in the process.

Soon after the death of Girot, the Magistrate is plagued by an apparent outbreak of poltergeist phenomena: a portrait of his wife is mysteriously transported from a storage room and hung on Cordier's wall; the words "hatred is evil" are found written on a dusty shelf; Girot's file is spirited onto the Magistrate's office desk. All of these occurrences are slyly staged in a way that makes Cordier doubt his own sanity. One night when he is alone going through Girot's file in his study, Cordier watches in horror as an invisible hand spills a bottle of ink all over the file. He then hears a demonic laugh in the room addressing him: "You deprived me of Girot's body ... now I will have yours." Cordier's body becomes possessed by the malignant being, who forces him to kill his little pet bird in a scene that recalls a similar avian murder in Tourneur's *Cat People*. "Do you still think I exist only in your mind?" the voice asks rhetorically before departing.

Fearing for his sanity, Cordier consults with police alienist Dr. Borman (Nelson Olmstead) about the bizarre events, but the psychiatrist thinks he has merely suffered a mild mental breakdown due to overwork and advises him to take a vacation and pursue his hobby of sculpting for awhile. While admiring a woman's portrait in the window of an art gallery, he is approached by the painting's subject, Odette du Classe (Nancy Kovack), who flirts with Cordier while offering her services as an artist's model. The Magistrate hires her at the exorbitant rate of ten francs an hour, but he does not know that Odette is married to Paul du Classe (Chris Warfield), the struggling artist who painted the portrait. Paul is unhappy with his wife posing for another man, but reluctantly accepts because they are in need of money.

Cordier is smitten with the vivacious Odette and falls in love with her during their art sessions. For her part, she has become desirous of the Magistrate's wealth and position and makes the decision to leave her husband for Cordier and rents an apartment for herself. The Magistrate's newfound romantic bliss is punctured by another visit from the evil spirit, which now calls itself "the Horla," and claims to be one of an invisible race of beings that covertly exist alongside humanity. The being preys upon the Magistrate's guilt over his wife's suicide after his son's accidental death, and even accuses him of murdering her indirectly. In mocking tones the Horla also informs Cordier that Odette is not the charming ingénue she seems, but the Magistrate is unconvinced. When Cordier proposes marriage she is forced to reveal that she is still married to Paul, so the Magistrate plots to use his legal powers to have the marriage annulled. As Paul confronts his wife at her apartment, the Horla possesses Cordier once more and sends him out to kill Odette, and after she and Paul have a heated argument, the husband storms out and Cordier creeps in to brutally knife her to death. Paul is arrested for the homicide and the Magistrate, knowing that Paul is innocent, refuses any clemency despite Jeanne's impassioned pleas.

The Horla then orders Cordier to kill Jeanne, and the entranced Magistrate is soon stalking her through the streets of Paris, but when the image of a cross is reflected in the murder blade the spell is broken. Upon regaining his senses, Cordier decides there is only one way out. Suspecting that the Horla (who appears to have some kind of material reality) can be destroyed by fire, he puts his worldly affairs in order before locking himself and the Horla in his study and setting the room on fire. 'How does terror feel?" the Magistrate taunts his oppressor before both of them are consumed in the blazing conflagration.

A highly underappreciated little gem, *Diary of a Madman*, although derivative of the AIP Poe product, is actually better than some of the AIP Corman Poe flicks. Horror veteran LeBorg directs with considerable verve and a fine feel for the historical period. Robert E. Kent's screenplay smoothly combines plot elements from the de Maupassant stories "The Horla" and "Diary of a Madman" into a seamless whole that melds a firsthand narrative of one man's descent into schizophrenia with a supernatural tale of spirit possession and poltergeist infestation. The screen presence of Vincent Price and the art direction of Daniel Haller both serve to invoke the elegant, fear-haunted universe of the Poe films. Price's performance is restrained and believable despite having to act opposite the offscreen dialogues of Joseph Ruskin as the invisible Horla, and he is ably supported by Nancy Kovack's sparkling portrayal of the vivacious but amoral Odette.

The film harks back to the costume noirs of the 1940s such as Brahm's *The Lodger* and Ulmer's *Bluebeard* with its period setting and murderous *homme fatal*. One big difference, however, is that *Diary of a Madman* contains supernatural elements like spirit possession. Reportedly, de Maupassant was suffering from the initial symptoms of a mental illness when he wrote these stories, and they are in some sense a chronicle of the affliction that would claim his life just five years later. There are indications that de Maupassant suffered from a condition known as "sleep paralysis," in which the subject has hallucinations that a malignant entity has entered the room and is trying to choke the sleeper to death. These hallucinations occur during the twilight state between sleep and full wakefulness, and the sleeper will awaken to find no one else in the room. The notion of the invisible Horla was surely inspired by an episode of this nightmarish sleep disorder. Stripped of its preternatural content, *Diary* can be read as a subjective noir journey into an individual's self-deluded madness and murder. The film's narrative is presented in a typical film noir fashion, with most of the action taking place in flashback accompanied by the protagonist's ironic voice-over narration. Over and above all the supernatural goings-on, the film presents a very human, very noir story of guilt, obsession, murder, madness, art, jealousy and betrayal.

The enormous commercial success of *Psycho* inspired a raft of imitators with titles inspired by various psychoses and neuroses, none of which remotely approached the quality of Hitchcock's masterwork. *Psychomania* (1963) featured murderous hijinks at a girl's school, while Hammer's *Paranoiac* (1963), scripted by Sangster, ripped off its plotline from *Scream of Fear*. Francis Ford Coppola's directorial debut, *Dementia 13* (1963), was a twisted tale of an axe murderer at a gothic castle, and in Hammer's *Nightmare* (1964), directed by Freddie Francis, Sangster regurgitated his earlier scripts once more. In a similar vein was Hitchcock wannabe William Castle's oddity *The Night Walker* (1964), a film that purported to explore the mysterious world of dreams.

The Night Walker begins with a "documentary" prologue that presents a montage of Freudian dream imagery while an offscreen narrator delivers a portentous monologue, asking the audience, "What are dreams?" and noting that "there's death in your dreams, too." As a montage of strange imagery unfolds, the unseen voice proclaims that "when you dream, you become a night walker," thus explaining the film's title and concept. The movie's narrative begins at the gloomy mansion of wealthy but sightless inventor Howard Trent (Hayden Rorke), who, because of his blindness, has wired the entire house for sound with sophisticated equipment and recorded his wife (Barbara Stanwyck, in her final theatrical film role) talking to an unknown lover in her sleep. Trent confronts his attorney, Barry Moreland (Robert Taylor), about his suspicions, as Irene is agoraphobic and never leaves the house and the lawyer is the only man who ever visits, but Moreland shoots back that Trent's blindness has exacerbated his insane jealousy. When Trent tries to discuss the matter with his wife, she flies into a rage, telling him, "My lover is only a dream but he's more of a man than you," before storming out of the house in a huff. Immediately after the spat, smoke begins pouring from Trent's attic laboratory and when he enters the lab he is killed in a tremendous explosion.

Although Trent's body has been completely vaporized by the explosion, Irene experiences a "nightmare" in which she is pursued through the house by his charred corpse. Understandably spooked, she decamps for a small apartment located behind Irene's Beauty Shop, a business that she owns and operates, but her strange dreams continue. Irene is visited by her dream lover (Lloyd Bochner), but soon she can't tell the difference between dream and reality anymore. During one of her nocturnal ramblings, her mysterious lover takes her to a strange chapel inhabited by mannequins where, in a funereal "wedding" ceremony, she is "married" to her dream suitor. In the aftermath of her bizarro dream experience she enlists Moreland's help in trying to prove that her nightmares are really happening. The two cruise around the streets of Los Angeles, where Irene recognizes an abandoned church as the scene of her mock wedding and finds the bogus wedding ring used in the ceremony. These clues prove that Irene is being gaslighted, but by whom and for what purpose? And has her husband faked his own death to avenge his jealousy, or is he a ghost? Who is Irene's mysterious dream lover? All of these loose ends are eventually tied up in an unlikely tangle of plot lines by the movie's end.

Back in the 1940s director William Castle had lensed most of the atmospheric *Whistler* series entries, but by the '60s Castle had become the horror film's greatest shlockmeister, producing and directing a string of gimmick-laden, juvenile terror fare that included *Macabre* (1958), *The House on Haunted Hill* (1959) and *The Tingler* (1959). The cigar-chomping Castle, who appears as the central character in Joe Dante's comedy-satire *Matinee* (1993), brought a carny sideshow sensibility to horror cinema the likes of which had not been seen since the heydey of Tod Browning's *Freaks* in the 1930s. By 1964, Castle had a serious case of Hitchcock envy after *Psycho* had made millions and revolutionized the horror film, but Castle's own directorial style had become flat and pedestrian, his visuals consisting mostly of static medium shots with little effort to use lighting or camera angles to conjure the expressionist shadows of horror or noir. There is no invocation of the oneiric shadow world so endemic to film noir since its inception in Boris Ingster's *Stranger on the Third Floor* (1940).

Robert Bloch, author of *Psycho*, constructed the script from a story by Elizabeth Kata, but the plot of *The Night Walker* is overly complex and frequently strains credulity. How does the blind Howard Trent conduct scientific experiments and operate a roomful of hi-tech machinery, for instance? And how can a house-bound Irene manage a business in absentia? The film's dream lover premise derives from the medieval concept of the incubus, a nocturnal being thought to be an alluring demon that was prone to sexually stimulating women in their dreams. Ultimately, *The Night Walker* presents the same drive-her-insane, *Gaslight*-type plotline that had become a tired cliché due to overuse. Los Angeles locations lend the film a black and white, documentary look typical of late-cycle "realist" noirs like *Kiss Me Deadly* (1955). Noir icon Barbara Stanwyck, who had portrayed the titular *femmes fatales* of *The Strange Love of Martha Ivers* (1946) and *The File on Thelma Jordan* (1950) and the mother of all evil noir women in the immortal *Double Indemnity* (1944), is clearly past her prime and woefully miscast as a romantic lead. La Stanwyck gets to scream her head off, act bewildered, blabber in her sleep and utter immortal lines like, "I can't wake up!" Playing opposite her is ex-hubby Robert Taylor, a veteran of noirs like *Johnny Eager* (1941), *The Bribe* (1949) and *Party Girl* (1958), who lends a stolid but otherwise dull screen presence to the proceedings. The film's horror hokum quickly falls by the wayside, leaving a noir mystery story that involves the familiar themes of jealousy, murder, larceny, deceit and high technology.

Veteran director William Wyler, who had lensed many well-known mainstream Hollywood movies, including *Wuthering Heights* (1939), *The Best Years of Our Lives* (1946) and *Ben-Hur* (1959), tackled the dark side of human behavior in the British-based production of *The Collector* (1965). Terence Stamp stars as psychotic loner Freddie Clegg, an ex–bank clerk whose winnings at a soccer pool have made him independently wealthy. He buys an old Tudor period house in a secluded area that contains a hidden chamber in which he installs modern furnishings and soundproofing, sealing it off from the outside world. Next, Freddie is observed tailing a young woman through the streets of London in his van. He cooly and cleverly chloroforms her on a deserted street and transports her to his house, where she is ensconced in the secret room.

The unfortunate woman, art student Miranda Gray (Samantha Eggar), awakens to find herself a prisoner in the strange domicile. Her captor explains that he has been obsessed with her since they lived together in the small town of Redding, and that he has been planning her kidnapping for a long time. There is no one within earshot to hear her scream in the soundproofed room, and no way for her to escape. While he is very firm

Freddie Clegg (Terrence Stamp) has an unhealthy obsession with Samantha Eggar in William Wyler's *The Collector* (1965).

in his desire to keep her imprisoned, he does not resort to violence or sexually assault her, despite being in a position to do so. "I want you to be my guest," he explains. "I want you to get to know me." He informs her that he intends to keep her imprisoned for four weeks, after which she will be free to go if she chooses not to stay with him.

Franklin and Miranda enter into a bizarre parody of a romantic relationship during her captivity. He is solicitous of her needs, bringing her books and art supplies that she requests in order to make her stay pleasant. The spirited Miranda does not back down from her captor and makes every effort to escape but the wily Franklin defeats all of her attempts. Sustained only by the hope that she will be freed at the appointed time, Miranda endures her imprisonment stoically while using her wits to mentally joust with her tormentor and manipulate him psychologically. Taking her on a tour of his home one day, Franklin reveals that he is a butterfly fancier and shows off his extensive collection of rare and beautiful preserved specimens, but instead of being impressed Miranda is appalled. "Think of all the living beauty you've ended," she spits at him, realizing that he thinks of her as one more exotic specimen caught inside of his killing jar.

In spite of a measure of intimacy that arises from their enforced closeness, Miranda fails to warm to Franklin at all. "You could fall in love with me if you tried," he laments.

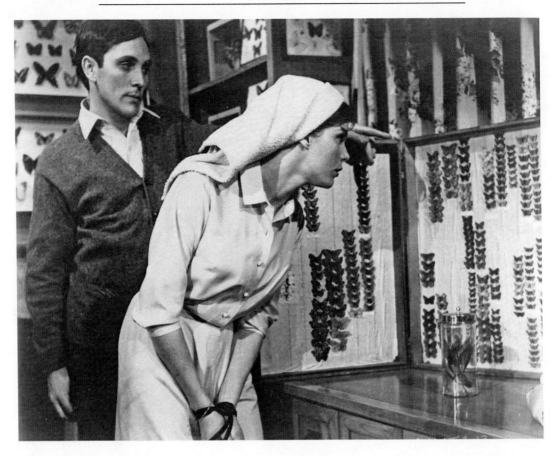

Terrence Stamp shows off his butterfly collection to Miranda Gray (Samantha Eggar) in *The Collector* (Columbia, 1965).

"You just don't try." She counters by calling him juvenile, retorting, "It's the sort of dream that young boys have when they reach puberty." In perhaps what is the film's most chilling line of dialogue, he replies, "There'd be a blooming lot more of this if more people had the time and the money." As Miranda's "freedom day" approaches, she has grave doubts about Franklin's promise to free her and wonders if she has the strength to endure her imprisonment and survive her captor's twisted game.

Wyler's offbeat psychological thriller has all but vanished into an undeserved obscurity today, perhaps because *The Collector* is a difficult film to watch. Claustrophobic and downbeat, with most of its action taking place within the tightly confined space of the hidden room, the film makes the audience share the trapped feeling of its female protagonist. Adapted from a novel by John Fowles (who would later pen *The French Lieutenant's Woman*) by Stanley Mann and John Kohn, the two-hour-plus film is basically a character study of two people. The film sustains itself on Wyler's direction of the two principals, who both turn in riveting performances. Samantha Eggar earned a Golden Globe Award for her portrayal of the imprisoned Miranda, while Terence Stamp is equally brilliant playing opposite her as the demented lepidopterist Freddie Clegg. The petulant, sexually repressed Clegg engages the audience's sympathies despite his foul deeds, yet he has the perverse charm of Anthony Perkins as Norman Bates in *Psycho* and Carl Boehm's Mark Lewis in *Peeping Tom*. Oddly, Freddie's character is perhaps even more similar to the psychopathic little girl in *The Bad Seed* in its mixture of childlike innocence and homicidal mania. One major criticism of *The Collector*, however, is that unlike *Psycho* or *Peeping Tom* it provides virtually no backstory about the reasons for Freddie's problems and deprives the character of psychological depth.

Like *Peeping Tom*, the film makes good use of London street locations that impart a documentary feeling to the proceedings in the manner of late-period realist noir. Stylistically, Wyler shoots using high-key lighting setups that are appropriate to a dramatic film rather than using the expressionistic shadows of horror or noir. Cinematic tension is expressed solely through dialogue and the dramatic interaction between the two characters, making *The Collector* sometimes seem like a horrific version of *Who's Afraid of Virginia Woolf?* (1966) as Freddie and Miranda go through a demented parody of a normal romantic relationship. Freddie is a typically obsessive noir protagonist and neo-gothic *homme fatal*, living in his intensely private world and sporting a hidden dungeon complete with female victim. The film also has affinities with other offbeat crime melodramas of the period that featured morbid British eccentrics and kidnapping plots, such as Bryan Forbes's *Séance on a Wet Afternoon* (1964) and Otto Preminger's *Bunny Lake Is Missing* (1965).

Karloff Returns

British cult director Michael Reeves had only three films to his credit before his untimely death in 1969. One of these was *The Sorcerers* (1967), in which a 23-year-old Reeves directed 70-year-old horror star Boris Karloff. Set in swingin' London of the 1960s familiar to fans of the *Austin Powers* comedies, Karloff plays "medical hypnotist" Dr. Marcus Monsarrat, who, along with his wife and assistant, Estelle (Catherine Lacey), has invented a machine that enables the telepathic transfer of sensations between two minds. Monsarrat scours London for a suitable experimental subject until he meets bored, callow youth Mike Roscoe (Ian Oglivy) in a Wimpy's hamburger joint and lures him to his home with the promise of a hallucinogenic experience that will relieve his ennui. At *chez* Monsarrat, Mike is strapped into the mind machine, where he undergoes an electronically induced psychedelic trip that unwittingly places him under the hypno-telepathic control of Marcus and Estelle. The elderly scientist then uses his hypnotic skills to induce amnesia about the session and on all subsequent mental takeovers by the couple.

Able to subjectively experience whatever Mike does, Marcus and Estelle soon become intoxicated by the vicarious feelings induced by their mind meld with the young man. Coveting an expensive fur coat Estelle sees in a shop window, the couple sends Mike out to steal it, and when Mike receives a slight wound on his hand during the robbery, both Marcus and Estelle receive a stigmata-like wound on exactly the same spot. On another occasion Estelle feels the need for speed and compels Mike to "borrow" a friend's motorcycle and go tearing down the highway at top speed with Mike's girlfriend, Nicole (Elizabeth Ercy), hanging on to him for dear life. Marcus, his hypnotic theories proven, wants them to stop living through the young man, but Estelle has become seduced by the pleasures of the mind link. "We all want to do things deep down inside ourselves, things we can't allow ourselves," she tells her husband, and now through the machine they are able to do these things without fear of consequences. When Marcus proposes to bring Mike back to the lab to deprogram his telepathic link, Estelle goes bonkers and destroys the mind-control device to prevent this from ever happening and incapacitates her husband so that he cannot interfere with her vicarious joys.

Meanwhile, Nicole and Mike's best friend, Alan (Victor Henry), has become deeply concerned with Mike's erratic behavior and amnesiac episodes, and things come to a head when Mike seemingly goes crazy and assaults Alan while under Estelle's control. Mike's weird "blackouts" intensify as Estelle vicariously savors the ultimate thrill — the murder of two young women. Alan and Nicole take their suspicions to the police, who begin an investigation of Mike and quickly suspect him of being the amnesiac serial killer. Events come to a climax as the demented Estelle makes Mike attack Alan with a knife, and when the police arrive Mike steals a car and drives off at high speed with the bobbies in hot pursuit. At this point Marcus summons his remaining psychic strength and abruptly wrests telepathic control of Mike away from Estelle and causes his car to crash and burn. The film's final scene shows the charred corpses of Marcus and Estelle in their apartment, the couple having burned to death subjectively through the power of the uncanny mind-meld.

This earnest exercise in low-budget film-making displays director Reeves's flawed but evolving cinematic style in his second feature. Scenes are repetitious and go on too long in order to play out screen time. In particular, several scenes that take place inside a rock club slow down the action considerably. The film's low-rent ambience and use of London locations lends *The Sorcerers* some of the same quasi-documentary verisimilitude that had enlivened *Peeping Tom* and *The Collector*. Reeves's reputation as a "youth director" has been blunted by the passage of time as the film's '60s-era milieu has dated badly. Oddly, sex rarely intrudes on the proceedings but the brutality of the two murders is lovingly depicted. Horror king Karloff, in one of his last major roles, carries on valiantly but is obviously struggling against advanced age and physical infirmities. His clichéd part as a kindly old mad scientist, a part that he had played in countless movies, is somewhat upstaged by the performance of character actress Catherine Lacey, who has a more interesting role as the perverse Estelle. Youthful lead Ian Oglivy is well-cast as the sensation-seeking psychedelic-era love child and enthusiastically expresses a range of emotions from bored petulance to excited homicidal dementia.

The screenplay, co-written by Reeves and Tom Baker from an idea by John Burke, is the film's strongest suit. Hypnotic mind control had been the subject of numerous horror and science fiction films, from *Svengali* (1931) to *Donovan's Brain* (1953) to *The Manchurian Candidate* (1962), but here the theme reflects the '60s-era notion of the generation gap, in which the old parasitically prey upon the young and send them out to do their dirty work. The motif of substitute or vicarious experience of another's senses is a potent concept that has risen to prominence recently in films like *Being John Malkovich* (1999), *Eternal Sunshine of the Spotless Mind* (2004), *Surrogates* (2009) and *Avatar* (2009). The premise of being freed to "do things we can't allow ourselves," touches on the fractured morality at the heart of noir and the will toward evil that is part of the human condition. Killers who commit their murders during periods of amnesiac blackouts are a staple of film noir, especially in noirs adapted from the works of mystery writer Cornell Woolrich, such as *Black Angel* (1946).

Peter Bogdanovich's directorial debut, *Targets* (1968), represents Karloff's final bow in an American A-picture, and is a fitting tribute to the great horror actor as well a harbinger of thematic trends to come within the horror genre. *Wunderkind* writer/director Bogdanovich reportedly got to make the movie because Karloff owed AIP producer/director Roger Corman three days' work. Instead of cranking out another Poe-inspired gothic melodrama, however, Bogdanovich opted to devise a modern story set in contemporary Los Angeles and inspired by the exploits of real-life serial killer Charles Whitman, a sniper who had shot several people to death at the University of Texas. Bogdanovich was assisted in his screenwriting task by the legendary neo-noir writer/producer/director triple threat Sam Fuller, whose noir works include *Pickup on South Street* (1952), *Shock Corridor* (1963) and *The Naked Kiss* (1963), but Fuller neither sought nor requested payment or screen credit for his work on the script.

Targets is structured around two separate narratives. In one, Karloff plays aging horror movie star Byron Orlok, who wants to retire from filmmaking because "all the good movies have been made." "I'm an antique, out of date, an anachronism," he laments. "The world belongs to the young. Let them have it." His director/scenarist, Sammy Michaels (Bogdanovich), wants Orlok to stay in show biz so he can lens his next script, but the erstwhile horrormeister has become mired in morbid reflection and self-pity. Pointing to a newspaper headline about a senseless violent crime, Orlok observes that "my kind of horror isn't horror anymore." Nonetheless, Sammy and Orlok's cute Asian assistant, Jenny (Nancy Hsueh), persuade him to attend a publicity event for his latest film (actually out-takes from Corman's *The Terror*) being held at the Reseda Drive-In in San Fernando Valley on the following evening.

The second narrative concerns insurance agent and Vietnam vet Bobby Thompson (Tim O'Kelly), a clean-cut young man with a penchant for firearms. Bobby lives at the home of his father (James Brown) and mother, Charlotte (Mary Jackson), with his wife, Ilene (Tanya Morgan). The family seems to lead a bland, middle-American existence until, for no discernable reason, Bobby shoots his wife and mother to death with a handgun one day, gathers up a huge cache of weapons and ammo, and leaves behind a note typed in red letters that reads: "I just killed my wife and my mother. I know they'll get me. But before that many more will die." His first stop is a nearby gas works, where he kills a number of passing motorists from a vantage point on top of a gas tank. Fleeing from the scene of the shootings, Bobby pulls into the Reseda Drive-In to elude the cops and waits for darkness to fall.

When night comes, Bobby begins to shoot people at the drive-in from his sniper's nest behind the screen, while, unknowingly, Orlok arrives for the promotional event. As creaky footage from *The Terror* unfolds on the screen, Bobby continues his killing spree while a clueless audience continues to watch the movie. When Jenny is wounded and Bobby begins to run low on ammo, Orlok spies the killer hiding in a corner and fearlessly approaches him. Catching Bobby between reloads, the aged horror star bitch-slaps the killer, disarming him so that he can be subdued. "Is this what I was afraid of?" Orlok muses in the aftermath.

Bogdanovich's brilliant screenplay and flawless directorial execution crafts a compelling thriller that works on a number of different levels. The film constitutes a heartfelt tribute to the life and career of the great Karloff, who is taking his final Hollywood bow in *Targets*. Faded horror movie luminary Byron Orlok resembles *Sunset Boulevard*'s Norma Desmond in reverse; he is a former film star who seeks to reject the cinema rather than shoehorn his way back into it. On another level the film is an indictment of American middle-class values, the banality of which presumably drives Bobby's homicidal acts. Bogdanovich also takes aim at the issue of gun control, showing the ease with which Bobby purchases gear at gun shops in two separate scenes. The film's biggest flaw is that it provides no backstory or rationale for Bobby's killing spree other than suggesting that his bland whitebread existence drove him to murder. On yet another level, *Targets* perfectly illustrates the metamorphosis of the horror film from the costume gothicism of Hammer and AIP to psychological horrors ripped from the pages of contemporary newspaper headlines, from Frankenstein's monster to an insane killer on the loose.

Karloff is superb in this homage to his long career, turning in a comic, warm-hearted performance as the garrulous Byron Orlok, and is ably assisted by his acting foil Bogdanovich. A brief excerpt from Howard Hawks's prison melodrama *The Criminal Code* (1931) that appears in the film is a reminder of the actor's early roles in 1930s-era gangster films such as *Graft* (1931), *The Guilty Generation* (1931), *Scarface* (1932) and *Behind the Mask* (1932), but the actor's identification with the screen image of Frankenstein's monster and his too-recognizable British accent precluded his appearance in film noir. The scenes depicting the mechanics and depredations of the film business seem to be modeled after Jean-Luc Godard's *Contempt* (1963). On the other hand, Tom O'Kelly delivers a very restrained, serious performance as the film's *homme fatal*, Bobby Thompson, and the character's fascination with firearms recalls a similar fascination by the principal characters in Joseph Lewis's classic noir *Gun Crazy* (1949). There are also affinities with Edward Dmytryk's *The Sniper* (1952), in which Arthur Franz portrays a psychotic long-distance lady-killer. The L.A. landscape in *Targets*, crisply rendered by ace cinematographer Lazlo Kovacs, provides a neo-noir urban backdrop for the deadly action.

While principal photography and post-production for *Targets* wrapped up in 1967, the film's commercial prospects were uncertain, and it had the misfortune not to be released until 1968, after the assassinations of Robert F. Kennedy and Martin Luther King earlier that year. This bad timing led to the film being a box-office flop with movie audiences, but it did launch Bogdanovich's career as an A-list director. His screenplay, with an assist from the iconoclastic Sam Fuller, incorporates many of the incidents from the Charles Whitman sniper murders into its plot. On August 1, 1966, Whitman, a clean-cut, 25-year-old engineering student at the University of Texas at Austin, shot and killed 14 people and wounded 32 from a sniper's nest on the roof of the 28-floor university administration building before being shot to death by police. Like the film's psycho-killer, Whitman had murdered his wife and mother on the previous evening. After Whitman's death, a malignant brain tumor was discovered that might possibly explain why this former altar boy and scoutmaster had become a mass-murderer.

Pray for Rosemary's Baby

Polish-born director Roman Polanski has always embraced a noir sensibility in exploring some of the darker regions of human nature in his films. His first Polish feature, *Knife in the Water* (1962), told the sordid tale of an erotic triangle that plays out on a small boat and ends in murder. In his first English-language film, the British-made *Repulsion* (1965), Polanski envisioned the terrifying subjective nightmare of a young woman's descent into insanity and homicide. Back in America, horror movie producer/director William Castle had obtained the galley proofs for Ira Levin's novel *Rosemary's Baby* and convinced Paramount studio execs to purchase the literary property before the book had even been published. The studio agreed, with the proviso that Castle himself should only produce, not direct, the film. Castle, in turn, managed to sign Polanski on as director and screenwriter for the project. The result would turn out to be one of the landmarks of the modern horror film and a Hollywood production about Satanism and witchcraft that itself seemed to be accursed.

Rosemary's Baby (1968) begins with one of the most impressive opening shots in cinema history. It starts with an establishing shot of Manhattan, and while the credits roll the camera slowly pans over the rooftops of New York until it glides over the eerie-looking 19th-century gothic spires of the Dakota apartment building (called the Bramford in the movie) to reveal two tiny figures approaching the building's entrance: aspiring actor Guy Woodhouse (John Cassavetes) and his wife Rosemary (Mia Farrow), who are

Newlyweds Rosemary and Guy Woodhouse (Mia Farrow and John Cassavetes) plan their future in *Rosemary's Baby* (Paramount, 1968).

being shown an apartment in the gloomy old place by the building's agent Mr. Nicklas (played by noir icon Elisha Cook, Jr.). The previous tenant, an older woman, has died suddenly and her furniture and personal effects are still in the apartment, from which Rosemary intuits some subtle wrongness, but they decide to rent the place anyway.

One night while doing her laundry in the building's spooky cellar, Rosemary meets another young woman, Terry Gionoffrio (Angela Dorian), a pregnant runaway who is being cared for by an elderly couple at the Bramford, the Castevets. Soon afterward, Terry takes a fatal plunge out of an apartment window and her death is ruled a suicide, and Guy and Rosemary are introduced to Roman Castevet (Sidney Blackmer) and his wife, Minnie (Ruth Gordon), during the police investigation of the incident. In the aftermath the Woodhouses strike up a social relationship with their next-door neighbors, who on the surface appear to be nothing more than a pair of aged, meddlesome eccentrics, but Rosemary slowly becomes aware that her husband seems to have some special relationship with the Castevets to which she is not privy.

Then, out of the blue, Guy gets a lucky break when the actor he is competing with for a coveted part in a play is suddenly stricken blind. Buoyed by this unexpected success, Guy proposes that they have a child, but on the night they have planned to conceive, Minnie arrives with a chocolate mousse dessert that Guy insists Rosemary eat, but she detects an odd aftertaste and feigns finishing it. That night Rosemary, feeling the effects of the drugged mousse, slips into a twilight state in which she cannot tell whether or not she is dreaming. She finds herself transported through a secret passage into the Castevets's apartment, where Guy, Roman, Minnie and a coven of witches are conducting a ceremony to conjure up the Devil. In a hallucinatory sequence, Rosemary perceives having sexual intercourse with a scaly Lucifer, who is made to look like her husband. Because she has not consumed all of the drug, she retains her memory of the event and is convinced that it really happened despite Guy's protestations that it was all just a dream.

When Rosemary becomes pregnant the Castevets get intimately involved in the process, insisting that she go to eminent OB/GYN practitioner Dr. Abraham Sapirstein (Ralph Bellamy), who treats her unusual pregnancy with strange herbal preparations, including a foul-smelling concoction called "tannis root." Rosemary, who is a bit of a *naïf*, nonetheless begins to have suspicions about her husband and the people surrounding her and consults her good friend Hutch (Maurice Evans), an avuncular older man who is a professional writer. Soon afterward, Hutch is the victim of a fatal hit and run, but still manages to deliver a book entitled *All of Them Witches* to her posthumously. The book contains information that suggests that the name Roman Castevet is an anagram for Steven Marcato, the son of an infamous Satan worshipper who once lived at the Bramford, and that tannis root is a fungus called "the Devil's pepper" traditionally used in witchcraft.

Her worst suspicions confirmed, Rosemary now believes that Guy is in league with the Castevets and a coven of witches in a conspiracy to obtain her baby for sacrifice in demonic rituals. She attempts to leave but is apprehended and brought back to the Bramford by Guy and Dr. Sapirstein, where she goes into labor and blacks out from a shot administered by the doctor. When Rosemary awakens she is no longer pregnant and is told that her baby died during delivery, but that night she hears a baby crying in the Castevets's apartment, picks up a knife and admits herself via the passageway into her

Rosemary (Mia Farrow) prepares to confront her diabolical offspring in *Rosemary's Baby* (Paramount, 1968).

neighbor's flat. She finds the coven, including her husband, assembled around a black bassinet cooing their adoration at the infant within. "Satan is his father, not Guy," Roman helpfully explains. "He came up from Hell and begat a son of mortal woman." Peering within, Rosemary looks upon the form of the baby Lucifer (which is not shown to the audience) and is so horrified by the sight of the infant's demonic eyes that she drops the knife. As visiting "Magi" arrive from around the world to adore the satanic child, Rosemary's maternal instincts prevail over her revulsion and she begins to rock the cradle of the newly born antichrist and accept an honored place within the perverse society of witches and warlocks.

Polanski's screenplay is one of the most faithful adaptations of a novel in screen history. Like Daphne du Maurier's *Rebecca* decades earlier, Ira Levin's novel was an enormous commercial success, and movie audiences mandated that the film version should resemble the book as much as possible. There are some points of similarity between *Rebecca* and *Rosemary's Baby* in that they are both modern gothics in which a shy, retiring heroine must square off against a powerful, seemingly supernatural force. The hapless Rosemary is deceived by all of the authority figures surrounding her, yet manages to unerringly perceive the truth and defy them. While the story is told through Rosemary's subjective viewpoint, there is enough ambiguity in the narrative to suggest that the weird goings-on may only be the pre-partum fantasies of an hysterical mother-to-be. Polanski's directorial manipulation of the material is superb as he utilizes New York locations to create a disturbing undertow of urban fear and angst that is one of the hallmarks of noir. The claustrophobic terrors of apartment living are brilliantly exploited as the director also does in *Repulsion* (1965) and *The Tenant* (1976). Note that there is no overt violence and very little gore in this horror smash hit. The horror is psychological, suggested rather than clearly shown. Even the appearance of the demonic baby is withheld from the viewer, yet audiences swore they saw its diabolical image when all that is really shown is a very brief dissolve depicting Rosemary's memory of Lucifer's yellow, cat-like eyes.

A wonderful mixture of newbies and Hollywood veterans in the cast bring this unlikely tale of witchcraft in Manhattan to life and, more importantly, make the fantastic premise entirely plausible. *Rosemary's Baby* was a popular and critical success, garnering a number of Golden Globe and Academy Award nominations. Mia Farrow's quirky yet sensitive portrayal of urban damsel-in-distress Rosemary Woodhouse, who is eventually overwhelmed by the natural and supernatural forces surrounding her, sustains the film, yet she is upstaged by Ruth Gordon's manic portrayal of the garrulous Minnie Castevet, whose prosaic, New York obnoxiousness is a façade for satanic evil. Gordon took both the Golden Globe Award and the Oscar for Best Supporting Actress that year. Veteran thesps Maurice Evans, Ralph Bellamy and Sidney Blackmer provide solid acting support, along with the presence of Elisha Cook, Jr., the distinctive character actor who was a part of film noir since its inception in *Stranger on the Third Floor* (1940) and *The Maltese Falcon* (1941) and countless other roles as a perennial noir loser. A neo-noir sensibility is provided by the presence of John Cassavetes, who had appeared in crime melodramas like Don Siegel's *Crime in the Streets* (1957) and Martin Ritt's *Edge of the City* (1957), in which he played similarly unpleasant, villainous roles.

An exercise in modern gothic like *Rebecca*, the film relocates the haunted castle to the noir urban megaspace of Manhattan in the 20th-century, while recycling such setpieces of the genre as the naïve heroine, the *homme fatal*, the hidden room and the supernatural secret. The narrative of *Rosemary's Baby* unfolds as a mystery story, its fantastic, even ridiculous premise slowly emerging from the midst of banal, everyday reality. Preternatural menace lurking on the mean streets of New York harks back to the Val Lewton horror noirs of the 1940s, particularly *The Seventh Victim* (1944), in which a woman is pursued by a coven of Manhattanite diabolists, as well as later films like *Cult of the Cobra* (1955) and *Jacob's Ladder* (1990).

Interestingly, *Rosemary's Baby* has a reputation as a "cursed" or "hexed" film because of a series of lethal disasters that befell its makers. In April 1969, the film's producer, William Castle, was rushed to the hospital with kidney failure, reportedly crying out, "Rosemary, for God's sake drop that knife," in his toxic delirium. Recuperating from a motorcycle accident at the same hospital was Krzysztof Komeda, the film's composer, who would die from a blood clot in his brain by the end of the month. Castle, who had directed *The Whistler* and its sequels, *The Night Walker* and several other psychological horror melodramas, also departed this world for that big movie studio in the sky soon afterward. Most shockingly, Polanski's pregnant wife, actress Sharon Tate, was brutally murdered in Los Angeles a year after the film's release by hippie cult members of Charles Manson's "family." The director was even questioned by the L.A. police about his possible associations with Satanic cult members while researching the film, but these alleged contacts were shown to be bogus, and the Sharon Tate murders were officially declared a case of life imitating art. Finally, the Dakota was the scene of the murder of ex–Beatle John Lennon, who was gunned down outside the gothic building by crazed gunman Mark David Chapman in 1980.

Back over the pond in Britain, the fledgling studio Amicus Productions was trying to steal some of the horror film market away from Hammer Films with a string of modest color horror features designed to compete with the Hammer product. *Scream and Scream Again* (1970), adapted from the 1966 sci-fi novel *The Disoriented Man* by Peter Saxon (a pseudonym for author W. Howard Baker) featured AIP horror star Vincent Price and Hammer horror mavens Christopher Lee and Peter Cushing in supporting roles. As the film begins, Olympic runner Ken Sparten (Nigel Lambert) is abducted while jogging through the streets of London and awakens to find himself in a strange "hospital" where one of his legs has been unaccountably amputated. The hapless athlete is kept incapacitated while his remaining limbs are excised during the course of the film, leaving him an armless, legless torso like one of the denizens of *Freaks*.

This is but one of several interweaving plotlines that serve as the basis of the film's construction. In a mythical Eastern European Soviet bloc country, a power struggle ensues

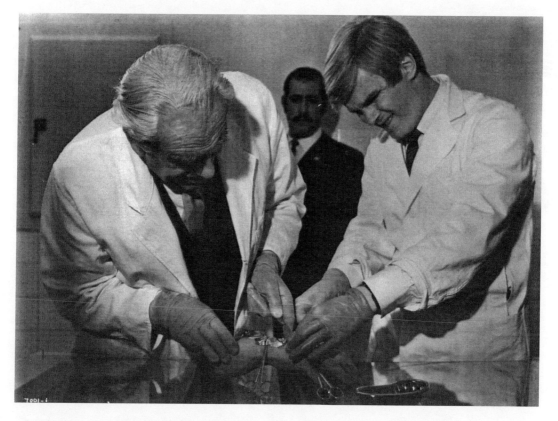

Prof. Kingsmill (Kenneth Benda, left) and Dr. David Sorel (Christopher Matthews) conduct an autopsy as Detective Supt. Bellaver (Alfred Marks) looks on, in *Scream and Scream Again* (Amicus, 1970).

between two high military officials, the brutal Konratz (Marshall Jones) and his rival Major Heinrich Benedek (Cushing), which ends in the murder of Benedek by Konratz, who seems to have superhuman powers. In another strand of the complex plot, London police are baffled by the "vampire murder" of a young girl whose body is found drained of blood. The cantankerous Detective-Superintendent Bellaver (Alfred Marks) is on the case, assisted by forensic physician Dr. David Sorel (Christopher Matthews). In the meantime, Konratz travels to London and meets with enigmatic government official Fremont (Christopher Lee) in Trafalgar Square as the two discuss an obscure espionage plot.

Superintendent Bellaver traces the dead girl to a London rock club and decides to set a "honey trap" for the killer by trying to lure him with a decoy policewoman. Their plan succeeds all too well as the decoy is hit on and kidnapped by groovy-looking hipster Keith (Michael Gothard). The killer drives to a secluded spot where he proceeds to drain the unfortunate decoy of her blood until Bellaver and his bobbies show up. When the police attempt to take the vampire killer into custody, the normal-looking Keith tosses the arresting officers around like tenpins with superhuman strength. He then gets back into his car and a typical cop movie car chase ensues, with Bellaver in hot pursuit, and when the police catch up with the vampire killer the second time they manage to physically subdue him and handcuff him to the bumper of a car, but Keith escapes by severing his hand and leaving it behind in the cuffs. The pursuit continues on foot until Keith runs onto the property of eminent scientist Dr. Browning (Price) and unhesitatingly hurls himself into a vat of acid.

The enigmatic Dr. Browning is allegedly conducting important germ-warfare research for the British government, but when Bellaver and Dr. Matthews try to investigate Browning they are told that the matter is closed and ordered by higher-ups to terminate the investigation. Dr. Matthews, however, has examined Keith's hand in the laboratory and found that its tissues have been strengthened by the addition of foreign substances, and decides to have a look around Browning's estate on his own recognizance. While he is away on his mission, Konratz pays a visit to the police station and kills Detective Bellaver with his bare hands. After snooping around Browning's digs, Matthews finally confronts the scientist in his elaborate laboratory, where Browning reveals the truth: he is plotting to create android doubles, or "composites" of world leaders that will be under his control and has been abducting victims like the Olympic runner to obtain quality material for his artificial humans. "God is dying all over the world," the mad doctor exults. "Man invented him, but Man doesn't need him anymore. Man is God now — as a matter of fact he always was!" As Browning sizes up Matthews as a limb donor, Konratz suddenly shows up at the lab and orders a halt to Browning's research because it has gained too much publicity. When Browning refuses, Konratz attacks the scientist who is revealed to be a composite himself, and the two struggle and fall into a vat of acid together while Matthews escapes.

This oddball little Amicus number has an overly complicated plot devised by scripter Christopher Wishing in which several strands are left dangling and tend to confuse the viewer. For instance, if Browning is responsible for creating the android composites, then who created *him*? While horror movie buffs could appreciate the teaming of '60s superstars Price, Lee and Cushing, the two Hammer luminaries only make brief appearances and their parts seem to have been written into the script merely to provide extraneous roles for the actors. Price delivers his usual hammy performance, but Alfred Marks steals

Espionage agents Konratz (Marshall Jones, left) and Fremont (Christopher Lee) meet in Trafalger Square in *Scream and Scream Again* (Amicus, 1970).

the show with his comically obnoxious portrayal of Inspector Bellaver as a typically unctuous British civil servant. Director Gordon Hessler does a pedestrian job, making no attempt to build dramatic mood in this cut-rate Amicus production.

The film's basic premise is highly derivative of Hammer's *Enemy from Space* (a.k.a. *Quatermass II*, 1957), in which a group of alien blobs land on Earth and try to covertly take over the British government, and the idea of a plot to replace world leaders with androids would later resurface in the American sci-fi thriller *Futureworld* (1976). *Scream and Scream Again* contains a surprising amount of police procedural, and Denis Meikle writes, "Hessler expends much effort on the police investigation, with long takes emphasizing the hustle-bustle of activity in an attempt to capture the pseudo-documentary approach of crime thrillers like Val Guest's *Hell Is a City* (1960) or *Jigsaw* (1962)."[3] The film's extensive scenes of battle between police and a vampiric being with preternatural strength very likely inspired similar scenes in the horror noir telefilm *The Night Stalker* (1972).

The Horror Noir Legacy of the '60s

The mega-success of *Psycho* (1960) moved the horror film away from supernatural motifs and nudged it into the realm of noir psychological terror. Many of the films that followed in this mode were among the finest entries in the history of the genre. George Franju's *Eyes Without a Face* (1960), Michael Powell's *Peeping Tom* (1960), William Wyler's *The Collector* (1965), Peter Bogdanovich's *Targets* (1968) and Roman Polanski's *Rosemary's Baby* (1968) are all examples of first-rate cinema lensed by world-class directors. On a less exalted level are cult faves and guilty pleasures like Seth Holt's *Scream of Fear* (1962), Reginald LeBorg's *Diary of a Madman* (1963), William Castle's *The Night Walker* (1964), Michael Reeves's *The Sorcerers* (1967) and Gordon Hessler's *Scream and Scream Again* (1969). The majority of these films were either made by European directors or shot in Europe, and therefore display a more sophisticated, European cinematic sensibility.

These films moved the horror genre in the direction of the modern gothic, the detective story, the mystery and the police procedural. Many of them seem to emulate the quasi-documentary approach of late-'50s classic noir, and shooting in London locations greatly enhances the urban, realistic feeling of *Peeping Tom, The Collector, The Sorcerers* and *Scream and Scream Again*, while *Eyes Without a Face* and *Rosemary's Baby* use Paris and New York in a similar fashion. All of these films deal with the familiar noir themes of murder, lust, obsession, deception, crime and madness, and with the exception of *Diary of a Madman* and *Rosemary's Baby*, none of them invoked the supernatural. Instead, *Eyes Without a Face, The Sorcerers* and *Scream and Scream Again* substitute the tech-noir horrors of science fiction and the perils of black technology. *Peeping Tom, The Collector* and *Targets*, in particular, were all excursions into the noir recesses of the criminal mind that constituted psychological profiles of highly disturbed homicidal individuals. These fine films are perfect examples of works that stand precisely on the cusp of film noir and the horror film.

10

Horror Noirs of the 1970s and 1980s

Many critics and genre film historians consider the 1970s a "golden age" of the horror film. The decade saw the release of many important, influential and seminal works that are now considered classics of horror, including William Friedkin's *The Exorcist* (1973), Tobe Hooper's *The Texas Chainsaw Massacre* (1974), Richard Donner's *The Omen* (1976), Brian de Palma's *Carrie* (1976), Wes Craven's *The Hills Have Eyes* (1978), John Carpenter's *Halloween* (1978) and Ridley Scott's *Alien* (1979). Genre films began to explore new themes that included demonic possession, psychic phenomena and religious apocalypse. In the wake of the release of George Romero's *Night of the Living Dead* in 1968, horror films had become more violent, daring and explicit in exploring unusual subjects. During the '70s, film noir had followed the trend toward obscurity that had prevailed in the 1960s. Relatively few genre films were made during the early part of the decade, but a neo-noir revival would begin in the mid-'70s with Roman Polanski's *Chinatown* (1974), Dick Richards's *Farewell, My Lovely* (1975), Arthur Penn's *Night Moves* (1975) and Martin Scorsese's *Taxi Driver* (1976).

While the '60s are considered the "turbulent decade," many of the contentious societal issues that had divided America came to a head during the '70s. Under President Richard Nixon the massacre of students at Kent State University in Ohio by national guardsmen in 1970 shocked the nation. Nixon was re-elected in a landslide in 1972 and secured an end to American involvement in the Vietnam War in the following year, but this was looked upon by the public as the first military defeat ever suffered by the United States. A scandal over files pilfered from Democratic national headquarters at the Watergate Hotel in D.C. and a threatened impeachment forced Nixon to resign in 1974, and in the aftermath of the end of the war and Watergate affair, the country seemed to slip into a state of somnolence during the remainder of the decade under the presidencies of Gerald Ford and Jimmy Carter. The American moviegoing public developed a taste for escapist horror and science fiction fare to offset the grim realities confronting the nation during those troubled times.

A Vampire in Las Vegas

By the 1970s elements of film noir began to be deliberately and self-consciously incorporated into the fabric of horror films. The first instance of this trend appeared in the ABC-TV telefilm *The Night Stalker* (1972), produced by Dan Curtis, whose highly successful daytime TV series *Dark Shadows* combined vampires and other supernatural creatures with soap opera. *The Night Stalker* starred Darren McGavin as Carl Kolchak, an irrepressible news reporter for the *Las Vegas Daily News*, who, as the film opens, is ensconced in a cheap motel room creating a tape recording of his narrative of recent events. "This is the story of one of the greatest manhunts in history," he intones as the events of the plot unfold in a typically noir flashback with periodic *Dragnet*-style voice-over monologues setting up or commenting on the action.

As the story proper opens, Kolchak is assigned to cover the murder of a Las Vegas showgirl whose body has been discovered stuffed into a garbage can in an alley right off the Strip. Using his contacts in law enforcement and among the city's shadowy denizens, he learns that the woman's body was entirely drained of blood. Not long afterward, the body of a second young woman is found in the middle of a sand pit, with no footprints of either murderer or victim, as if she was hurled about 30 feet by someone with tremendous strength. When an autopsy reveals that the second victim was also drained of blood, an incredulous Kolchak submits his article on the "vampire killings" to his editor, Tony Vincenzo (Simon Oakland), who refuses to run it out of fear it will create a public panic.

Intrepid newshound Carl Kolchak (Darren McGavin) wards off a Vegas vampire in *Kolchak: The Night Stalker* (ABC-TV, 1972).

The intrepid news reporter also runs afoul of Vegas law enforcement, who also move to put a lid on his story about "some screwball who imagines he's a vampire" simply because, "it's bad for business."

As the bodies continue to pile up, Kolchak stays on the case, getting information from his contacts, including his main squeeze, casino worker Gail Foster (Carol Lynley), detective Bernie Jenks (Ralph Meeker) and chronic gambler and real estate agent Mickey Crawford (played by venerable noir icon Elisha Cook, Jr.). One night as Kolchak drives around listening to the police band on his car radio, he hears of a robbery in progress at the blood bank of a local hospital, and arrives on the scene to find cops and orderlies grappling with a cadaverous individual in a business suit. The reporter watches in amazement as the man hurls orderlies and policemen around with superhuman strength and, impervious to bullets, escapes from the cops in a hail of gunfire. The police get a make on the car he uses to escape, and by tracing the license number find out the identity of the vampire killer, which is revealed at a press conference to be one Janos Skorzeny (Barry Atwater), a 70-year-old Romanian individual who has been sought in connection with a number of homicides on two continents for over 30 years. Oddly, even after witnessing Skorzeny's inhuman feats, the D.A.'s office refuses to treat the case as if they are hunting a real vampire because it would compromise "the image of law enforcement in Vegas," and continue to use "standard police procedures" to bring Skorzeny to justice.

Kolchak, however, suspends his disbelief and assumes that they are up against the real deal and arms himself with a Van Helsing–type medical bag containing a crucifix, a wooden stake, a hammer and other paraphernalia of the vampire hunter's trade. Finally, he gets a tip from Mickey about a broken-down fixer-upper in town that has recently been sold to a mysterious individual. Arriving at the house, Kolchak calls Jenks for backup, but invades the vampire's lair well before the cops arrive to obtain exclusive pictures for his news article. He snoops through the gloomy old place to discover a fridge full of stolen blood packs, a drawer containing wigs, mustaches and other disguises, a coffin and one of the vampire's victims, a woman tied to a bed who is being used as a "human blood bank." Unfortunately, Skorzeny unexpectedly returns and stalks Kolchak through the house until Jenks bursts in, and the detective and the newsman use the crucifix and the risen sun to subdue the vampire. Police backup arrives just as Kolchak is driving a stake through Skorzeny's heart, and in the aftermath, Vincenzo refuses to run Kolchak's exclusive article on the vampire killer, while the D.A.'s office threatens him with a murder rap for dispatching Skorzeny. He is forced to sign a false statement exonerating him of the killing and must leave town immediately, and we are back to Kolchak relating the story of the manhunt to his tape recorder as shown in the beginning of the movie.

The Night Stalker's meld of supernatural vampire chills and realistic police procedural proved to be a hit with audiences, as the telefilm received the highest ratings ever recorded for a made-for-TV movie. Its morbid subject matter is leavened with a good dose of humor, courtesy of star Darren McGavin's breezy portrayal of eccentric newshound Carl Kolchak, and by the film's jaunty, noir-inspired dialogue as penned by veteran horror writer Richard Matheson. The Kolchak character was the creation of novelist Jeff Rice, whose unpublished book *The Kolchak Papers* provided the basis for Matheson's tightly plotted teleplay. Director John Llewellyn Moxey keeps the chills and the chuckles flowing along smoothly, crafting a minor masterwork of low-budget film-making which offers a worm's-eye, documentarian view of the noir underbelly of Vegas. McGavin's Kolchak is an engaging fellow who emerges as a crusading, journalistic everyman whose signature seersucker suit and porkpie straw hat are indicators of his proletarian milieu. Barry Atwater's Janos Skorzeny is a memorable screen vampire who has no lines of dialogue yet manages to project an intense sense of menace via facial expression. The photogenic Carol Lynley provides some romantic interest, but her character takes no active part in the plot and her performance limited to a few minor dialogue scenes.

Classic film noir is consciously evoked both by *The Night Stalker*'s supporting cast and by its setting and themes. Ralph Meeker, who played Detective Jenks, had starred as Mickey Spillane's extra-hard boiled private eye Mike Hammer in Robert Aldrich's atomic noir *Kiss Me Deadly* (1955), one of the best of the late period noirs. Meeker is a long way from his Hammer persona here, though, as little of the actor's intensity shines through. And, of course, the presence of the venerable Elisha Cook, Jr. as Mickey the gambler is also meant to signify the universe of noir. Cook, whose forté was playing soft-boiled losers in many classic noirs, has an amusing exchange with McGavin at a gaming table. "Has the idea of winning ever occurred to you?" McGavin queries, to which Cook replies, incredulously, "Winning?" The film's Las Vegas setting recalls the casino backdrops in *The Shanghai Gesture* (1941), *Gilda* (1946) and *Johnny O'Clock* (1947), among others. Newspaper reporters acting as amateur sleuths are archetypal noir characters that go back to *Stranger on the Third Floor* (1940), and crusading, big-city journalists speaking truth to power are another noir staple. Kolchak spends a fair amount of screen time driving around the city at night while delivering a droll voice-over narration in typically noir fashion. Matheson's teleplay sparkles with sophisticated noir-esque dialogue: "Don't sit there like a cheap gonef guzzling my beer," Kolchak chides Jenks at one point, and in another scene Kolchak, drink in hand, wryly observes, "I really ought to light a candle to Ben Hecht." The film also explores the deeper noir theme of corruption in high places as the movie's Vegas bigwigs scramble to keep the truth about the vampiric mass-murders from the public's knowledge so as not to affect the city's casino business or tarnish the image of local law enforcement.

The film proved to be so successful that it inspired a 1973 ABC-TV sequel entitled *The Night Strangler*, in which Kolchak and his editor, Vincenzo (Simon Oakland) travel to Seattle where they encounter a serial strangler who returns to plague the city after a hundred-year hiatus, and much of the film was shot in the eerie confines of Seattle's Underground City. Producer Dan Curtis directed from a second Richard Matheson script and the interesting cast included Margaret Hamilton, Wally Cox and John Carradine. A 1974–1975 television series produced by Universal, *Kolchak: The Night Stalker* followed, with McGavin and Simon Oakland reprising their original roles as Kolchak and Vincenzo. The series soon devolved into a "monster-of-the-week" format, in which a different creature was featured in each episode. Chris Carter has cited the Kolchak series as an inspiration for his own highly successful show *The X-Files*, where McGavin appeared in several episodes as Arthur Dales, the "father of the X-Files."

Another nosy news reporter went digging for the truth about a weird murder mystery in director Brian De Palma's homage to Alfred Hitchcock, *Sisters* (1973). The movie begins with a segment of a reality TV show called *Peeping Tom* where contestant Danielle (Margot Kidder) must guess the responses of Philip Woode (Lisle Wilson) to a voyeuristic situation. After the show, the French-Canadian Danielle and African American Philip hit it off, and the couple repair to Danielle's apartment in New York City's borough of Staten Island for a night of hot sex. Philip awakens the following morning to overhear an argument between Danielle and her twin sister, Dominique, going on in an adjacent room. Hearing that it is the sister's birthday, Philip steps out to buy a birthday cake as a peace offering for the ladies and has it inscribed with both their names. When he returns to the apartment, however, he is brutally attacked by Dominique (or is it Danielle?) with a knife and killed. At this point a man named Emile (William Finley), who is supposedly Dominique's husband, bursts into the room and begins helping Dominique conceal all traces of the crime, hiding Philip's body inside a folding sofa-bed.

The murder happens to be witnessed by Grace Collier (Jennifer Salt), a news reporter for a local paper, from her apartment across the street. She immediately calls the police, and Detective Spinelli is dispatched to the scene, but by the time they arrive Danielle and Emile have hidden all the evidence. The one clue, the birthday cake, is accidentally destroyed, and while Grace notes the bakery's address on the box, the police feel that they have nothing to investigate. Grace's reporter's instinct has been aroused, however, and she hires private investigator Joseph Larch (Charles Durning) to assist her in gathering information for what she thinks might be an important story. Illegally breaking into Danielle's apartment, Larch finds a medical file on Danielle that indicates she was formerly a Siamese twin and that her sister, Dominique, is currently living at a nearby mental institution.

As the plot gets curioser and curiouser, Grace travels to the institute where the operation took place and begins snooping around, but she is apprehended by Emile, who is head doctor at the institute, and is committed to the institution against her will. She is kept heavily sedated with hypnotic drugs that enable Emile to brainwash her into believing that Woode's killing never took place and that the entire affair was just a misunderstanding. "There was no body because there was no murder," Emile insists. In a hallucinatory dream sequence brought on by the effect of the drugs, Grace apprehends the truth: that the evil twin Dominique died during the separation operation and Danielle is keeping her sister's personality "alive" psychologically out of guilt. Whenever a man tries to make love to Danielle, Dominique emerges to create mayhem, as was the case with Philip Woode. Then, as Grace looks on helplessly, Emile attempts to have sex with Danielle, at which point Dominique comes forth and grabs a scalpel to administer the unkindest cut of all to Emile's manhood. In the aftermath of these weird events Grace is rescued from the asylum but suffers a mental breakdown as a result of her experiences. When questioned about the whereabouts of Philip's body by the police, she succumbs to Emile's post–hypnotic suggestion, mindlessly repeating the phrase, "There was no body because there was no murder."

De Palma's clever homage to the Hitchcock thriller, written by the director and co-scripter Louisa Rose, recycles plot elements from *Rear Window* and *Psycho* with wit and charm. The hilly, urban waterfront landscape of Staten Island is even used as a stand-in for the similar-looking San Francisco setting of *Vertigo*. Hitchcock's erstwhile composer Bernard Herrmann devised an eerie, brooding score reminiscent of his work on *Vertigo* and *Psycho* that is one of the best of his later works. Unfortunately, De Palma attempts to "out–Hitch" the master by utilizing '70s-era nudity, explicit blood and gore and split screens, with mixed results. Like *Psycho*, *Sisters* shifts viewpoints between a number of different players as the film's plot advances, a technique that serves to emotionally distance the characters from the audience. A cast of near-unknowns turn in solid performances in which Jennifer Salt's portrayal of the aggressive newswoman who suffers a mental breakdown as a result of her ordeal stands out, and recalls Vera Miles's role as Henry Fonda's shattered wife in Hitchcock's tale of crime and mistaken identity, *The Wrong Man* (1957).

In spite of its derivative nature, *Sisters* is an effective thriller in its own right that contains many horror and noir motifs. Foremost is the theme of the evil twin, which is associated with the doppelganger and with possession by spirits of the dead. As in *Cat People* or *Psycho*, the homicidal alternate personality manifests itself during sexual activity as a jealous rage. The crusading journalist striving to uncover an unpleasant truth being covered up by the power structure is another archetypal noir character that inhabits classic noirs from *Stranger on the Third Floor* (1940) to *Beyond a Reasonable Doubt* (1956). Amateur sleuths who investigate murders that the police won't bother with are another noir staple familiar from works as diverse as *Phantom Lady* (1944) and *Black Angel* (1946) to *The Leopard Man* (1943) and *Psycho* (1960) Charles Durning's role as P.I. Joseph Larch, who received his detective training at the "Brooklyn School of Modern Investigation," offers a comic takeoff on the clichéd private investigator character. The horrific situation of an individual being consigned to and imprisoned in a mental hospital against their will as part of a criminal scheme is another sub-plot that appears in a number of classic noirs and neo-noirs, including *Murder, My Sweet* (1944), *Shock* (1946), *The Return of the Whistler* (1948) and *Shock Corridor* (1963).

Exorcise This

William Peter Blatty's 1971 supernatural thriller *The Exorcist* was a runaway bestseller whose enormous popularity demanded a lavish screen treatment. Accordingly, Blatty became producer and screenwriter on the film version, and William Friedkin, the Oscar-winning director of the fast-paced neo-noir *The French Connection* (1971), was assigned to direct. The resulting film version of *The Exorcist* (1973) would become a major cultural event and a significant milestone in the history of the horror film.

The plot revolves around Regan MacNeil (Linda Blair), the blandly normal adolescent daughter of Chris MacNeil (Ellen Burstyn), a famous movie star who has taken up temporary residence in a town house in Washington, D.C., while shooting a film in the area. For no apparent reason, Regan becomes possessed by a demon from ancient Iraq, causing an outbreak of supernatural happenings at the MacNeil household. Heavy pieces of furniture move around by themselves while the girl's body is subjected to a psychic assault by the invading entity. The possessed girl also acquires superhuman abilities such as telepathy, a knowledge of foreign languages, and preternatural strength. The story unfolds as a supernatural mystery as the uncanny nature of her affliction is slowly revealed through a seemingly endless battery of physical and psychological tests until all the prognoses of modern medical science are exhausted and Chris turns in desperation to the Catholic Church for help.

As Regan descends into the horrors of full-blown possession her physical appearance becomes grotesquely altered and she continually slips in and out of consciousness while being kept heavily sedated by her doctors. Then Chris returns home one night to find Regan alone in the house and learns from her assistant, Sharon Spencer (Kitty Winn), who soon arrives from a trip to the pharmacy, that she left Regan with Chris's director, Burke Dennings (Jack MacGowran), who happened to drop by for a visit. Dennings, an irascible, foul-mouthed alcoholic who had previously insulted Chris's Teutonic servant Karl (Rudolph Schundler) in a drunken tirade at a house party, is notoriously irresponsible and is nowhere to be found. Chris finds the window in Regan's room wide open and soon learns that Burke has been found dead at the bottom of a steep flight of stairs nearby (dubbed the "Hitchcock Steps" for their resemblance to a similar stairway in *The Parradine Case*) in a case of accidental death.

The emphasis of the story shifts to that of the title character, Father Damien Karras (Jason Miller), a Jesuit priest and psychologist at a nearby Catholic university. Karras, a rugged former amateur boxer, is bitterly conflicted and losing his faith after the recent death of his impoverished Greek mother. One day while jogging around the university's track he is approached by D.C. homicide detective William Kinderman (Lee J. Cobb) about the death of Burke Dennings, which the detective suspects is tied to a recent outbreak of desecrations occurring at Karras's church. He tells Karras that Denning's corpse was found with its head turned completely around and that this injury was unlikely to have been caused by the fall. Kinderman speculates that only a very powerful man could have done this, and that Dennings may have been hurled out of one of the windows of the MacNeil home by the same individual. Karras is questioned as to whether there may be a disturbed priest on the campus who could be responsible for what may be a ritual witchcraft killing and the desecrations, but Karras assures Kinderman that this is not the case. The detective and the priest strike up an instant friendship, and Kinderman turns out to be a film buff who compares Karras to John Garfield in the classic film noir *Body and Soul* (1947).

Next, Kinderman pays a visit to Chris and questions her at length, learning that Regan was alone in the house with Dennings on the night of the director's death. Considering the sedated adolescent unlikely to have accomplished the feat, his detective's instinct is nonetheless aroused. Chris, however, is certain that her demon-possessed offspring is responsible, and is crushed by the thought that her daughter may be charged with Murder One. In desperation, she approaches Karras and pleads for his help as both a psychologist and a priest. After examining Regan and interviewing the personality which has invaded her and witnessing firsthand the anomalous phenomena surrounding her, Karras is convinced that her case meets the criteria for exorcism and approaches his superiors at the diocese for permission to conduct the ritual. The Church consents, but insists that the ceremony be conducted by the aged Father Lancaster Merrin (Max Von Sydow), a veteran Jesuit with field experience in exorcism from his missionary work, with Karras assisting.

During the exorcism the two priests go mano a mano with the demon-possessed child in Regan's bedroom as all hell breaks loose in a whirlwind of levitation, telepathy, psychokinesis, potty-mouth obscenities and flying vomit. Father Merrin drops dead from a heart attack induced by the strain, and while Karras contends with the demon alone, Kinderman shows up at the door. As the exorcism reaches its climactic point, Karras himself becomes possessed and in a final act of will sacrifices himself by throwing himself through the same window through which Denning had transited, and dies at the bottom of the Hitchcock Steps. Chris and Kinderman burst into the room to find Regan restored to herself once more, a broken window and Karras's corpse outside, as Kinderman ponders the enigmatic events. The original theatrical version of the film ends with Karras's friend, Father Dyer (played by real-life Jesuit Fr. William O'Malley) saying goodbye to a cured Regan as she and Chris leave D.C. for L.A., but a "director's cut" re-release restores the novel's original ending in which Kinderman arrives to pay his respects and winds up inviting Dyer to the movies, quoting Bogart's line to Claude Rains at the end of *Casablanca* (1942): "Louie, I think this is the beginning of a beautiful friendship."

One of the landmarks in the history of the horror movie, *The Exorcist* was a runaway mega-hit that reportedly grossed $120 million at the box-office against Warner Bros.'s production costs of about $12 mil despite its R-rating and unusual subject matter. The film was nominated for Academy Awards for best picture, director, leading actress, and supporting actor and actress, but only won for best adapted screenplay and sound. Blatty's screenplay refined the main thrust of the plot while eliminating many of the extraneous subplots that would have slowed down the action of the film, while Friedkin's direction utilizes some of the neo-noir realism that had enlivened *The French Connection*. Bravura performances by principals Ellen Burstyn, Jason Miller, Max Von Sydow and Linda Blair emphasize the human dimensions of the drama against which the fantastic events are set and makes them believable.

The noir aspects of the film revolve around Kinderman's homicide investigation, which is ultimately a side show for all the supernatural activity, human drama and theological ramblings of the plot. The casting of Lee J. Cobb, a veteran of the classic films noir like *Call Northside 777* (1947), *Johnny O'Clock* (1947), *The Dark Past* (1949) and *Party Girl* (1958), among others, (not to mention the horror noir *Gorilla at Large*), deliberately invokes the universe of noir. The Kinderman character had a much larger role in Blatty's novel and first draft screenplay. Originally, the film contained noiresque scenes in which Kinderman visits the District's morgue to examine Dennings's corpse, and one in which he investigates Karl's daughter, who is a heroin addict, in a red herring subplot which was entirely edited out of the finished film. Although Kinderman's homicide investigation is an essential part of the action, Friedkin and Blatty correctly reasoned that movie audiences would already know that Regan was Dennings's killer, thereby voiding any mystery or suspense over the killing, so these were written out. As originally conceived, Kinderman was an ethnic Jewish detective fond of spouting Yiddish phrases, but his ethnicity was toned down to avoid drawing similarities with TV's Italian-American homicide cop *Columbo*. The Kinderman character would return to the screen, played by George C. Scott, in Blatty's sequel, *Exorcist III: Legion* (1990).

ESP and Murder

The "detective vs. the supernatural" subplot of *The Exorcist* may have inspired *Psychic Killer* (1975), a low-budget horror/mystery thriller about a paranormal murderer. Jim Hutton stars as Arnold Masters, a psychotic mama's boy who is serving time for the murder of a doctor who refused to operate on his mother, who has died of neglect while Arnold has been imprisoned. As the film opens, Arnold, who is confined to the prison's hospital, freaks out over his mother's death and has to be restrained in a scene that dimly recalls Jimmy Cagney's similar jailhouse outburst in *White Heat* (1949). While the other inmates consider Arnold a nut job, he is befriended by an enigmatic West Indian inmate named Emilio (Stack Pierce), who claims to have the power to project his will outside of his body using a magical amulet. He tells Arnold that he is preparing to take revenge on the pimp who turned his daughter to prostitution, and the next day he informs Arnold that he has taken his vengeance. "I carved my name on his chest," he says before scaling the prison fence and jumping to his death. Afterward, Arnold finds an item in the newspaper that confirms Emilio's account of the pimp's death, and is surprised when the West Indian leaves Arnold the magic amulet that enables the out-of-body experiences.

When Arnold is unexpectedly sprung from the joint when another perp confesses to the murder for which he was imprisoned, he returns to his mama's house and embarks on a campaign of revenge against those he holds responsible for letting his mother die. Using the power of the amulet, he launches a psychic attack on Dr. Paul Taylor (Whit Bissell), whom he strangles to death via telekinesis. Next up are perverse nurse Martha Burnson (Mary Charlotte Wilcox), who is scalded to death by boiling water in her shower stall and crooked attorney H.B. Sanders (Joseph Della Sorte), crushed by a cornerstone at a construction site. All of these seemingly accidental deaths assume a new significance when the arresting officer in the Arnold Masters case is killed in a freak car crash and homicide detective Lt. Jeff Morgan (Paul Burke) discovers that all of the deceased have some connection to Arnold.

An aggressive investigator, Morgan finds that the ex-con has solid alibis for the times of death, but his instincts tell him that Arnold is somehow responsible and he orders a stakeout of Arnold's residence from an adjacent house. The detective clearly observes Arnold in a catatonic trance inside his home while the murders are being committed, including the brutal killing of neighborhood butcher Lemonowski (played by film noir bad boy Neville Brand) who is found hanging in his meat locker like a butchered side of beef. Baffled by these strange events, Lt. Morgan consults Dr. Gubner (Nehemiah Persoff), a parapsychologist at a local university, where he learns that Arnold may be able to travel outside his body and use psychokinesis to commit his crimes. Realizing that no jury will ever convict Arnold of the murders on the basis of paranormal evidence, Morgan devises a plan. The next time Arnold is observed going into one of his trances, Morgan calls the coroner's office and has Arnold declared legally dead, as his body is in a zombified state indistinguishable from death. Acting as judge, jury and executioner, the detective sends Arnold's inert body to a crematorium, where the psychic killer is incinerated before he can free himself.

Psychic Killer is a minor but earnest low-budget thriller crafted by director Raymond Danton, who directs the actors well but exhibits little in the way of visual flair. Co-written by Danton, Greydon Clark and Mike Angel, the screenplay combines police procedural with supernatural mystery in a manner similar to *The Night Stalker* and *The Exorcist*. The character of hard-nosed homicide cop Lt. Morgan, as realized in the aggressive performance of Paul Burke, drives the film, while Jim Hutton's demented mama's boy Arnold Masters references Norman Bates in *Psycho*. Note that the intrepid detective Morgan, unlike other horror noir sleuths, has no problem following the serial killer's supernatural clues to a logical conclusion and taking action instead of being paralyzed by unbelief. The hard-charging homicide detective is a stereotypical film noir figure, and classic noir is also invoked by the casting of Neville Brand, whose schizoid villainy had enlivened *D.O.A* (1950), *Kiss Tomorrow Goodbye* (1950) and *Kansas City Confidential* (1952) and a number of other classic noirs, in a brief but memorable role as the butcher, Lemonowski. The film deals with the intriguing theme of crime and ESP, a subject that has been treated in a number of interesting melodramas from *Shadow of a Doubt* (1943) to *Manhunter* (1986).

Murder and psychic phenomena were combined once more in the A-list production of *Eyes of Laura Mars* (1978), a stylish horror noir thriller starring Oscar-winner Faye Dunaway as the titular character, a chic Manhattan fashion photographer whose violent and sexually explicit imagery has made her a successful but controversial figure. As the film begins, Laura has a vivid nightmare of the murder of her colleague, editor Doris

Michelle (Lisa Taylor, left) and Lulu (Darlene Fleugel) model a homicide-chic layout in *Eyes of Laura Mars* **(Columbia, 1978).**

Spenser (Meg Mundy), in her Manhattan apartment. That night, Laura attends the gala opening of a new exhibit of her photographs at a gallery-cum-discotheque where her arty photo spreads depicting sex and murder draw both admiration and revulsion. One of Laura's models explains the thrust of the artist's work thus: "Okay America, okay world, you are violent, you are pushing all this murder on us ... so we'll use murder to sell deodorant so that you'll just get bored with murder."

Unfortunately, murder rears its ugly head at the party as homicide detectives arrive to announce the murder of Doris Spenser. Laura is quizzed by NYPD gumshoe John Neville (Tommy Lee Jones), who seems to take a professional interest in her work. When she learns of the similarities between her dream and Doris's death, Laura is horrified, but the visions of murder keep coming. While conducting a shoot at Manhattan's busy Columbus Circle, she is overwhelmed by psychically witnessing the killing of another associate, Elaine Cassell (Rose Gregorio), on the stairs of a nearby apartment building. Rushing to the murder scene she breathlessly tells the police that she is a witness to the crime, but admits that she was not actually present when the murder took place. "What'd you see it with, a telescope?" scoffs one of the cops, and Laura is unable to provide a description of the perpetrator because she sees the killings strictly from the murderer's point of view.

Under further questioning by Neville, another enigma crops up. The detective shows her a series of classified police photos of unsolved murder scenes that have never been published side by side with her photographs and points out that the layouts of the bodies

Homicide detective John Neville (Tommy Lee Jones, left center) pursues suspect Tommy Ludlow (Brad Dourif) down the mean streets of New York in *Eyes of Laura Mars* (Columbia, 1978).

and objects are practically identical to those in her pictures. Unable to rationally explain the similarities, Laura confides that she "began to see images of murder and violence" and incorporated these into her work. The body count of her colleagues continues to mount up, however, as the "Eyes Killer," (so-called because the victim's eyes are stabbed out), continues on a murderous rampage, each killing preceded by one of Laura's pre-cognitive visions. Her effete agent, Donald Phelps (Rene Auberjonois), gets it in an elevator, while lesbo airhead models Lulu (Darlanne Fluegel) and Michelle (Lisa Taylor) are dispatched inside their apartment. Suspicions fall on Laura's alcoholic ex-husband Michael Reisler (Raul Julia) and her chauffeur/gofer Tommy Ludlow (Brad Dourif), an ex-con with a rap sheet for armed robbery and assault with a deadly weapon. Or is the killer the character one would least suspect?

Irwin Kershner directs with a fine feeling for the urban landscape of New York that recalls the urban grit of 1970s-period neo-noirs like *The French Connection* (1971) and *Taxi Driver* (1976). The film smoothly melds realistic police procedural and crime melodrama with the fantastic world of ESP, although the intriguing premise of Laura's second sight is not explored in any depth. The surreal demimonde of the period's Studio 54-era decadent glitterati provides a grotesque backdrop of sexuality and violence that enlivens the mystery and horror while scoring points about the issue of violence being used "to sell deodorant," in our society. Written by cult director John Carpenter, who would go on to lens horror classics like *Halloween* (1978) and *The Thing* (1982), the screenplay was heavily revised by David Goodman and producer Jon Peters, and probably not for the better. *Eyes of Laura Mars* begins with a fascinating notion of precognitive art imitating life imitating art, but fails to sustain much in the way of suspense.

One of the film's primary weaknesses is in the performances of its two principal actors. Faye Dunaway, who had won the Oscar for her role in *Network* (1976) two years earlier, has little to do except look glamorous and bug out her eyes and flare her nostrils during her psychic interludes, while nascent star Tommy Lee Jones seems oddly miscast as an NYPD homicide cop. The film's supporting characters, however, are straight out of classic film noir, including the foppish dragster Donald Phelps, the hedonistic lesbian models Lulu and Michelle, failed alcoholic writer Michael Reisler (as played by a doe-eyed Raul Julia) and the brooding ex-con Tommy Phelps, (portrayed by the ever-sinister Brad Dourif).

1980s Horror Noir

The decade of the 1980s was one of general decline of the horror film. In the wake of John Capenter's enormously successful *Halloween* (1978), the genre became dominated by seemingly endless sequels and imitations. *Halloween* would eventually inspire seven sequels and was followed by the highly derivative *Friday the 13th* (1980) with ten sequelae and *Nightmare on Elm Street* (1984) with seven. These formulaic retreads, aimed at a juvenile market, took the genre in a decidedly lowbrow direction, although offbeat and unusual horror films continued to be made from time to time. Noir, on the other hand, was going through a period of revival as renewed popularity and interest as a deeper regard for the classic films emerged and neo-noir film-making forged ahead with remakes of *The Postman Always Rings Twice* (1981), *Out of the Past* (as *Against All Odds*, 1984) and *D.O.A.* (1989) and updated revampings of noir themes in genre fare such as Lawrence Kasdan's *Body Heat* (1981), Joel Coen's *Blood Simple* (1984), Richard Tuggle's *Tightrope* (1984), Richard Marquand's *Jagged Edge* (1985) and Walter Hill's *Johnny Handsome* (1989). Another significant trend was the development of the tech-noir subgenre that combined elements of noir with science fiction in popular and acclaimed techno-thrillers like *Escape from New York* (1981), *Blade Runner* (1982) and *The Terminator* (1984).

Urban blight and societal concerns over soaring crime rates in America's major cities would help drive the popularity of neo-noir, tech-noir and horror noir during this period. By the early 1980s wide swaths of American cities like New York had been turned into toxic slums, danger zones where violence and drug addiction thrived. The advent of crack cocaine, a potent new form of the drug that was thought to be more addictive and cause more violent behavior in addicts, was blamed for the soaring crime rates and urban disintegration, and these concerns in turn were reflected in popular culture.

Urban Predators

A case in point was writer/director Michael Wadleigh's *Wolfen* (1981), a modern urban update of the werewolf legend. As the film opens, yuppie billionaire Christopher

Vanderveer (Max M. Brown), along with his wife and bodyguard, are brutally killed in Battery Park on the southern tip of Manhattan Island in the early hours of the morning after a groundbreaking ceremony for an urban renewal project in the South Bronx. Quirky homicide detective Dewey Wilson (Albert Finney) is assigned to the case, along with equally loopy medical examiner Whittington (Gregory Hines), but the cops are baffled by the killings, which involve dismemberment and cannibalism. Wilson's superiors in the department, along with a hi-tech security firm hired to protect Vanderveer, suspect a Weathermen-type violent political group is responsible for the murders, but Whittington's forensic work soon turns up contrary evidence, including the unusual nature of the wounds and animal hairs found on the victims. The mystery deepens when identical wounds and hairs are found on a homeless junkie murdered in the slums of the South Bronx, in the same area that Vanderveer had conducted the groundbreaking ceremony for the development project.

Teamed with savvy police psychologist Rebecca Neff (Diane Venora), Wilson pursues these elusive clues to a ruined church at the project site. When the hairs are identified as those of a wolf, Wilson and Whittington decide to stake out the area, and during a late-night vigil Whittington is killed by an unseen creature. Fluid moving camera work combined with a solarization process that renders the images in glowing false colors simulates

High steel: Native American construction worker Eddie Holt (Edward James Olmos, right) ascends the Manhattan Bridge in *Wolfen* (Orion, Warner Bros., 1981).

the creature's point of view seen through infrared night vision. Thinking that there may be some connection to Native American political activist groups, Wilson seeks information from one of his contacts, ex-con Indian Eddie Holt (Edward James Olmos) and meets with the construction worker on his vertiginous eyrie on the "high steel" atop the Manhattan Bridge. Eddie tells him about Native "shapeshifters" who are able to change into various animals through magical means, adding, "I can shift with the best of them," but on a subsequent occasion Wilson watches Eddie participate in a ritual wherein he runs around naked and howls at the moon but does not transform into a wolf. "It's all in the head," Eddie tells Wilson in lieu of becoming a werewolf.

Then Wilson's police superiors produce a wolfskin found at the lair of a political anarchist group and declare the case closed, but Wilson knows better as the wolf creatures begin to stalk him and Rebecca. Desperate for answers, he approaches Eddie and his Native American elders and is told, "It isn't wolves, it's Wolfen," an ancient tribe of highly intelligent super-wolves who have been forced to leave their vanishing wilderness haunts and hunt human prey in the cities. "It is all a hunting ground," they explain, noting that the Wolfen killed Vanderveer in order to prevent the urban renewal of their territory. Eddie is dubious about Wilson's chances of going up against the pack and tells him, "You don't have the eyes of the hunter, you have the eyes of the dead." As the Wolfen close in on Wilson and Rebecca, the detective must find a way to communicate with the creatures in order to stay alive.

Made during a revival of werewolf-themed horror fare in 1981 that also included *An American Werewolf in London* and *The Howling*, *Wolfen* takes a much more subtle tack in its combination of horror and crime thriller motifs. Director Wadleigh, best known for his rockumentary *Woodstock* (1970), uses vivid NYC locations from the dizzying top of the Manhattan Bridge to the burned-out no-man's land of the Bronx. The grisly scenes that take place at the city morgue and medical examiner's office have a particularly chilling verisimilitude. Taking a cue from *Halloween*, Wadleigh makes highly effective use of the SteadiCam hand-held camera device, along with false-color thermography techniques, to simulate the creature's "wolf-eye view" of the proceedings. Based on horror writer Whitley Strieber's 1978 debut novel about mutant wolves, *The Wolfen*, screenwriters Wadleigh, David Eyre and Eric Roth (uncredited) inserted an extraneous subplot involving Native American mysticism and shapeshifting that deepens the mystery surrounding the strange events but ultimately proves to be a red herring. As a horror film, *Wolfen*'s biggest flaw is that the wolf-creatures, when finally revealed to the audience, are merely a pack of trained wolves that are not particularly fear-inspiring.

The film's most horrific image, however, is that of the ruined Bronx church standing in the middle of a field of rubble amid the ghostly shells of abandoned apartment buildings. Looking like the bombed-out moonscape of Dresden or Nuremburg after World War II, this very real image of fallen faith and urban desolation is ultimately more terrifying than any Hollywood monster. This imagery expresses real-world concerns about 1980s-era urban angst typified by films like *Fort Apache: The Bronx*, made in the same year (1981). *Wolfen*'s horror noir city of night is a haunted realm in which the forces of law and order battle against rampaging predators. Unfortunately, the film's emphasis on politically correct ecological concerns and Native American mysticism tend to undermine this disturbing concept. Star Albert Finney seems oddly out of place as a long-haired Brit homicide detective working on the New York police force, while female co-star Venora shows some big city grit and would later be cast opposite De Niro and Pacino in Michael Mann's crime thriller *Heat* (1995). Actor/dancer Gregory Hines provides comic relief and quirky noir characterization in his screen debut as the souled-out coroner Whittington. All in all, *Wolfen* is a prime example of horror noir, its werewolf theme melding smoothly with mystery and police procedural motifs in a haunting urban setting that recalls the stylish thrillers produced by Val Lewton in the '40s.

Writer/director Paul Schrader, best known to film noir aficionados as the screenwriter of Martin Scorsese's neo-noir *Taxi Driver* (1976) and his seminal 1972 essay "Notes on Film Noir," tackled a remake of the Val Lewton/Jacques Tourneur classic in the remake of *Cat People* (1982). Schrader and scripter Alan Ormsby relocate the action to 1980s New Orleans, as Irina Gallier (Natassja Kinski) reunites with her brother, Paul (Malcolm McDowell), after the siblings have been separated from birth and reared by different sets of foster parents. Paul lives in a big spooky old house with maternalistic Cajun servant and enabler Female (pronounced "fe-MALL-ee") (Ruby Dee), and as soon as Irina moves in it becomes obvious that Paul has affections for his sister that are anything but brotherly. Soon afterward, a prostitute in a seedy hotel/brothel is mauled by a black panther, and zoo curator Oliver Yates (John Heard) and his assistant Alice Perrin (Annette O'Toole) are called in to trap the animal, which they capture and cage at the New Orleans zoo. At the same time, Paul mysteriously disappears and Irina is unaccountably drawn to the panther's cage.

While working late one night Oliver spies Irina sketching the cat in the semi-darkness long after the zoo has closed. Confronting her, he becomes fascinated with the young woman and as romantic sparks fly he agrees to get her a job at the zoo's gift shop. A few days later the newly caged panther shows a streak of viciousness by mauling a zoo attendant to death and the big cat manages to escape before Oliver can put it down. Then Paul mysteriously reappears to reveal the truth to Irina: they are both were-panther shapeshifters who transform into panthers after making love to a normal human and cannot change back until they kill someone. Paul suggests to Irina that they enter into an incestuous liaison because their were-cat magic dictates that this is the only way that two cat people can have sex without metamorphosing. Irina, who is still a virgin, is appalled by his proposition and flees out into the street to flag a passing cop car. While snooping around Paul's house, the police find a grisly panther's den of cages and human remains hidden in the basement. Female is arrested but Paul escapes and Irina flees to Oliver's house for succor.

While Irina prepares to surrender her virginity to Oliver, the jealous Paul stalks his rival in feline form, but Oliver is prepared and shoots the were-cat to death. The couple is free to consummate their union, and after making love to Irina she changes into the panther but spares Oliver's life and runs out into the street. Police track the cat to a bridge, where it escapes by jumping in the water and swimming away. Oliver, however, tracks the panther down and finds Irina transformed into human form once more after committing another murder. The unusual situation is finally resolved when Oliver ties her to a bed as the two copulate once more in order to let her "be with her own," and the film ends with Irina, in her cat form, installed in a cage at the zoo and being cared for by a doting Oliver.

Joe Creigh (Ed Begley, Jr.) and Irena Gallier (Natassja Kinski) stray too close to the panther's cage in Paul Schrader's remake of *Cat People* (Universal, 1982).

Schrader's remake of the '40s horror noir classic dispenses with all the *presque vu* subtlety of the original in favor of graphically depicted sex and violence. While entire scenes (such as the famous swimming pool sequence) are duplicated in Alan Ormsby's script in a homage to the original, Schrader fails to create much in the way of horrific mood or dark atmosphere. The uniquely noir aspects of the wicked voodoo city of New Orleans are not exploited, as they would be just a few years later in Alan Parker's *Angel Heart* (1987); in fact, Schrader's Big Easy is treated in a picturesque, travelogue fashion that fails to horrify. Explicit gore effects are substituted for the unseen terrors of the night and the gratuitous nudity, both male and female, seems merely exploitative and contributes little to the film's overall effect. Principals McDowell, Kinski and Heard are all one-dimensional characters who fail to engage the audience's interest or sympathy. Kinski is particularly lackluster in her portrayal of the cat woman that is devoid of any mystery or allure. The kinky brother/sister incest subplot injects a note of noir that is not sufficiently developed. Giorgio Moroder's quirky score, which included a song by British rocker David Bowie, won a Golden Globe Award.

Whitley Strieber, whose debut novel had brought the werewolf legend into a contemporary New York milieu in 1981's *Wolfen*, inspired a similar treatment of the vampire theme in his novel *The Hunger*, as lensed by director Tony Scott in 1983. Euro glam-star

Catherine Deneuve portrays urban vampire Miriam Blaylock, a wealthy Manhattan socialite who lives in a fortress-like gothic mansion with her vampire husband, John (David Bowie). Note that these are not the traditional type of Transylvanian bloodsucker, but rather embody vampirism as a modernistic science-fiction concept. While there are no coffins filled with earth, crucifixes, garlic, destruction by sunlight or extruding canines in evidence, Strieber's vampiric mutants drink blood that they access by means of a blade to the victim's throat, are extremely long-lived and possess hypnotic and telepathic powers of mind.

The film opens with a creepy sequence in which Miriam and John pick up a goth couple at a decadent rock club and murder them during a sex party to the accompaniment of Bauhaus's song, "Bela Lugosi's Dead." After feeding, the deadly couple return home to incinerate the remains of their prey in an industrial-strength furnace housed in the mansion's basement. The idyllic sex-and-death lifestyle of the vampiric predators is shattered, however, when John, who is several hundred years old, begins to age extremely rapidly. He enlists the aid of Dr. Sarah Roberts (Susan Sarandon), a scientist who is studying human aging and longevity at a Manhattan research facility, but she is unable to alleviate his condition. Becoming too feeble to overpower his prey, John returns home and murders Alice Cavender (Beth Ehlers), an adolescent girl from the neighborhood who comes over for a music lesson and disposes of her desiccated corpse in the usual fashion. When Miriam returns home, however, she finds John has aged so rapidly that he has become a dead-alive husk that she installs in a coffin inside a secret room that contains the zombified bodies of her other "lovers" from centuries past.

Intrigued by John's case, Sarah pays a visit to his address and encounters Miriam instead. The bisexual vampire lady immediately takes a shine to the attractive doctor and uses her mental influence to seduce her, and the two become "blood sisters" as Sarah is compelled to mingle her blood with Miriam's. Returning home to her live-in boyfriend and colleague, Dr. Tom Haver (Cliff DeYoung), Sarah, as a result of the transfusion, begins to experience drug withdrawal-type symptoms that are part of the process of turning her into a vampire. She confronts Miriam about her mysterious illness but collapses and is placed in the mansion's guest room. Soon afterward Tom comes to the mansion looking for Sarah and is led to the upstairs room where Sarah, her transformation complete, is consumed by "the hunger" and bleeds him dry. Sarah is devastated by Tom's death and by her own vampiric state, however, and the human part of her conspires to exact a terrible revenge upon Miriam with an assist from Miriam's living-dead former lovers.

The Hunger was a refreshingly modern take on the vampire film, which had been mired in a 19th-century British milieu for decades in a seemingly endless series of Dracula movies produced by Hammer and other English studios. Gone were the fangs, operatic capes and Central European locales favored by the previous century, which were replaced by the sex, drugs and rock 'n' roll of the MTV generation by screenwriters Ivan Davis and Michael Thomas. One theme from the classic vampire tale that translated well to a modern idiom was the lesbian-vampire angle, a motif that goes back to Sheridan Le Fanu's story "Carmilla" (1872), later filmed by Hammer as *The Vampire Lovers* (1970) and its sequels, *Lust for a Vampire* (1970) and *Twins of Evil* (1971).

Director Tony Scott, the brother of famed British film director Ridley Scott, acquits himself well in his first feature. Critics have noted points of similarity between Ridley's tech-noir opus *Blade Runner* (1982), released just a year earlier, and *The Hunger*. The film's interior lighting setups exhibit what has been called "the Ridley look," consisting of diffuse, pastel backgrounds punctuated by dark silhouettes and smoke. Miriam Blaylock's mansion rooms are ornate and tastefully adorned with dramatic statuary and bric-a-brac in a manner similar to interior spaces in Ridley's films such as *Blade Runner*, *Gladiator* and *Hannibal*. Like his brother, Tony Scott's directorial style has been criticized as being a triumph of form over substance, but here the film-maker's vivid style creates a dazzling vision of darkness and violence. Also, like *Blade Runner*, the primary characters are superhuman beings who suffer from "accelerated decrepitude" and are desperately seeking to extend their life-spans.

Catherine Deneuve's classic features capture some of the allure of Strieber's deadly vampiress, but her performance is wooden and her character remains distant. Pop star David Bowie is surprisingly effective in his role as the betrayed, disintegrating lover, even when he must act under heavy layers of Dick Smith's elaborate makeup, while Susan Sarandon drew kudos from the gay community for the film's sensual lesbian love scenes. *The Hunger* emerges as a noir study of obsession, perversity and murder, and with the supernatural element purged from the plot, Miriam and John might as well be two clever homicidal psychopaths on a perpetual sex-and-murder spree. Immortal vamp Miriam Blaylock is a monstrous *femme fatale*, described in Strieber's novel as, "A divine creature. A *thing* of the gods. Irresistible and fatal."[1] The film's action is set against the neo-noir landscape of 1980s New York and, like *Eyes of Laura Mars* and *Wolfen*, exploits the tortured urban angst of the decadent Big Apple.

It isn't often that a novelist gets to direct (and script) a film version of his own novel, but that's just what happened with Norman Mailer's *Tough Guys Don't Dance* (1987). The action takes place in Provincetown, a tourist mecca and gay enclave located on the tip of Cape Cod, during the winter off-season. Ryan O'Neal plays Tim Mallon, a hard-drinking ex-con and failed writer who is being supported by his rich-bitch wife Patty Lariene (Debra Sandlund). As the film opens, Patty has been missing for about three weeks and Tim's father, Dougy Madden (played by noir super-heavy Lawrence Tierney), pays a sudden, unannounced visit. Portly and bald after a bout of chemotherapy, Dougy is still a tough guy who has sensed that his son is in some kind of trouble and wants to help out before cashing in. As Tim confides in his father the recent events of his life unfold in flashbacks punctuated by Tim's voice-over monologue.

It seems that Provincetown was once known as "Helltown" in centuries past and was formerly an anarchic den of pirates and prostitutes. "In certain houses," Tim informs us, "you can still hear the cries of slaughtered sailors." Patty Lariene has become troubled by ghosts from Helltown because "two dead whores keep whisperin' to me," and arranges a séance with a local medium, Stoodie (Stephan Morrow). During the séance both the medium and Patty see identical visions of Patty with her head cut off, which she takes as a warning to leave town. After the abrupt departure of his wife, Tim meets an odd couple from out of town at a local bar, the seductive Jessica Pond (Frances Fisher), who claims to be a performer in "triple X-rated" movies and her dour companion, Lonnie Pangborn (R. Patrick Sullivan), who have flown in from California for a real estate deal. After a wild night of booze and coke, Tim awakens with a vague memory of having had sex with

Jessica as Lonnie watched, but with total amnesia for what might have gone on during the rest of the escapade. He is further unnerved to find unexplained bloodstains inside his car.

Tim soon gets a call from P-town's whacked-out chief of police, Capt. Alvin Luther Regency (Wings Hauser), who informs him that Lonnie's body has been found in the trunk of their rented car, the victim of an apparent suicide, while Jessica has gone missing. At dusk, when Tim checks out his marijuana stash hidden in a burrow deep in the woods, he pulls out a blonde-haired severed head wrapped in a plastic bag, but in the poor light he does not know if it is Jessica's or Patty Lariene's. Later, trying to ascertain the identity of the dead woman, he checks the stash again and finds a second woman's head in the hole. Knowing now that both his wife and Jessica are dead, and suspecting that he is being set up for the murders, he takes both heads with him and stashes them in his cellar. Tim also rekindles a romance with an old flame, Madeline Falco (Isabella Rossellini), who is now unhappily married to Regency, and learns from her that Patty Lariene was having an affair with her husband.

As Tim's flashback concludes, the narrative moves to the present, where Dougy, who

Tim Mallon (Ryan O'Neal, left) gets some tough love from Dougy Madden (noir veteran Lawrence Tierney) in Norman Mailer's *Tough Guys Don't Dance* (Cannon Films, 1987).

has had long experience with affairs of violence, comes to his son's rescue. He volunteers to dispose of the evidence, and returns from a "fishing excursion" on a small boat to announce, "I just deep-sixed two heads." Tim, investigating multiple murders in which he might be the killer, finds out that Jessica, Lonnie, Regency and Patty Lariene were involved in a $2 million coke deal with Provincetown's wealthy homosexual bad boy Wardley Meeks III (John Bedford Lloyd). Wardley is also involved in a plot to blackmail Regency by using Jessica's headless corpse to tie him to the murders. Tim and Dougy must unravel the unnervingly complex web of homicide and deceit in order to clear Tim of the murder of Patty Lariene and the others.

Mailer's twisted blend of horror, homicide, humor and homophobia has been called a "demented film noir," and "Norman Mailer's best film, adapted from his worst novel," among other things, by critics. Working with an A-list Hollywood cast and crew for the first time, Mailer performs surprisingly well in the director's chair and his pacing and direction of the actors is professional and surprisingly effective. Mailer uses the sounds of the sea, crying gulls, the eerie moan of the wind, the crashing of the surf, to build aural tension in counterpoint to the visuals. Cinematographer John Bailey does a fine job of capturing the moodiness and subtle terror of P-Town's washed-out winter seascape. With the exception of lead Ryan O'Neal, who seems oddly miscast in the role of a lowlife ex-con scribbler, the rest of the actors turn in memorably quirky performances, notably Wings Hauser as one of the most demented cops in screen history, Frances Fisher's trashy seductress and John Bedford Lloyd's Southern-accented gay villain. Isabella Rossellini is more subdued here than in her more flamboyant role in David Lynch's *Blue Velvet* (1986), while Debra Sandlund's blonde *femme fatale* projects man-devouring menace as the film's "unredeemed redneck" Patty Lariene.

The noir heart of the film, however, is in the casting of the formidable Lawrence Tierney as Dougy in a role that clearly dominates the film. Tierney, who starred in memorable crime melodramas such as *Dillinger* (1945), *The Devil Thumbs a Ride* (1947) and *The Hoodlum* (1951), has been described by Barry Gifford as being "the wickedest-looking big lug in B-movie history.... He's in his sixties now, fat and completely bald ... but that mean look was still in his eyes; that bad-to-the-bone, never-give-in visage. There is no daylight in that face."[2] The actor's tough-as-nails screen presence as a hulking ex-thug is easily the best thing about the film and injects a much-needed heft and film noir gravitas to the proceedings.

Arguably the most problematic element of *Tough Guys Don't Dance* is Mailer's eccentric screenplay, which sparkles with bizarro lines of dialogue such as, "Your knife is in my dog," "I feel demented tonight," and "I just deep-sixed two heads." At one climactic point Ryan O'Neal keeps repeating, "Oh man, oh god, oh man, oh god, oh man, oh god," in a passage that is considered one of the most ludicrous lines of dialogue in screen history. The film's wacky denouement, in which Tierney and O'Neal deep-six murdered bodies from a small boat accompanied by "Pomp and Circumstance" graduation music, is hilarious. All this having been said, the film deftly combines a standard film noir plot revolving around an alcoholic amnesiac investigating murders in which he may be the killer with the horror elements of ghosts, séances and severed heads. The main theme is the demonic aspect of human (especially male) sexuality that leads these "unspeakable sleazos" (in Mailer's words) to jealousy, drug addiction and murder.

Voodoo Noir

Writer/director Alan Parker's *Angel Heart* (1987) walked the line between the universes of classic film noir and otherworldly voodoo. Set in January 1955, the film follows the exploits of hard-boiled, shabby New York private eye Harry Angel (Mickey Rourke), who is hired on a missing person case by mysterioso Frenchman Louis Cyphre (Robert De Niro). Cyphre, it seems, had a contract with a 1940s-era crooner named Johnny Favorite, who suffered neurological injuries during World War II and has been confined to an upstate mental hospital ever since for "radical psychiatric treatment." Because Favorite was reduced to an amnesiac vegetable, Cyphre's contract was never honored, but recently suspicions have arisen about Johnny having died or been released, and Cyphre wants Harry to locate Johnny alive or dead. The weird Frenchman sports shoulder-length hair, claw-like nails and operates out of an eerie run-down Pentecostal church in Harlem, but money talks and Harry is on the job.

Harry travels to the upstate loony bin to discover that Favorite was transferred out back in '43, and he strongarms Dr. Albert Fowler (Michael Higgins), the drug-addicted physician who treated Johnny into revealing that Favorite checked out with a man named Edward Kelly and an unidentified woman, and that he was paid a yearly sum to falsify Johnny's continued presence at the hospital. He also learns that Johnny's features have been altered via reconstructive facial surgery so that nobody knows what he looks like. Soon afterward, the junkie doc comes up dead, an apparent suicide, and Harry traces Favorite to New Orleans through some old contacts. Fortified with a cool five thou from Cyphre, Harry travels from the Big Apple to the Big Easy in search of his quarry.

In New Orleans, Harry tracks down Favorite's associates to try to ascertain his whereabouts. He contacts Margaret Krusemark (Charlotte Rampling), a fortune teller, and guitarist Toots Sweet (played by real-life bluesman Brownie McGhee), but learns little. Trying to trace another of Johnny's acquaintances, voodoo priestess Evangeline Proudfoot, he finds instead her grave and her 17-year-old daughter, Epiphany (Lisa Bonet), who claims that Fortune was her father. One night Harry trails Toots out into the bayous where he watches the musician and Epiphany taking part in a grisly voodoo ceremony. The next day Harry wakes up to find New Orleans detective Sterne (Eliott Keener) searching his hotel room and learns that Toots has been brutally murdered and he is a potential suspect. Visiting Margaret, he finds that she has also been killed and her heart cut out of her chest. Harry meets with Cyphre at a local church and complains that Johnny's bad luck "is starting to rub off on me," and that he is being set up to take the rap for the killings.

Returning to his hotel Harry finds Epiphany there, and winds up having sex with her in a wild scene in which they are covered in blood while copulating. The final revelation of the mystery comes when Harry confronts "Ed Kelly," the man who sprung Favorite from the asylum, who is in reality Margaret's father, Ethan Krusemark (Stocker Fontelieu). Harry learns that Favorite was a satanist who made a deal with the Devil to attain stardom, but then tried to renege by assuming the identity of a soldier who he murdered in a ritual killing back in 1943. In other words, Harry is Johnny, the man he has been looking for all along, and that he has committed all the murders under the direction of Louis Cyphre (read: Lucifer). As the amnesia is lifted, Harry/Johnny becomes cognizant of his crimes, including the final murders of Ethan and Epiphany, as Cyphre comes to claim his soul at last and his damnation is complete.

Angel Heart is the first movie to deliberately combine elements of supernatural horror and classic film noir, mixing voodoo and satanism with a Philip Marlowe-type private eye protagonist into a captivating whole. Faithfully adapted from the novel *Falling Angel* by William Hjorstberg, Parker's screenplay relocates the action in the second half of the film to New Orleans. Parker's direction, assisted by the crisp camerawork of cinematographer Michael Seresin, employs beautifully composed visuals that alternate from bleak expressionist shadows to brightly lit exteriors, and there is a fine feeling for period detail in the use of timeless locations like Harlem and Coney Island in New York and the French Quarter of New Orleans. Composer Trevor Jones contributes an eerie score that utilizes "actual" or "stage" music (the music that the characters in the film are hearing) such as voodoo drums, gospel music and delta blues, whenever possible. These African American musical soundscapes accompany Harry Angel throughout his voyage to self-discovery and damnation.

The affable Mickey Rourke, who would later garner acclaim for his performance in *The Wrestler* (2007), easily carries the film in the lead role of grotty Chandlerian private detective Harry Angel. Harry is portrayed as an unscrupulous tough guy with a mean streak, but ultimately comes off as a likeable, sympathetic character. His gradual transformation into the sadistic murderer and satanist Johnny Favorite therefore seems to ring a false note. Co-star and "Cosby kid" Lisa Bonet, long associated with the popular television sitcom *The Cosby Show*, achieved notoriety for scenes in which she drank chicken blood and writhed in the throes of spirit possession during a voodoo ceremony, and for her blood-soaked, softcore sex scene with Rourke that tarnished her wholesome TV image. Robert De Niro's performance as the devilish Cyphre is cool and understated yet projects the powerful sense of hidden authority and subtle menace of a seasoned Mafia don.

Many motifs taken from classic noir are woven into the fabric of the film's plot, including amnesia, plastic surgery and the notion of a killer who is investigating the mystery of homicides that he himself has committed. Harry Angel is struggling with his

Falling Angel: Mickey Rourke as fated P.I. Harry Angel in Alan Parker's *Angel Heart* (TriStar, 1987).

sense of identity and striving to recover lost memories in an existential quest to discover the ultimate truth about himself. Critics have pointed out thematic similarities between *Angel Heart* and Ridley Scott's future noir *Blade Runner*, released just two years earlier. Both of these feature Philip Marlowe–type detectives in fantastic urban settings struggling against inhuman forces of science or magic. Slavoj Zizek writes, "Both films deal with memory and subverted personal identity: the hero, the hardboiled investigator, is sent on a quest ... whose final outcome is that he himself was from the very beginning implicated in the object of his quest. In *Angel Heart*, the hero ascertains that the dead singer is none other than himself.... In *Blade Runner*, he is told that he himself is a replicant,"[3] or artificial human. Like *Blade Runner*, *Angel Heart*

Robert De Niro as the diabolical Louis Cyphre in *Angel Heart* (TriStar, 1987).

achieves a near-perfect meld of film noir and the fantastic. There are also distant echoes of Jacques Tourneur's horror noir *I Walked with a Zombie* (1943), which also combined mystery and voodoo.

"Two Bodies ... Two Minds ... One Soul"

In his non-fiction book *Evil Twins*, crime writer John Glatt states, "Although cases of evil twins are very rare in the annals of criminology they do occur and are usually far more mysterious and complex than other cases of routine homicide.... A common thread of all these cases is the strange, almost unearthly power that twins can exert over each other."[4] Canadian horrormeister David Cronenberg tackled the special relationship between twins in *Dead Ringers* (1988), a horror noir thriller loosely based on the bizarre real-life exploits of twin New York gynecologists Cyril and Stewart Marcus.

Identical twin doctors Elliot and Beverly Mantle (both played by Jeremy Irons) jointly operate an upscale state-of-the-art fertility clinic in Toronto. Their relationship is abnormally close even for twin brothers, as the two live together and even share the same women without anyone being the wiser. The Mantles are brilliant scientists and conduct original research in their field and work together closely as a team. The extroverted Eliott, the elder of the twins, deals with professional politics and makes public appearances while the shy and retiring Beverly conducts the research. Their relationship is strained, however, when neurotic actress Claire Niveau (Geneviève Bujold) becomes a patient at the clinic. Claire, a hard-edged, promiscuous drug addict with masochistic tendencies, wants to have a child but upon examination is found to have a "trifurcate uterus," a rare, freakish condition in which her womb is divided into three parts, which renders her unable to have children. The charismatic Eliott soon seduces Claire, then shunts her off on Beverly as per their usual practice of sharing women, even among their patients. After Beverly has enjoyed Claire's favors while pretending to be Eliott, his brother demands to know the details of their tryst. "You haven't had any experience until I've had it too," Eliott reminds him, but Beverly insists on keeping his relationship with Claire private.

A rift develops between the twins over Claire as Beverly continues to see her. Under her influence he starts doing drugs and abuses his medical ethics by writing prescriptions for amphetamines and barbiturates. Claire begins to fall deeply in love with Beverly, but remains blissfully unaware that he has a twin until she hears it from a friend. She demands to meet Eliott and humiliates the twins over dinner at a posh restaurant, spitting out the accusation that "you can't get it up unless your brother's watching?" before storming off. Beverly's relationship with Claire resumes after a brief hiatus, however, but she observes, "You two have never come to terms with the way it really does work between you."

When Claire must go out of town on a film shoot for ten weeks, Beverly begins to use more drugs and suffers a mental breakdown when a phone call to Claire is answered by one of her assistants and he fantasizes that she is having an affair during a pharmaceutically induced delusion. He rapidly deteriorates into an obsessive madness, becoming unable to perform his duties as a physician and commissioning a local metalworker to create a set of grotesque gynecological tools designed specifically for "working on mutant women." When he attempts to use the instruments to perform surgery he is stripped of his medical license, further exacerbating his downward spiral of self-destructive behavior.

Beverly's drugged-out condition begins to affect Eliott via some strange telepathic link between the twins as Eliott begins to follow his brother into addiction in order to get "synchronized" with Beverly. The two wander through Beverly's apartment, which is now strewn ankle-high with garbage and refuse, in a stoned haze. Claire, returning to Toronto after the film shoot is concluded, is appalled by Beverly's decrepit condition, but is repulsed when she discovers his obscene medical tools. In the end, the twins descend into their hellish private world together until they decide to use Beverly's surgical instruments to "separate Siamese twins" in a bizarre ritual murder/suicide. "Separation can be a terrifying thing," Beverly says as he performs the operation on Eliott that will sever the bond between the twins forever.

After the visceral awfulness of *The Fly* (1986) and Cronenberg's other horror films, *Dead Ringers* represented a departure for the acclaimed Canadian director. The film is primarily a psychological study of the insular world of the twins who share a special bond that serves to exacerbate their freakish medical and sexual obsessions. Typical of Cronenberg's *oeuvre*, *Dead Ringers* exploits the "body horrors" of gynecology, especially in scenes depicting surgery in which the twins are attired in flowing red outfits that resemble

Evil twins: Twin doctors Beverly (left) and Elliot Mantle, both played by Jeremy Irons, flank Claire Niveau (Geneviève Bujold) in *Dead Ringers* (20th Century–Fox, 1988).

priestly robes worn during some strange religious ceremony. The creepy medical implements resemble medieval instruments of torture and seem designed to inflict pain rather than healing. Cronenberg is in fine directorial form, coaxing strong performances from the actors and pacing the narrative so there is very little screen time wasted.

Jeremy Irons delivers two riveting performances as Eliott and Beverly Mantle, portraying minute differences between the twins that are so subtle as to be almost subliminal. Eliott, the older, more dominant twin is droll and acerbic while Beverly (who is really the film's protagonist) comes off as being warmer and more vulnerable. Note that Cronenberg does not resort to the clichéd "good twin" versus "evil twin" narrative dichotomy, but instead explores the dramatic tension summarized in the film's tag line, "two bodies, two minds, one soul." Irons is perfectly matched with Geneviève Bujold's portrayal of the cynical, world-weary Claire in one of her finest performances. Color-saturated cinematography by Peter Suschitzky gives the film an exquisite look, while composer Howard Shore contributes a brooding score that invokes the work of Bernard Herrmann.

Cronenberg's screenplay, co-written with Norman Snider, is a much more sophisticated treatment of the theme of malignant twins than Brian De Palma's gimmick-laden *Sisters* (1973). Adapted from the novel *Twins* by Bari Wood and Jack Geasland, *Dead Ringers* incorporates many details culled from the true crime case of twin gynecologists Cyril and Stewart Marcus. During the 1960s the two prominent Manhattan physicians were estranged from each other when Cyril married, but when the marriage fell apart he drifted into a deep depression and began using drugs heavily, a practice which his brother Stewart soon emulated. The drugs took their toll on the twins' medical practice, and by 1975 they were living together in a filthy apartment on New York's upscale Sutton Place, hopelessly addicted to self-prescribed drugs. The Marcus brothers were found dead together inside their apartment, having died while trying to detox from barbiturate addiction by going cold turkey, which is worse than trying to kick a heroin habit. *Dead Ringers* is a compelling noir study of obsession, drug addiction, medical malpractice, perverse sexuality and the doppelganger.

In the shadow of the neo-noir revival of the 1980s, the horror-noir hybrid form had matured and ripened into a series of memorable films that included *Wolfen*, *The Hunger*, *Angel Heart*, *Tough Guys Don't Dance* and *Dead Ringers*. But a new type of criminality was about to emerge in the following decade in the person of Doctor Hannibal ("The Cannibal") Lecter.

11

The Noir Horrors of Hannibal the Cannibal

Cannibal psychiatrist Dr. Hannibal Lecter was the literary creation of novelist Thomas Harris and first appeared in the author's 1981 crime thriller *Red Dragon*. While Dr. Lecter was a memorable but minor character in that book, he assumed a central narrative significance in Harris's sequels, *The Silence of the Lambs* (1988), *Hannibal* (1999) and *Hannibal Rising* (2006). All of these books were eventually filmed, but it was Jonathan Demme's screen version of *The Silence of the Lambs* (1991) that transformed Lecter into a major American cultural icon.

During the 1980s and '90s the figure of the serial killer had assumed a cultural resonance in the wake of the well-publicized exploits of real-life mass-murderers such as David Berkowitz (a.k.a. the "Son of Sam"), Ted Bundy, the "Zodiac" killer, the "Green River" killer, John Wayne Gacy and Jeffrey Dahmer, among others. The serial killer was a figure of dread, an angel of darkness who dealt death in secret from the shadows, an archetypal villain that had long been a staple of film noir. Philip Simpson has written, "The 'serial killer' ... is a confabulation of Gothic/romantic villain, literary vampire and werewolf, detective and 'pulp' fiction conceits, film noir outsider, frontier outlaw, folkloric threatening figure and 19th-century pseudo-sociological conception of criminal types given contemporary plausibility."[1] As major American cities descended into crime and anarchy, the serial killer emerged as a cinematic emblem of these anarchic, threatening social forces.

In *Red Dragon*, Lecter is presented to the reader as a brilliant psychologist and surgeon who has violated his Hippocratic Oath by murdering nine victims. He is described as a "Renaissance Prince," a highly sophisticated European of high learning and culture who nonetheless possesses an atavistic homicidal streak. Lecter's nemesis in *Red Dragon*, FBI agent Will Graham, offers his insights into the doctor's personality thus: "Dr. Lecter is not crazy, in any common way we think of being crazy. He did some hideous things because he enjoyed them. But he can function perfectly well when he wants to.... They say he's a sociopath because they don't know what else to call him. He has some of the characteristics of what they call the sociopath. He has no remorse or guilt at all.... His electroencephalograms show some odd patterns, but they haven't been able to tell much from them."[2] In other words, Lecter takes human evil to the next level and his super-sociopathy is so off the charts that it cannot be measured. Pressed to describe the doctor further, Graham states, "He's a monster. I think of him as one of those pitiful things that are born in hospitals from time to time. They feed it, and keep it warm, but they don't put in on the machine and it dies. Lecter is the same way in his head, but he looks normal and nobody could tell."[3]

The psychotic medico ghoulishly feasts upon his victims (as did Jeffrey Dahmer), which has earned him the sobriquet of "the Cannibal." He is ensconced in a hi-tech cell at a maximum security prison that serves as a shrine to his evil sainthood, where he is consulted by various supplicants, mainly psychiatrists and law-enforcement types who try to tap into Lecter's perverse wisdom. At times he seems to exhibit psychic powers that further enhance his aura of inhuman dread, and he possesses a super-keen animal-like sense of smell that enables him to detect subtle nuances of his environment. His profound knowledge of psychology allows him to manipulate those around him effortlessly. In short, Lecter is a superhuman figure of towering malevolence.

All of the books and films featuring Lecter are police procedurals in which dedicated FBI agents race against time to prevent further mass-murders from occurring. The forensic skills that the Agency wields during these manhunts are much more sophisticated than anything employed by local law enforcement and utilize hi-tech devices like computers, lasers, methane probes and the like. Lecter is usually paired with a second psychotic character (i.e., the "Tooth Fairy" in *Red Dragon*, "Buffalo Bill" in *The Silence of the Lambs* and Mason Verger in *Hannibal*) and assumes the role of being another detective or forensic consultant working to crack these baffling homicide cases. He is thought to have a mental conduit into the minds of these other serial slayers and alone can comprehend their bizarre, inhuman logic and speak their special language. Lecter also exemplifies the noir character of the evil psychiatrist, a figure familiar from films noir such as *Nightmare Alley* and horror noirs like *Cat People*.

Manhunter

The first film in which Lecter appeared was Michael Mann's *Manhunter* (1986), a slick crime melodrama based on Harris's novel *Red Dragon* and directed by the creator of the stylish 1980s TV cop show *Miami Vice*. William Petersen portrays the legendary FBI profiler Will Graham, who has left the Bureau after bagging Lecter and sustaining severe physical and psychological wounds in the process. Leading an idyllic existence on the Florida coast with his wife, Molly (Kim Greist), and son, Kevin (David Seaman), Will is coaxed out of retirement by his former superior, Jack Crawford (Dennis Farina), to catch the so-called "Tooth Fairy," a vicious killer who has brutally murdered two families in different cities without apparent motive and has earned his moniker by biting the skin of his victims post-mortem. The FBI is baffled by the case and Crawford hopes to tap into Graham's intuitive detection skills that enabled him to catch Lecter. Because the Tooth Fairy kills during the cycle of the full moon, the Bureau is desperate to nail the serial killer before he strikes again.

While employing standard police investigative procedures, Graham also uses unorthodox methods that appear to be psychic. He eerily retraces the killer's steps through the victim's houses, recreating the murders in his mind in order to "catch the scent" of his quarry. "What are you dreaming?" he asks, as if trying to communicate with the Tooth Fairy on some telepathic wavelength. Then, in order to "recover the mindset," Graham pays a visit to Dr. Lecter (here spelled 'Lecktor' for some unknown reason and played by Scottish actor Brian Cox) in his maximum-security cell. The wily Lecter is still smarting from his capture as he verbally jousts with Graham during their meeting, his mocking hauteur and mordant wit cutting his captor like a knife. Graham tries to get the doctor interested in the Tooth Fairy case, but Lecter is evasive and provides no useful insights into the crimes. Realizing that Graham has met with him merely to "get the old scent back again," Lecter suggests to Graham: "Smell yourself."

After the visit Lecter cleverly jimmies one of the prison phones while he is ostensibly calling his lawyer and, via subterfuge, manages to obtain Graham's home address in Florida. Then, during a routine search, a letter from the Tooth Fairy to Lecter written on toilet paper is discovered inside one of the doctor's books. Signed "Avid Fan," the note proclaims, "I know that you alone can understand what I am becoming." Using state-of-the-art forensic techniques, FBI experts are able to ascertain that the two mass-murderers are communicating through ads in the tabloid newsrag *The National Tattler*. Graham and Crawford hatch a plot to bait the Tooth Fairy by having lowlife *Tattler* reporter Freddie Lounds (Stephen Lang) run an unflattering article on the killer that suggests he is a sexual pervert in the hope that he will go after Graham, but the killer abducts Lounds instead. The hapless reporter awakens inside the killer's lair, where an entire wall is decorated by an enormous picture of the surface of the planet Mars. Lounds is confronted by the Tooth Fairy himself, who is in reality one Francis Dolarhyde (Tom Noonan), a tall, monstrous figure wearing a grotesque mask fashioned from a pair of panty hose. The killer forces Lounds to audiotape a retraction of the "facts" presented in the *Tattler* article and then returns him to the abduction site, burning him to death as he is strapped into a flaming wheelchair.

In the meantime the FBI has decoded a message sent from Lecter to the Tooth Fairy in an ad in the *Tattler* that gives away Graham's home address and urges his fellow murderer: "Kill them all, save yourself." As Molly and Kevin are removed to a secure location, the action shifts to following Dolarhyde, who works as a technician in a St. Louis film processing plant where he has access to the infra-red film stock he uses to make home movies of his atrocities under low-light conditions. Dolarhyde unexpectedly enters into a romantic relationship with a blind co-worker, Reba McClane (Joan Allen), a gentle soul who seems to offer him a chance at leading a normal life, but all hopes are dashed when he thinks he sees Reba with another man. He abducts Reba, intending to kill her for betraying him inside his sanctum sanctorum, but by this time Graham has had a flash of insight that has revealed the riddle of the Tooth Fairy's identity. While watching 8mm home movies of the murdered families he realizes that the killer must have also seen the films and thus the perpetrator must work at the film processing company where they are sent to be developed. In the movie's action-filled climax, Graham and Crawford desperately race to stop the Tooth Fairy before he brutally murders Reba as Graham's "sixth sense" directs them to the killer.

Writer/director Michael Mann imbues *Manhunter* with a palpable sense of lurking dread that is one of the hallmarks of noir. Essentially faithful to the plot of Harris's novel, Mann's screenplay downplays the book's emphasis on the Tooth Fairy's obsession with the art and poetry of William Blake and changes and simplifies the novel's ending. Mann's stylish execution crafts a smooth, arty thriller that sustains suspense throughout its complex

William Petersen as FBI profiler Will Graham in *Manhunter* (Warner Bros., 1986).

plot and police procedural details that might otherwise bore the audience. The director also coaxes fine, believable performances out of his cast of unknowns. William Petersen's restrained performance as the wounded psychic manhunter easily carries the film, with an able assist from co-star Dennis Farina. Petersen would go on to play a similar role in the TV police series *CSI*, while Farina, who in real life was an ex–Chicago police officer, made a new career for himself portraying cops and criminals, the most memorable of which was his role as a Miami gangster in Barry Sonnenfeld's comic noir *Get Shorty* (1995).

As Hannibal "Lecktor," Brian Cox's performances is invariably judged against Anthony Hopkins's Oscar-winning performance in *Silence of the Lambs* and its sequels and inevitably comes up short in comparison. It should be noted, however, that Lecter's role in *Manhunter* is much more circumscribed, and that Cox only appears onscreen in three scenes. *Manhunter* is also the only film featuring Lecter in which the doctor is not the prime mover, or *homme fatal*, of the plot. Cox's more restrained interpretation of the part was reportedly based on the Scottish serial killer Peter Manuel. Most of the film's menace is provided by Tom Noonan as the Tooth Fairy, a hulking, Frankenstein-like monster, who combines some of Lecter's insane cleverness with brute muscle into a terrifying whole. Noonan is said to have requested that no one in the cast be allowed to see him until their scenes together were filmed, a technique that created a genuine fear of him on the set.

While the film was a box-office flop in its original release, *Manhunter* has since been lauded as a "cult" film and its many virtues extolled on the internet and elsewhere. Author Thomas Harris began his writing career as a crime reporter, and his intimate knowledge of law enforcement procedures lends both novel and film a chilling verisimilitude. Fictional FBI agents Will Graham and Jack Crawford were inspired by the real-life exploits of FBI profiler John Douglas, who developed the sophisticated investigative techniques depicted in *Manhunter* and its sequels. In his non-fiction book *Mind Hunter* (1996), Douglas explicates the psychological techniques he invented and refined during his extensive personal interviews with notorious serial killers like David Berkowitz and Charles Manson. Director Mann would later lens the acclaimed crime caper movie *Heat* (1995), and *Manhunter* would be remade by Brett Ratner as *Red Dragon* (2002). While *Manhunter* would eventually be overshadowed by its sequels, there are some aficionados of the Lecter movies who consider it the best of the lot.

The Silence of the Lambs

Despite the tepid public response to *Manhunter*, Harris's sequel to *Red Dragon* was optioned before his new novel was even published. Jonathan Demme, who had previously been associated with comedy films, was brought in to direct a cast that included no big Hollywood names. The result was *The Silence of the Lambs* (1991), the sleeper hit of the year and the most acclaimed horror film in screen history.

The film's protagonist is FBI agent-in-training Clarice Starling (Jodie Foster), a young, ambitious woman who is struggling to overcome the disadvantages of a poor family background and compete in the male-dominated culture of the Bureau. Starling's training is interrupted by a summons from her boss, Jack Crawford (played here by Scott Glenn), who begins by asking her the curious question, "Do you spook easily, Starling?" Crawford ostensibly wants her to interview Hannibal Lecter, who he describes as "our most prized asset," and convince him to fill out a psychological questionnaire for the Bureau's behavioral research effort, but his real motive is to get Lecter's input on another serial killer dubbed "Buffalo Bill" because he "skins his humps," that is, he flays the young women who are his victims. His hope is that Lecter will respond to Starling's femininity and loosen his tongue.

Dispatched to the Baltimore mental hospital where Lecter is kept imprisoned, Agent

Dr. Hannibal Lecter (Anthony Hopkins) advises FBI agent Clarice Starling (Jodie Foster) about the fine points of serial homicide in Jonathan Demme's *The Silence of the Lambs* (Orion, 1991).

Starling experiences a fearful encounter with Lecter (here played to demonic perfection by the distinguished Welsh actor Anthony Hopkins). Housed in a hi-tech plexiglas enclosure like a specimen in some deranged human zoo, Lecter dispenses nuggets of demented wisdom and tantalizing tidbits of information while he mocks and intimidates Starling with his rapier-like wit. "A census taker once tried to test me," the doctor confides. "I ate his liver with some fava beans and a nice chianti." Nevertheless, Lecter gives her a clue that leads to the discovery of a severed head in exchange for personal information about her past. When the pupa of a death's head moth is discovered in the throat of one of Buffalo Bill's victims and a second moth pupa is found inside the severed head, it becomes clear that Lecter has some inside knowledge about the serial killer. "I'm offering you a psychological profile of Buffalo Bill based on the case evidence," Lecter suggests, trying to parlay his cooperation into a change of accommodations. He suggests that the killer is attempting to fashion a "woman suit" from the skins of his victims and that he may be a pathological transvestite or a transsexual.

While the FBI is trying to cut a deal with Lecter, Buffalo Bill strikes again, but this time he abducts the daughter of a U.S. senator, Catherine Martin (Brooke Smith), which ignites a firestorm of political pressure on the FBI to catch the serial killer. In the meantime, Catherine is placed inside a pit in Bill's basement as he prepares to harvest her hide. The twisted mass-murderer, whose real name is Jame Gumb (Ted Levine), is depicted as a stereotypical effeminate homosexual who swishes through his bizarre domain accompanied by his pet poodle named Precious. Aside from making "woman suits," Gumb's other hobby is raising rare moths inside a room kept in total darkness where he works using infra-red goggles. The moth pupae placed inside the throats of his victims are a symbol of his sexual transformation.

Trying to enhance his own career, the mental hospital's administrator, Dr. Chilton (Anthony Heald) cuts his own deal with Senator Ruth Martin (Diane Baker), who is desperate to save her daughter's life. Lecter is to be transferred to a prison facility in the senator's home state of Tennessee in exchange for information that will lead to the capture of Buffalo Bill. Imprisoned inside an enormous cage in an old courthouse building in Memphis, the doctor starts singing like a bird as Crawford and the FBI begin to follow up on his leads. Starling, however, remains unconvinced and visits the doctor in Memphis and in another of their tense confrontations extracts some key information in exchange

A masked Lecter (Anthony Hopkins) is escorted out of the psychiatric hospital by orderly Barney Matthews (Frankie Faison, extreme right) in *The Silence of the Lambs* (Orion, 1991).

for her traumatic recollections about the slaughter of lambs on a farm during her child-hood.

After she leaves, Lecter uses a tool made from a pilfered pen to slip out of his hand-cuffs and brutally murders three of his guards and two paramedics during his escape. In the meantime Starling tracks down Jame Gumb through a sewing connection and correctly deduces his address while the FBI, acting on Lecter's bogus information, raids an empty house. Alone, she must confront Buffalo Bill as serial killer and FBI agent play a deadly game of cat and mouse amid the swarms of moths and "woman suits" that are part of Bill's macabre domain.

Nobody in Hollywood expected *The Silence of the Lambs* to achieve mega-hit status, but Demme's offbeat, horrific thriller rang a chime with movie audiences. The director quickly divests himself of his comic style and plunges full force into this demented noir tale of madness and murder. Demme's visual style veers between neo-noir expressionist shadows and gritty realism, the psychotic inner worlds of Lecter and Buffalo Bill alter-nating with scenes of clinical FBI crime investigations. The director shot the FBI scenes on location at the Bureau's headquarters in Quantico, Virginia, and this sterile, bureau-cratic setting becomes a visual metaphor for the logic, sanity and order standing in oppo-sition to the chaos of the homicidal milieu of the killers. The entire film is suffused with a mood of suffocating imprisonment of characters caught in dark webs of their own mak-ing: Lecter is confined inside his hi-tech dungeon; Catherine Martin is held captive in a bloody pit of horror; Buffalo Bill lives inside his morbid private world of perverse sexuality and death; and Starling is struggling to overcome the oppression of the male-dominated FBI bureaucratic culture.

What really made the film so effective, however, was the acting, spearheaded by Anthony Hopkins's magnetic performance as Lecter. Seldom has an actor realized a screen role so perfectly as Hopkins made author Harris's deranged character leap off the page, his Welsh-accented speaking voice providing just the right verbal flair for the part. He plays the character as being physically immobile with an unblinking hypnotic stare, and although Hopkins's performance dominates the film, Lecter appears onscreen for only about 17 minutes. Jodie Foster's Clarice Starling presents the perfect dramatic foil for Hopkins with her combination of toughness and vulnerability. Her performance is superbly understated and her West Virginia drawl flawless. While Scott Glenn's portrayal of Bureau bigwig Jack Crawford is lackluster, Ted Levine shines as the homicidal Buffalo Bill and Brooke Smith doles out gut-wrenching fear as Bill's abductee and prospective skin donor Catherine Martin.

If noir is defined as the exploration of human perversity, then *The Silence of the Lambs* is drawn in the darkest shades of black. The Oscar-winning screenplay by Ted Tally is very faithful to Harris's story and captures the novel's bleak mood perfectly, and whole passages of the book's creepy dialogue are lifted verbatim. Harris reportedly mod-eled the character of Buffalo Bill on real-life serial killers like Ed Gein (who had also pro-vided the inspiration for *Psycho*'s Norman Bates) and Ted Bundy. The film displays a noir preoccupation with perverse psychiatry, both in the Lecter character and in the FBI profilers trying to psychologically decode the motives of the serial killers. Lecter and Buf-falo Bill represent a force of human chaos that is at the heart of noir, yet their extreme morbidity and practice of ritualized violence tip them over into the domain of horror as well. Hannibal the Cannibal seems hardly human; his vast, malignant intellect and quasi-telepathic powers of mind make him resemble a sorcerer or extraterrestrial. He represents a force of evil beyond our comprehension, and as such is one of the most memorable screen villains of all time.

The Silence of the Lambs was an enormous popular and critical hit, sweeping the top five Academy Awards for Best Picture, Best Actor (Anthony Hopkins), Best Actress (Jodie Foster), Best Director (Jonathan Demme), and Best Adapted Screenplay (Ted Tally), making it the most acclaimed horror film in Oscar history. Although it presented a strong female protagonist in the person of the tough-as-nails Clarice Starling, some feminist critics proclaimed that the film denigrated women with its unending stream of mutilated female victims. Gay critics were appalled by the stereotypically negative portrayal of transvestite Buffalo Bill, causing protests of the film by activists around the country. In truth, there is a strain of homophobia that runs through Harris's works, as all of the "secondary" serial killers (the Tooth Fairy in *Red Dragon*, Buffalo Bill in *Silence* and Mason Verger in *Hannibal*) are portrayed as gay or having a hazily- defined sexuality, while both Lecter and his nemesis Clarice Starling also exhibit a degree of sexual ambiguity.

Hannibal

Despite the popularity of his previous work, Harris did not generate a sequel to *The Silence of the Lambs* until 11 years later, when *Hannibal* was published in 1999. Italian Producer Dino De Laurentiis immediately snapped up the property for a cool $10 mil, but problems arose over the novel's bizarre content, in which Clarice Starling and Hannibal Lecter end up as lovers. Screenwriter Steven Zaillian, who had won an Oscar for *Schindler's List*, was called in to doctor the script, but the film's violent plot caused director Jonathan Demme and star Jodie Foster to pass on the project. Foster in particular was incensed by the story's transformation of Clarice Starling. "The movie worked because people believed in her heroism," she complained in an interview. "I won't play her with negative attributes she'd never had." Actress Julianne Moore replaced Foster as Agent Starling. The old cannibal himself, Anthony Hopkins, was persuaded to return as Lecter, however, and the distinguished British director Ridley Scott, fresh from his triumph on the Oscar-winning epic *Gladiator* (2000), was signed on to helm the project. Scott, who had directed the tech-noir masterwork *Blade Runner* (1982) and the crime melodramas *Someone to Watch Over Me* (1987) and *Black Rain* (1989), would bring his exquisite visual style to bear on the horrors of *Hannibal* (2001).

In the sequel Clarice Starling has been suspended from the FBI after she takes some bad publicity from a badly botched drug raid in D.C. Her nemesis is oily FBI bureaucrat Paul Krendler (Ray Liotta), who bears a special animus against Starling because she has refused his romantic advances. After a mysterious phone call, however, Krendler relents and re-assigns Starling to the still-open Hannibal Lecter case. The phone call is from one of Lecter's surviving victims, the ultra-rich Mason Verger (Gary Oldman), whose wealth enables him to corrupt Krendler and others within the Bureau. Verger, an insane pedophile who is crippled and severely disfigured after his encounter with Lecter, is obsessed with getting revenge and has offered a $3 million bounty on the internet for information leading to Lecter's apprehension. He has no intention of giving Lecter to the authorities, however, but plans to exact a terrible vengeance on his enemy.

Cut to Florence, Italy, where the rumpled Italian detective Inspector Rinaldo Pazzi (Giancarlo Giannini) believes that he has located Lecter, who is posing as Renaissance scholar and museum curator Dr. Fell. Convinced that Fell is Lecter, Pazzi decides to sell him to Verger and claim the reward rather than deliver him to the FBI, but in order to do this he must obtain a fingerprint from his suspect. In order to accomplish this, he lines up a petty thief to pick Lecter's pocket, and obtains the prints but callously allows the man to die from a knife wound inflicted by Lecter. The fingerprints are a match and Verger dispatches his men to abduct Dr. Fell, but the wily killer smells a rat and murders Pazzi by hanging and disemboweling him in a Florentine plaza. Lecter manages to elude Verger's men and returns to the United States using one of his phony identities.

Back in the States, Verger suspects that Lecter has returned and compels Krendler to suspend Starling from the FBI on trumped-up charges. She is kept under surveillance by Verger's men until she receives a call from Lecter requesting that she visit Washington's Union Station for a meeting. The two of them talk on cell phones while she walks through the vast inner spaces of the station and do not actually meet, but Verger's thugs have followed her and take Lecter prisoner. Starling witnesses the kidnapping and realizes that Verger intends to torture his foe to death, and wanting him brought to justice instead,

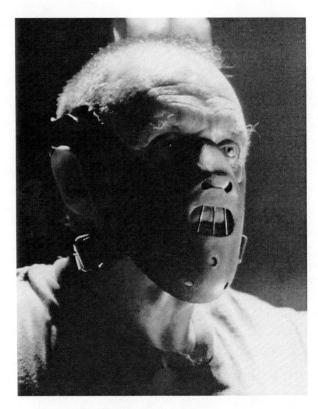

rides off to the rescue. Arming herself, she infiltrates the Verger estate and comes upon a bizarre scene: Lecter is going to be placed in a kind of amphitheater where Verger will watch as the doctor is eaten alive by a herd of monstrous pigs that have been specially trained for this purpose.

Before the giant swine can be released, Starling bursts in and shoots the pig wranglers while freeing Lecter, but is rendered unconscious by an animal tranquilizer dart fired by one of Verger's henchmen. Lecter carries Starling away in his arms, untouched by the pigs who begin feasting on the bodies of Verger's men instead. When Verger and his henpecked physician, Dr. Cordell (Zeljko Ivanek), appear, Lecter convinces the doctor to dump Verger into the pigpen for spite. "You can always say it was me," Lecter helpfully suggests as the despised Verger is hoisted by his own petard and turned into pig chow. Starling is

Lecter (Anthony Hopkins) is back in the mask again in *Hannibal* (MGM, 2001).

taken to Krendler's country house where Lecter tends to her wounds. She awakens in an upstairs bedroom where she hears voices downstairs and calls the police before going down to investigate. Krendler and Lecter are seated in the dining room, which is elegantly set for an elaborate meal, but she soon finds that the main course is portions of Krendler's brain. Lecter has sawn off the top of Krendler's skull and is slicing off bits of brain tissue, frying them and feeding them to an oblivious Krendler, who is obviously suffering from brain damage. Horrified by this awful scene, she attacks Lecter with a candlestick but is overcome, yet the serial murderer chooses not to harm her and escapes once more before the FBI and police can arrive. In the mind-numbing aftermath, Hannibal is last seen as a passenger on an airplane offering a child a piece of Krendler's brain.

Although *Hannibal* did a brisk business at the box-office, it did not approach the commercial or critical success of *The Silence of the Lambs*. The main problem is the basic story line, as derived from Harris's novel, which transforms the Lecter/Starling duet into a macabre variation on *Beauty and the Beast*. The notion of a May-December relationship between Starling and Lecter strains credulity, as does casting the fearful Hannibal the Cannibal in the role of a romantic leading man. One critic even sarcastically suggested retitling the film, "When Hannibal Met Sally." A number of scenes, including the disemboweling of Pazzi, Verger being devoured by the filthy hogs and Krendler unwittingly snacking on his own brain were shocking and even revolting rather than suspenseful. The narrative is episodic, initially following Starling's travails, then switching locations and protagonists in the Florence interlude, then returning to Starling again in the final act. Scriptwriter Zaillian does improve on the novel's perverse ending, in which Starling and Lecter become lovers and escape to Buenos Aires together, and replaces it with a scenario that seems much more in keeping with Starling's character from *Silence*.

Director Ridley Scott, assisted by cinematographer John Mathieson, crafts a film of great visual beauty, especially in the scenes shot on location in the picturesque city of Florence, but Scott's artful style is not appropriate to the film's horrific subject matter. The gritty, murky visuals of *Silence* have been replaced by the splendors of Scott's gorgeous cinematic palette but this approach works against creating a mood of lurking terror. Instead of a descent into a murderer's mental netherworld, *Hannibal* offers the audience vistas of classical opera and the glories of old-world art and architecture. In his second go-around as Lecter, Anthony Hopkins is ten years older than he was in the previous film and seems to have lost some of the lean and mean menace of the cannibal monster as the actor has mellowed into middle-age. Somehow the Lecter character seemed more frightening in the earlier films when his evil was imprisoned and more accessible for inquiry into his demented interior world.

As feminist FBI heroine Clarice Starling, Julianne Moore delivers a mediocre performance that is inferior to Jodie Foster's intense Oscar-winning performance in the role in *Silence*. It must be noted, however, that Starling's character is not as central to the plot of *Hannibal* as it was to the previous film, thereby diluting the impact of the heroine's part in the sequel. Ray Liotta, so villainous as a heavy in gangster fare like *Goodfellas* (1990), enlivens the scenes he's in as the oily FBI bureaucrat Krendler, but he's afforded very little screen time. British actor Gary Oldman, as the film's obligatory second madman Mason Verger, steals the picture, his horrific visage upstaging even Lecter's when clad in his pugnacious hockey mask. Oldman's elaborate makeup, which made the actor appear grotesquely disfigured, was devised by makeup artist Greg Cannom and consisted of an elaborate silicon appliance that took five hours to attach to Oldman's face. Physically feeble but possessing great power through his vast wealth, the Mason Verger character is a perfect foil for Lecter.

There is less emphasis on police procedural techniques in *Hannibal* than in the first two Lecter outings. The gorgeous, wide-open vistas of Florence contrast with the confined noir spaces of *Silence*. *Hannibal* also reflects a change in public attitude about the FBI in the wake of the tarnishing of the Bureau's image during the Ruby Ridge and Waco debacles in the 1990s. The all-American camaraderie of the Bureau depicted in *Silence* has been replaced by the toxic FBI corporate culture represented by Krendler that is responsible for oppressing the female agent. Still, like the earlier Lecter films, *Hannibal* combines thematic elements of the crime melodrama with the horror film.

The Hannibal *Prequels*

After *Hannibal*, producer Dino De Laurentiis, who still owned the rights to the Lecter character, engineered a third go-round for Hopkins as the character in a remake of Harris's first novel in the series, *Red Dragon* (2002), which had already been filmed by Michael Mann as *Manhunter* in 1986. De Laurentiis made no secret of his disdain for the earlier version and promptly brought in screenwriter Ted Tally, who had won the Oscar for his script for *Silence*, to fashion a prequel designed to expand Lecter's role in the original. In order to create a work that was different from *Manhunter*, Tally incorporated some backstory material on Lecter gleaned from Harris's *Silence* and restored two key scenes from *Red Dragon* that had been deleted from *Manhunter*.

Red Dragon begins with a pre-credit sequence set in 1980 Baltimore, at a celebratory dinner party being given by Lecter after a performance of the city's symphony orchestra. The guests comment on the desultory performance of one of the orchestra's flautists while they unknowingly dine on the man's flesh, which has been prepared as *haute cuisine* by the cannibal doctor for his cultured guests. After the party breaks up Lecter receives a visit from FBI profiler Will Graham (Edward Norton), who is using Hannibal as a forensic consultant on a murder case. During the meeting Graham receives a spontaneous insight that IDs Lecter as the killer, whereupon Lecter attacks and grievously wounds him, but Graham fights back and shoots the doctor so that he can be captured. Lecter is convicted of multiple murders and receives concurrent life sentences without the possibility of parole while Graham, after recuperating from his mental and physical wounds, quits the Bureau and goes to live in Marathon, Florida, with his wife, Molly (Mary-Louise Parker), and son, Josh (Tyler Patrick Jones).

Graham is persuaded to come out of retirement by his old boss, Jack Crawford (Harvey Kietel), to stalk the Tooth Fairy serial killer, who has already murdered two entire families. Stumped for clues, Graham approaches Lecter, who is imprisoned in his dungeon at the Baltimore psychiatric hospital familiar to audiences from *Silence*. Lecter goes through his usual creepy shtick while confronting Graham but delivers little useful information about his fellow serial killer, and the visit inspires Lecter to obtain Graham's home address via a clever subterfuge. The Tooth Fairy is Francis Dolarhyde (Ralph

FBI profiler Will Graham (Edward Norton, right) consults Dr. Lecter (Anthony Hopkins) about the "Tooth Fairy" murders in *Red Dragon* (MGM, 2002).

Fiennes), a St. Louis film technician who lives in a decrepit old building that was formerly a nursing home run by his family. Dolarhyde has a strange fascination with the art of William Blake, and with Hannibal. When a note from the Tooth Fairy is accidentally discovered in Lecter's cell, Graham and Crawford know that the two killers are communicating through personal ads in *The Tattler*, a national tabloid. Decoding Lecter's latest personal ad, they learn that Lecter has passed Graham's home address to his fellow murderer, causing Graham's family to be temporarily moved to a secure location.

Trying to flush out the Tooth Fairy, Crawford and Graham arrange with sleazeball tabloid writer Freddy Lounds (Philip Seymour Hoffman) to publish a provocative article about the killer in the *Tattler*. The Bureau's hope is that the Fairy will retaliate by going after Graham, but he kidnaps Lounds instead. The hapless Lounds is forced to look upon Dolarhyde's naked hide, which is tattooed with grotesque Red Dragon–like designs running down his back. Lounds is returned to the *Tattler*'s parking lot strapped to a flaming wheelchair and later dies of his wounds. The action then shifts to Dolarhyde's newfound romance with Reba McClane (Emily Watson) a blind co-worker at the film development lab who seems to soften the killer's homicidal tendencies for awhile. In an effort to neutralize the forces within him, Dolarhyde travels to the Brooklyn Museum in New York, where he subdues a curator and devours the watercolor painting that has obsessed him, William Blake's *The Great Red Dragon and the Woman Clothed in the Sun*. The Dragon emerges once more, however, when he thinks he sees Reba with another fellow worker, Ralph Mandy (Frank Whaley), causing Dolarhyde to shoot Mandy dead and abduct Reba to the nursing home.

In the meantime Graham and Crawford have traced the Tooth Fairy to the St. Louis film lab and have identified Dolarhyde as their suspect. As they race to his residence, Dolarhyde sets the place on fire and apparently shoots himself dead in front of Reba, although the blind woman cannot actually witness this. She is saved from the fire as the house explodes, and afterward a charred corpse is discovered inside. Believing that the Tooth Fairy is dead, Graham and his family return to Florida, but Graham receives word from the Bureau that the burned body found in Dolarhyde's home was Ralph Mandy's and that the killer may still be at large. Right on cue Dolarhyde shows up at Graham's home and captures Kevin, holding a knife to the boy's throat, but Graham cleverly manipulates the killer psychologically, causing him to free the child and attack him. The Dragon is killed by Graham in the ensuing gunfight, with an assist from Molly's marksmanship and the FBI monster-slayer recovers from his wounds and is made whole once more. Back in his Baltimore cell, Lecter is about to be introduced to Clarice Starling as the series cycles back onto itself.

Despite the presence of Hopkins as Lecter in *Red Dragon*, many critics consider the film an inferior remake of *Manhunter*. In truth, the retread lacks the verve of the original, and seems to be merely a commercial vehicle designed to provide Hopkins with one last turn in the Lecter role. The acting is uninspired and Edward Norton, who had played unusual roles in films like *American History X* (1998) and *Fight Club* (1999), is woefully miscast as profiler Will Graham, his twerpy mannerisms and monotonous delivery of dialogue being wrong for the part. Trying to part company with *Manhunter*, the quasi-psychic Graham is demystified into being nothing more than a clever policeman, and the character is also shorn of the sensitivity and vulnerability he displayed in the original. Even Hopkins seems to have lost much of his enthusiasm for the Lecter role despite having his screen time extended in the remake, and Ralph Fiennes as the Dragon lacks the menace of Tom Noonan in the original. The rest of the cast and director Brett Ratner do a work-manlike but mediocre job.

Hannibal the Cannibal (Anthony Hopkins) is kept on a short leash in *Red Dragon* (MGM, 2002).

While Harris's novel *Hannibal* rang down the curtain on the further misadventures of the cannibal psychiatrist, in 2006 Harris produced a prequel to the three Lecter novels entitled *Hannibal Rising* that developed backstory narratives about Lecter's early life that had been alluded to in *Hannibal*. The De Laurentiis production company lensed the film version in Prague which was released in 2007, and for the first time author Harris became involved in a screen adaptation of one of his works by writing the screenplay. *Hannibal Rising* presented the cannibal's origin story and provided insights into his twisted mentality.

In 1944 Lithuania, eight-year-old Hannibal Lecter (Goran Kostic) and his little sister Mischa (Helena Lia Tachovska) are caught up in the horrors of World War II. Fleeing from the retreating Nazis, the aristocratic Lecter family takes refuge in their country lodge, but both of their parents are killed in the conflict, leaving Hannibal and Mischa to fend for themselves. Their situation becomes dire when a group of Lithuanian SS-wannabe collaborators discover the lodge and take refuge there. The motley crew of brutal thugs includes the leader, Grutas (Rhys Ifans), Kolnas (Kevin McKidd), Dortlich (Richard Brake) and Milko (Ivan Marevich). When food becomes scarce, the militiamen descend into barbarity by killing and eating Mischa, an act that severely traumatizes Hannibal, who nonetheless manages to survive the war.

Eight years later a grown-up Hannibal (Gaspard Ulliel) escapes from a Lithuanian orphanage and transits the Iron Curtain to arrive in France at the estate of his wealthy uncle, who is recently deceased. He is adopted by his mysterious and beautiful Japanese aunt, Lady Murasaki (Gong Li), who becomes a surrogate mother to the boy and teaches him about martial arts and other Oriental practices. Young Hannibal's bloodlust and cannibalistic instincts are brought to the fore when he murders a loutish butcher who has insulted his aunt in public and decapitates him with a samurai sword. Investigating the homicide, police Inspector Popil (Dominic West) notes that parts of the victim's face have been removed, presumably to be eaten by the killer.

A sudden reversal in the family's fortunes causes Lady Murusaki to lose the Lecter estate, forcing her to move to an apartment in Paris while Hannibal attends medical school. He injects himself with a truth serum that allows him to recover his childhood memories and identify the collaborators who murdered and consumed Mischa. The rest of the film chronicles Hannibal's revenge on the ex–Nazis who are now respected members of French society and beyond the reach of the law. One by one his enemies are dispatched in various gruesome ways until only the ringleader, Grutas, is left. The brutal Grutas, a black marketer who traffics in women, tries to turn the tables on Hannibal by kidnapping the Lady Murusaki and keeping her imprisoned on his houseboat. Hannibal undergoes his baptism of blood as he delivers his vengeance unto his foes and travels to America to begin his long career of homicide, cannibalism and medical malpractice.

Easily the least of the five movies featuring Lecter, *Hannibal Rising* attempts to make the character sympathetic and provide some kind of justification for his evil deeds. It's hard to feel this way about Lecter when he is shown with his leering lips dripping with the blood of his victims, even if they are despicable Nazi symps. The militiamen resort to cannibalism because they are starving to death, while Hannibal exacts his pound of flesh just for fun. As Lecter, Gaspard Ulliel has the impossible task of filling the shoes of Oscar-winner Anthony Hopkins and predictably comes up short, but the young actor does project a sense of brooding screen menace in the film's key sequences of violence and mayhem. Thomas Harris, scripting from his own novel, fashions a story that is part war movie, part espionage thriller and part horror movie, but the violent action frequently comes off as being gratuitously sadistic. Director Peter Webber makes stylish use of photogenic European locations but the film's pacing is tepid and its running time over-long. *Hannibal Rising* has the ambience of postwar noirs such as Carol Reed's *The Third Man* (1949), and Dominic West cuts a dashing 1940s-era Gallic noir figure as Inspector Popil.

Lecter's Legacy of Evil

It is undeniable that Thomas Harris created one of the greatest villains in literary history in Hannibal Lecter, paralleled only by the inhuman menace in Bram Stoker's *Dracula* in the late 19th-century. Like Dracula, Lecter is a predatory killer who murders casually and without a hint of conscience. Both physically consume parts of their victim's bodies, and both have superhuman powers of mind that enable them to dominate their prey. They both embody elements of Gothic mystery. And, like Dracula, Lecter's evil persona was greatly amplified by the cinema, as Tod Browning's *Dracula* (1931) and Jonathan Demme's *The Silence of the Lambs* (1991), though separated by six decades, are both milestones in the history of the horror film. A recent poll of members of the American Film Institute rated Hannibal Lecter as the number-one villain in American movies, and the critical and popular success of *The Silence of the Lambs* opened the door to a raft of serial killer thrillers produced during the 1990s. It was also largely responsible for the bizarre cult of the serial killer that emerged in American culture at this time. The inception of the internet created an electronic forum for aficionados of mass mayhem to exchange views, as web sites devoted to the dark deeds of famous murderers sprang up like poisonous fungi and objects they once owned became pricey collector's items. This phenomenon was referenced in a scene in *Hannibal* in which Mason Verger purchases Lecter's hockey mask from a dealer for a six-figure sum.

The *Red Dragon* DVD includes a special feature entitled, "Into the Mind of a Killer," in which real-life FBI profiler John Douglas, who was the inspiration for the Will Graham character in the film, offers his insights into Lecter's psychology using the analytic skills he developed for the FBI's behavioral science unit. Douglas stresses that serial killers are made, not born, and are created by severe childhood traumas similar to those suffered by the young Lecter as depicted in *Hannibal Rising*. Lecter is said to have an "antisocial personality" that centers around a fantasy that can never be fulfilled, and the resolution of this fantasy provides the inspiration for all of the killer's homicidal deeds. In Lecter's case his fantasy revolves around the murder and cannibalism of his sister, Mischa, and it is revealed in *Hannibal Rising* that Lecter himself also partook of Mischa's flesh. He seeks to somehow reverse time and bring Mischa back to life. Although the secondary killers in the Lecter films (the Tooth Fairy in *Manhunter* and *Red Dragon*, Buffalo Bill in *The Silence of the Lambs* and Mason Verger in *Hannibal*) are all depicted as being homosexual or of dubious sexuality, Hannibal himself appears to be nominally hetero. His only relationship with a member of the opposite sex, apart from his quasi-incestuous obsession with the Lady Murusaki, is his platonic fascination with Clarice Starling. One gets the impression that the doctor's vast intellect precludes his having much of an interest in human sexuality of any stripe.

Hannibal Lecter stands as a noir criminal for the ages, a monster whose protean intellect and utter lack of humanity make him a uniquely disturbing individual. Using sophisticated psychology combined with a savage lust for violence, Lecter embodies the anti-social impulses that exist within us all. As we study his monumental evil from afar, within the comforts of our universe of reason and order, Hannibal merely snorts, "Smell yourself," for we are all endowed with a capacity for wickedness. As Thomas Harris writes in *Hannibal*: "But this we all share with the doctor: In the vaults of our hearts and brains, danger waits. All the chambers are not lovely, light and high. There are holes in the floor of the mind, like those in a medieval dungeon floor.... Nothing escapes from them quietly to ease us. A quake, some betrayal by our safeguards, and sparks of memory fire the noxious gases— things trapped for years fly free, ready to explode in pain and drive us to dangerous behavior."[4]

12

The Mean Streets of Hell

Horror films in the beginning of the decade of the 1990s continued to flounder in the mediocrity of seemingly endless sequels of the once-popular genre franchises in films like *Freddy's Dead: The Final Nightmare* (1991), *Jason Goes to Hell: The Final Friday* (1993) and *Halloween 6: The Curse of Michael Myers* (1995). As some of these titles suggest, these repetitive horror series entries had pretty much run out of steam, although Wes Craven's *Scream* (1996) and its sequels would breathe new life into the slasher film. The horror film was poised to go in new directions later in the decade, however, with innovative fare that included the docu-terrors of *The Blair Witch Project* (1999) and a sophisticated revival of the supernatural ghost story in *The Sixth Sense* (1999). The mega-success of *The Silence of the Lambs* (1991) also served to re-orient the genre in a new direction in which mystery and police procedural themes merged with horror in films such as *Se7en* (1995), *Fallen* (1998) and *The Bone Collector* (1999), in which urban cops stalked mysterious serial killers down the mean streets of hell.

Neo-noir reached new heights of critical acclaim and audience popularity during the '90s as the genre explored new themes such as incest in Steven Frears's *The Grifters* (1990), explicit sexuality in Paul Verhoeven's *Basic Instinct* (1992) and John Dahl's *The Last Seduction* (1993), African American noir in Carl Franklin's *Devil in a Blue Dress* (1995) and black comedy in the Coen Brothers's *Fargo* (1996). Curtis Hanson's retro-noir *L.A. Confidential* (1997) featured a stellar cast and garnered two Academy Awards, but the most important neo-noir of the decade was surely writer/director/producer Quentin Tarantino's radical *Pulp Fiction* (1994), which redefined the structures of film narrative in its exquisitely complex, Oscar-winning screenplay and also made a ton of money at the box-office. Other memorable noirs of the decade included Martin Scorsese's remake of *Cape Fear* (1991), the Coens' *Miller's Crossing* (1990), David Lynch's *Wild at Heart* (1990), Tarantino's *Reservoir Dogs* (1992) and Bryan Singer's *The Usual Suspects* (1995).

As related in Chapter 10, William Peter Blatty's novel *The Exorcist* contained a mystery-crime subplot revolving around homicide detective Lt. William F. Kinderman's investigation of the murder of film director Burke Jennings. The Kinderman character, played by Lee J. Cobb in the 1973 film version, had his part severely cut back in the movie as this aspect of the plot became de-emphasized. In 1983 Blatty's sequel, entitled *Legion*, was published, which combined the serial killer thriller with supernatural mystery and made Lt. Kinderman into the lead character in the piece. After languishing in development hell for a number of years, Blatty got to script and direct his novel, which was released in 1990 as *Exorcist III: Legion*.

The story takes place 15 years after the events of *The Exorcist*, where a series of baffling murders has struck Georgetown. Lt. Kinderman (here played by George C. Scott) visits a murder scene where an African American man of his acquaintance has been brutally murdered in the idiosyncratic manner of the "Gemini Killer" a serial murderer who had been executed 15 years earlier. The victim has been decapitated, his right index finger cut off, and the astrological sign for Gemini carved into the palm of his left hand, details that had never been released to the public. Later that day movie-lover Kinderman and his cinema buddy Father Dyer (the amiable priest from the first movie, played here by Ed Flanders) attend a showing of *It's a Wonderful Life* at a revival house and share memories of Father Karras (Jason Miller), who had died during the exorcism of Regan McNeil 15 years earlier.

Soon afterward a priest is found murdered in a church in the same manner as the victims of the Gemini Killer, causing Kinderman to have concerns about Dyer, who has been admitted to a local hospital for a routine checkup. That night Kinderman has a strange dream in which he visits Dyer in a vast train depot that is a kind of waiting room for Heaven, where winged angels oversee human souls on their way to the Kingdom and Dyer tells him, "I'm not dreaming." The next day Dyer is found murdered at the hospital, all his blood having been drained and neatly arranged in an array of plastic hospital cups. The words "It's a Wonderful Life" are written on the wall of his room in the priest's blood, the word "wonderful" being spelled with an extra "l" in the manner of the Gemini Killer. Another oddity is that the fingerprints found at all three murder scenes do not match up, indicating that the killings were committed by three different people.

Kinderman learns from the hospital's psychiatric director, Dr. Temple (Scott Wilson), about an inmate known only as "Patient X," an unidentified man found wandering the streets 15 years earlier who has been in a catatonic state until very recently, when he awakened to claim that he is the Gemini Killer. Confronting Patient X in his padded cell, he finds that the body of Father Damien Karras, thought to have been dead for a decade and a half, has been possessed by the spirit of the Gemini, James Venamun (Brad Dourif), who appears as his true self to the audience. The Karras/Venamun entity claims responsibility for the murders, which seems unlikely as he is confined to a high-security cell at the hospital. The next morning, however, Dr. Temple and a nurse are found murdered in the psychiatric wing in a manner implicating the Gemini.

When he returns to the patient's cell for another interview, Venamun reveals to Kinderman that the demon who possessed Regan McNeil 15 years earlier was greatly angered about being deprived of a dwelling place, and installed the just-executed Gemini killer's soul into the body of the dying exorcist Father Karras just for spite. Venamun's spirit is able to leave his body and take control of elderly patients in the psychiatric wing who suffer from senile dementia and use their bodies to commit the killings, which explains the variety of fingerprints found at the murder sites. When Kinderman decides to take a look at the patients in the ward, he is unknowingly stalked by a spirit-possessed old woman crawling upside-down on the ceiling like a fly, but the detective escapes unharmed. The demonic goings-on reach a boiling point when one of the hospital's chaplains, Father Morning (Nicol Williamson), attempts an exorcism and is nearly killed by psychic forces unleashed by the powers of Hell. Kinderman arrives on the scene and is also overwhelmed by the supernatural maelstrom until Morning succeeds in exorcising Venumun's spirit from Karras's body. The dead-alive Karras begs the detective to end his torment, and Kinderman complies by blowing his brains out with his police revolver. In an epilogue, Karras's body is given a proper burial and the long-suffering priest is mourned by Kinderman.

Blatty acquits himself surprisingly well in the director's chair, and while *Exorcist III* falls far short of its famous progenitor, the film is still a stylish and effective horror noir thriller. It's certainly a much better job than his previous directorial effort, the semi-intelligible crypto-Gothic "thriller" entitled *The Ninth Configuration* (a.k.a. *Twinkle, Twinkle, "Killer Kane,"* 1979). Blatty builds mood and suspense nicely throughout the movie and uses scenic Georgetown locations to good effect as a realistic metropolitan backdrop for the mysterious murders. The juxtaposition of actors Brad Dourif and Jason Miller taking onscreen turns as the Gemini Killer is a tad confusing, however, and the frequent verbal confrontations between Kinderman and the Gemini are plodding and repetitious, although these scenes seem to anticipate similar interviews between a detective and a serial killer in *The Silence of the Lambs*, released in the following year. Blatty's screenplay contains a number of loopy and allegedly comic scenes, however, including the sequence filmed inside the heavenly train station, which comes complete with an angelic '40s-era swing band kicking out Glenn Miller tunes. *Exorcist III* also suffers from an alteration in the novel's ending to include an exorcism, a change insisted on by the studio, that results in a greatly weakened denouement.

Unfortunately, despite an interesting cast *Exorcist III: Legion* fails in the acting department, the worst offender being Oscar-winner George C. Scott in the lead role of Kinderman, who gives a tepid portrayal of the veteran homicide detective. Perennial weirdo Brad Dourif steals the show as the Hannibal Lecter–like Gemini Killer Venumun, who travels from body to body, but the rest of the cast turn in indifferent, forgettable performances. This is particularly true of Jason Miller as Father Karras, who was so effective as the title character in *The Exorcist* and seems to have been inserted here merely to have an actor from the first movie present onscreen. The film also contains several silly and inexplicable cameo appearances by a number of celebrities, including actor Samuel L. Jackson, basketball stars Patrick Ewing and John Thompson, cable-TV personality Larry King, ex–U.S. Surgeon General C. Everett Koop and male supermodel Fabio (as an angel). In its conception at least, *Exorcist III* skillfully melds the horrors of demon possession with old-school noir police procedural into a supernatural mystery story that recalls the novel version of *The Exorcist*.

Another offbeat horror noir released that year was British director Adrian Lyne's *Jacob's Ladder* (1990). Tim Robbins stars as Jacob Singer, who, in the film's opening scenes is an American soldier fighting in the Mekong Delta during the Vietnam War in 1971. During a firefight Jacob's unit is hit by some mysterious gas and Jacob becomes disoriented and is separated from his unit when he receives a bayonet wound to the gut. Abruptly, he awakens from what is apparently a dream on a grimy New York City subway train. It is five years later and he is now a postman returning home after working the night shift. The train is eerily empty except for a couple of ghostly looking passengers, and when he disembarks at his stop he realizes he cannot exit the station and has to cross the tracks, where he is almost run down by an approaching train and sees people with weird faces staring out of the windows at him.

Jacob is divorced from his first wife, Sarah (Patricia Kalember), who has custody of his two sons from their marriage, while a third son, Gabe (Macaulay Culkin), was killed in an auto accident before Jacob left for 'Nam. After the breakup of their marriage, Jacob has moved in with his hot-blooded Latina girlfriend, Jezzy (Elizabeth Pena), in a ratty New York walk-up. While on the surface everything about his life seems normal, Jacob begins to experience vivid "dreams" and spontaneous flashbacks about being back in Vietnam. His chiropractor, Louie (Danny Aiello), who also acts as a mentor and confidante, tries to put his body and mind back into alignment while intimating that Jacob is undergoing something far deeper. "It's a deep adjustment," Louie tells him during a chiropractic session, but Jacob continues to see "demons" stalking him. He is almost run over by a car full of mysterious men and attends an orgiastic dance party where the dancers, including Jezzie, appear to morph into a mass of grotesque monsters. Jacob becomes gravely ill with a high fever after the party and must be placed in a bathtub full of ice water as an emergency measure to bring his fever down, the shock of which causes him to lose consciousness.

When he awakens he inexplicably finds himself in bed with his first wife, Sarah, as if their divorce had never taken place and his son Gabe is alive once more. Jacob tells Sarah about his "dream" of living with Jezzie, but he soon "wakes up" to find himself in the bathtub once more. After his recovery, Jacob gets a call from one of his Army buddies, Paul Gruninger (Pruitt Taylor Vince), and when the two meet, Paul confesses that he has been suffering from strange dreams and frightening hallucinations after his service and suspects malfeasance by the U.S. Army. After their meeting Paul is killed when his vehicle explodes in an apparent car bombing as Jacob watches in horror. At Paul's funeral the other platoon members confess their suspicions about being guinea pigs in some clandestine Army experiment and contact shyster lawyer Geary (*Seinfeld*'s Jason Alexander in an early role) in a bid to launch a class-action lawsuit against the government. When the other former troopers mysteriously withdraw from the suit, Jacob confronts Geary, who informs him that official records show that his unit never served in 'Nam, but were discharged after participating in "war games" in Thailand.

Jacob Singer (Tim Robbins) is subjected to bizarre medical experiments in *Jacob's Ladder* (Carolco/TriStar, 1990).

In a state of total bewilderment, Jacob continues to yo-yo back and forth between his life with Jezzie, his alternate existence with Sarah and his "memories" of being wounded in Vietnam. Then he is kidnapped by three men in a government limousine, presumably espionage agents, who rough him up and warn him about continuing his inquiry before throwing him out of the car. While he is unconscious his ID is stolen by a man dressed as Santa Claus. In the film's most nightmarish sequence, Jacob is taken to a bizarre "hospital" for emergency treatment and wheeled down filthy corridors strewn with severed body parts, where he is subjected to a surgical procedure that seems more like an autopsy. When he protests that he wants to go home, the lead doctor blandly tells him, "This is your home, you're dead. You've been killed, don't you remember?" Jacob awakens to find himself recuperating in a public hospital, where Louie arrives to rescue him and offer solace. While performing another chiropractic adjustment, Louie begins discussing the philosophy of Christian mystic Meister Eckhart. "The only thing that burns in Hell is the part of you that won't let go of life, your memories, your attachments," he explains to Jacob. "So, if you're frightened of dying and you're holding on, you'll see devils tearing your life away. But if you've made your peace, then the devils are really angels, freeing you from the earth."

As he ponders Louie's advice, Jacob is contacted by a mysterious individual named Michael Newman (Matt Craven), who claims to be a "hippie chemist" unwillingly recruited by the government to produce a super-hallucinogen dubbed "The Ladder," a noxious drug that had the effect of greatly enhancing human aggression. Michael reveals that Jacob's unit was unwittingly dosed with The Ladder and began killing one another, and Jacob is still suffering from flashbacks and hallucinations from the lingering effects of the drug. In the end, however, all the layers of illusion are stripped away to reveal the truth: all of his postwar life is a reverie experienced in Jacob's mind as he is dying in a field hospital in Vietnam.

Jacob's Ladder was the brainchild of screenwriter Bruce Joel Rubin, who was inspired by American horror writer Ambrose Bierce's 1886 short story, "An Occurrence at Owl Creek Bridge," a similarly themed tale of the last moments of a Civil War soldier's life. The story was made into a short film by Robert Enrico and shown on American television as an episode of *The Twilight Zone* in 1964. Rubin also drew inspiration from the Buddhist text *The Tibetan Book of the Dead*, which details the worlds of illusion experienced by the soul as it is dying. A film noir take on this idea provides the basis for John Boorman's *Point Blank* (1967), in which Lee Marvin plays a violent gangster who is shot at point blank range in a cell on Alcatraz and somehow "survives" to wreak vengeance on his betrayers, but the film suggests that his revenge is merely a figment of his imagination that he experiences while he is dying. Rubin also wrote *Ghost* (1990), another story revolving around ideas about life after death, but his screenplay for *Jacob's Ladder* is a much deeper and more disquieting treatment of this theme that was later echoed in M. Night Shyamalan's popular supernatural thriller *The Sixth Sense* (1999), a similar narrative about a bewildered man who doesn't know he's a ghost. Another possible influence was Herk Harvey's cult classic *Carnival of Souls* (1962), in which a drowning woman imagines that she is being pursued by ghostly figures. Rubin's script is beautifully constructed as a psychological and metaphysical horror story that takes place in the borderland between life and the afterlife and unfolds as an existential mystery.

Director Lyne employs the same realistic style he uses in films like *Fatal Attraction*

(1987) and *Unfaithful* (2002) to create Jacob's cinematic netherworld, a simulacrum of New York City inhabited by the ghosts and demons of Jacob Singer's mind. This realism is ultimately what makes the film convincing as the eerie events of the narrative are played out against this prosaic urban backdrop. Lyne envisions New York as a gritty necropolis, a noir city of the mind's eye, a suffocating maze of drab streets, cramped apartments and dank hospitals, and Brian Morris, who had worked as art director on Alan Parker's *Angel Heart*, assisted Lyne in crafting the dark urban milieu of the film. Tim Robbins portrays Jacob Singer as an affable everyman who tragically descends into his own private hell, while co-stars Elizabeth Pena and Danny Aiello provide deft touches of ethnic authenticity. Well conceived, finely acted and beautifully directed, *Jacob's Ladder* constitutes a minor classic of the horror film and represents a unique philosophical and metaphysical take on the genre.

Like *The Seventh Victim* and *Wolfen*, *Jacob's Ladder* exploits the myriad terrors of its mega-urban New York environment and like Alex Proyas's nightmarish sci-fi noir *Dark City* (1998) posits a city of shadows from which there is no escape. Jacob's existential dilemma is fraught with a typically noir nightmare surrealism, a web of fate in which the protagonist is helplessly caught. Writer Bruce Joel Rubin explains his concept of the film thusly: "The horror of the movie would be in the revelation that hope is hell's final torment, that life is a dream that ends over and over with the final truth, that life was never real, that we are all creatures trapped in eternal suffering and damnation."[1]

Raymond Chandler Meets H.P. Lovecraft

The era of American pulp fiction in the 1930s produced a number of renowned writers who worked in the various genres of the pulp magazines. Raymond Chandler wrote hard-boiled crime stories for pulps like *Black Mask* and created the primordial private eye hero Philip Marlowe, who would later star in the classic noir novels *The Big Sleep* and *The Long Goodbye*, among others. Howard Philips Lovecraft wrote arcane horror stories for *Weird Tales* magazine about strange gods who wish to permeate our reality in his cycle of horror stories referred to as the "Cthulhu Mythos." The pulp universes of Marlowe and Cthulhu intersected in a pair of mystery/comedy/horror thrillers made for cable television by HBO Pictures and executive-produced by Gale Ann Hurd, who had worked with James Cameron on the sci-fi classics *The Terminator* and *Aliens*. These films were set in an alternate-world Los Angeles in which magic has emerged as an alternative form of technology and the protagonist is a typically hard-boiled film noir private eye with the genre-meld moniker of "Philip Lovecraft."

The first film, *Cast a Deadly Spell* (1991), is a sendup of Chandler's premiere Marlowe novel, *The Big Sleep*. Fred Ward stars as Philip Lovecraft, a typically world-weary P.I. who disdains the use of magic in his private and professional life despite the conventional wisdom that magic "makes everything easier." Decrying a world where murders can be committed by voodoo dolls or sorcerous spells, Lovecraft shuns magic for undisclosed "personal reasons," which puts him at a severe disadvantage. There are some who appreciate Lovecraft's principled stand, however, as one character observes, "You're the only guy I know walking around without a magic wand up his ass." Forever down on his luck, Lovecraft shares his typically seedy office with African American voodoo practitioner Hypolite Kropotkin (Arnetia Walker), who runs a dancing school next door.

Chandlerian private eye Phillip Lovecraft (Fred Ward, left) squares off against sorcerer Amos Hackshaw (David Warner) in *Cast a Deadly Spell* (HBO, 1991).

As the film opens, Lovecraft is summoned to the mansion of the ultra-wealthy Amos Hackshaw (David Warner), whose twin obsessions are book collecting and preserving the virginity of his precocious 16-year-old daughter, Olivia (Alexandra Powers). Hackshaw hires Lovecraft to find a rare book of magic spells that has been stolen from his library by his former chauffeur, Larry Willis (Lee Tergesen). The book is called the *Necronomicon* (familiar to H.P. Lovecraft's readers as the dread grimoire of the mad Arab Abdul Alhazred), and Hackshaw wants it retrieved ASAP. On his way out of the Hackshaw estate, Lovecraft has a close encounter with the maidenly yet worldly-wise Olivia, who is kept in seclusion on the rich man's palatial estate and whose hormones are kicking in big time. Olivia is yearning to experience the joys of womanhood, but the private detective is able to keep his cool in the face of her surprisingly sophisticated flirtations while they trade witty verbal banter in the time-honored noir tradition of Bogart and Bacall.

That evening, at a swanky nightclub called the Dunwich Room, would-be criminal Mickey Locksteader (Ken Thorley) is trying to fence Hackshaw's copy of the *Necronomican* to the suave gangster and club owner Harry Bordon (Clancy Brown), but when the book is found to be a bogus copy, Bordon dispatches the dwarfish sorcerer Tugwell (Raymond O'Connor) and hulking undead henchman Zombie (Jaime Cardriche) to settle the score. The hapless Locksteader is murdered in a men's room by Tugwell using "the death by a thousand paper cuts," a whirling mass of papers that reduce Locksteader to a bloody pulp. Meanwhile, Lovecraft finds a clue at Willis's vacated apartment that leads him to the Dunwich Room in search of Locksteader's elusive girlfriend named Lily Sirwar. At the nightclub Lovecraft renews his acquaintance with an old flame, sultry songstress Connie Stone (Julianne Moore), but fails to come up with any clues. He does come to Bordon's attention, however, and Tugwell is sent to murder Lovecraft by passing him a paper inscribed with a runic spell that summons a demon, but the attempt is unsuccessful.

Lovecraft eventually figures out that "Lily Sirwar" is really Larry Willis in drag, but as he tracks the cross-dressing thief to his hotel room and retrieves the *Necronomicon*, the private eye is followed by Bordon's henchmen, who appropriate the book and take Lovecraft back to their boss for good measure. The gangster reveals that, with the spell-book in his possession once more, Hackshaw is preparing to summon the dread demon Yog-Sottoth from the void and offer the virgin Olivia to it as a human sacrifice. Driving out to the Hackshaw estate that night for the ceremony with Connie and Lovecraft in tow, Bordon gloats that he will be Hackshaw's number-one guy in the coming world that will be dominated by black magic, but in the event the hard-hearted Connie kills Bordon, wishing to take his place, and double-crosses Lovecraft. Olivia is trussed up and offered to the slimy Yog-Sottoth, who duly emerges from the void when summoned by Hackshaw's spells to claim its prize, but instead of accepting the sacrifice, the demon turns on Hackshaw and consumes him. It is later revealed that the spell failed because Olivia had been secretly deflowered by LAPD detective Lt. Grimaldi (Peter Allas), who had been assigned to stake out the Hackshaw estate and wound up trysting with the girl. In the end the world is saved by an act of statutory rape committed by a policeman and Connie is taken into custody for Borden's murder.

Cast a Deadly Spell combines the film noir universe of Chandler with the eldritch horrors of Lovecraft by injecting a third element of humor to unite the two disparate elements. The clever script by Joseph Dougherty does full justice to both pulp fiction traditions in comic fashion. Some of the amusing horror noir tropes include a werewolf being grilled by aggressive cops in a back room at the station house, L.A. tract housing being built by zombie labor (referred to as "applied industrial thaumaturgy") and tranced-out policemen holding hands in a séance to obtain psychic evidence. Director Martin Campbell evokes the dark urban mood of film noir where appropriate while never losing his comic timing, but the film's horrors are played strictly for laughs and its gremlins, demons and werewolves are of the comic book variety.

As Philip Lovecraft, Fred Ward ably projects the strengths and weaknesses of the film's Chandlerian private eye protagonist. His breezy performance is also perfectly suited to bring out the laughs. The Lovecraft character subscribes to Philip Marlowe's lofty moral codes, especially in his refusal to use magic. "I'm my own man," he proclaims with steely conviction. "Nobody owns a mortgage on my soul. I own it free and clear." One feels that Marlowe, caught in Phil Lovecraft's position, would have felt exactly the same way. Romantic interest Julianne Moore makes for a beautifully icy, redheaded *femme fatale* nightclub singer, while perennial heavy Clancy Brown exudes oily menace as the mustachioed 1940s mobster Harry Bordon. British actor David Warner is perfectly cast as the typically acerbic Chandlerian rich man and Alexandra Powers is charmingly innocent, yet worldly wise as Olivia. All in all, *Cast a Deadly Spell* is a witty, funny meld of classic film noir and Lovecraftian horror sporting a great cast and a highly literate script.

Three years later HBO produced a sequel entitled *Witch Hunt* (1994), in which neo-noir stalwart Dennis Hopper took over the role of Philip Lovecraft. Paul Schrader, writer of *Taxi Driver* (1976) and director of *Cat People* (1982), was at the helm and John Dougherty, who had written the previous film, contrived the script as an homage to Chandler's 1950s-era Marlowe novel *The Long Goodbye*, in which Marlowe is involved in an investigation of Hollywood's film business. *Witch Hunt* is set in 1953, when private investigator Lovecraft (Hopper) is still coping with his dislike of magic ("Never touch the stuff, myself"), and this time he's not alone. Senator Larson Crockett (Eric Bogosian) is leading a McCarthyite crusade against magic by claiming it is "un–American," and is set to hold Congressional hearings on the matter in the light of new laws that have just been passed authorizing capital punishment for practitioners of the magical arts that are deemed to be subversive.

One day a beautiful woman named Kim Hudson (Penelope Ann Miller) arrives at Lovecraft's office and turns out to be the wife of big shot movie mogul N.J. Gotleib (Alan Rosenberg). Kim has suspicions that her hubby is cheating on her with a young actress and hires Lovecraft to keep tabs on Gotleib. In order to take the measure of the man, the private eye tags along with his witchy-woman neighbor Hypolite Kropotkin (played here by Sheryl Lee Ralph) on a trip to Gotleib's studio, where she uses her magic to resurrect the shades of William Shakespeare and Mark Twain to work in the studio's story department (!). While at the studio Lovecraft runs into a fellow P.I. named Finn Macha (Julian Sands), who does use magic in his practice and is working security for Gotleib. The two have a cordial chat but Lovecraft wonders what Macha has been hired to do for the studio head.

That night Lovecraft tails Gotleib to a secluded house he owns in the Los Feliz area of L.A. but hangs back. "The last thing I needed," he confides in voice-over, "was to get turned to stone or wind up with the body of a goat." His fears are well-founded, however, when he is put to sleep by magical means and wakes up clueless the next day. Meanwhile, over at the studio, Gotleib is subjected to a shrinking spell and is reduced to doll-size, whereupon he is chewed to death by his two pet Dobermans. "Somebody put the big whammy on Gotleib and cut him down to size," one policeman observes while the mogul's diminutive remains are being scraped into a lunch box. At that moment Senator Crockett shows up to exploit the murder as an example of the evils of magic before the TV cameras. After shooting the TV spot, Crockett approaches Lovecraft about joining his anti-magic movement, but the P.I. declines. In the aftermath of Gotleib's murder, Kim instructs Lovecraft to find out who killed her husband.

Lovecraft, assisted by Hypolite's magic skills, visits a Malibu beach house owned by Gotleib only to find it has been wiped clean not only of fingerprints but of psychic "vibes" as well. Returning to survey the Los Feliz house, Lovecraft gets nailed by a trio of thugs and taken inside (the interior was filmed at the famous Ennis-Brown House, a futuristic structure designed by Frank Lloyd Wright and used to great effect in movies like *Blade Runner* and *Black Rain*). He discovers that the place is, in reality, a high-class bordello run by madam Vivian Dart (John Epperson, a.k.a. "Lypsinka" in drag), where magic is used to enhance the client's erotic experiences. As he is observing all this, Lovecraft runs into Finn Moxa, who is now working for Dart and escorts him outside, without incident, as a professional courtesy.

All of this intrigue is related to Senator Crockett's "No More Magic in Hollywood" crusade, which he hopes will propel him into the White House. Crockett holds televised public hearings in L.A. and Kim, called as a witness in the matter of Gotleib's sorcerous murder, is made to wrongly implicate Hypolite as her husband's murderer. Acting as judge, jury and executioner, Crockett orders the "murderer and consort of the Devil," Hypolite, to be publicly burned at the stake during a massive anti-magic rally being held the next day. Unfortunately for the Senator, Crockett makes the mistake of trying to cross Finn Moxa, who retaliates by using his magic to reveal Crockett's noxious "inner self" while he is making his big speech at the rally, and Hypolite is freed unharmed. It turns out that Valerie Dart and Moxa have been involved in a scheme to blackmail the Senator over the accidental death of one of Dart's prostitutes during a bout of rough sex (an obvious reference to a similar plotline in *Godfather II*). In the film's climax, Lovecraft must overcome his aversion to magic and draw upon his own latent magical powers to defeat Moxa, who has kidnapped Kim and is threatening to murder her.

Screenwriter Joseph Dougherty, who had penned *Cast a Deadly Spell*, delivers another charming, funny and highly literate script that sparkles with witty noir dialogue, cleverly references movies like *Targets*, *Sunset Boulevard* and *Godfather II*, and satirizes the McCarthyite "witch hunt" Hollywood blacklists of the early 1950s. Dougherty also tones down the emphasis on H.P. Lovecraft's transcendental horrors of the "Cthulthu Mythos" in the sequel in favor of a more generic concept of magic. The main problem with *Witch Hunt*, however, is in Paul Schrader's execution. Eschewing the confined spaces, expressionist angles and shadowy, low-key lighting that are the stylistic hallmarks of film noir, Schrader instead shoots most scenes in bright pastel tones and in full daylight. Lovecraft's office, for instance, is airy and modern and decorated in glowing turquoise, a design scheme that is diametrically opposed to Philip Marlowe's cramped and dingy workplace or of Lovecraft's earlier digs in *Deadly Spell*. *Witch Hunt* also lacks the star power of the first film. Dennis Hopper, so effective playing wicked, charismatic villains in films like *Blue Velvet* (1986) and *Speed* (1994), is miscast in the role of P.I. Lovecraft, and brings none of the charm shown by Fred Ward to the part. It's left to supporting players Julian Sands as the sorcerous private eye Finn Moxa and John Epperson as the bizarro madam of the magical whorehouse to provide some acting flair as typically noir grotesques. Both *Cast a Deadly Spell* and *Witch Hunt* are light-hearted, delightful excursions into a hazy, crazy borderland between classic film noir and fantastic horror.

Lord of Illusions

British writer/director Clive Barker rose to prominence as the author of popular horror fiction that would ultimately evolve into the *Hellraiser* (1987) and *Candyman* (1992) film franchises. Acting as co-producer, scenarist and director, Barker adapted his horror noir private eye character Harry D'Amour for the big screen in *Lord of Illusions* (1994). Barker has described D'Amour as being inspired by Dashiell Hammett's Sam Spade, Raymond Chandler's Philip Marlowe and Carl Kolchak in *The Night Stalker*. D'Amour is as hard-boiled and street- tough as they come in film noir, but also has an instinct for getting his nose into a big stinking pile of supernatural trouble.

Lord of Illusions opens with an ominous title that proclaims, "There are two worlds of magic. One is the glittering domain of the illusionist. The other is a secret place, where magic is a terrifying reality. Here men have the power of demons, and death itself is an illusion." The action begins deep in the Mojave desert in 1982, where demonic messiah Nix, a.k.a. "The Puritan" (Daniel Von Bargen) holds his acolytes in thrall by demonstrating his magical control over fire inside the cult's ratty compound, which is adorned with awful images of death and dread. Suddenly, Nix's former chief disciple, Philip Swann (Kevin J. O'Connor), arrives at the compound with a hit squad of ex-cultists who are on a mission to rid the world of the black sorcerer's evil after he has kidnapped a 12-year-old girl to use as a human sacrifice. A gun battle and a magical conflict ensue, in which Nix is killed by Swann and his dark wizardry confined to the netherworld by Swann's powers.

Thirteen years later, in New York, private investigator Harry D'Amour (*Quantum Leap*'s Scott Bakula) is recovering from his last assignment in his apartment/office, where a lurid headline in the tabloid *New York Post* proclaims in bold type: PRIVATE EYE IN BROOKLYN EXORCISM DRAMA. Harry, who, according to the *Post* article "has been linked with occult activities on several occasions," is unexpectedly offered a more mundane job investigating a case of insurance fraud in Los Angeles. Traveling to the Left Coast, D'Amour tails his suspect to a fortune teller's digs in a rundown L.A. office building, where he discovers the seer, Caspar Quaid (Joseph Latimore), pierced with knives by two of Nix's former cultists. Harry fights off the two goth punks, and Quaid, who was formerly one of Swann's team that took out Nix, warns Harry that the Puritan is returning and tells him that "you must walk the line between Heaven and Hell" before dying.

Hearing about D'Amour's involvement with the homicide in the news, Swann's wife Dorothea (Famke Janssen) contacts Harry. She is concerned about Quaid's strange prophecy and wants to hire D'Amour to keep an eye on her husband, offering him five thou a day for his services, to which Harry replies, "Do I get lunch?" Swann is now a famous illusionist who has been hard at work developing a new trick for his act, but it appears that some of his stage magic is not an illusion. Harry and Dorothea attend Swann's gala performance at L.A.'s Pantages Theater, where, after an elaborately baroque stage show, Swann unveils his new illusion, which involves falling swords on a rotating table. Something goes terribly wrong with the trick, however, and Swann is killed when the swords fatally impale him. Fearing that remnants of the Puritan's cult may have somehow been responsible for Swann's death, Dorothea keeps Harry on the case, and he promises to "dig in places the cops wouldn't look."

One of those places is the "magician's circle," a gathering of illusionists that convenes at L.A.'s Magic Castle. Pretending to be a professional stage magician, Harry attends the meeting, where he befriends a young conjurer named Billy Who (Lorin Stewart). After the meeting, the iconoclastic Billy helps D'Amour break into the Castle's Repository, a hidden room where all the trade secrets of the magician's fraternity are kept. Harry retrieves files on Nix and his cult, and their worst fears are justified when they are assailed by a series of terrifying hallucinations projected at them by the Puritan's magic. The private eye eventually learns that Dorothea is, in reality, the 12-year-old girl that Swann rescued from Nix 13 years earlier. He also tracks down Swann, who is still alive and hiding in seclusion, having arranged the illusion of his own death because he feared the return of Nix. In the meantime the former cultists have heard the call of Nix from beyond the grave and are coming from all over the country for a reunion at Nix's compound. Then the brutal cult leader Butterworth (Barry Del Sherman) kidnaps Dorothea and transports her out to the Mojave, where he exhumes Nix's body and resurrects him to life. Realizing what has happened, Swann and D'Amour join forces and race out to the desert to rescue Dorothea and do battle with the newly risen Nix and his demented followers.

Barker, directing from his screenplay adaptation of his short story "The Last Illusion," had a large measure of creative control over the film. The script emphasizes the tangled relationship between real magic, illusion and religion. Nix represents an antichrist figure who dies and is reborn, wields awe-inspiring miraculous powers, and proclaims, "I was born to murder the world." Nix and his demented disciples were reportedly based on serial killer Charles

Scott Bakula as P.I. Harry D'Amour in *Lord of Illusions* (United Artists, 1995).

Harry D'Amour (Scott Bakula) and Dorthea (Famke Janssen) invade the domain of an evil cult leader in *Lord of Illusions* (United Artists, 1995).

Manson and his homicidal "Family." Visually, Barker deliberately avoided using noirish visuals in *Lord of Illusions*. "The movie *isn't* an homage to noir," he stated in an interview. "I deliberately sat down with the DP [Ronn Schmidt] and said, 'Look, we're not going to do what *Angel Heart* did brilliantly,' which was to reference noir visually. You know, sunlight through venetian blinds falling on a desk with a P.I. with a slouch hat on. It wasn't going to look like a Raymond Chandler novel."[2] Instead, the film conjures a neo-noir visual sensibility, a hard-edged realism punctuated with intensely color-saturated shadows. Barker also makes effective use of computer animation to depict Nix's terrifying illusions and elaborate make-up and visual effects by Thomas C. Rainone to enhance the film's ghastly sense of dread.

Scott Bakula's straight-up performance as hard-hitting private eye Harry D'Amour easily carries the film and creates a believable borderline figure that stands at the juncture of the two genres. *Lord of Illusions* continues the tradition of self-consciously created genre-melding characters such as Carl Kolchak, Harry Angel and Philip Lovecraft. This super hard-boiled horror noir P.I. must not only face off against psychotic criminals but must also confront the terrors of the occult as well, and could well be described as being a sort of "Van Helsing with a gun." Bakula's D'Amour is more of a Sam Spade than a Philip Marlowe, a tough-as-nails noir private detective who's inclined to dish it out rather than take it, and does so with great relish. Character actor Daniel Von Bargen exudes an eerie supernatural menace as the loathsome Nix, the film's titular lord of illusions and is ably assisted by Barry Del Sherman as Nix's gothic cult creature Butterworth. The one false note is struck by comic actor Kevin J. O'Connor, who bears a resemblance to comedian Jim Carrey and is sorely miscast in the crucial role of Swann. In comparison with the similarly themed *Angel Heart*, *Lord of Illusions* is less arty but perhaps more accessible and lacks *Angel Heart*'s nihilistic, downbeat thematics.

Meet John Doe

During the 1990s the big screen was assaulted by a multitude of serial killers after the commercial and critical success of *The Silence of the Lambs*. Films like *Henry, Portrait of a Serial Killer* (1990), *Kalifornia* (1993) and *Natural Born Killers* (1994) exploited the serial killer mystique and created a new cultural icon. As in *Silence*, a new breed of law-enforcement agents would arise to do battle with these ultra-violent purveyors of cultural chaos. A classic example of this conflict took place in David Fincher's serial killer thriller *Se7en* (1995).

The action takes place over a period of exactly seven days in the dank, haunted metropolis of New York. Morgan Freeman stars as William Somerset, a seasoned NYPD homicide detective who has just one week left before he retires and leaves the cursed city behind forever. His replacement is brash upstart David Mills (Brad Pitt), an ambitious young Turk looking to make a name for himself in the department. Somerset and his newbie partner are confronted with a series of brutal and enigmatic murders that illustrate the medieval concept of the "Seven Deadly Sins." An obese man is force-fed until he bursts as an example of Gluttony; a crooked lawyer has a pound of his flesh excised as an example of Greed; a pederast is discovered strapped to a bed in which he is kept barely alive to illustrate Sloth. The grotesquerie and premeditated sadism of the killings make a vivid impression on rookie Mills and even appall the veteran Somerset, who has presumably seen it all in his years on the force.

New York City's hellish environs are taking a toll on Mills's wife, Tracy (Gwyneth Paltrow), a teacher who is shocked by the awful conditions in inner-city schools. She confides to her husband's partner that, unknown to Mills, she is pregnant and considering an abortion because she doesn't want to bring a child into this horrific urban environment. Back on the case, Somerset approaches a clandestine FBI contact who furnishes him with illegally obtained information from a government database that tracks the book-borrowing habits of public library users. Mills and Somerset use the information to track down an individual named "Jonathan Doe" to a seedy apartment and when the killer starts shooting at them, Mills chases Doe down an alleyway where he is nearly killed by his mysterious assailant. Using a ruse to gain entrance to Doe's place without a warrant (and without revealing the illegal source of his FBI info), the methodical Somerset pores over Doe's extensive records of the murders, including literally thousands of notebooks detailing the serial killer's bizarre, homicidal thoughts. "John Doe," as he is now called, seems to have no job, no personal history and has mutilated the tips of his fingers so as to leave no fingerprints. While in Doe's apartment, Mills and Somerset receive a phone call from the killer who taunts the detectives about further Deadly Sin murders that he is poised to commit.

Doe is not just boasting as the homicide cops soon discover a prostitute murdered with a sex toy as an emblem of Lust, and a beautiful model who has her nose "cut off to

Homicide detectives William Somerset (Morgan Freeman, top) and David Mills (Brad Pitt, bottom) investigate a series of baffling murders in *Se7en* (New Line Cinema, 1995).

spite her face" to illustrate Pride. Then, unexpectedly, Doe (Kevin Spacey) wearing a bloody T-shirt, turns himself in to the police. The bald-headed, soft-spoken Doe claims that he has committed his final two murders based on the sins of Wrath and Envy, and insists that Somerset and Mills accompany him to the murder site, an offer that the officers cannot refuse. The two detectives escort Doe out to the murder scene in the back seat of a car being discretely shadowed by a police helicopter, and on the long drive out of the city the killer rambles on about his religious philosophy. Doe claims to have been "chosen" by God to illustrate the wicked ways of the world by staging the elaborate murders based on the Deadly Sins. Arriving at their destination, a cluster of high-tension electrical towers that cleverly prevent the copter from landing or hovering nearby, Doe enacts the final sins of Envy and Wrath that he hopes will present an immortal allegory of sinfulness to the wicked world.

Se7en was ideally suited to director Fincher's bleak visual style that captures stark, brooding images of a modern Gothic city of decay and dread. The film's New York cityscape is curiously devoid of familiar landmarks and place indicators. Instead, the action takes place in a generic urban landscape of back alleys, fire escapes, sex clubs and seedy apartments that constitute any city's dark underbelly. As Kirsten Moana Thompson notes, "*Se7en*'s setting is a neo-noir moodpiece in a city that is no place.... Art design makes the city space purposively anonymous, with no details in the street signs, costumes, police cars or helicopters to identify the metropolis's name, location or temporal setting."[3] Like the dark metropolis depicted in *Blade Runner*, the city is doused in a melancholy perpetual rain and is haunted by the myriad cries of its denizens and the rattle and hum of its heavy, complex machinery, but as Joe Kane observes, "*Se7en* presents a view of a modern metropolis as a Dantean inferno, without resorting to dystopian sets."[4] Fincher's cinematographer Darius Khondji utilized a silver-retention process called bleach bypass or CCE that rebonds the silver leached out during normal film processing to the print to produce the deep blacks and desaturated colors that give the film its distinctive horror noir ambience. Horror movie makeup ace Rob Bottin contributed the graphic designs for the killer's grotesque victims, and the scene in which the Sloth victim's ostensibly rotting corpse lurches to sudden life is a moment of pure cinematic terror.

The film's dramatic matrix is a two-character piece centering around "good cop" Freeman versus "bad cop" Pitt, in which Freeman appears to be bland and detached as a foil to Pitt's violent histrionics. The interplay between the two actors seems lively and organic, although Freeman appears perhaps a bit too laid back in light of the film's ghastly revelations. Gwyneth Paltrow's performance is confined to a few low-key dialogue sequences, while a bald-headed, emaciated-looking Kevin Spacey practically steals the movie with his understated portrayal of the enigmatic serial killer John Doe.

One of the flaws in scenarist Andrew Kevin Walker's screenplay, however, is that it provides almost nothing in the way of backstory about John Doe. Unlike earlier excursions into serial killer territory such as *Manhunter* or *The Silence of the Lambs*, the murderer is not shown during the act of killing, making him seem oddly detached from his foul misdeeds. He is a cypher, his fingerprints and societal identity having been obliterated, and even his name "John Doe" is but a legal term for anonymity. Doe's motivations have something in common with those of Martin Scorsese's neo-noir figures Max Cady (Robert De Niro) in *Cape Fear* (1991) and Travis Bickle (De Niro, again) in *Taxi Driver* (1976), both of whom are on a self-deluded, religiously inspired crusade of murderous retribution, and Doe's original prototype is surely Harry Powell (Robert Mitchum), the macabre preacher/killer in *The Night of the Hunter* (1955), who is also on a faith-based mission to rid the world of society's undesirables. Like the murderous sniper in *Targets* (1968), Doe is also driven to commit mayhem because of the sheer banality of American culture. Some of John Doe's diabolical exploits, obviously inspired by those of fellow genius cum homicidal maniac Hannibal Lecter, tend to strain credulity, such as the enactment of the deadly sin murders in a time frame that exactly coincides with Somerset's last seven days on the job. Still, despite its faults, *Se7en* is a masterful thriller that skillfully combines noir elements of mystery and police procedural with the ghoulish conventions of the horror film.

Cops on the Mean Streets of Hell

The cops versus serial killer movie formula was given a supernatural twist in *Fallen* (1998). Denzel Washington plays Philadelphia homicide detective John Hobbes, whose career has just taken a quantum leap after he has bagged the notorious serial killer Edgar Reese (Elias Koteas). Invited to the killer's execution, which is to be filmed by a legal rights group, Hobbes observes that Reese appears jocular, even playful, as he is led to the gas chamber singing the Rolling Stones's rock anthem, "Time Is on My Side," and cryptically telling Hobbes, "What goes around, goes around." The murderer also gives Hobbes a cryptic riddle about some former officers of the Philly police force. As the poison fumes overcome Reese inside the execution chamber, the audience sees a subjective view as the killer's spirit leaves his body and travels into the body of a jail guard and from there the evil spirit migrates from body to body by touch.

A string of brutal murders follows, all of which exhibit the distinctive M.O. of the deceased killer. Hobbes and fellow homicide detectives Jonesy (John Goodman) and Lou (James Gandolfini) are baffled but their superior, Lt. Stanton (Donald Sutherland) has a pet theory that a cop is involved. Examining Reese's riddle leads Hobbes to investigate a former policeman, one officer Milano, who committed suicide under mysterious circumstances 30 years earlier. Reese is drawn to the officer's daughter, Gretta Milano (Embeth Davidtz), a theologian at a local college, who eventually reveals the truth: Reese was possessed by an immortal demon named Azazel who can move from body to body and the evil spirit is stalking Hobbes from beyond the grave. Anyone Hobbes sees on the street can now be the killer, although the demon cannot take over Hobbes directly because of the detective's purity of spirit.

As the murder investigation continues, Hobbes brings in an expert linguist to analyze Reese's speech on the execution film, and the killer's unknown tongue is identified as Syrian Aramaic, a language spoken in the Ancient Near East in Biblical times. After being taunted by Azazel, who confronts him in a series of different bodies, Hobbes is manipulated into killing a schoolteacher who, possessed by the demon, pulls a gun on him. Hobbes is immediately suspended from the force and becomes the prime suspect in the murders, but goes on the run rather than face charges. Knowing that Azazel can only survive for a limited time outside of its host body, the wily detective strives to lure the demon into a trap where it can be destroyed, even if he must sacrifice his own life in the process.

In trying to combine the detective and supernatural horror genres, *Fallen* manages to fail on both counts. The main problem is Nicholas Kazan's highly derivative screenplay, which recycles plot elements from *Exorcist III* and *Se7en*, as well as from the sci-fi horror flick *The Hidden* (1987), which features an alien serial killer that can move from body to body. Kazan's script also includes a number of extraneous scenes highlighting problems in Hobbes's family life that tend to slow down the main action considerably. There is a terrible misuse of film noir-style voice-over narration that has Hobbes uttering ridiculously portentous lines like, "Evil is eternal and knows no bounds." Journeyman director Gregory Hoblit, whose debut feature was the courtroom mystery thriller *Primal Fear* (1996), fails to imbue the work with the proper moods of suspense or dread. Unlike the grotesque murders depicted in *Se7en*, the film's homicide scenes are bloodless and antiseptic. Future Oscar-winner Denzel Washington does his level best to imbue some life into the proceedings as the noble protagonist Hobbes, but the rest of the interesting cast, including John Goodman and Donald Sutherland, deliver mediocre performances. Elias Koteas, in a role that seems to have been written for Robert De Niro, provides some brief flashes of thespic power as the demon-possessed killer Edgar Reese.

Like *Se7en*, the film's action takes place inside a generic neo-noir metropolis, a city that seems oddly outside of time or place. As in other serial killer thrillers, the emphasis is on combining police procedural with the trappings of the horror film, although *Fallen*'s meld of supernatural and detective motifs doesn't quite gel. There's no noirish moral ambiguity about the Hobbes character, who is as straight-arrow a cop as ever served on any Hollywood police force. Although the notion of a demonic murderer inhabiting many bodies is at times genuinely creepy, it also tends to dilute Azazel's aura of primordial evil and divorces his actions from human psychological motivations.

Denzel was pulling some heavy overtime tracking down diabolical serial killers, because in the following year he also played the protagonist of *The Bone Collector* (1999). In this one he plays ace NYPD criminologist Lincoln "Linc" Rhymes, who has been wounded in the line of duty and is now a quadriplegic being cared for at home by nurse Thelma (Queen Latifah). Surrounded by a tangle of beeping life-support equipment and police computers, Linc is still able to access the Department's systems and use his undamaged mind to do useful detective work. Unfortunately, Linc's condition is degenerative and he is waiting for the seizure that will make him a vegetable and is considering assisted suicide when a string of bizarre murders brings his talents to the fore once again. The deadly chain of events begins when wealthy couple, Alan and Lindsay Rubin (Gary Swanson and Olivia Birkelund), are kidnapped from JFK airport by a mysterious cab driver and transported to an undisclosed location. Soon afterward Alan's body is discovered partially buried beneath an Amtrak rail line by beat cop Amelia Donaghy (Angelina Jolie), whose resourceful police work preserves vital evidence at the crime scene. Impressed by what he perceives as officer Donaghy's "natural instinct for forensics," Linc insists that the street-smart Amelia be brought into the investigative team he is forming to solve the murders against the wishes of his superior, Captain Howard Cheney (Michael Rooker).

Aided by his police cohorts, detectives Kenny Solomon (Mike McGlone), Eddie Ortiz (Luis Guzmán) and Paulie Sellitto (Ed O'Neill), Linc's forensic team skillfully sift through the evidence, which indicates that the killer has an affinity for turn of the century sites for his murders. The killer, his face obscured by a ski mask, is shown dragging Lindsay through an underground maze of pipes and machinery as Linc deduces that she is being imprisoned beneath the Woolworth Building in the Wall Street area of NYC. Linc dispatches Amelia downtown with the police rescue team but they are too late as Lindsay is placed in front of a large steam pipe by the killer and scalded to death. Linked to Linc via a cell phone hookup, Amelia is expected to "walk the grid" while relaying the crime scene data to the criminologist, but balks at sawing off the hands of Lindsay's horribly scalded corpse in order to obtain the handcuffs for evidence. She does manage to collect a bloody bone and a piece of paper with some unreadable markings found at the murder scene, however.

Soon afterward the enigmatic cabbie abducts another victim, a young male student at NYU, whose body is later found gnawed to death by rats in an abandoned slaughterhouse with a finger bone removed and another cryptic piece of paper. Then a grandfather and granddaughter are picked up at Grand Central Station and are whisked away by the cabbie killer to a fate certain. In the meantime, Linc has deciphered an image culled from the mysterious scraps of paper deliberately left as clues by the killer as representing the graphic logo of an old publishing house that once specialized in mystery fiction. Amelia manages to locate an old book bearing the publisher's imprint entitled "The Bone Collector," and realizes that the killer is re-enacting the gruesome homicides depicted in the book. This allows the police to locate the grandfather and granddaughter tied to a pier in Lower Manhattan in time to save the child's life, but Linc's unorthodox methods provoke Captain Chaney to take Linc and Amelia off the case. Undeterred, Amelia pursues further clues that lead her to an old subway station in Lower Manhattan, but this is just a ruse to get her out of the way as the killer invades Linc's apartment and goes after the helpless, bedridden criminologist.

The Bone Collector, like the equally derivative *Fallen*, illustrates how clichéd and formulaic the serial killer thriller had become. Adapted by scenarist Jeremy Iacone from a crime novel by Jeffery Deaver, the screenplay is overlong, frequently confusing to the viewer and offers the same stock situations (the fiendishly clever serial murderer, the brilliant and diligent detective, the game of cat and mouse between the two) that hark back to *Manhunter* (1986). The screenplay's most glaring flaw is in revealing the killer to be an unlikely, minor character, and the audience never learns exactly what his motivation is for re-enacting the murders from the old book. The working relationship between the immobile Linc and his enabler Amelia is a dim echo of Rex Stout's detective novels (and film adaptations) about agoraphobic sleuth Nero Wolfe and his can-do sidekick Archie Goodwin, and also self-consciously references the relationship between Clarice Starling and her FBI superior Jack Crawford in *The Silence of the Lambs*.

While the emphasis is on hi-tech police procedural, the grisly nature of the murders tips the film over into the realm of horror, and the film's underground locations, a labyrinthine netherworld of darkened corridors that constitutes a city of darkness beneath the familiar metropolis, engender a deep sense of claustrophobia and dread. Director Phillip Noyce does a workmanlike but uninspired job with this stereotypical material, while stars Denzel Washington as the suicidal, self-pitying quadriplegic detective and Angelina Jolie as a typically Noo Yawk beat cop turn in engaging, sympathetic performances that almost manage to redeem the film. Supporting cast members Queen Latifah, Ed O'Neill and Luis Guzmán provide the movie's requisite urban ethnic grit, but Michael Rooker, who had portrayed the homicidal title character in *Henry, Portrait of a Serial Killer* (1990) gives a quietly sinister performance as the reactionary police captain Cheney.

New Directions for a New Millennium

By the end of the 1990s the serial killer thriller had clearly run out of steam. The Hannibal Lecter franchise, representing the most important works of the sub-genre, continued on with diminished expectations in *Hannibal* (2001) and *Red Dragon* (2002), but the thrill was gone. As Kendall R. Phillips observes, "By the end of the 1990s, Hannibal Lecter had become the same kind of ubiquitous cultural monster that Freddy Krueger had been at the end of the 1980s. The films, while successful, had begun to lose their horrific edge."[5] The serial killer movie had started to fold in upon itself by the mid–1990s in a spate of movies that featured multiple murderers. In *Copycat* (1995), for instance, a serial murderer lovingly re-creates the crimes of others of his ilk such as Ted Bundy, The Boston Strangler and the Son of Sam, while the sci-fi noir *Virtuosity* (1995) featured a cybernetic monstrosity who has been programmed to be an amalgam of many of the famous serial killers of the past. While films on this theme continued to be made going into the next decade, such as *Mindhunters* (2004) and *Suspect Zero* (2004), the horror film began to slide back into a series of slasher film franchises aimed at a youth market, including *Scream* (1996) and *Saw* (2004) and their numerous sequels. The horror genre was afflicted with a series of tepid remakes of horror classics from prior decades, including

The Haunting (1999), *House on Haunted Hill* (1999), *Thirteen Ghosts* (2001), *The Texas Chainsaw Massacre* (2003) and *Dawn of the Dead* (2004). It was clearly time for the horror noir film to tack in a new direction.

Chris Carter's popular television series *The X-Files* had run from 1993 to 2001 and spawned a feature film, *The X-Files: Fight the Future* (1998). The sci-fi-oriented show revolved around the exploits of intrepid FBI agents Fox Mulder (David Duchovny) and Dr. Dana Scully (Gillian Anderson), who are assigned to investigate anomalous phenomena for the Bureau. Most of the shows and the 1998 movie centered around an exploration of the UFO enigma and the story arc involving the alleged abduction of Mulder's sister by aliens years earlier, but some episodes also delved into the mysteries of ESP and other strange anomalies. A second *X-Files* movie had languished in development hell for a number of years following the demise of the series due to various contractual disputes, but was finally released as *The X-Files: I Want to Believe* in 2008. The new film dispensed with the alien theme and instead was a parapsychological murder mystery.

Six years after the events of the final TV program have transpired, former agent Mulder (Duchovny) is hiding from the FBI to avoid being hauled in on charges before the Bureau. When FBI agent Monica Bannan (Xantha Radley) is kidnapped from her home in the wintry backwater town of Somerset, West Virginia, the Bureau approaches Scully (Anderson), who is now working as a pediatrician in a Catholic children's hospital, about bringing Mulder back into the fold. It seems that an eccentric former priest, Father Joseph Crissman (Billy Connolly), who claims to receive psychic visions from God, has been assisting the FBI on the missing person case and has recently led them to the discovery of a severed human arm from another victim on a frozen lake bed. The Bureau wants Mulder to work with Father Joe on the case because of his expertise in working with psychics during his stint on the X-Files unit.

Scully locates Mulder in a remote country house, where she persuades him to aid in the hunt for the missing agent because, "It could have been you once, or me," and adds that the Bureau will drop all charges against him in return for his cooperation. Mulder and Scully are flown to D.C. where they are briefed by Dakota Whitney (Amanda Peet), the agent in charge of the investigation. It turns out that Father Joe is a pedophile who was defrocked for sexually assaulting altar boys and is now living in a sex-offender housing facility. When Scully and Mulder escort the psychic priest out to the crime scene to receive impressions of the crime via ESP, Mulder is convinced he is genuine when the priest's eyes bleed after he experiences a vision. Father Joe later leads the team to a severed head and a cache of body parts frozen in the ice in the rear of the property, and insists that the killers are surrounded by barking dogs. This contention is confirmed when traces of a canine tranquilizer are found in one of the severed arms.

Soon afterward a young woman, Cheryl Cunningham (Nicki Aycox), is abducted after leaving a public swimming pool by the brutal Jank Dacyshyn (Callum Keith) and transported to a scuzzy-looking laboratory/hospital facility, where she is locked in a cage alongside a kennel full of barking dogs. A discarded medical ID bracelet found in the abducted girl's car leads them to Dacyshyn, who works as a courier for an organ transplant outfit that is involved in illegal organ smuggling. When the FBI attempts to question him, Dacyshyn flees to a construction site where agent Whitney is killed while giving chase. Following various leads, Mulder manages to track the Russian to his laboratory, where he is taken prisoner by the Russkies and beholds the solution to the mystery. Dacyshyn is conducting grotesque head-transplantation experiments designed to graft the head of his gay lover, Franz Tomczeszyn (Christopher "Fagin" Woodcock), onto Cheryl Cunningham's body. Before Mulder can be recycled for his body parts, Scully and FBI agent Walter Skinner (series regular Mitch Pileggi), their former superior at the X-Files unit, arrive to rescue Mulder, dispatch Dacyshyn and Tomczeszyn, and close down the bizarre medical experiment for good. In the aftermath, Father Joe has a seizure and dies and Mulder and Scully are seen rowing toward a green, tropical island far away from the film's snowbound landscape.

Co-produced and directed by series originator Chris Carter from a screenplay by Frank Spotnitz, the film comes off as a feature-length version of one of the *X-Files* TV shows. Carter imbues the film with some of the sense of paranoia and lurking dread that characterized the show, but the convoluted script slows down the mystery and police procedural action with extraneous soap-opera subplots concerning Scully and Mulder's romantic relationship and some business about Scully performing a risky operation on a terminally ill child. Carter's direction is sluggish while Spotnitz's script is often as confusing as episodes of the TV show used to be. Fans of the series, however, were pleased to see David Duchovny, Gillian Anderson and Mitch Pileggi reprise their roles in the second *X-Files* theatrical feature, and the movie ends on a pleasant romantic note as Mulder and Scully sail off into the sunset together. Billy Connolly turns in a strong performance as the tortured psychic priest Father Joe, while Callum Keith is grimly sinister as the brutal Slav Dacyshyn.

The film's departure from the extraterrestrial motifs of the show's mythic story arc shifts the thematic focus from paranoia and conspiracy theory to the realms of crime melodrama and horror. *I Want to Believe*'s wintry landscape, filmed in Vancouver and Pemberton, British Columbia, recalls the snowbound milieu of the Coen Brothers' black-comic noir *Fargo* (1996). The emphasis on black medicine is another horror noir theme familiar from films like *Eyes Without a Face*, but the movie's strangest subplot involves the grafting of a man's head onto a woman's body, an idea which seems like a macabre version of Buffalo Bill's "woman suit" in *The Silence of the Lambs* and is grotesquely homophobic. Similarly, the defrocked pederast priest Father Joe introduces a further note of sexual perversion.

Writer/director and neo-noir deity Martin Scorsese, veteran of many serious and highly acclaimed crime melodramas, including *Mean Streets* (1973), *Taxi Driver* (1976), *Goodfellas* (1990), *Cape Fear* (1991), and *The Departed* (2006), for which he was awarded Best Picture and Best Director Oscars, turned his attention to the horror film in the unusual psychological thriller *Shutter Island* (2010). Adapted from a 2003 novel by mystery writer Dennis Lehane, the film is set during the classic noir era of 1954 and stars Leonardo Di Caprio as U.S. marshal Teddy Daniels. As the film begins, Teddy and fellow marshal Chuck Aule (Mark Ruffalo) are riding the ferry out to Shutter Island, a barren rock 11 miles out to sea from Boston that houses a psychiatric hospital for the criminally insane. Teddy and Chuck are there to find an inmate who has mysteriously escaped from a locked cell, and are greeted by the asylum's head honcho, Dr. John Cawley (Ben Kingsley), who seems curiously uncooperative. When the patient suddenly re-appears just as mysteriously, the two marshals have plenty of questions but no answers. They are prevented from leaving the island, however, when a sudden hurricane blows in and they are forced to ride out the storm at the asylum.

Flashbacks reveal that Teddy is deeply troubled in the aftermath of liberating Dachau concentration camp as a soldier during World War II, and by the recent death of his wife, Dolores (Michelle Williams), in an apartment fire. Teddy also reveals to Chuck that he has an ulterior motive for accepting the Shutter Island assignment. In reality he is looking for demented serial arsonist Andrew Laeddis (*Fallen's* Elias Koteas), whom he believes is responsible for setting the fire that killed his wife. He has reason to believe that Laeddis is an inmate at the hospital and is out to get revenge for his wife's death. Upon coming to the island, however, Teddy has begun to experience debilitating migraines and terrifying nightmares in which he is haunted by images of Laeddis, his wife and the corpses of the Dachau dead.

When the storm causes a power outage, the hospital erupts into anarchy and Teddy uses the hiatus to explore the hitherto forbidden corners of the island, including "Ward C" the facility for ultra-violent criminals. He is startled when one of the inmates tells him, "You ain't investigating nothing—you're a rat in a maze." Later, while trying to reach the island's antique lighthouse, he discovers a woman living in a seaside cave (Patricia Clarkson), who claims to be a former doctor at the hospital. She tells him that Dr. Cawley is conducting illegal mind control experiments on the patients inside the lighthouse that involve brain surgery and psychotropic drugs. These procedures are designed to erase their memories and create pliant "ghosts" who will act as Manchurian candidates to do the government's bidding. As the mystery deepens, Teddy begins to experience frightening hallucinations in which Dolores and the war dead appear before him like avenging spirits. As the film progresses it becomes unclear whether Teddy is seeing drug-induced illusions or if he has more profound problems with his sanity, which leads the story to its unexpected conclusion.

Scorsese's script, as derived from Lehane's novel is an exercise in modern gothic noir, a nightmarish landscape comprised of crumbling architecture, dread secrets, insane characters, ghosts and swarms of rats. The isolated setting of the rugged island and the claustrophobic asylum environment creates an atmosphere of despair and dread that suffuses the film. *Shutter Island's* ghosts are psychological, rather than supernatural, in nature in the manner of Hitchcock's thrillers like *Vertigo* and *Psycho*. Scorsese's directorial execution, however, is frequently plodding and emotionally unengaging, and fails to generate enough sympathy for its main character, the tormented Teddy Daniels. The film's dismal setting and its downbeat, enigmatic ending make for a less than uplifting filmgoing experience.

Lead players Di Caprio and Kingsley go through the motions without much emotion and get only mediocre support from Mark Ruffalo and screen veteran Max Von Sydow (playing an ex–Nazi doctor) in throwaway roles. Oddly, the film's most memorable performances are by actors who portrayed serial killers in other movies. Elias Koteas, who played the demonic murderer Edgar Reese/Azazel in *Fallen*, shines in his brief but creepy role as firestarter Andrew Laeddis, who is adorned by a Frankenstein-like stitched-up scar running down the middle of his face, while Ted Levine, who portrayed the serial killer Buffalo Bill in *The Silence of the Lambs*, has a similarly minor but memorable part as the hospital's Gestapo-esque warden. Robbie Robertson contributes an unnerving score that incorporates the moody sounds of fog horns and gulls of the film's oceanic setting.

The movie's early 1950s setting as well as the trenchcoat-and-slouch-hat iconography of Di Caprio and Ruffalo's cop outfits, deliberately evoke the milieu of classic-era film noir. Thematically, *Shutter Island*'s asylum setting recalls noirs like Alfred Werker's *Shock* (1946) and Sam Fuller's *Shock Corridor* (1963), while the plot device of an individual being wrongly confined to a mental hospital against their will is featured in a number of noirs, including *Murder, My Sweet* (1944), *Spellbound* (1945), *The Return of the Whistler* (1948) and *Sisters* (1973). *Shutter Island* also recalls the nightmare odysseys of self-revelation endured by the haunted protagonists of the horror noirs *Angel Heart* and *Jacob's Ladder*. In interviews about the film, Scorsese cited Jacques Tourneur's *Cat People* and *I Walked with a Zombie* as major influences, bringing the horror noir cycle full circle into the 21st-century.

During the 1990s and early 2000s the serial killer thriller prevailed as the dominant form of horror noir. The Hannibal Lecter films, as well as effective horror noirs like *Exorcist III*, *Se7en*, *Fallen* and *The Bone Collector*, brought these human monstrosities squarely into the popular imagination in their deft combination of mystery, gothicism, body horror and police procedural. In her book *Apocalyptic Dread*, Kirsten Moana Thompson explains, "Consequently, popular representations of the serial killer draw upon archetypal figures of horror — the vampire, the devil, the wolfman, the sorcerer and the cannibal.... The compelling and repulsive elements of the fictional serial killer, whether it be the cultured, gentlemanly Hannibal Lecter or in the spookily clever master planner John Doe ... are intensified by the sensational and florid characterizations that foreground the serial killer's godlike hyperintelligence, strength, insight and ubiquity. Both fascinated and repelled by them, we dread the serial killer because, in reality, they are occult."[6]

Conclusion:
Horror and Film Noir —
The Dark Genres

Horror and film noir have a lot in common. Both genres share a common preoccupation with the dark side of human existence, with fear, madness, fate and murder amid the looming shadows of night. Both are populated by grotesque, monstrous characters with homicidal motives caught in a labyrinthine netherworld, a nightmare landscape of the mind, a dark web from which there is no escape.

Film noir emerged from a milieu of horror literature, from the primordial 19th-century gothic mysteries of Poe, Stevenson, Collins, Wilde and Conan Doyle. In *The Strange Case of Dr. Jekyll and Mr. Hyde*, Robert Louis Stevenson created the first noir city of night in his vision of Victorian London as a dark urban landscape fraught with violence, mystery and peril. This template for the dark cities that would later emerge in the German Expressionist films of the silent and early sound era, and later, the American films noir of the 1940s, is an image that has endured into the horror noir thrillers of the 21st century. Unlike the glittering futuristic cities of tech-noir, the horror noir night cities are dark, diseased and utterly mournful monuments to despair as pictured in modern films like *Wolfen*, *Jacob's Ladder* and *Se7en*. These doom-laden urban hells are common to both horror and film noir.

Both genres deal with human monstrosities, with agents of chaos whose schizophrenic and psychopathic mentalities threaten the established social order. They represent aberrations, enigmas to be exorcised, formulas for human evil that must be destroyed. These homicidal sociopaths come in all shapes and sizes, from the outwardly sweet little girl in *The Bad Seed* to the cultured serial murderer Hannibal Lecter in *The Silence of the Lambs*. They are every bit as monstrous as Frankenstein, Dracula or the Creature from the Black Lagoon. Both horror and noir peer unblinkingly into the depths of the evil that lurks in the hearts of men (and women) like that dread harbinger of doom, the Shadow.

The shadow worlds of film noir were initially created for the horror film. Expressionism, imported from Germany to Hollywood with the diaspora of Deutschland's finest cinematic talent, brought the terrors of the haunted screen to America. During the 1930s, Universal's horrormeisters devised the familiar visual stylistics that were later adapted for use in film noir. Then, during the formative years of classic noir in the early '40s, RKO's Val Lewton/Jacques Tourneur horror noir thrillers brought the darkness of the old world into a contemporary urban environment, an approach that would have a profound influence on the genesis of noir. An emphasis on psychology rather than the supernatural in these films and in many horror movies that followed this innovative trend drew the two genres closer together. During this same period the gothic and costume noirs combined historical melodrama with madness and homicidal criminality that echoed the styles and themes of modern film noir.

As the 1950s progressed into the terrors of the atomic age the decade also spawned several highly unusual horror/mystery thrillers like *The Bad Seed, The Night of the Hunter* and *Diabolique* that stood at the cusp between the two genres. The '60s witnessed the triumph of psychological horror and human criminality over the supernatural horror film in memorable case studies such as *Psycho, Peeping Tom, The Collector* and *Targets*. During the decades that followed, a number of horror thrillers deliberately referenced film noir in works like *Kolchak: The Night Stalker, Psychic Killer, Wolfen, Angel Heart, Cast a Deadly Spell, Witch Hunt* and *Lord of Illusions*. The coming of Hannibal Lecter in *Manhunter* and *The Silence of the Lambs* presaged the advent of the grim serial killer-themed horror movies that followed, including *Se7en, Hannibal, Fallen, Red Dragon* and *The Bone Collector*, all of which combined urban police procedural, abnormal psychology and murderous criminality into a popular and intriguing horror-noir meld. Lecter, an inhumanly cruel yet protean being with quasi-occult powers, would eventually be enthroned in critical opinion as the number-one screen villain of all time in an indication of the ascendancy of the horror noir form.

During the era of classic noir a number of memorable actors were associated with both genres, a list that includes Peter Lorre (*The Face Behind the Mask, The Beast with Five Fingers*), Lon Chaney, Jr. (*The Inner Sanctum Mysteries, Son of Dracula*), and Laird Cregar (*The Lodger, Hangover Square*). In later decades, noir stalwarts like Vincent Price (*Diary of a Madman, Scream and Scream Again*), Raymond Burr (*Bride of the Gorilla, Gorilla at Large*), and Elisha Cook, Jr. (*Rosemary's Baby, Kolchak: The Night Stalker*), would also join the roster. Well-known noir icons would eventually be deliberately and self-referentially cast in horror noir roles, including Ralph Meeker (*Kolchak: The Night Stalker*), Neville Brand (*Psychic Killer*), Lawrence Tierney (*Tough Guys Don't Dance*), Robert De Niro (*Angel Heart*) and Dennis Hopper (*Witch Hunt*).

Some of film noir's finest directors also produced their share of acclaimed and seminal horror noirs. While Jacques Tourneur (*Cat People, I Walked with a Zombie, The Leopard Man* and *Experiment Perilous*) is the most notable example, others include Robert Siodmak (*Son of Dracula, The Spiral Staircase*), Edgar G. Ulmer (*Bluebeard*), Alfred Hitchcock (*Rebecca, Psycho, Vertigo*), John Brahm (*The Undying Monster, The Lodger, Hangover Square*) and Stuart Heisler (*The Monster and the Girl*). More recent examples of noir luminaries producing works of horror would include Paul Schrader (*Cat People, Witch Hunt*), Adrian Lyne (*Jacob's Ladder*) and David Fincher (*Se7en*).

Many works of horror noir are counted among the most significant and illustrious films in the history of the horror genre. This tally includes Rouben Mamoulian's *Dr. Jekyll and Mr. Hyde*, Tod Browning's *Freaks*, Jacques Tourneur's *I Walked with a Zombie*, Henri-Georges Clouzot's *Diabolique*, Charles Laughton's *The Night of the Hunter*, Georges Franju's *Eyes Without a Face*, Alfred Hitchcock's *Psycho*, Michael Powell's *Peeping Tom*, Roman Polanski's *Rosemary's Baby*, William Friedkin's *The Exorcist* and Jonathan Demme's *The Silence of the Lambs*, this last being the most acclaimed horror picture in the history of the genre, garnering five Oscars, including Best Picture.

On a slightly less exalted level are finely wrought exercises in filmic fear crafted by some of the cinema's most talented directors, including Michael Curtiz's *The Mystery of the Wax Museum*, Robert Siodmak's *The Spiral Staircase*, Joseph L. Mankiewicz's *Dragonwyck*, George Cukor's *Gaslight*, William Wyler's *The Collector*, Peter Bogdanovich's *Targets* and Martin Scorsese's *Shutter Island*. Then there are a group of wonderfully well-made thrillers such as Robert Florey's *The Face Behind the Mask*, Edgar G. Ulmer's *Bluebeard*, John Brahm's *The Lodger*, Albert Lewin's *The Picture of Dorian Gray*, Robert Day's *The Haunted Strangler*, Tony Scott's *The Hunger* and David Cronenberg's *Dead Ringers*. Finally, there are cult faves and guilty pleasures like A. Edward Sutherland's *Murders in the Zoo*, Jean Yarbrough's *House of Horrors*, Francis D. Lyon's *Cult of the Cobra*, Albert Band's *I Bury the Living*, John Llewellyn Moxey's *Kolchak: The Night Stalker*, Norman Mailer's *Tough Guys Don't Dance* and Martin Campbell's *Cast a Deadly Spell*.

These and the other works discussed stand at the cinematic juncture of criminality and monstrosity, night and fate, dream and surrealism, ghosts and darkness, where the fear-drenched shadow realms of horror and film noir comingle to intrigue and delight us. Film's evil twins, horror and noir, will surely continue to morph into new and frightening forms in the years to come.

Filmography

Alias Nick Beal (1949) Director: John Farrow. Producer: Endre Boehm. Screenplay: Jonathan Latimer. Cast: Ray Milland, Thomas Mitchell, Audrey Totter, George Macready, Daryll Hickman, Fred Clark, King Donovan, Nestor Pavia. USA (Paramount). B&W. 93m. DVD: Unavailable.

The Amazing Mr. X (a.k.a. *The Spiritualist*) (1948) Director: Bernard Vorhaus. Producer: Ben Stoloff. Screenplay: Crane Wilbur. Cast: Turhan Bey, Lynn Bari, Cathy O'Donnell, Richard Carlson. USA (Eagle Lion). B&W. 70m. DVD: Alpha Video.

Angel Heart (1987) Director/Screenplay: Alan Parker. Producers: Alan Marshall, Elliot Kassner. Cast: Mickey Rourke, Robert De Niro, Lisa Bonet, Charlotte Rampling, Brownie McGhee, Kathleen Wilhoite. USA (Tristar). Color. 113m. DVD: Lion's Gate.

The Bad Seed (1956) Director/Producer: Mervyn LeRoy. Screenplay: John Lee Mahin. Cast: Nancy Kelly, Patty McCormack, Henry Jones, William Hopper, Eileen Heckart, Jesse White. USA (Warner Bros.) B&W. 129m. DVD: Warner Home Video.

The Beast with Five Fingers (1946) Director: Robert Florey. Producer: Wesley Anderson. Screenplay: Curt Siodmak. Cast: Peter Lorre, Robert Alda, Andrea King, J. Carrol Naish, Victor Francen. USA (Warner Bros.) B&W. 89m. DVD: Unavailable.

Bluebeard (1944) Director: Edgar G. Ulmer. Producer: Leon Fromkiss. Screenplay: Pierre Gendron. Cast: John Carradine, Jean Parker, Nils Asther, Ludwig Stossel, George Pembroke.

USA (PRC). B&W. 74m. DVD: Miracle Pictures.

The Bone Collector (1999) Director: Phillip Noyce. Producer: Dan Jinks. Screenplay: Jeffrey Deaver. Cast: Denzel Washington, Angelina Jolie, Queen Latifah, Ed O'Neill, Michael Rooker, Luis Guzmán. USA (Universal) Color. 117m. DVD: Universal.

Bride of the Gorilla (1951) Director/Screenplay: Curt Siodmak. Producer: Jack Broder. Cast: Raymond Burr, Barbara Payton, Lon Chaney, Jr., Tom Conway, Woody Strode. USA (Realart). B&W. 76m. DVD: St. Clair Vision.

The Brute Man (1946) Director: Jean Yarbrough. Producer: Ben Pivar. Screenplay: Dwight V. Babcock, George Bricker, Abraham Grossman. Cast: Rondo Hatton, Tom Neal, Jan Wiley, Jane Adams, Donald Macbride, Peter Whitlen. USA (PRC/Universal). B&W. 90m. DVD: Cheezy Flicks.

Calling Dr. Death (1943) Director: Reginald Le Borg. Producer: Ben Pivar. Screenplay: Edward Dien. Cast: Lon Chaney, Jr., J. Carrol Naish, Patricia Morison, David Bruce, Fay Helm, Holmes Herbert. USA (Universal). B&W. 63m. DVD: Universal.

Cast a Deadly Spell (1991) Director: Martin Campbell. Producer: Gale Ann Hurd. Screenplay: Joseph Dougherty. Cast: Fred Ward, Julianne Moore, David Warner, Clancy Brown, Arnetia Walker. USA (HBO) Color. 96m. DVD: Unavailable.

Cat Girl (1957) Director: Alfred Shaughnessey. Producers: Lou Rusoff, Herbert Smith. Screenplay: Lou Rusoff. Cast: Barbara Shelley, Robert Ayres, Kay Callard. UK (AIP) B&W 69m. DVD: Unavailable.

Cat People (1942) Director: Jacques Tourneur. Producer: Val Lewton. Screenplay DeWitt Bodeen. Cast: Simone Simon, Kent Smith, Jane Randolph, Tom Conway, Jack Holt. USA (RKO). B&W. 73m. DVD: Warner Home Video.

Cat People (1982) Director: Paul Schrader. Producer: Charles Fries. Screenplay: Alan Ormsby. Cast: Malcolm McDowell, Natassja Kinski, John Heard, Ruby Dee, Ed Begley, Jr. USA (Universal). Color. 118m. DVD: Universal.

The Collector (1965) Director: William Wyler. Producers: John Kohn, Jud Kinberg. Screenplay: Stanley Mann, John Kohn. Cast: Terrence Stamp, Samantha Eggar. USA/UK (Columbia) Color. 119m. DVD: Sony Pictures Home Entertainment.

Conflict (1945) Director: Curtis Bernhardt. Producer: William Jacobs. Screenplay: Arthur T. Horman, Dwight Taylor. Cast: Humphrey Bogart, Alexis Smith, Sydney Greenstreet, Rose Hobart, Charles Drake. USA (Warner Bros.). B&W. 86m. DVD: Unavailable.

Cult of the Cobra (1955) Director: Francis D. Lyon. Producer: Howard Pine. Screenplay: Cecil Maiden, Richard Collins. Cast: Faith Domergue, Richard Long, Marshall Thompson, William Reynolds, David Janssen, Jack Kelly. USA (Universal). B&W. 90m. DVD: Universal.

Dead Man's Eyes (1944) Director: Reginald Le Borg. Producers: Ben Pivar, Will Cowan. Screenplay: Dwight Babcock. Cast: Lon Chaney, Jr., Acquanetta, Jean Parker, Thomas Gomez, Paul Kelly, Jonathan Hale. USA (Universal). B&W. 64m. DVD: Universal.

Dead Ringers (1988) Director/Producer/Screenplay: David Cronenberg. Producer: Marc Boyman. Screenplay: Norman Snider. Cast: Jeremy Irons, Genevieve Bujold, Stephen Lack, Barbara Gordon. Canada (20th Century–Fox). Color. 113m. DVD: Warner Home Entertainment.

Devil Bat's Daughter (1946) Director/Producer: Frank Wisbar. Screenplay: Griffin Jay.

Cast: Rosemary La Planche, John James, Michael Hale, Molly Lamont, Nolan Leary, Monica Mars. USA (PRC). B&W. 67m. DVD: Image Entertainment.

Diabolique (*Les Diaboliques*) (1955) Director/Producer/Screenplay: Henri-Georges Clouzot. Screenplay: Georges Geronimi, Rene Masson, F. Grendel. Cast: Simone Signoret, Vera Clouzot, Paul Meurisse. France (Seven Arts). B&W. 107m. USA: The Criterion Collection.

Diary of a Madman (1963) Director: Reginald Le Borg. Producer/Screenplay: Robert E. Kent. Cast: Vincent Price, Nancy Kovak, Chris Warfield, Ian Wolfe, Stephen Roberts. USA (United Artists). Color. 96m. DVD: Unavailable.

Dr. Jekyll and Mr. Hyde (1932) Director/Producer: Rouben Mamoulian. Screenplay: Samuel Hoffenstein, Percy Heath. Cast: Fredric March, Miriam Hopkins, Rose Hobart, Holmes Herbert, Halliwell Hobbes, Edward Norton, Tempe Piggott. USA (Paramount). B&W. 96m. DVD: Warner Home Entertainment.

Dr. Jekyll and Mr. Hyde (1941) Director/Producer: Victor Fleming. Screenplay: John Lee Mahin. Cast: Spencer Tracy, Ingrid Bergman, Lana Turner, Donald Crisp, Ian Hunter, Barton MacLane, C. Aubrey Smith. USA (MGM). B&W. 113m. DVD: Warner Home Entertainment.

Dr. Renault's Secret (1942) Director: Harry Lachman. Producer: Sol M. Wurtzel. Screenplay: William Bruckner, Robert F. Metzler. Cast: J. Carrol Naish, John Shepperd, Lynne Roberts, George Zucco, Mike Mazurki. USA (20th Century–Fox). B&W. 58m. DVD: 20th Century–Fox Home Entertainment.

Dracula's Daughter (1936) Director: Lambert Hillyer. Producer: E.M. Asher. Screenplay: Garett Ford. Cast: Gloria Holden, Otto Kruger, Margueritte Churchill, Nan Gray, Irving Pichel, Edward Van Sloan. USA (Universal). B&W. 71m. DVD: Universal.

Dragonwyck (1946) Director/Producer/Screenplay: Joseph L. Mankiewicz. Cast: Gene Tierney, Vincent Price, Walter Huston, Glenn Langan, Anne Revere, Spring Byington. USA

(20th Century–Fox). B&W. 103m. DVD: 20th Century–Fox Home Entertainment.

The Exorcist (1973) Director: William Friedkin. Producer/Screenplay: William Peter Blatty. Cast: Ellen Burstyn, Max Von Sydow, Linda Blair, Jason Miller, Lee J. Cobb, Jack MacGowran. USA (Warner Bros.). Color. 122m. DVD: Warner Home Entertainment.

Exorcist III: Legion (1990) Director/Screenplay: William Peter Blatty. Producer: Carter De Haven, Jr. Cast: George C. Scott, Jason Miller, Brad Dourif, Ed Flanders, Zorah Lampert. USA (20th Century–Fox). Color. 105m. DVD: Warner Home Entertainment.

Experiment Perilous (1944) Director: Jacques Tourneur. Producer/Screenplay: Warren Duff: Cast: Hedy Lamarr, George Brent, Paul Lukas, Albert Dekker, Olive Blakeney, George N. Neise. USA (RKO). B&W. 91m. DVD: Unavailable.

Eyes of Laura Mars (1978) Director: Irvin Kershner. Producer: Jon Peters. Screenplay: John Carpenter, David Goodman. Cast: Faye Dunaway, Tommy Lee Jones, Brad Dourif, Raul Julia. (Columbia) Color. 104m. DVD: Sony Home Entertainment.

Eyes Without a Face (*Les Yeux sans visage,* a.k.a. *The Horror Chamber of Dr. Faustus*) (1959) Director: Georges Franju. Producer: Jules Borkon. Screenplay: Georges Franju, Jean Redon, Pierre Boileau, Thomas Narcejac, Claude Sautet. Cast: Pierre Brasseur, Edith Scob, Alida Valli. France/Italy (Lopert). B&W. 84m. DVD: The Criterion Collection.

The Face Behind the Mask (1941) Director: Robert Florey. Producer: Wallace McDonald. Screenplay: Allen Vincent, Paul Jarrico. Cast: Peter Lorre, Evelyn Keyes, George E. Stone, Don Beddoe. USA (Columbia) B&W. 69m. DVD: Unavailable.

Fallen (1998) Director: Gregory Hoblit. Producers: Charles Roven, Dawn Steel. Screenplay: Nicholas Kazan. Cast: Denzel Washington, John Goodman, Donald Sutherland, Elias Koteas, James Gandolfini.USA (Warner Bros.). Color. 124m. DVD: Warner Home Entertainment.

Freaks (1932) Director/Producer: Tod Browning. Screenplay: Willis Goldbeck, Leon Gordon, Edgar Allen Woolf, Al Boasberg. Cast: Wallace Ford, Olga Baclanova, Henry Victor, Harry Earles, Daisy Earles. USA (MGM) B&W. 64m. DVD: Warner Home Entertainment.

The Frozen Ghost (1945) Director: Harold Young. Producer: William Cowan. Screenplay: Bernard Schubert, Luci Ward. Cast: Lon Chaney, Jr., Martin Kosleck, Evelyn Ankers, Elena Verdugo, Douglas Dumbrille, Milburn Stone. USA (Universal) B&W. 61m. DVD: Universal.

Gaslight (1944) Director: George Cukor. Producer: Arthur Hornblow, Jr. Screenplay: John Van Druten, Walter Reisch, John Balderston. Cast: Ingrid Bergman, Charles Boyer, Joseph Cotten, Angela Lansbury, Dame May Whitty. USA (MGM). B&W. 114m. DVD: Warner Home Entertainment.

Gorilla at Large (1954) Director: Harmon Jones. Producer: Robert L. Jacks. Screenplay: Leonard Praskins, Barney Slater. Cast: Raymond Burr, Anne Bancroft, Cameron Mitchell, Lee J. Cobb, Lee Marvin. USA (20th Century–Fox). Color. 84m. DVD: 20th Century–Fox Home Entertainment.

Hangover Square (1945) Director: John Brahm. Producer: Robert Bassler. Screenplay: Barre Lyndon. Cast: Laird Cregar, Linda Darnell, George Sanders, Glenn Langan, Alan Napier. USA (20th Century–Fox). B&W. 77m. DVD: 20th Century–Fox Home Entertainment.

Hannibal (2001) Director: Ridley Scott. Producers: Dino de Laurentiis, Martha de Laurentiis. Screenplay: David Mamet, Steven Zallian. Cast: Anthony Hopkins, Julianne Moore, Ray Liotta, Gary Oldman, Giancarlo Giannini. USA (MGM). Color. 132m. DVD: MGM/UA.

Hannibal Rising (2007). Director: Peter Webber. Producers: Dino De Laurentiis, Martha De Laurentiis. Screenplay: Thomas Harris. Cast: Gaspard Ulliel, Li Gong, Dominic West, Rhys Ifans, Richard Brake, Kevin McKidd. USA (MGM). Color. 117m. DVD: The Weinstein Company.

The Haunted Strangler (1958) Director: Robert Day. Producer: John Croydon. Screenplay: Jan Read, John C. Cooper. Cast: Boris Karloff, Anthony Dawson, Elizabeth Allen, Jean Kent. UK (Anglo Amalgamated/MGM). B&W. 81m. DVD: Image Entertainment.

House of Horrors (1946) Director: Jean Yarbrough. Producer: Ben Pivar. Screenplay: George Bricker. Cast: Rondo Hatton, Martin Kosleck. Robert Lowery, Virginia Grey, Kent Taylor, Alan Napier, Bill Goodwin. USA (Universal/PRC). B&W. 65m. DVD: Universal.

The Hunger (1983) Director: Tony Scott. Producer: Richard A. Shepard. Screenplay: Ivan Davis, Michael Thomas. Cast: Catherine Deneuve, Susan Sarandon, David Bowie, Dan Hedaya, Cliff De Young, Bessie Love, John Pankow, Willem Dafoe. USA (MGM) 94m. DVD: Warner Home Entertainment.

I Bury the Living (1958) Director: Albert Band. Producer/Screenwriter: Albert Band, Louis Garfinkle. Cast: Richard Boone, Theodore Bikel, Peggy Maurer, Russ Bender. USA (United Artists). B&W. 76m. DVD: Alpha Video.

I Walked with a Zombie (1943) Director: Jacques Tourneur. Producer: Val Lewton. Screenplay: Curt Siodmak, Ardel Wray. Cast: Tom Conway, Frances Dee, James Ellison, Edith Barrett, Darby Jones, Christine Gordon, Sir Lancelot. USA (RKO) B&W. 69m. DVD: Warner Home Entertainment.

Jacob's Ladder (1990) Director: Adrian Lyne. Producer: Alan Marshall. Screenplay: Bruce Joel Rubin. Cast: Tim Robbins, Elizabeth Pena, Danny Aiello, Perry Lang, Jason Alexander, Matt Craven, Macaulay Culkin. USA (Carolco Tristar) Color. 115m. DVD: Lion's Gate.

Kolchak: The Night Stalker (1972) Director: John Llewelyn Moxie. Producer: Dan Curtis. Screenplay: Richard Matheson. Cast: Darren McGavin, Carol Lynley, Simon Oakland, Ralph Meeker, Claude Aikens, Kent Smith, Barry Atwater. USA (ABC-TV). Color. 73m. DVD: Universal.

The Leopard Man (1943). Director: Jacques Tourneur. Producer: Val Lewton. Screenplay: Ardel Wray. Cast: Dennis O'Keefe, Jean Brooks, Margo, James Bell, Abner Biberman, Ben Bard, Margaret Landry, Tula Parma. USA (RKO). B&W. 66m. DVD: Warner Home Entertainment.

The Lodger (1944) Director: John Brahm. Producer: Robert Bassler. Screenplay: Barre Lyndon. Cast: Laird Cregar, Merle Oberon, George Sanders, Sir Cedric Hardwicke, Aubrey Mather. USA (20th Century–Fox). B&W. 84m. DVD: 20th Century–Fox Home Entertainment.

Lord of Illusions (1995) Director/Producer/Screenplay: Clive Barker. Producer: JoAnne Sellar. Cast: Scott Bakula, Kevin J. O'Connor, Famke Janssen, Daniel Von Bargen. USA (United Artists) Color. 121m. DVD: MGM Home Entertainment.

Manhunter (1986) Director/Screenplay: Michael Mann. Producer: Richard Roth. Cast: William Petersen, Kim Griest, Dennis Farina, Brian Cox, Tom Noonan, Stephen Lang. USA (Warner Bros.) Color. 118m. DVD: MGM Home Entertainment.

The Mark of the Whistler (1944) Director: William Castle. Producer: Rudolph C. Flothow. Screenplay: George Bricker. Cast: Richard Dix, Janis Carter, Porter Hall, Paul Guilfoyle, Matt Willis. USA (Columbia). B&W. 60m. DVD: Unavailable.

The Mask of Diijon (1946) Director: Lew Landers. Producers: Max Alexander, Alfred Stern. Screenplay: Arthur St. Clair, Griffin Jay. Cast: Erich von Stroheim, Jeanne Bates, William Wright, Mauritz Hugo. USA (PRC). B&W. 73m. DVD: Image Entertainment.

The Monster and the Girl (1941) Director: Stuart Heisler. Producer: Jack Moss. Screenplay: Stuart Anthony. Cast: Ellen Drew, Robert Paige, Paul Lukas, George Zucco, Rod Cameron, Onslow Stevens. USA (Paramount). B&W. 65m. DVD: Unavailable.

Murders in the Zoo (1933) Director: A. Edward Sutherland. Screenplay: Philip Wylie, Seton I. Miller. Cast: Lionel Atwill, Kathleen Burke, Randolph Scott, Charlie Ruggles, Gail Patrick. USA (Paramount). B&W. 62m. DVD: Universal.

Mysterious Intruder (1946) Director: William Castle. Producer: Rudolph C. Flothow. Screenplay: Eric Taylor. Cast: Richard Dix, Barton MacLane, Nina Vale, Regis Toomey, Mike Mazurki. USA (Columbia). B&W. 61m. DVD: Unavailable.

The Mystery of the Wax Museum (1933). Director: Michael Curtiz, Producer: Henry Blank. Screenplay: Don Mullany, Carl Erickson. Cast: Lionel Atwill, Fay Wray, Glenda Farrell, Arthur Edmund Carewe. USA (Warner Bros.). B&W. 77m. DVD: Warner Home Entertainment.

Night Has a Thousand Eyes (1948) Director: John Farrow. Producer: Endre Boehm. Screenplay: Barre Lyndon, Jonathan Latimer. Cast: Edward G. Robinson, Gail Russell, John Lund, Virginia Bruce, William Demarest. USA (Paramount). B&W. 81m. DVD: Unavailable.

Night Monster (1942) Director/Producer: Ford Beebe. Screenplay: Clarence Upton Young. Cast: Lionel Atwill, Bela Lugosi, Ralph Morgan, Leif Erikson, Nils Asther. USA (Universal). B&W. 80m. DVD: Universal.

The Night of the Hunter (1955) Director: Charles Laughton. Producer: Paul Gregory. Screenplay: James Agee. Cast: Robert Mitchum, Shelley Winters, Lillian Gish, Billy Chapin, Evelyn Varden, Corey Allen, Peter Graves. USA (United Artists). B&W. 93m. DVD: MGM/UA.

The Night Walker (1964) Director/Producer: William Castle. Screenplay: Robert Bloch. Cast: Barbara Stanwyck, Robert Taylor, Hayden Rorke, Lloyd Bochner, Rochelle Hudson. USA (Universal). 86m. DVD: Unavailable.

Nightmare Alley (1947) Director: Edmund Goulding. Producer: George Jessel. Screenplay: Jules Furthman. Cast: Tyrone Power, Joan Blondell, Coleen Gray, Helen Walker, Mike Mazurki. USA (20th Century–Fox). B&W. 110m. DVD: 20th Century–Fox Home Entertainment.

Peeping Tom (1960). Director/Producer: Michael Powell. Producer: Albert Fennell. Screenplay: Leo Marks. Cast: Carl Boehm, Moira Shearer, Anna Massey, Maxine Audley, Shirley Ann Field, Pamela Green. UK (Anglo Amalgamated/Astor.) Color. 109m. DVD: The Criterion Collection.

The Picture of Dorian Gray (1945) Director/Screenplay: Albert Lewin. Producer: Pandro S. Berman. Cast: Hurd Hatfield, George Sanders, Angela Lansbury, Donna Reed, Peter Lawford, Bernard Gorcey. USA (MGM) B&W and Color. 110m. DVD: Warner Home Entertainment.

Pillow of Death (1945) Director: Wallace Fox. Producer: Ben Pivar. Screenplay: George Bricker. Cast: Lon Chaney, Jr., Brenda Joyce, Rosalind Ivan, Clara Blandick, Edward Bromberg. USA (Universal) B&W. 66m. DVD: Universal.

The Power of the Whistler (1945) Director: Lew Landers. Producer: Leonard S. Picker. Screenplay: Aubrey Wisberg. Cast: Richard Dix, Janis Carter, Jeff Donnell, Loren Tindall, Tala Birell. USA (Columbia) B&W. 66m. DVD: Unavailable.

Psychic Killer (1976) Director: Ray Danton. Producer: Mardi Rustam. Screenplay: Greydon Clark, Mike Angel, Ray Danton. Cast: Jim Hutton, Paul Burke, Whit Bissell, Neville Brand, Aldo Ray, Nehemiah Persoff. USA (Avco Embassy). Color. 90m. DVD: MPI.

Psycho (1960) Director/Producer: Alfred Hitchcock. Screenplay: Joseph Stefano. Cast: Anthony Perkins, Janet Leigh, John Gavin, Martin Balsam, Vera Miles, Simon Oakland. USA (Paramount). B&W. 109m. DVD: Universal.

Rebecca (1940) Director: Alfred Hitchcock. Producer: David O. Selznick. Screenplay: Robert E. Sherwood, Joan Harrison. Cast: Joan Fontaine, Laurence Olivier, George Sanders, Judith Anderson, Nigel Bruce, Leo G. Carroll. USA (Selznick Studios). B&W. 130m. DVD: MGM/UA.

Red Dragon (2002) Director: Brett Ratner. Producers: Dino Di Laurentiis, Martha Di Laurentis. Screenplay: Ted Tally. Cast: Anthony Hopkins, Edward Norton, Julianne Moore, Harvey Keitel, Ralph Fiennes. USA (MGM). Color. 124m. DVD: Universal.

The Return of the Vampire (1944) Director: Lew Landers. Producer: Sam White. Screenplay: Griffith Jay. Cast: Bela Lugosi, Matt Willis, Frieda Inescort, Nina Foch, Miles Mander. USA (Columbia). B&W. 69m. DVD: Sony Pictures Home Entertainment.

Return of the Whistler (1948) Director: Ross Lederman. Producer: Rudolph C. Flothow Screenplay: Edward Bock, Maurice Tombragel. Cast: Michael Duane, Lenore Aubert, Richard Lanc, James Caldwell, Ann Shoemaker, Wilton Graff. USA (Columbia) B&W. 60m. DVD: Unavailable.

Rosemary's Baby (1968) Director/Screenplay: Roman Polanski. Producer: William Castle. Cast: Mia Farrow, John Cassavetes, Ruth Gordon, Sidney Blackmer, Ralph Bellamy, Patsy Kelly, Charles Grodin. USA (Paramount). Color. 136m. DVD: Paramount Pictures.

Scream and Scream Again (1970) Director: Gordon Hessler. Producer: Milton Subotsky. Screenplay: Christopher Wicking. Cast: Vincent Price, Christopher Lee, Peter Cushing, Michael Gothard, Judy Huxtable. UK (Amicus). Color. 94m. DVD: MGM/UA.

Scream of Fear (1961) Director: Seth Holt. Producer/Screenplay: Jimmy Sangster. Cast: Susan Strasberg, Ann Todd, Christopher Lee. Ronald Lewis. UK (Hammer) 81m. DVD: Sony Pictures Home Entertainment.

The Secret of the Whistler (1946) Director: George Sherman. Producer: Rudolph C. Flothow. Screenplay: Raymond L. Shrock. Cast: Richard Dix, Leslie Brooks, Mary Currier, Michael Duane, Mona Barrie. USA (Columbia). B&W. 68m. DVD: Unavailable.

Se7en (1995). Director: David Fincher. Producers: Arnold Kopelson, Phyllis Carlyle. Screenplay: Andrew Kevin Walker. Cast: Morgan Freeman, Brad Pitt, Kevin Spacey, Gwyneth Paltrow, Richard Roundtree. USA (New Line Cinema). Color. 127m. DVD: Warner Home Entertainment.

The Seventh Victim (1943) Director: Mark Robson. Producer: Val Lewton. Screenplay: Dewitt Bodeen. Cast: Jean Brooks, Kim Hunter, Tom Conway, Isabel Jewell, Hugh Beaumont. USA (RKO). B&W. 71m. DVD: Warner Home Entertainment.

The Shadow (1940). Director: James W. Horner. Producer: Larry Darmour. Screenplay: Ned Dandy, Joseph O'Donnell, Joseph P. Poland. Cast: Victor Jory, Vera Ann Borg, Roger Moore, Jack Ingram, Frank La Rue. USA (Columbia) B&W. Serial in 15 Chapters. DVD: Unavailable.

The Shadow (1994). Director: Russell Mulcahy. Producers: Willi Bar, Martin Bregman, Michael Scott Bregman. Screenplay: David Koepp. Cast: Alec Baldwin, John Lone, Ian McKellan, Penelope Ann Miller, Jonathan Winters. USA (Universal) Color. 108m. DVD: Universal.

Shadow of a Doubt (1943) Director: Alfred Hitchcock. Producer: Jack H. Skirball. Screenplay: Thornton Wilder, Sally Benson, Alma Reville. Cast: Teresa Wright, Joseph Cotten, Macdonald Carey, Henry Travers, Patricia Collinge. USA (Universal). B&W. 108m. DVD: Universal.

She-Wolf of London (1946) Director: Jean Yarbrough. Producer: Ben Pivar. Screenplay: George Bricker. Cast: June Lockhart, Sara Haden, Jan Wiley, Lloyd Corrigan, Martin Kosleck. USA (Universal). B&W. 62m. DVD: Universal.

Shutter Island (2010) Director/Producer: Martin Scorsese. Producers: Bradley J. Fischer, Mike Medavoy, Arnold W. Messer. Screenplay: Laeta Kalogridis, Steven Knight, Cast: Leonardo Di Caprio, Ben Kingsley, Mark Ruffalo, Michelle Williams, Max Von Sydow, Elias Koteas, Ted Levine. USA (Paramount). Color. 138m. DVD: Paramount.

The Silence of the Lambs (1991) Director: Jonathan Demme. Producers: Kenneth Witt, Edward Saxon, Ron Bozman. Screenplay: Ted Tally. Cast: Anthony Hopkins, Jodie Foster, Scott Glenn, Ted Levine, Anthony Heald. USA (Orion) Color. 118m. DVD: Image Entertainment/MGM UA.

Sisters (1973). Director/Screenplay: Brian De Palma. Producer: Edward R. Pressman. Screenplay: Louisa Rose. Cast: Margot Kidder, Jennifer Salt, Charles Durning, William Finley. USA (American International) Color. 92m. DVD: The Criterion Collection.

Son of Dracula (1943) Director: Robert Siodmak. Producer: Ford Beebe. Screenplay: Eric Taylor, Curt Siodmak. Cast: Lon Chaney, Jr., Louise Allbritton, Robert Paige, Evelyn Ankers, Frank Craven. USA (Universal) B&W. 82m. DVD: Universal.

The Sorcerers (1967) Director/Screenplay: Michael Reeves. Producers: Patrick Curtis, Tony Tenser. Screenplay: Tom Baker. Cast: Boris Karloff, Catherine Lacey, Ian Oglivy, Susan George, Elizabeth Ercy. UK (Amicus/ Allied Artists). Color. 87m. DVD: Unavailable.

The Spiral Staircase (1946) Director: Robert Siodmak. Producer: Dore Schary. Screenplay: Mel Dinelli. Cast: Dorothy McGuire, George Brent, Ethel Barrymore, Kent Smith, Rhonda Fleming, Elsa Lanchester. USA (RKO). B&W. 84m. DVD: Sony Pictures Home Entertainment.

Strange Confession (1945) Director: John Hoffman. Producer: Ben Pivar. Screenplay: M. Coates Webster. Cast: Lon Chaney, Jr., Brenda Joyce, Milburn Stone, Lloyd Bridges, J. Carrol Naish. USA (Universal). B&W. 63m. DVD: Universal.

Sunset Boulevard (1950) Director/Screenplay: Billy Wilder. Producer/Screenplay Charles Brackett. Screenplay: D.M. Marshman, Jr. Cast: William Holden, Gloria Swanson, Erich von Stroheim, Nancy Olson, Fred Clark. USA (Paramount). B&W. 115m. DVD: Paramount Pictures.

Supernatural (1933) Director/Producer: Victor Halperin. Producer: Edward Halperin. Screenplay: Harvey Thew, Brian Marlow. Cast: Carole Lombard, Randolph Scott, Vivienne Osborne, H.B. Warner. USA (Paramount). B&W. 60m. DVD: Unavailable.

Targets (1968) Director/Producer/Screenwriter: Peter Bogdanovich. Cast: Boris Karloff, Peter Bogdanovich, Tim O'Kelly, Nancy Hseuh, Sandy Baron, Mike Farrell, Dick Miller. USA (Paramount). Color. 92m. DVD: Paramount Pictures.

The Thirteenth Hour (1947) Director: William Clemens. Producer: Rudolph Flothow. Screenplay: Edward Bock, Raymond L. Shrock. Cast:

Richard Dix, Karen Morley, Mark Dennis, Regis Toomey, John Kellogg. USA (Columbia). B&W. 65m. DVD: Unavailable.

Three Strangers (1946) Director: Jean Negulesco. Producer: Wolfgang Reinhardt. Screenplay: John Huston, Howard Koch. Cast: Sydney Greenstreet, Peter Lorre, Geraldine Fitzgerald. USA (Warner Bros.) B&W. 92m. DVD: Unavailable.

Tough Guys Don't Dance (1987) Director/ Screenplay: Norman Mailer. Producers: Menahem Golan, Yoram Globus. Cast: Ryan O'Neal, Lawrence Tierney, Wings Hauser, Isabella Rosellini, Debra Sandlund. USA (Canon Films). Color. 110m. DVD: MGM/UA.

The Undying Monster (1942) Director: John Brahm. Producer: Brian Foy. Screenplay: Lillie Hayward, Michael Jacoby. Cast: James Ellison, Heather Angel, John Howard. USA (20th Century–Fox). B&W. 63m. DVD: 20th Century–Fox Home Entertainment.

The Unholy Three (1930) Director: Jack Conway. Producer: Irving Thalberg. Screenplay: Waldemar Young. Cast: Lon Chaney, Lila Lee, Elliott Nugent, Harry Earles, Ivan Linow, John Miljan. USA (MGM). B&W. 90m. DVD: Unavailable.

The Unseen (1945) Director: Lewis Allen. Screenplay: Raymond Chandler, Hagar Wilde. Cast: Gail Russell, Joel McCrea, Phyllis Brooks, Herbert Marshall, Isobel Elsom, Norman Lloyd. USA (Paramount). B&W. 81m. DVD: Unavailable.

Vertigo (1958) Director/Producer: Alfred Hitchcock. Screenplay: Alec Coppel, Samuel Taylor. Cast: James Stewart, Kim Novak, Barbara Bel Geddes, Tom Helmore. USA (Paramount). Color. 120m. DVD: Universal.

The Voice of the Whistler (1945) Director/ Screenplay: William Castle. Producer: Rudolph C. Flothow. Screenplay: William H. Petit. Cast: Richard Dix, Lynn Merrick, Rhys Williams, James Cardwell, Tom Kennedy. USA (Columbia). B&W. 60m. DVD: Unavailable.

Weird Woman (1944) Director: Reginald LeBorg. Producer: Ben Pivar. Screenplay: Brenda

Weisberg. Cast: Lon Chaney, Jr., Evelyn Ankers, Anne Gwynn, Elizabeth Russell. USA (Universal). B&W. 84m. DVD: Universal.

The Whistler (1944) Director: William Castle. Producer: William C. Flothow. Screenplay: Eric Taylor. Cast: Richard Dix, J. Carroll Naish, Gloria Stuart, Alan Dinehart, Joan Woodbury. USA (Columbia) B&W. 60m. DVD: Unavailable.

Witch Hunt (1994). Director: Paul Schrader. Producer: Gale Ann Hurd. Screenplay: Joseph Dougherty. Cast: Dennis Hopper, Penelope Ann Miller, Julian Sands, Eric Bogosian, Lypsinka, Christopher John Fields. USA (HBO). Color. 100m. DVD: Unavailable.

The Wolf Man (1941) Director/Producer: George Waggner. Screenplay: Curt Siodmak. Cast: Lon Chaney, Jr., Claude Rains, Evelyn Ankers, Bela Lugosi, Maria Ouspenskaya, Ralph Bellamy. USA (Universal). B&W. 70m. DVD: Universal.

Wolfen (1981) Director/Screenplay: Michael Wadleigh. Producer: Rupert Hitzig. Screenplay: David Frye. Cast: Albert Finney, Edward James Olmos, Tom Noonan, Gregory Hines. USA (Orion/Warner Bros.). Color. 114m. DVD: Warner Home Entertainment.

The X Files: I Want to Believe (2008) Director/Producer/Screenplay: Chris Carter. Producer/Screenplay: Frank Spotnitz. Cast: David Duchovny, Gillian Anderson, Amanda Peet, Billy Connolly, Mitch Pileggi. USA (20th Century–Fox). Color. 104m. DVD: 20th Century–Fox Home Entertainment.

Chapter Notes

Introduction

1. James M. Cain, *Double Indemnity* (New York: Vintage, 1978), p. 94.
2. Ibid., p. 125.
3. Quoted in Eric Somer, "The Noir Horrors of *Cat People*," in Alain Silver and James Ursini, eds., *Film Noir Reader 4* (New York: Limelight, 2004), p. 192.
4. Jeremy Dyson, *Bright Darkness: The Lost Art of the Supernatural Horror Film* (London: Cassell, 1997), p. 137.
5. Quoted in Eric Somer, "The Noir Horrors of *Cat People*," *Film Noir Reader 4*, p. 193.
6. Ibid., p. 193.

Chapter 1

1. Alain Silver, and Elizabeth Ward, eds., *Film Noir: An Encyclopedic Reference to the American Style* (Woodstock: Overlook Press, 1979), p. 209.
2. Ibid., p. 204.
3. Donald Spoto, *The Dark Side of Genius: The Life of Alfred Hitchcock* (New York: Ballantine, 1983), p. 276.
4. Arthur Lyons, *Death on the Cheap: The Lost B-Movies of Film Noir* (New York: Da Capo, 2000), p. 139.

Chapter 2

1. Robert Louis Stevenson, *The Strange Case of Dr. Jekyll and Mr. Hyde* (London: Penguin, 2002), introduction by Robert Mighall, pp. xxx–xxxi.
2. Ivan Butler, *Horror in the Cinema* (New York: A.S. Barnes, 1970), p. 64.
3. Carlos Clarens, *An Illustrated History of the Horror Film* (New York: Capricorn Books, 1967), p. 70.
4. Kenneth Anger, *Hollywood Babylon II* (New York: Plume, 1985), p. 87.
5. Joe Kane, *The Phantom of the Movies' Videoscope* (New York: Three Rivers, 2000), p. 106.
6. Butler, *Horror in the Cinema*, p. 159.
7. Roy Milano, *Monsters: A Celebration of Classics from Universal Studios* (New York: Del Ray, 2006), p. 124.

8. Ibid., p. 137.
9. Jeremy Dyson, *Bright Darkness*, p. 93.

Chapter 3

1. Lyons, *Death on the Cheap*, p. 40.
2. Quoted in Eric Somer, "The Noir Horrors of *Cat People*," *Film Noir Reader 4*, p. 193.
3. Ibid., p. 191.
4. Chris Fujiwara, *Jacques Tourneur: The Cinema of Nightfall* (Baltimore: Johns Hopkins University Press, 1998), p. 3.
5. Ibid., p. 72.
6. Joel E. Siegel, *Val Lewton: The Reality of Terror* (New York: Viking Press, 1973), p. 32.
7. Lyons, *Death on the Cheap*, p. 2.
8. Fujiwara, *Jacques Tourneur*, p. 74.
9. Dyson, *Bright Darkness*, p. 111.
10. Quoted in Eric Somer, "The Noir Horrors of *Cat People*," *Film Noir Reader 4*, p. 195.
11. Michel Perez, "The Puritan Despair," in Roy Huss and T.J. Huss, eds., *Focus on the Horror Film* (Englewood Cliffs, NJ: Prentice-Hall, 1972), p. 134.
12. Fujiwara, *Jacques Tourneur*, p. 242.
13. Perez, *Focus on the Horror Film*, p. 132.
14. Fujiwara, Jacques Tourneur, p. 87.
15. Ibid., p. 98.
16. Siegel, *Val Lewton*, pp. 116, 119.
17. Fujiwara, *Jacques Tourneur*, p. 99.
18. Ibid., pp. 106–107.
19. Manny Farber, "Val Lewton and the School of Shudders," in *Focus on the Horror Film*, p. 142.
20. Barry Gifford, *The Devil Thumbs a Ride and Other Unforgettable Films* (New York: Grove, 1988), p. 75.
21. Siegel, *Val Lewton*, p. 121.
22. Ibid., pp. 71–72.
23. Quoted in Eric Somer, "The Noir Horrors of *Cat People*," *Film Noir Reader 4*, p. 192.

Chapter 4

1. Stephen King, *Danse Macabre* (New York: Berkeley, 1981), p. 118.
2. Gerald Nachman, *Raised on Radio* (Berkeley: University of California Press, 2000), p. 310.

3. John Stanley, *I Was a TV Horror Host* (Pacifica, CA: Creatures at Large, 2007), p. 14.

4. Jon Tuska, *The Detective in Hollywood* (New York: Doubleday, 1978), p. 283.

5. Ibid., p. 287.

6. Ibid., p. 288.

7. Ibid., p. 286.

8. Gerald Nachman, *Raised on Radio*, p. 310.

9. John Stanley, *I Was a TV Horror Host*, p. 15.

10. Alan Warren, "Calling Dr. Death," in Gary J. Svelha and Susan Svelha, eds. *Lon Chaney, Jr.: Midnight Marquee Actors Series* (Baltimore: Luminary, 2005), p. 99.

11. Ibid., p. 97.

12. Carlos Clarens, *An Illustrated History of the Horror Film*, p. 101.

13. Bryan Senn, "Weird Woman," in Svelha, *Lon Chaney, Jr.*, p. 147.

14. Michael H. Price, and Kerry Grammill, "Strange Confession," in Svelha, *Lon Chaney, Jr.*, p. 180.

Chapter 5

1. William K. Everson, *More Classics of the Horror Film: Fifty Years of Great Chillers* (Secaucus, NJ: Citadel, 1986), p. 84.

2. Bruce Dettman, "Son of Dracula," in *Lon Chaney, Jr.*, p. 123.

3. Gifford, *The Devil Thumbs a Ride*, p. 71.

Chapter 6

1. Gregory William Mank, *Hollywood Cauldron: Thirteen Horror Films from the Genre's Golden Age* (Jefferson, NC: McFarland, 1994), p. 166.

Chapter 8

1. Donald Spoto, *The Dark Side of Genius: The Life of Alfred Hitchcock*, p. 351.

2. Ibid., p. 341.

3. Ibid., p. 276.

4. Ibid., p. 349.

5. Ibid., p. 404–405.

6. Ibid., p. 434.

7. Eddie Muller, *Dark City: The Lost World of Film Noir* (New York: St. Martin's, 1998), p. 191.

8. Spoto, *The Dark Side of Genius*, p. 503.

9. François Truffaut, with Helen G. Scott, *Hitchcock* (New York: Simon & Schuster, 1983), p. 308–309.

Chapter 9

1. Raymond Durgnat, "Eyes Without a Face," in Huss, ed., *Focus on the Horror Film*, pp. 88–89.

2. Ibid., p. 91.

3. Denis Meikle, *Vincent Price: The Art of Fear* (London: Reynolds & Hearn, 2003), p. 163.

Chapter 10

1. Whitley Streiber, *The Hunger* (New York: Pocket Books, 1981), p. 146.

2. Barry Gifford, *The Devil Thumbs a Ride*, p. 52.

3. Slavoj Zizek, in Joan Copjec, ed., *Shades of Noir* (London: Verso, 1993), p. 200.

Chapter 11

1. Quoted in Kendall R. Phillips, *Projected Fears: Horror Films and American Culture* (Westport, CT: Praeger, 2004), p. 152.

2. Thomas Harris, *Red Dragon* (New York: Dell, 1981), p. 53.

3. Ibid., p. 54.

4. Thomas Harris, *Hannibal* (New York: Delacorte, 1999), p. 253.

Chapter 12

1. Bruce Joel Rubin, *Jacob's Ladder* (New York: Applause Books, 1990), p. 150.

2. Joe Kane, *The Phantom of the Movies' Videoscope*, p. 68.

3. Kirsten Moana Thompson, *Apocalyptic Dread: American Film at the Turn of the Millennium* (New York: State University of New York Press, 2007), p. 107.

4. Kane, *The Phantom of the Movies' Videoscope*, p. 383.

5. Kendall R. Phillips, *Projected Fears*, p. 161.

6. Thompson, *Apocalyptic Dread*, p. 111.

Bibliography

Anger, Kenneth. *Hollywood Babylon II.* New York: Plume, 1985.

Ashley, Mike. *Who's Who in Horror and Fantasy Fiction.* New York: Taplinger, 1977.

Butler, Ivan. *Horror in the Cinema.* New York: A.S. Barnes, 1970.

Cain, James M. *Double Indemnity.* New York: Vintage, 1978.

Clarens, Carlos. *An Illustrated History of the Horror Film.* New York: Capricorn Books, 1967.

Copjec, Joan, ed. *Shades of Noir.* London & New York: Verso, 1993.

Dyson, Jeremy. *Bright Darkness: The Lost Art of the Supernatural Horror Film.* London: Cassell, 1997.

Everson, William K. *More Classics of the Horror Film: Fifty Years of Great Chillers.* Secaucus, NJ: Citadel, 1986.

Fujiwara, Chris. *Jacques Tourneur: The Cinema of Nightfall.* Jefferson, NC: McFarland, 1998.

Gifford, Barry. *The Devil Thumbs a Ride and Other Unforgettable Films.* New York: Grove, 1988.

Glatt, John. *Evil Twins.* New York: St. Martin's, 1999.

Harris, Thomas. *Hannibal.* New York: Delacorte, 1999.

_____. *Red Dragon.* New York: Dell, 1981.

Hefferman, Kevin. *Ghouls, Gimmicks and Gold: Horror Films and the American Movie Business, 1953–1968.* Durham: Duke University Press, 2004.

Hirsch, Foster. *Detours and Lost Highways: A Map of Neo-Noir.* New York: Limelight, 1999.

Huss, Roy, and T.J. Huss, eds. *Focus on the Horror Film.* Englewood Cliffs, NJ: Prentice-Hall, 1972.

Hutchinson, Tom, and Roy Pickard. *Horror: A History of Horror Movies.* Secaucus, NJ: Chartwell Books, 1984.

Kane, Joe. *The Phantom of the Movies' Videoscope.* New York: Three Rivers, 2000.

King, Stephen. *Danse Macabre.* New York: Berkley Books, 1981.

Lyons, Arthur. *Death on the Cheap: The Lost B-Movies of Film Noir.* New York: Da Capo, 2000.

Mank, Gregory William. *Hollywood Cauldron: Thirteen Horror Films from the Genre's Golden Age.* Jefferson, NC: McFarland, 1994.

Meikle, Denis. *Vincent Price: The Art of Fear.* London: Reynolds & Hearn, 2003.

Milano, Roy. *Monsters: A Celebration of Classics from Universal Studios.* New York: Del Ray Books, 2006.

Muller, Eddie. *Dark City: The Lost World of Film Noir.* New York: St. Martin's, 1998.

Nachman, Gerald. *Raised on Radio.* Berkeley: University of California, 2000.

Phillips, Kendall R. *Projected Fears: Horror Films and American Culture.* Westport, CT: Praeger Books, 2004.

Rubin, Bruce Joel. *Jacob's Ladder.* New York: Applause Books, 1990.

Siegel, Joel E. *Val Lewton: The Reality of Terror.* New York: Viking, 1973.

Silver, Alain, and James Ursini, eds. *Film Noir Reader 4.* New York: Limelight, 2004.

Silver, Alain, and Elizabeth Ward, eds. *Film Noir: An Encyclopedic Reference to the American Style.* Woodstock: Overlook, 1979.

Skal, David J. *The Monster Show: A Cultural History of Horror.* New York: W.W. Norton, 1983.

Spoto, Donald. *The Dark Side of Genius: The Life of Alfred Hitchcock.* New York: Ballantine Books, 1983.

Stanley, John. *Creature Features: The Science Fiction, Fantasy and Horror Movie Guide.* New York: Boulevard Books, 1997.

_____. *I Was a TV Horror Host.* Pacifica, CA: Creatures at Large, 2007.

Stevenson, Robert Louis. *The Strange Case of Dr. Jekyll and Mr. Hyde.* London: Penguin Books, 2002.

Streiber, Whitley. *The Hunger.* New York: Pocket Books, 1981.

Svelha, Gary J., and Susan Svelha, eds. *Lon Chaney, Jr.: Midnight Marquee Actors Series.* Baltimore: Luminary, 2005.

Thompson, Kirsten Moana, *Apocalyptic Dread: American Film at the Turn of the Millennium.* New York: State University of New York Press, 2007.

Truffaut, François, with Helen G. Scott. *Hitchcock.* New York: Simon & Schuster, 1983.

Tuska, Jon. *The Detective in Hollywood.* New York: Doubleday, 1978.

Weldon, Michael J. *The Psychotronic Encyclopedia of Film.* New York: Ballantine Books, 1983.

_____. *The Psychotronic Video Guide.* New York: St. Martin's, 1996.

Index